Introduction

The *Flea Market Trader* is a unique price guide, geared specifically for the convenience of the flea market shopper. Several categories have been included that are not often found in general price guides, while others on antiques not usually seen at flea markets have been omitted. The new categories will serve to introduce you to collectibles that are currently coming on, the best and often the only source for which is the market place. As all of us who religiously pursue the circuits are aware, flea markets are the most exciting places in the world to shop; but unless you're well-informed on current values those 'really-great' buys remain on the table. Like most pursuits in life, preparation has its own rewards; and it is our intention to provide you with the basic tool of education and awareness toward that end. But please bear in mind that the prices in this guide are meant to indicate only a general value. Many factors determine actual selling prices -- values vary from one region to another, dealers pay various wholesale prices for their wares, and your bargaining skill is important, too.

We have organized our listings into general categories for easy use; if you have trouble locating an item, refer to the index. We assume that prices quoted by dealers are for mint items unless damage is noted. So our listings, when no condition code is present, reflect prices of items in mint condition. NM stands for minimal damage, VG indicates that the items will bring 40% to 60% of its mint price, and EX should be somewhere between the two. Nothing is listed in poorer condition than VG. Glassware is assumed clear unless a color is noted. Only generally accepted abbreviations have been used. Photos other than those we have taken are acknowledged on page 4, and we would like to take this opportunity to thank each author, dealer, and auction house who allowed us to use their photographs.

The Editors

3

Photo Credits

Blue Willow, Mary Frank Gaston, pg 310

Brian-Riba Auctions, Inc., Historical Ephemera, P.O. Box 53, Main St., South Glastonbury, CT 06073, pg 27,61,81,222

Carnival Chalk Prizes, Thomas G. Morris, pg 64

Children's Dishes, Margaret and Kenn Whitmyer, pg 77

Children's Glass Dishes and Furniture, Doris Anderson Lechler, pg 78

Col. Doug Allard, P.O. Box 460, St. Ignatius, MT 59865, pg 161,162

Collector's Encyclopedia of Depression Glass, Vol. 6 and 7, Gene Florence, pg 103,104,108

Collector's Encyclopedia of Fiesta, 6th Edition, Sharon and Bob Huxford, pg 126,127

Collector's Encyclopedia of Hall China, Margaret and Kenn Whitmyer, pg 148

Collector's Encyclopedia of Nippon, 3rd Edition, Joan Van Patten, pg 204

Collector's Encyclopedia of Noritake, Joan Van Patten, pg 205

Collector's Encyclopedia of Occupied Japan, 2nd Edition, Gene Florence, pg 207

Collector's Encyclopedia of Pattern Glass, Mollie Helen McCain, pg 213,217

Collector's Guide to Country Stoneware and Pottery, Don and Carol Raycraft, pg 280

Collector's Guide to Paper Dolls, Mary Young, pg 210,211

Du Mouchelles, 409 Jefferson Ave., Detroit, MI 48226, pg 82

Garths Auctions, Inc., 2690 Stratford Road, Box 369, Delaware, OH 43015, pg 235

Glassworks Auctions, P.O. Box 187, East Greenville, PA 18041, pg 137

Goofus Glass, Carolyn McKinley, pg 144

Head Vases, Kathleen Cole, pg 153

Illustrated Guide to Cookie Jars, Ermagene Westfall, pg 192,193

Metal Molds, Eleanore Bunn, pg 196

Petretti's Coca-Cola Collectibles Price Guide, Alan Petretti, pg 86,87

Railroad Collectibles, 2nd Edition, Stanley Baker, pg 239,240

Richard A. Bourne, Co., Inc., Estate Auctioneers & Appraisers, Box 141, Hyannis Port, MA 02647, pg 58,83

Scouting Collectibles, R.J. Sayers, pg 266

Standard Baseball Card Price Guide, Gene Florence, pg 32,34

Standard Encyclopedia of Carnival Glass, Bill Edwards, pg 64-67

Standard Knife Collectors Guide, Stewart and Ritchie, pg 174

Straight Razor Collecting, Robert Doyle, pg 241

300 Years of Kitchen Collectibles, Vols. 1 and 2, Linda Campbell Franklin, pg 147

Revised Seventh Edition

Flea Market Trader

Edited by
Sharon & Bob Huxford

COLLECTOR BOOKS
A Division of Schroeder Publishing Co., Inc.

The current values in this book should be used only as a guide. They are not intended to set prices, which vary from one section of the country to another. Auction prices as well as dealer prices vary greatly and are affected by condition as well as demand. Neither the Editors nor the Publisher assumes responsibility for any losses that might be incurred as a result of consulting this guide.

ABC Plates

Popular in the 1800s as well as the early years of this century, plates with the ABCs in their borders encouraged children toward learning their letters even during meal time. They were made from a variety of materials, but examples in earthenware with a colorfully-printed central motif are most collectible, especially those dealing with sports, transportation, or a famous person, place, or thing.

Lost, crying girl, 8½", $95.00.

Bowl, Ride a Stick Horse..., Wood, Burslem, 6½"..................**25.00**
Cup, florals, embossed alphabet, strap handle **165.00**
Mug, Crusoe at Work, Brownhills, 1877, EX **55.00**
Mug, gold trim, alphabet rim, marked Germany...........**25.00**
Mug, Jack in the Corner, Staffordshire, 2¾"........................**90.00**
Mug, letter W, Christ with cross, 2¾"................................**115.00**
Mug, W is for whipping, Staffordshire..............................**110.00**
Plate, birds on left, alphabet on right, 6"...........................**38.00**
Plate, boys crossing stile, Staffordshire **80.00**
Plate, Canary, Bullfinch & Goldfinch, multicolor **55.00**

Plate, children at play, multicolor, Staffordshire, 6¾" **65.00**
Plate, Children Teach Dog To Be Polite, Staffordshire.......**45.00**
Plate, clock with Roman numerals, numerals & alphabet band, glass, 7" **35.00**
Plate, Cock Robin, tin **65.00**
Plate, dogs chase stag, multicolor, 7"...................................**40.00**
Plate, fox & duck, printed alphabet, 6½"...........................**40.00**
Plate, Gathering Cotton, Staffordshire, 5½"......................**195.00**
Plate, girl swings, tin, 6¼"....**45.00**
Plate, girls gardening, blue transfer, Staffordshire............**40.00**
Plate, Highland Dance, Staffordshire, 5¼".........................**85.00**
Plate, Hold Your Hand Out..., teacher & boy, Edge Malkin, 4½" **110.00**
Plate, How Glorious Is Our Heavenly King, 6¼" **58.00**
Plate, Independence Hall, glass, dated 1776-1876..........**150.00**
Plate, Little Bo-Peep, numbers 1-9, alphabet rim, glass **55.00**
Plate, Matrimonial Ladder, couple in park, Staffordshire ..**200.00**
Plate, puppets, brown transfer, 6¾" **40.00**
Plate, That Girl Wants the Pup Away, 5½" **85.00**
Plate, tiny beads on underside & border, glass, 5"..............**32.00**
Plate, Willie & His Rabbit, multicolor, 5½" **65.00**
Plate, 1000 Eye, clock in center, alphabet rim, glass, 6" ..**65.00**
Plate, 3 Dutch children, deaf signs, transfer, 6¼" **150.00**

Abingdon Pottery

Produced in Abingdon, Illinois, from 1934 to 1950, this company made vases, cookie jars, utility ware, and lamps.

Ash tray, #306 ....**12.00**
Ash tray, #615, black gloss ...**15.00**
Bookend, #305, sea gull, turquoise matt, 6", pair **40.00**
Bookend, #441, horse's head, black gloss, pair **50.00**
Bowl, #432, Fern Leaf, 15" ...**40.00**
Bowl, #529, Tai Leaf, 16"......**30.00**
Candle holder, #126, Classic, blue gloss, pair **17.00**
Candle holder, #404, triple, Chain, beige **42.00**
Cookie jar, #471, Old Lady, decorated **60.00**
Cookie jar, #549, Hippo, undecorated, 8".........................**50.00**

Cookie jar, #677D, Daisy **25.00**
Cookie jar, #694, Bo Peep **65.00**
Cornucopia, #569D, blue, decorated **25.00**
Figurine, #3906, shepherdess & fawn..............................**230.00**
Figurine, #469, Dutch boy, white matt **25.00**
Flower basket, #582, plain or decorated, 8" **25.00**
Flowerpot, #150D, Columbine, decorated **12.00**
Flowerpot, #347, egg & dart, undecorated, 7", pair.....**30.00**
Pitcher, #200, ice lip, all colors except red matt, 2-qt......**20.00**
Pitcher, #202, ice lip, all colors other than yellow gloss, 2-quart...............................**20.00**
Tea tile, #400, geisha, turquoise gloss **80.00**
Vase, #319, Modern, turquoise, 7" **40.00**
Vase, #351, Capri, turquoise matt **40.00**

Cookie jar, Humpty Dumpty, $45.00.

Cookie jar, #611, Jack-in-the-Box, undecorated, 11".............**40.00**
Cookie jar, #651, Locomotive, cream with red & black .**55.00**
Cookie jar, #659D, Mother Goose, goose by side...................**95.00**
Cookie jar, #663, Humpty Dumpty, decorated........**45.00**
Cookie jar, #663, Humpty Dumpty, undecorated **35.00**
Cookie jar, #664, Pineapple, decorated **40.00**

Vase, Laurel, #442, 6", $35.00.

Vase, #420, Fern Leaf, undecorated, 7¼" **15.00**
Vase, #444, dolphin, pink, 6" ..**16.00**
Vase, #516, Acadia **20.00**
Vase, #563, blue, decorated, urn shape...............................**18.00**

Vase, #591, pink **10.00**
Wall pocket, #457, Ionic, undecorated, 9" **15.00**
Wall pocket, #586D, calla lily, decorated, 9" **30.00**

Advertising Collectibles

Since the late 1800s competition among manufacturers of
retail products has produced mul-
titudes of containers, signs, trays,
and novelty items, each bearing a
catchy slogan, colorful lithograph
or some other type of ploy, all fla-
grantly intent upon catching the
eye of the potential customer. In
their day, some were more successful than others; but today it is
the advertising material itself
rather than the product that rings
up the big sales–from avid collectors and flea market shoppers,
not the product's consumers!

See also Coca-Cola; Labels;
Planters Peanuts.

Ad Cards

**Clark's ONT Spool Cotton,
Leading Women of the World,
$5.00.**

Aultman Steam Threshers, 4-sec-
tion fan, rare **30.00**
Baker's Cocoa, EX **10.00**
Bicycle Playing Cards, king &
cycle, mechanical **30.00**
Castoria, Barnum's Circus,
Jumbo & baby, 1885.......**15.00**
Clark Powers, black & white vio-
lin, EX............................**10.00**
Dr Kilmer's Female Remedy,
ladies on veranda...........**10.00**
Eagle Brewery, Vincennes IN, factory view, EX **16.00**
Electric Lustre Starch, Red Riding Hood, mechanical **15.00**
Exodus, 2 Black tramps, hold-to-
light, brown & white, jew-
eler's ad **15.00**
Frank Matthew's Stable, carriage
& 2 horses, ca 1845........**25.00**
Gold Baking Powder, French
franc/stamped envelopes on
front, 1888, EX **20.00**
H Clausen & Son Brewing, multicolor scenes, 1876...........**40.00**
Huntley & Palmers Biscuits,
explorer & Indians.........**60.00**
Jones' Superlative Flour, NYC,
baby in cradle made from
flour barrel **16.00**
Kentucky Derby, Louisville
Jockey Club, Spring.......**15.00**
Lemp Brewery, St Louis, Fallstaff
with beer, mechanical....**32.00**
Mellins' Food, mother & children,
diecut, 8".........................**20.00**
NY Coffee House, Portland, Rail-
road flares & firefighting
equipment......................... **5.00**
Peabody's Dry Goods, couple on roller
skates, Massachusetts, EX..**12.00**
Philadelphia Best Brewing, lady
on black ground, 5" **30.00**
Pope's Rifle Air Pistol, 2 women,
testimonials....................**40.00**
Pratt's Astral Oil, Statue of Liberty, EX **15.00**
Rodger's Photographer, boy &
grasshopper....................**15.00**

Schlitz Brewery, bird's eye view of brewery, EX...... **9.00**
Singer Sewing Machines, native costumes, set of 14.........**55.00**
Soapine, sailor washing whale, whale shape....................**15.00**
Standard Java Coffee, 2-sided, boy on donkey.................**15.00**
Stevens Point Brewing, Stevens Point Wisconsin, multicolor view, EX.........................**16.00**
Terrific Fidelity Casualty, accident & crime scenes.......**20.00**
Toledo Brewing & Malting, political comic, 1884, EX........**25.00**
Warner's Yeast, children view comet through canister..**15.00**
Waterbury Watch, man looks over wall................................**26.00**
Wheat Bitters, bottle in varied settings, 1880s, set of 5..**25.00**

Woolson Spice Co. of Toledo, 'Offer Expires Jan. 1, 1896,' $6.50.

Banks

AC Spark Plug, horse on tub, rubber wheels, slush-cast metal, EX................................**150.00**
Betsy Ross Tea, tin & paper .**16.00**
Big Boy Restaurant, EX **15.00**
Budweiser Barley Malt Syrup, tin can, EX **55.00**

Calumet, black and cream on red, 4", $95.00.

Campbell Kids, cast iron, worn paint, 3¼".....................**190.00**
Chevrolet, car, 1953 ....**65.00**
Gem Furnace, cast iron, worn paint, M-2364, 4⅝".......**105.00**
Grapette, clown......................**17.50**
Kentucky Fried Chicken, Colonel Sanders figure, 12½"......**15.00**
Kodak, box camera shape, cast iron, 1900, 4x5x3"........**275.00**
Osborn Molding machines, pig, cast iron, M-625, 4"......**255.00**
Stevens, Jr Cash Register, with key, EX..........................**145.00**
Van Camps Pork 'N Beans, can form, NM **10.00**
Van Dyk Teas, Lincoln Logs cabin form **125.00**
White Rose, tin......................**35.00**
8 O'Clock Coffee, tin **10.00**

Book Marks

Borden's Malted Milk, country scene, 1890, 6", EX **8.00**

Chase Pianos, snow scene, 1890s, 5", EX............................... **9.00**
Eastman's Extract of Wild Roses, girl amid roses, 1888, 7". **8.00**
Esty Organ & Piano Co, baby 1890s, 5" **9.00**
Palmer's Candy, lovely woman, ca 1908, EX **5.00**
Presbyterian Sabbath School, sailing scene, 1880s, 5"... **5.00**
Richardson's Music & Card Store, snow scene, 5½", EX........ **6.00**

Calendars

Benjamin & Hastings Insurance, cardboard & tin, 1916, 19x13", EX.....................**25.00**
Buckeye Fire Insurance, lady, 1889, 28x20".................**275.00**
Clark's Thread, 1891.............**45.00**
Cloe's Real Estate, girl & dog in car, San Diego, 1946 ......**12.50**
Deering Farm Implements, 1905, 20x15", EX **55.00**
DeLaval Cream Separators, boy with fish, 1921, EX **78.00**
Dionne Quints, Springtime, 1942, 15x12", EX......................**18.00**
Dupont, tin, 1900, 2", VG **45.00**
Esquire, Vargas girl, unsigned, 1947, EX **65.00**
Ferd Neumer Lager Beer, man tasting beer, 1887, EX .**175.00**
Gerlach-Barclow, Here He Comes, trifold, 1931, 22x46" **32.00**
Hercules Powder, 1915, July & August sheets...............**165.00**
Laflin & Rand, 1900, pocket size, EX **200.00**
Libby, 1908, 21x17", EX......**155.00**
Lipton Tea, girl in pink drinking tea, 1901, framed & matted, EX **65.00**
Mendote Candy Factory, diecut, 1903 ....**95.00**
Morrison Machines, Black boys on fence, 1895, EX..............**55.00**

Musselman, outdoor girl riding, 1921, M..........................**22.00**
Planters Mills, Cape Girardeau MO, 1905 ....**38.00**
Rexall Drugs, 1925, EX **30.00**
Shemp Bros, diecut, 1913 .....**95.00**
Snap-On Tools, 1988, M........**15.00**
Sports Illustrated, girls in swim-suits, 1986, NM..............**12.50**
T Clark Carriage Repository, winter scene, 1909, VG........**15.00**
Winchester, complete pad, 1927, 10x21", EX.....................**60.00**
Youth's Companion, 1899 .....**25.00**

Clocks

Baird's Jolly Tar, 1890s.......**825.00**
Bell Bourbon, metal, EX.....**900.00**

Black Cat Shoe Dressing and Superba Shoe Polish, wood with tin face, 28" x 24", poor condition, $695.00.

Blatz Beer, iron, standup **55.00**
Calvert Whiskey, electric light-up, working, VG **22.50**
Dr Pepper, black & beige, in green frame, 15" dia **100.00**
Frostie Root Beer, metal with fluorescent bulb...............**150.00**
General Electric, refrigerator, metal, 9" **165.00**

Kuppenheimer Clothes, gold and foil messages, 23x23" ..**165.00**
RCA, neon, reverse-painted metal case, 11" square............**150.00**
Rival Dog Food....................**65.00**
St Joseph's Aspirin, neon ...**300.00**
Strauss Bros, America's...Tailors, Chicago IL, Art Nouveau, 34x18"..........................**625.00**
Vantage Cigarettes, round, battery operated, NM.........**35.00**

Cheerios, bee, 14"..................**22.00**
Chicken of the Sea, mermaid, 1974, EX **18.00**
John Deere, deer, green, stuffed cloth, EX........................**27.50**
Munsingwear Underclothing, penguin, vinyl, 1970, 7".......**16.00**
Procter & Gamble, Pogo Possum, vinyl, 1969, 5"................**16.00**
Quaker Oats, Captain Crunch, M in package **18.00**

Dolls

Energy Scotsman, 17", $15.00.

A&W Root Beer, bear, EX.....**30.00**
Amway, Woodsey Owl, EX....**20.00**
Birds Eye Foods, Merry, Minx & Mike, 1953, set of 3........**65.00**
Brach Candy, Scarecrow Sam, NM.................................**25.00**
Breck Shampoo, Bonnie, vinyl, 9", NM.................................**20.00**
British Overseas Airline, stewardess, M in package **12.00**
Budweiser Beer, turtle bean bag with logo **12.00**
Campbell's Kids, Cheerleader, 1957, EX........................**45.00**

Fans

Acme Beer, blonde with beer glass, 1933, 9½", EX.......**14.00**
Bee Brand Spices, McCormick & Co, cardboard................**10.00**
Ford Motor Company, cardboard with wood handle, EX....**12.50**
Overland Auto Sales, Jackson MI, cardboard, early, EX **15.00**
Putnam Dye, multicolor Art Deco design **15.00**
Singer Manufacturing, apple blossoms & bluebirds **12.50**

Match Holders

Bengal Furnaces, furnace & Bengal tiger, tin, 3½x5", EX...**85.00**
Ceresota Flour, small boy, tin, 3½"x5"..........................**175.00**
General Electric, refrigerator figural **90.00**
Holsum, The Sanitary Bread, loaf, tin, 3½x5" **125.00**
Hoodley & Bennett, black & green paint on metal, 3½x6" ...**30.00**
Merry War Lye, girl doing wash, tin, 4x5½" **165.00**
Red Cross Stoves & Furnaces, painted brass & celluloid, 1900s **165.00**
Reliance Baking Powder, woman & child, tin, 4x5½" **155.00**
W Avery & Son, horse form, brass, hallmark, 1890s, EX **65.00**

Willis & Wilson, paper whisk broom, 10", $35.00.

Dutch Boy Paints, lead **20.00**
Fontius Shoes, clear glass, 3"
    diameter, EX **10.00**
Glidden & Joy Varnish, black &
    white, 3" diameter **12.50**
HJ Heinz, brass, '39, EX **10.00**
Moorman's Feed, pig on block, felt
    bottom, 2", EX **15.00**
Norvell Shapleigh Hardware, St
    Louis MO, 2½x4" **15.00**

Buster Brown Shoes, 5½" diameter, $125.00.

Match Safes

American Steam Packing, sil-
    vered brass/celluloid, Indian
    head, 1900s **165.00**
Anheuser Busch, large eagle on
    letter A, silver, EX........**110.00**
Barker Brand Clothing, silvered
    brass, hinged lid, ca 1900,
    1½x2" **175.00**
Berlin Iron Bridge Company, cel-
    luloid **75.00**
Bowler Bros Breweries, cellu-
    loid/metal, Whitehead &
    Hoag, light wear.............**30.00**
Chicago Pneumatic Tools, nickel
    & brass **25.00**
Ingersoll-Sergeant, silvered
    brass/celluloid, 1900s...**165.00**
Leather Workers Union, silvered
    brass/celluloid, 1890s...**185.00**

Paperweights

Chalmer's Motor Company, fac-
    tory & cars, bronze.........**68.00**
Chevrolet Motor Company, early
    car on wood base, 5" **20.00**

Pin-Backs

Atlantic City, Auditorium & Con-
    vention Hall, 1900s........**65.00**
Berry Brothers Varnishes, chil-
    dren & dog, 1900s, 2" **28.50**
Buster Brown Blue Ribbon Shoes,
    boy & dog, Meek, 1" **65.00**
Chiquita, midget, Cuban Atom, ca
    1890s, 2", EX **27.50**
GE Full Range Radio Round-Up,
    man on horse with lasso,
    1940s, 1¼" **35.00**
High Admiral Cigarettes, Hard to
    Beat, 1890s, ⅞" **10.00**
Oscar Mayer Canned Wieners,
    brown, yellow & red, 1930s,
    1¼" **45.00**
Ringham's Best Brand Tools, mul-
    ticolor, ca 1915, 1"..........**40.00**
Sharples' Separator, mother &
    child, EX color, 1¼" **12.50**

Stephenson Union Suits, ca 1920,
EX **16.00**
Union-Made Cigars, light blue
union label & flags, 1900s,
1¼", EX **15.00**
Vote for Philip Morris, 3-color,
1940s, 1¼", VG **15.00**

Pocket Mirrors

Angelus Marshmallows, 2 cherubs
with product **68.00**
Brer Rabbit Syrup, rabbit holds
product, EX **150.00**
Ceresota Flour, color scene, black
letters, celluloid, 2" **25.00**
Ceresota Flour, small boy cutting
bread, EX........................**60.00**
Indian Motorcycle, orange &
black, 3x2", VG...............**22.50**
Invincible Junior, black & white
photo of woman, celluloid,
1920s, VG **22.00**
Nehi Ginger Ale, rum keg.....**12.50**
Peninsular Stove, Ranges & Fur-
naces, factory scene, celluloid,
EX **32.00**

Signs

**Cadbury Cocoa, 18th-century
scene with a royal coach, 19" x 24",
$240.00.**

Berghoff Beer, tin, hunting dogs
on point, 13x21", EX **75.00**
Bucking Bronco Coal, cardboard,
metal frame, 20x42".......**60.00**

Burgomaster Beer, sheet metal,
13" diameter, EX............**40.00**
Cadbury's Chocolate, color decal
between 2 panes of glass,
12x9", VG......................**75.00**
City of New York Insurance,
reverse-painted on glass,
framed, 21x15".............**155.00**
Coleman's Pale Dry Ginger Ale, 4-
color, tin, 12x24", M.......**20.00**
Cook's Beer, man smoking &
riverboat, tin with cardboard
back, 30x24" **125.00**
Cook's Gold Blume Beer, self-
framed tin oval, 14x18" ..**60.00**
Donald Duck Bread, D Duck, multicolor, tin, 27x40", VG.**120.00**
Dupont Powder, self-framed tin,
1903, 23x33", EX..........**400.00**
Gollams Ice Cream, boy with
cone, double-sided porcelain,
28x20", EX....................**125.00**
Grape Nuts, To School..., girl &
dog, self-framed tin......**200.00**
Harvey's Home Made Chocolate,
Deco style, electric light-up,
9x19"..............................**70.00**

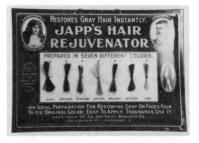

**Japp's Hair Rejuvenator, with
color samples, 9" x 13", $350.00.**

Kato Beer, eagle, glass, convex,
15" **110.00**
La Reforma Cigars, reverse-
painted, 10x14", EX.......**85.00**
Lime Cola, embossed tin, 1937,
3x24", M........................**45.00**
Mason's Old Fashioned Root Beer,
4-color, tin, 20x27" **20.00**

Paul Jones Whiskey, game & rifle, tin, in wood frame, 34x49", EX...................50.00

Pennzoil, black on yellow, double-sided steel, 31x22" 35.00

Pepsi Cola, red, white & blue, cap shape, 19" diameter.......90.00

Pet Ice Cream, Schmidt's of Philadelphia, 2-color neon, 19x12", EX.....................75.00

Peter Pan, 3-color, embossed tin, 20x29", M........................65.00

Royal Crown Cola, embossed tin, 1936, 22x34", EX............85.00

Shaefer Hat Works, Los Angeles, cardboard, wood frame, 1923, 23x27"...........................45.00

Val Blatz Brewing, still life, self-framed tin, 22x28".......500.00

Western Ammunition, hunting scene, embossed tin, 1930s, 13x19", EX....................135.00

Western Union, Send Telegrams by Telephone, paint on porcelain, 9x18" 65.00

Winchester, paper shot shells, cardboard, standup, foldout, 50x34"...........................100.00

Wrigley's Gum, 4 packs, silver leaf print, tin, 11x7" 95.00

Thermometers

Baugh's Fertilizers, 3-color paint on wood, 12" 17.50

Biltrite, red, white & yellow, shoe in center, tin, 13x6" 30.00

Camel Cigarettes, red, yellow & white, tin, 13½x6", EX ..12.50

Chesterfield Cigarettes, 3-color paint on tin, 13x6", EX ..12.50

Fatima Cigarettes, blue & white, porcelain on steel, Pat 1915, 17x7"...............................70.00

Five Star Anti-Freeze, bear at top, 3-color paint on tin, 21", EX 55.00

Hughes' Fuel Oil, green & white, wood, 15", EX 22.50

Mail Pouch, blue & white, porcelain on steel, 38x8".......165.00

Marvels, product at top, 3-color paint on tin, 12" 25.00

NuGrape, white with purple & yellow on tin, 16", EX 48.00

Orange Crush, Crushy figure at top, Deco style, tin, 10"..30.00

Red Seal Dry Battery, red, white & blue, porcelain on steel, 1915, EX 80.00

Royal Crown Cola, The Heat Is On!, yellow & red, 25"....25.00

Taxi Auto Supplies, touring car, wood, glass rod & barometer, 12", VG 30.00

Tums, blue & red, yellow & white letters, tin, 9x4", VG......25.00

5 Roses Flour, porcelain, 1920s, 38x8", EX......................60.00

Tin Containers

Hills Brothers Coffee, copyright 1922, 7", $40.00.

Azeura Talc, floral design, round with lift lid, EX 6.50

Bendsorp's Cocoa, red & gold, canister, 14x11"....................38.00

Bliss Coffee, 4x5", EX **15.00**
Buckingham Tobacco, sample
size, EX.........................**110.00**
Buffalo Peanut Butter, pail,
small, EX.......................**50.00**
Bunte Marshmallows, Bunte Kid,
1914, EX.......................**165.00**
Campfire Marshmallows, beige,
red & blue, 6x10", EX..**175.00**
Chesterfield Cigarettes, canister,
'50s, EX..........................**25.00**
Dixie Queen Plug Cut, lady's por-
trait, canister, VG **90.00**
Dr Sayman's Healing Salve, sam-
ple size, VG....................... **5.00**
El Roi Tan Cigars, pocket size,
5x3½x1", EX **20.00**
Esso Motor Oil, red, white & blue,
pail, bail handle, 9½".....**10.00**
Holiday Tobacco, Christmas paper
label, canister, EX..........**20.00**
La Fendrich Cigars, man with
gold medals, 5x4x1".......**30.00**
Lucky Strike Cigarettes, Flat
'50s, EX...........................**12.50**
Ocean Blend Tea, ship & Indian,
Ceylon, 6x7", M **35.00**
Peach Tobacco, pocket size ...**45.00**
Picobac, hand with leaf, M ...**70.00**
Rumford Baking Powder, sample
size, VG...........................**12.50**
Squirrel Peanut Butter, 4" diame-
ter **38.00**
Tuxedo, man smoking, round-top
canister, '10, 6x5", EX....**38.00**
Union Leader, eagle, white rib-
bon, recessed lid, EX......**12.00**
Velvet Tobacco, pipe, pocket size,
EX **6.00**
Yum Yum Smoking Tobacco, farm
boy, pail.........................**155.00**

Tip Trays

Ballentine & Sons, 3 rings on
wood-grain background, 5"
diameter, NM **42.00**
Bartel's, watchman with pitcher,
pre-prohibition, 4".........**140.00**

CD Kenny, girl praying, 4" ...**85.00**
Clover Brand Shoes, Black boy
with watermelon, VG **85.00**
Co-Operative Foundry Red Cross
Stoves & Ranges, 4½" diame-
ter **25.00**
Columbus Brewing, portrait of
Columbus **155.00**
Cortez Cigars, 6x4", VG........**22.50**
DeLaval Cream Separators, 4¼",
EX...................................**65.00**
Evervess Sparkling Water, parrot,
6x4", VG.........................**66.00**
Hotel Belleview, Washington DC,
porcelain, 1912, M.........**32.00**
Kings Puremalt, Panama Pacific
Expo, multicolor, EX......**60.00**
Lucky Lager, western hemisphere
& boat, 4x6", EX............**27.00**
Marilyn Monroe, nude portrait, 4"
diameter, NM **28.00**
Mount Vernon Evaporated Milk,
oval, 4½", EX **35.00**
National Cigar Stands, woman in
pink, gold trim, EX **85.00**
Pep-To-Lac, dark-haired lady with
large earrings.................**65.00**
S&S Ginger Ale, NM.............**36.00**
Stagmaier Brewing, factory view,
4" diameter, NM...........**110.00**
Yuengling's Beer, 1900s, 4"...**88.00**

Trays

Bavarian Brewing, Deco flowers,
1908, 13¼x13¼", EX **50.00**
Cheon, For Iced Tea..., geisha with
tray, 4" diameter, NM **50.00**
Double Cola, girl holding two
glasses, 1960s, 13¼" diame-
ter, NM **12.00**
Heine Beer, Dutch Boy, Compli-
ments of...Union, EX **75.00**
Hires Root Beer, Best Drink on
Earth, 5¢, 13", EX........**400.00**
La Verdo Cigars, courting couple,
oval, 14x17", EX...........**155.00**
Orange Julep, lady with parasol,
1920s, 10½x13¼"..........**100.00**

Pepsi Cola, Pepsi kids singing, rectangular, NM.............**18.00**

Red Raven, lady embracing large black bird, 1910s, 12" diameter, EX............**145.00**

Rheingold Extra Dry Brewery, red, black & white, 13" diameter, EX **22.00**

Miscellaneous

Box, Egypt Lacquer, Egyptian princess on label, wooden, dovetailed.......................**20.00**

Coffee measure, Hills Bros Coffee, M.......................**5.00**

Display, Copenhagen Chew, red, black & gold, tin, hanging, 9", VG **28.00**

Display box, Kellogg's Corn Flakes, 16x20x7", NM .**100.00**

Display rack, Pertussin Cough Medicine, tin, countertop, 4x11x6", EX.......................**45.00**

Display razor, Griffon XX, silvery blade, black handle, 29".**25.00**

Door push, Ex-Lax, multicolor, plastic, 3½x7½", pair......**20.00**

Map, Grace Lines premium, full color, 1933, 32x24", EX..**12.50**

Mirror, Buckingham Bros, gold lettering, beveled glass, 12" diameter.......................**200.00**

Mirror, Carstairs, red letters, painted wood frame, 18x24", EX.**35.00**

Mirror, Cluett, Peabody & Co, reverse painted, stand-up back, 16x11" **95.00**

Mirror, Eclipse Electrotype & Engraving, white with brown details, 4" **15.00**

Mirror, Lucas Paint, silver letters, wood frame, 24x25".......**30.00**

Mirror, Magnet Pale Ale, reverse-painted letters, heavy, 22x34", EX.......................**45.00**

Mirror, Simonds on Draught, gold letters on black frame, 10x8", EX **55.00**

Pencil clip, Star Brand Shoes, ca 1900, EX **8.00**

Pencil sharpener, Baker's Chocolate, girl figural, metal, 2", EX **25.00**

Pin, lapel; Smith & Wesson, pistol shape, silver metal.........**25.00**

Plaque, Walter Baker & Co Ltd Chocolate & Cocoa, lady with cup, 16x18".......................**30.00**

Plaque, Watson North Undertaker, metal with worn brass finish, 6x14" **50.00**

Tape measure, Edison Mazda Lamps, celluloid, Whitehead & Hoag, EX **15.00**

Tile, Malt Kepler Essence, milk glass, in wood frame, 7½x11", EX.......................**50.00**

Lunch box, Green Turtle Cigars, 4½" x 7½" x 5½", $200.00.

Akro Agate

This company operated in Clarksburg, West Virginia, from 1914 to 1951, manufacturing marbles, novelties, and children's dishes, for which they are best known. Though some were made in clear solid colors, their most popular, easy-to-identify lines were produced in a swirling opaque type of glass similar to that which was used in the production of their marbles. Their trademark was a flying eagle clutching marbles in his claws.

Stippled Band, Small; see listings for specific values.

Chiquita, creamer, opaque turquoise, lavender, or caramel, 1½" **12.00**

Chiquita, saucer, transparent cobalt blue, 3⅛" **2.00**

Chiquita, sugar bowl, baked-on colors, open, 1½".............. **8.00**

Chiquita, teapot, opaque turquoise or lavender, with lid, 3"...............................**35.00**

Concentric Rib, creamer, opaque green, 1¼"......................... **5.00**

Concentric Rib, cup, opaque colors besides green or white, 1¼". **5.00**

Concentric Rib, sugar bowl, opaque green or white, 1¼" **4.50**

Concentric Rib, teapot, opaque green or white, 3½" **9.00**

Concentric Ring, cereal bowl, transparent cobalt, 3⅜" ..**28.00**

Concentric Ring, creamer, marbleized blue, 1⅜" **45.00**

Concentric Ring, cup, opaque lavender or yellow, 1⅜"..**30.00**

Concentric Ring, cup, transparent cobalt, 1¼" **24.00**

Concentric Ring, plate, solid opaque colors, 4¼"........... **6.00**

Concentric Ring, sugar bowl, transparent cobalt, with lid, 1⅞" **45.00**

Concentric Ring, transparent cobalt blue, 3¼" **5.00**

Interior Panel, creamer, pink or green lustre, 1⅜" **14.00**

Interior Panel, cup, marbleized red & white, 1¼" **20.00**

Interior Panel, plate, marbleized blue & white, 3¾"............ **7.00**

Interior Panel, sugar bowl, azure blue or yellow, 1¼" **27.00**

Interior Panel, teapot, lemonade & oxblood, with lid, 3¾"..**47.00**

J Pressman, cup, transparent cobalt blue, ribbed, 1½"... **4.00**

J Pressman, plate, transparent red or brown, 1½"...........**30.00**

J Pressman, sugar bowl, baked-on colors, with lid, 1½" **10.00**

J Pressman, teapot, transparent green, with lid, 1½"........**30.00**

Miss America, creamer, marbleized orange & white..**32.00**

Miss America, plate, marbleized orange & white **20.00**

Miss America, sugar bowl, forest green, with lid................**48.00**

Octagonal, cereal bowl, lemonade & oxblood, 3⅜"...............**20.00**

Octagonal, tumbler, pumpkin, yellow, or lime green, 2" **12.00**

Raised Daisy, teapot, blue or green, open, 2⅜" **40.00**

Raised Daisy, tumbler, blue, no embossed pattern, 2" **55.00**

Stacked Disc, creamer, pumpkin, 1¼" **12.00**

Stacked Disc, sugar bowl, pumpkin, 1¼" **14.00**

Stacked Disc, teapot, opaque green or white, with lid, 3⅜" **9.00**

Stacked Disc & Interior Panel, cereal bowl, marbleized blue, 3⅜" **35.00**

Stacked Disc & Interior Panel, creamer, opaque solid colors, 1¼" **14.00**

Stacked Disc & Interior Panel, sugar bowl, transparent green, 1¼".......................**40.00**

Stacked Disc & Interior Panel, tumbler, transparent cobalt, 2" **8.00**

Stippled Band, creamer, transparent amber, 1¼" **8.00**

Stippled Band, cup, transparent azure, 1½" **18.00**

Stippled Band, saucer, transparent green, 3¼" **2.00**

Stippled Band, sugar bowl, transparent amber, lid, 1⅛" ...**18.00**

Stippled Band, tumbler, transparent green, 1¾" **7.00**

Aluminum

From the late 1930s until early in the 1950s, kitchenwares and household items were crafted from aluminum, usually with relief-molded fruit or flowers on a hammered background. Today many find these diversified items make an interesting collection. Especially desirable are those examples marked with the manufacturer's backstamp or the designer's signature.

Tray, cherry branches, marked Wendell August Forge, 16" long, $25.00.

Bowl, pea pod handle, Everlast, with lid **12.50**

Butter tub, with lid & bail handle, 4" **20.00**

Candy dish, leaf form, hammered, unmarked **7.50**

Garden ornament, rabbit, cast, 12", EX............................**55.00**

Ice bucket, hammered, crockery lining, EX **28.00**

Pitcher, plain, hammered, water size................................**10.00**

Teapot, octagonal, wood handle, Wagner Ware, 10x7" **28.00**

Tray, embossed decoration, Farberware, EX **12.50**

Tray, engraved florals, hammered, 11x11" **10.00**

Animal Dishes with Covers

Popular novelties for part of this century as well as the last, figural animal dishes were made by many well-known glass houses in milk glass, slag, colored opaque, or clear glass. These are preferred by today's collectors, though the English earthenware versions are highly collectible in their own right.

Atterbury duck reproduction, any color, unmarked **75.00**

Baby Moses on cattail or reed base, 6¼" long...............**185.00**

Bambi, powder jar, carnival glass, Jeannette Glass **15.00**

Bird with berry, milk glass, Greentown....................**300.00**

Bull's head, mustard jar, milk glass, with tongue ladle, Atterbury......................**200.00**

Cat on tall hamper, transparent colored **200.00**

Chick in egg on sleigh, milk glass, 5¼" **50.00**

Chick on eggs, milk glass, dated August 6, 1889 on lid...**165.00**

Dog, milk glass, Westmoreland Specialty **65.00**

Donkey, powder jar, clear **12.50**

Duck, blue opaque, Atterbury, dated 1887, 11" **450.00**

Duck on cattail base, milk glass, 5½" long **85.00**

Duck soap dish, clear with painted bill, 1930s **10.00**

Elephant, standing, trunk up, clear, 9" long...................**45.00**

Fish on collared base, clear frosted...........................**150.00**

Fox, beaded base, blue opaque, Westmoreland, large......**95.00**

Fox, ribbed lid, lacy base, milk glass, 6¼".......................**165.00**

Hand & dove, milk glass, Atterbury, patent date..........**110.00**

Hen on basketweave base with woven edges, colored, 5⅝" long **45.00**

Hen on diamond basketweave nest, chocolate glass **400.00**

Hen with chicks on basketweave base, milk glass, Wright, medium size **25.00**

Lion, British; milk glass **95.00**

Lion on ribbed base, milk glass, Aug 6, 1889 in lid.........**135.00**

Lion on ribbed base, milk glass, no date.............................**65.00**

Quail on scroll base, milk glass, unknown maker.............**65.00**

Rabbit, lacy base, white carnival, Westmoreland, large......**85.00**

Swan, milk glass, marked Vallerysthal, 5½" long, $125.00. (Beware of Taiwan reproductions.)

Rat on egg, milk glass, Vallerysthal **175.00**

Rooster, goofus glass, wide-rib milk glass base, 5½".......**45.00**

Santa on sleigh, milk glass, Westmoreland **40.00**

Swan, clear frosted, marked Vallerysthal....................**95.00**

Swan on block, milk glass ..**110.00**

Appliances

Old electric appliances are collected for nostalgic reasons as well as for their unique appearance and engineering. Especially interesting are early irons, fans, vacuum cleaners, and toasters. Examples with Art Deco styling often bring high prices at today's auctions and flea markets.

Sunbeam toaster, chrome with black trim, $45.00.

Coffeepot, Edison General Electric Hotpint, chrome.....**12.50**

Fan, Emerson, early 1900s...**35.00**

Fan, table; Solar Cub, AC Gilbert, 6", EX original...............**65.00**

Mixer, Lindstrom, with original glass bowl, 1920s, EX **8.00**

Mixer/juicer, General Electric, hinged frame, 1919, EX.**90.00**

Percolator, Farberware, Bakelite handle, EX.....................**35.00**

Percolator, Royal Rochester, chrome, wood handles, Pyrex lid, 15" **50.00**

Toaster, General Electric D12, porcelain base, patented 1908, EX **80.00**

Toaster, Marion Giant Flip Flop #66, EX **45.00**

Toaster, Universal #946, steel doors **32.00**

Vacuum cleaner, Bellows, EX paint **95.00**

Waffle iron, Manning-Bowman, Deco styling, Bakelite handles, 11" dia **80.00**

Ash tray, chrome with black enamel trim, 7", $12.00.

Art Deco

The Art Deco movement began at the Paris International Exposition in 1925 and lasted into the 1950s. Styles of apparel, furniture, jewelry, cars, and architecture were influenced by its cubist forms and sweeping, aerodynamic curves. Sleek greyhounds and female nudes (less voluptuous than Art Nouveau nudes), shooting stars and lightning bolts, exotic woods and lush fabrics–all were elements of the Art Deco era. Today's fashions, especially in home furnishings, reflect the movement; and collectors delight in acquiring authentic examples to recreate the posh Art Deco environment.

Adding machine, Streamline by Victor, Bakelite **120.00**

Ash tray, ceramic with cobalt glaze, 4½".......................**28.00**

Ash tray, depression glass with suits of cards, each.......... **8.00**

Bookends, brass finish on metal, Scotty dogs, Frankart, 7", pair **75.00**

Bookends, comical dog, NuArt, pair **32.00**

Bookends, nude with arched back, bronze wash, 7", pair **80.00**

Bowl, multicolor leaves on orange, gold trim, 11" **35.00**

Box, porcelain, hand-painted abstracts, octagonal **160.00**

Box, powder; frosted green glass, semi-nude finial, 8½" **70.00**

Box, white Bakelite, brass frame, 7¾x5" **25.00**

Chair, bentwood, black webbing, Bruno Matheson **350.00**

Cheese dish, chrome, round, Chase, 14"......................**30.00**

Cigarette lighter, elephant figural, chrome **75.00**

Clock, digital, bronze, Silvercrest, ca 1930s, 19" long **165.00**

Coat rack, rectangular with mirror, scrolled ironwork, 64" long **200.00**

Cocktail set, chrome with black bands, 5-piece...............**130.00**

Cocktail shaker, chrome plated, etched grapevines, 12".**155.00**

Cocktail shaker, chrome-plated penguin form, 11½x8" ..**185.00**

Cocktail, dancing nude supports pink glass bowl, 5" **40.00**

Compact, navy plastic, hand painting on silver bar, France..............................**95.00**

Compact, sterling with hand-chased florals **85.00**

Figurine, Cinderella, ceramic with glossy finish, ca 1940s, 12"..................................**125.00**

Figurine, pink flamingo, porcelain, 10½".........................**42.00**

Figurine, wolfhounds, ceramic, Germany, 1940s, 13" ...**250.00**

Flower frog, nude on foliage, porcelain, 7¾" **45.00**

Grooming set, plastic, 10-piece in leather case **20.00**

Hair brush, engraved girl on gold-tone, EX **15.00**

Ice bucket, chrome, round base, lucite hdls, 10" **100.00**

Ice bucket, glass with chrome handle, 6" **35.00**

Jar, powder; camphor glass, supported by nudes at base **75.00**

Lamp, chrome gazelles on black glass base, with conical shade, 9" **55.00**

Lamp, Harlequin playing lute, green crackle globe **70.00**

Lamp, 2 minstrels at lamppost, plaster, hobnail shade....**50.00**

Mirror, pot-metal nude figure on faux marble base **140.00**

Pen holder, horse on pedestal, bronze, on teardrop base, 6x4½x3½".........................**95.00**

Plaque, nude with 2 greyhounds, heavy metal, 9x12½"....**125.00**

Plate, hand-painted & incised fish, Longwy-style pottery, 10"....................................**95.00**

Punch set, ruby glass with chrome trim, 7-piece **155.00**

Purse, large white plastic beads in pentagon shape..........**18.00**

Sconce, gold iridescent shade with molded geometrics, 9" holder **42.00**

Teakettle, Pyrex, long spout, applied handle, 1919......**35.00**

Tray, chrome & wood with lucite hdls, Ernst Hagerstrom, 21" long **120.00**

Tumbler, chrome holder, cobalt blue glass insert, 2½".....**14.00**

Waste basket, blue mirror **55.00**

Tea set, chrome, marked EPNS, 3-piece, with pair of 6" candlesticks, $375.00.

Autographs

Autographs of famous people from every walk of life are of interest to students of Philography, as it is referred to by those who enjoy this hobby. Values hinge on many things–rarity of the signature and content of the signed material are major considerations. Autographs of sports figures or entertainers often sell at $5.00 to $15.00 for small signed photos. Beware of forgeries. If you are unsure, ask established dealers to help you.

Andrews Sisters, three signatures on black & white photo, 1951 ....**25.00**

Armstrong, Neil; signature on 3x5" card.........................**32.00**

Arnold, Eddy; signature on 8x10" black & white photo.......**27.50**

Autry, Gene; inscribed signature on 8x10" photo, M **27.50**

Bachrach, Louis Fabian; signed on typed letter, 1958......**28.00**

Ball, Lucille; signature on 5x7" photo, NM......**15.00**

Bench, Johnny; signature on 4x6" photo......**10.00**

Blanc, Mel; signature on 4x6" color photo......**22.00**

Britton, Barbara; signature on typed letter, 1940s, EX..**20.00**

Buckley, William F; signature on 5x7" photo......**22.00**

Crawford, Joan; inscribed signature on 8x10" black & white photo, ca 1940......**60.00**

Cronkite, Walter; signature on 3x5" card......**35.00**

Eastwood, Clint; signature on 4x6" card......**10.00**

Eisenhower, Mamie Dowd; full signature on White House card, NM......**55.00**

Gleason, Jackie; inscribed signature on 8x10" photo with Steve McQueen......**68.00**

Goldwater, Barry; signature on 6-page typescript......**22.00**

Grayson, Kathryn; signature on 3½x5" photo......**10.00**

Greenwood, Charlotte; signature on sepia color scene from Oklahoma......**42.00**

Hartman, David; signature on 7x9" photo......**18.00**

Hoffman, Dustin; signature on photo, as Tootsie......**28.00**

Hooper, Harry; signature on 4x6" photo......**18.00**

Ives, Burl; full signature on 4x6" card......**20.00**

Kelly, Gene; signature on 5x7" photo......**16.00**

Knowland, William; inscribed signature on 5x7" photo, as CA senator......**10.00**

Lancaster, Burt; signature on color still, 1974......**28.00**

Landry, Tom; signature on 4x6" photo......**10.00**

Loren, Sophia; signature on 4x6" photo......**12.00**

Love, John; signature on envelope cover......**8.00**

Mantle, Mickey; signature on 8x10" photo......**40.00**

Montana, Joe; signature on 8x10" black & white photo......**25.00**

Murphy, Bob; inscribed signature on 5x7" photo......**18.00**

Niven, David; signature on 4x6" photo, 1930s, EX......**78.00**

Preble, Admiral George Henry; signature on letter, dated 1881, 2 pages......**40.00**

Retton, Mary Lou; signature on 3x5" card......**12.00**

Rich, Buddy; signature on 8x10" photo, 1948......**25.00**

Rinehart, Mary Roberts; signature on card......**22.00**

Rogers, Ginger; signature on card, 1954......**17.50**

Russell, Rosalind; signature on handwritten note......**12.50**

Schmidt, Helmut; signature on 5x7" photo......**40.00**

Shepard, Cybil; signature on card with 8x10" photo......**20.00**

Simpson, OJ; signature on 8x10" black & white photo......**17.50**

Smith, Alfred; signature as Governor of NY on typed letter, 1930......**22.50**

Stern, Isaac; signature on 1971 program......**16.00**

Stewart, James; signature on 8x10" black & white photo, as General......**48.00**

Stratemeyer, General George E; signature on typed letter, 1946......**32.00**

Sutton, Don; signature on 5x7" black & white photo, early Dodger years......**32.00**

Swanson, Gloria; signature & inscription on album page..**15.00**

Thomas, Betty; signature on 4x6" card with small photo....**10.00**

Thomas, Frankie; signature on movie still, 1935.............**36.00**

Truman, Bess; signature on printed message.............**27.50**

Tucker, Tommy; inscribed signature on 8x10" black & white photo...............................**28.00**

Tunney, Gene; clipped signature, large, bold.......................**32.00**

Welch, Racquel; signature on 11x14" lobby card, 1968.**32.00**

Westmoreland, General; signature on 3x5" card **7.50**

Woodward, Joanne; signature on 4x6" card.........................**12.50**

Young, Loretta; signature on magazine photo cover, 1930..**27.50**

Tony Sarg, on illustrated letterhead, hand-drawn and colored elephant at close of letter responding to photo request, $400.00.

Automobilia

Many are fascinated with vintage automobiles, but to own one of those 'classy chassis' is a luxury not all can afford! So instead they enjoy collecting related memorabilia such as advertising, owners' manuals, horns, emblems, and hood ornaments. The decade of the 1930s produced the items that are most in demand today, but the fifties models have their own band of devoted fans as well. Usually made of porcelain on cast iron, first-year license plates in hard-to-find excellent condition may bring as much as $200.00 for the pair.

Ash tray, Dodge Family Day, aluminum, 1949 .... **8.00**

Ash tray, United Motors, glass, touring car logo, 6x6".....**22.00**

Ash tray, US Royal Master Air Ride, tire with glass insert, EX................................**22.50**

Banner, Pyro Anti-freeze......**18.00**

Book, Vintage Motorcars, David Wise, 1972, NM **12.00**

Booklet, Amazing Tydol Facts, well illustrated, 1934, 16 pages, NM **6.50**

Booklet, Champion Spark Plugs, 1940s, 24 pages, EX........ **5.00**

Bud vase, carnival glass, missing bracket, pair...................**80.00**

Clicker toy, Quaker State Motor Oil, with logo **8.00**

Coat hook, DeSoto-Plymouth, slips over window glass .. **7.50**

Gearshift knob, simulated onyx with brass medallion in center, EX **28.00**

Key ring, Phillips 66, shield shape with logo, 3-color............. **6.00**

Keychain identification tag, Oldsmobile & Viking, celluloid, EX............................**16.50**

Letter opener, Pontiac, hammered brass, enameled emblem, 1930s, 9" **80.00**

Letter opener, Texaco, simulated pearl handle with logo, chrome blade **14.00**

Manual, owner's; DeSoto, 1953, M....................................**38.00**

Manual, owner's; Studebaker, 1925, VG **48.00**

Medallion, Chevrolet, Pikes Peak Champion Truck, brass .**30.00**

Model, Pontiac promotional, 2-door sedan, 1954, EX...**135.00**

Motometer, Minute-Man 6....**45.00**

Pencil, mechanical; Interstate Oil, EX **2.50**

Pennant, Buick, black letters on yellow felt, 6" long **2.50**

Plymouth for 1953, fold-out, $10.00.

Radiator cap mascot, Dodge, blue & white enamel, 1918....**25.00**

Radiator cap mascot, eagle wings, brass, 9¼" wide **30.00**

Radiator cap mascot, Franklin lion, M...........................**200.00**

Radiator cap mascot, DeSoto, 1928 ....**200.00**

Record, Chevrolet promotional, message performed by Ben Cartwright, 1964............**10.00**

Ruler, Buick Authorized Service, cardboard, 6", NM **6.50**

Ruler, Hupp Corporation, plastic, 6" **15.00**

Ruler, Studebaker Cars & Trucks for Quality & Economy, plastic, 6".................................**12.50**

Spark plug, Champion X for Model-T, 2-piece, 4 for....**55.00**

Stick pin, Mercedes, 3-point star, EX **15.00**

Tire gauge, US Gauge, dial type, 0-80 lbs, with original pouch, EX..**36.00**

Autumn Leaf

Autumn Leaf dinnerware was a product of the Hall China Company, who produced this extensive line from 1933 until 1978 for exclusive distribution by the Jewell Tea Company. The Libbey Glass Company made coordinating pitchers, tumblers and stemware. Metal, cloth, plastic, and paper items were also available. Today, though very rare pieces are expensive and a challenge to acquire, new collectors may easily reassemble an attractive, usable set at a reasonable price.

Baker, oval, Fort Pitt **70.00**
Bean pot, handles, 2¼-qt **85.00**
Bowl, coupe soup **10.00**
Bowl, cream soup **18.00**
Bowl, salad **14.00**
Bowl, vegetable; oval, with lid, 10" **35.00**
Bowl, vegetable; 9"................**60.00**
Bread box, metal **125.00**
Bud vase, 6".........................**150.00**
Butter dish, ¼-lb **125.00**

Butter dish, 1-pound, $165.00.

Cake safe, metal, motif on top & sides, 5"...........................**25.00**
Canister, metal, round, with matching lid, 7" **25.00**
Canister, metal, square, set of 4: 8½" & 4½" **115.00**
Casserole, Royal Glas-Bake, shallow, with clear lid **20.00**

Casserole, 10-oz...................... 8.00
Clock, original works 350.00
Coffee maker, all china with
    insert, 5-cup 175.00
Coffee percolator/carafe, Douglas,
    with warmer base, M...200.00
Cup & saucer......................... 8.00
Cup & saucer, St Denis.........18.00
Custard cup........................... 4.00
Flatware, stainless, each 10.00
Granulator, metal, no decal..35.00
Gravy boat.............................15.00
Hot pad, oval 10.00
Marmalade jar, 3-piece.........45.00
Mug, Irish coffee 45.00
Picnic thermos, metal 250.00
Pitcher, jug; 5½-pint.............18.00
Place mat, set of 8, M in original
    package.........................195.00
Plate, 10" 10.00
Plate, 6" 4.00
Plate, 7" 4.00
Plate, 8" 8.00
Plate, 9" 7.00
Platter, 11½"..........................14.00
Platter, 13½"..........................16.00
Sauce dish, serving; Douglas,
    Bakelite handle 125.00
Sugar bowl, New Style 12.00
Tablecloth, cotton sailcloth with
    gold stripe, 54x72" 70.00
Tablecloth, plastic...............125.00
Teapot, Aladdin 38.00
Teapot, Newport..................115.00
Tidbit tray, 2-tier..................35.00
Toaster cover, plastic, fits 2-slice
    toaster............................25.00
Tray, metal, oval 55.00
Tumbler, Brockway, 16-oz.....18.00
Tumbler, gold frost etched, footed
    bottom, 6½-oz 45.00
Warmer base, round.............90.00

Aviation Collectibles

Collectors of aviation memorabilia search for items dealing
with zeppelins, flying machines–
aircraft of any type, be it experi-
mental, commercial, civilian, or
military. From airplane parts and
pilot's gear to photos and magazines, there is a multitude of
material relative to this area of
interest.

Album, Zepellin-Weltfahrten, soft
    cover, 1933, VG 155.00
Book, Lindbergh, the Lone Eagle,
    Beamish, 1st edition 25.00
Book, Story of the Airship, many
    photos, 1932, EX 35.00
Book, Thirty Seconds Over Tokyo,
    1st edition, EX...............15.00
Bookmark, Lindbergh woven in
    silk 40.00
Brochure, Beechcraft Bonanza, ca
    1948, 6-page 17.50
Cigarette lighter, Pan American
    Air Lines 15.00
Crochet panel, Spirit of St Louis,
    24x12" 60.00
Decal, Eaglerock Aircraft, yellow
    & blue with gray eagle...22.00
Flyer, Continental Aircraft,
    describes engine, ca 1935, 6-
    page 17.50
Game, Flight to Paris, Lindbergh
    cover, 1920s, EX 15.00
Helmet, flight; leather, 1920s,
    EX.................................40.00
Menu, Pan American, Maxim's
    Paris, 1960, 10x14"........17.50
Model, Spirit of St Louis, cellu-
    loid, EX..........................55.00
Pencil case, tin, Charles Lind-
    bergh, EX.......................47.50
Photograph, Amelia Earhart,
    early, 8x10"....................25.00
Program, Bremen Fliers, Boston,
    May, 1928, 20-page 12.00
Ring, American Airlines Junior
    Pilot 6.00
Sign, Whitney Aircraft Chains,
    tin, 1940s, 9x23" 48.00
Stock, canceled certificate,
    United, 1960s, EX..........24.00

Zeppelin, tin litho, mechanical, by Tipp, Germany, 24", EX, $450.00.

Textbook, Naval Aviation, Henry Woodhouse, 1917, 287-page, EX **75.00**

Timetable, Hindenberg, 3-fold, French, EX **20.00**

Avon

Originally founded under the title California Perfume Company, the firm became officially known as Avon Products, Inc., in 1939, after producing a line of cosmetics marketed under the Avon name since the mid-twenties. Among collectors they are best known not for their cosmetics and colognes but for their imaginative packaging and figural bottles. Also collectible are product samples, awards, magazine ads, jewelry, and catalogues.

1960 Persian Wood Toilet Water, 2-oz., $12.00; 1969 Petite Flower Cologne, $9.00; 1956 Pine Bath Oil, 4-oz., $27.00.

Ariel perfume, octagonal bottle & cap, 1933, M **48.00**

Ballad perfume, bottle with gold cord & lable, with stopper, 3-dram **95.00**

Bishop chess piece decanter, 1975-1978, 3-oz, M **3.50**

Brushless shaving cream, green & black tube, 1930s, VG....**22.00**

Candy Cane Twins, 2 cameo lipsticks on candy cane box, 1966 ....**27.50**

Christmas Trio for Men, 1964, M in box **27.50**

Circle of Pearls, 1957, 2-oz, M in box..................................**65.00**

Classic Style set, black & gold box, 1958, NM **17.50**

Cotillion perfume, gold cap, 1935, ¼-oz, M in box **78.00**

Demonstrator kit, deodorant & soap, 1942, M in box **48.00**

Doubly Yours hand cream, 2 tubes in rose box, 1954, M **18.00**

Evening Lights set, gold purse, 3 cosmetics, 1965 ....**18.00**

Face Powder Sample, metal can, 1936-1943, EX................ **7.50**

Fluffy cleansing cream, pink tube, 1947, EX........................**18.00**

Happy Hours set, cuckoo clock on box, 1958, 2-oz, M **35.00**

Honeysuckle Floral Duet Set, rollette & bar of soap, 1972, M in box **6.00**

Kwick foaming shave cream, green & white can with red top, 10-oz **7.50**

Lilac Soap, cellophane wrapper, 1955, M in box...............**18.00**

Lotion Lovely, gold painted label, 1964, 8-oz, NM **2.00**

Oland spray talc, upside label on can, 7-oz, 1970s.............. **4.50**

Quaintance Soap, 3 blue bars with embossed bows, 1950s, M in box..........................**38.00**

Rapture perfume oil, green glass & cap, 1960s, M in box.... **6.00**

Spongaroo soap & sponge, kangaroo shapes, 1966, VG.....**10.00**

Sweetest One Baby Set, soap, powder & lotion, 1962-1964, M in box **42.00**

Ultra Fluff set, dusting powder & puff, 1970, M in box.......**12.50**

Unforgettable Heirloom, gold & white tray, 1½-oz............**35.00**

Vigorate after shave, clear glass with white cap, 1959-1960, 8-oz, NM **30.00**

Witch hazel cream, green tube, 1923, EX.........................**30.00**

Azalea China

Manufactured by the Noritake Company from 1916 until the mid-thirties, Azalea dinnerware was given away as premiums to club members and home agents of the Larkin Company, a door-to-door agency who sold soap and other household products. Over the years, seventy chinaware items were offered as well as six pieces of matching hand painted crystal. Early pieces were signed with the blue 'rising sun' Nippon trademark, followed by the Noritake M-in-wreath mark. Later, the ware was marked Noritake, Azalea, Hand Painted, Japan.

Bonbon, #184, 6¼"................**45.00**

Bowl, deep, #310 ....**50.00**

Bowl, fruit; #188, 7¾" **325.00**

Bowl, oatmeal; #55...............**18.00**

Butter chip, #312 ....**40.00**

Butter dish, #314 ....**90.00**

Cake plate, #10 ....**50.00**

Candy jar, #313 ....**525.00**

Casserole with lid, #16 ....**75.00**

Celery tray, #99, 12" **50.00**

Coffeepot, AD; #182 ....**500.00**

Creamer & sugar bowl, AD; open, #123 ....**100.00**

Cruet, #190.........................**175.00**

Cup & saucer, #2 ....**18.00**

Cup & saucer, AD; #183........**25.00**

Egg cup, #120 ....**40.00**

Mustard jar, #191 ....**48.00**

Creamer and sugar set #7, $50.00; Cup and saucer #2, $18.00.

Pitcher, milk; #100, 1-qt **175.00**
Plate, #4, 7½" **10.00**
Plate, grill; 3-compartment, #338,
  10¼" **95.00**
Platter, #17, 14"....................**55.00**
Platter, #186, 16" **325.00**
Platter, #311, 10" **180.00**
Relish, #194, 7" **70.00**
Sandwich tray, #112..............**60.00**
Saucer, fruit; #9 ....**10.00**
Shakers, #89, pair.................**25.00**
Spoon holder, #189................**75.00**
Tea tile, #169 ....**45.00**
Teapot, gold finial, #400 ....**420.00**
Toothpick holder, #192..........**90.00**
Vase, fan form, #187 ....**125.00**

Badges

'Wild West' badges and those
once worn by officials whose posi-
tions no longer exist–City Constable, for instance–are tops on the
lists of today's badge collectors.
All law-enforcement badges are
considered collectible as well.
Badges have been made in many
materials and styles since the
1840s when they came into general use in this country. They
were usually of brass or nickel silver, though even silver and gold
were used on special order. Stars,
shields, octagonals, ovals, and
disks are the most common
shapes.

Bellmore Fire Department, silver
  metal, 1880s, 2" **75.00**
Chauffeur, Kansas, sunflower
  shape, brass, undated but old,
  M **48.00**
Chauffeur, Minnesota, brass &
  enamel, 1934 ....**25.00**
Chauffeur, New York, brass, 1923,
  EX **18.00**
Constable, Boston, city seal, black
  incised letters, 1940s **48.00**

Department of Water Supply,
  Detroit MI, metal, EX ...**20.00**
Deputy Sheriff, CA, silver metal
  & black enamel, 6-pointed
  star, EX...........................**50.00**
Deputy Sheriff, Wayne County,
  bronze tone, 1900, 2½"...**48.00**
Deputy Special Officer, Bureau of
  Indian Affairs, shield shape,
  2"....................................**50.00**
Essex Veteran Firemen's Assn,
  silver metal, 1900, 2½" ..**48.00**
Fireman Engine #1, Franklin
  NH, silver metal, 1900, 2",
  VG...................................**45.00**

**14k fire badges, left: $400.00;
right: $325.00.**

Hamilton MA Fire Department,
  47 Yrs of Service, gold tone,
  1940s, VG **25.00**
Honorary Deputy Sheriff, Dorch-
  ester Co, silver metal, 1920s,
  2", EX..............................**55.00**
Meter Maid, silver metal, star
  center, eagle atop **5.00**
Naval Police, Seabees emblem,
  #d, 1940s **80.00**
Police Lieutenant, MO, gold tone,
  state seal & eagle, 3½"...**45.00**
Police Reserve, NYC, gold tone, ca
  WWI, EX...........................**75.00**
Police Sergeant, Pecos TX, gold
  tone, state seal, eagle atop,
  EX **45.00**
Security Agent, Texas, brass,
  2½x1¾", M **55.00**
Southwest Security Special Offi-
  cer, gold tone, 6-pointed star,
  M....................................**35.00**

Special Officer, gold tone, brass
pin on back, 1900, 2½"...**50.00**
Volunteer Firemen's Assn, NYC,
silvered brass, early.....**110.00**

Banks

The most popular (and expensive) type of bank with today's collectors are the mechanicals, so called because of the antics they perform when a coin is deposited. Over three hundred models were produced between the Civil War period up to the first World War. On some, arms wave, legs kick, or mouths open to swallow up the coin–amusing nonsense intended by the inventor to encourage and reward thriftiness. The registering bank may have one or more slots and, as the name implies, tallies the amount of money it contains as each coin is deposited. Many old banks have been reproduced–beware! Condition is important; look for good original paint and parts.

Some of the banks listed here are identified by C for Cranmer, D for Davidson, L for long, and M for Moore, oft-used standard reference books.

Mechanical Banks

Always Did 'Spise a Mule, D-251,
jockey, Pat 1897 ...... **1,250.00**

Bad Accident, D-20, cast iron, 10"
long, $1,650.00.

Bamboula, D-21 .... **1,000.00**
Boy on Trapeze, D-60, painted
cast iron, VG **1,600.00**
Cabin, D-93, painted cast iron, 4",
VG.................................**375.00**
Dog on Turntable, D-159, nickle-
plated cast iron, NM....**350.00**
Elephant with howdah, D-173,
man pops up, 5½".........**650.00**
Fisherman, cast iron, polychrome
paint, 12¼" **95.00**
Gem Bank, D-206, nickel-plated
cast iron, EX.................**525.00**
Hall's Excelsior, D-228, painted
cast iron, 3¾", EX.........**275.00**
Home Bank, D-242, cast iron, no
dormers, EX **800.00**
Indian & Bear, D-257, painted
cast iron, original feathers,
VG............................. **1,350.00**
Joe Socko, D-262 ....**750.00**
Jolly Nigger with High Hat, D-
272, aluminum, EX......**275.00**
Lion & 2 Monkeys, D-300, painted
cast iron, repairs, 10"...**950.00**
Southern Comfort, soldier shoots
coins, modern, 8x6"........**75.00**
Strike, cast iron, polychrome
paint, 11½".....................**95.00**
Tammany, D-455, cast iron, worn
polychrome paint, 5¾" .**250.00**
Tank & Cannon, N-5430, alu-
minum, EX **275.00**

Trick Pony, 7½", VG, $850.00.

Teddy & the Bear, D-459, painted cast iron, 7½", VG **1,200.00**

William Tell, D-565, painted cast iron, VG **600.00**

2 Frogs, D-200, painted cast iron, Stevens 1822, VG........**650.00**

Registering Banks

Astronaut Daily Dime **20.00**

B&R Mfg, NY, 10¢ register ..**10.00**

Bean Pot, M-951, 5¢ register, painted cast iron, 4".....**155.00**

Bed Post, M-1305, 5¢ register, EX **65.00**

Beehive Savings, M-681, nickel-plated cast iron, paint traces, 5" **125.00**

Bucket, 1¢ register, cast iron, Japan, patent applied for, 2¾" **80.00**

Daily Dime Clown.................**16.00**

Honeycomb, C-105, 5¼" **100.00**

Junior Cash, M-930, nickel-plated cast iron, 4¼", VG **65.00**

Kettle, painted nickel-plated cast iron, 5¢ register, 3½"......**20.00**

Rockford Nat'l Bank, 10¢ register, EX **24.00**

Statue of Liberty **10.00**

Trunk, Phoenix, M-947, 10¢ register, nickel plate, worn paint, 5" **95.00**

Wee Folks, Money Box, tin litho, square, English, 5".........**50.00**

Still Banks

Admiral Dewey Bullet, EX ...**70.00**

Air Mail, M-848, cast iron, polychrome paint, 6⅜" **350.00**

Amish Boy, holds pig, sits on hay bale, EX **75.00**

Apple, L-904, cast iron, yellow paint, 5½" **750.00**

Aunt Jemima, M-175, painted white metal, 5¼", EX **65.00**

Baby Emerging from Eggshell, C-535, EX **35.00**

Barrel, M-916, nickel-plated cast iron, worn, 5½" long **65.00**

Barrel, Sunny Future, New York NY, 3½" **8.00**

Battleship Maine, M-1439, painted cast iron, minor wear, 10¼" **350.00**

Beggar Boy, L-643, boy kneels, holds hat, 7", EX **65.00**

Black Boy on Pot, chalkware, 13", M...................................**30.00**

Boy Scout, M-45, paint traces on cast iron, 5⅞".................**80.00**

Bulldog, M-405, painted cast iron, worn, 3½".....................**125.00**

Camel, W-202, small...........**235.00**

Carpet Bag, C-352, bronze, 3½", EX **45.00**

Cat, W-248, cast iron **175.00**

Clown, M-211, gold- & red-painted cast iron, 6" **95.00**

Cow, M-553, brass, 5⅜" long.**15.00**

Dog on Pillow, M-443, paint traces on cast iron, 5½".............**90.00**

Duck on Tub, L-354, cast iron, Hubley, 5⅜" **115.00**

Elephant, M-472, gray-painted cast iron, 4" long **25.00**

Elephant with Howdah, M-457, gold-painted cast iron, worn, 2⅜" **35.00**

Fido, M-193, polychrome-painted cast iron, modern, 4⅞" ..**45.00**

Foxy Grandpa, M-320, painted cast iron, worn, 5½" **295.00**

Garage, M-1010, 2-car, painted cast iron, worn, 2½" **85.00**

Home Savings, M-1236, painted cast iron, worn, 3½" **105.00**

Horse, M-532, gold-painted cast iron, 3" **115.00**

Horse, W-86, small..............**225.00**

Humpty Dumpty, L-747, cast iron, 6", VG **350.00**

Jackie Robinson, metal.......**150.00**

Lamb, M-595, white-painted cast iron, worn, 3⅛" **95.00**

Lion, M-755, painted cast iron, 5⅛", EX...........................**35.00**

Lion, gold-painted cast iron, 4" x 5", $40.00.

Lion on Tub, M-746, gold-painted cast iron, 5½", EX...........**65.00**

Mourner's Purse, L-1481, lead, 1902, 5", EX....................**55.00**

Owl, M-597, polychrome-painted cast iron, 4¼", EX.........**155.00**

Pirate Chest, tin **32.00**

Polar Bear, standing, cast iron, no painting..........................**95.00**

Puppy, M-416, polychrome-painted cast iron, 4⅝"....**65.00**

Rabbit, M-568, paint traces on cast iron, 3¾"..................**65.00**

Radio, M-833, red-painted cast iron, nickel-plated door, 4½", EX **75.00**

Rumplestiltskin, L-832, cast iron, 6", VG **325.00**

Safe, Young American, with key, 1890s, NM **145.00**

Sailor, M-27, painted cast iron, worn, 5¼" **105.00**

Scotty, M-419, painted cast iron, 5", M **75.00**

Security Safe Deposit, combination lock **35.00**

Sheep, M-595, cast iron, no paint, 4¼" long **55.00**

Stag, M-737, gold-painted cast iron, 9"...........................**85.00**

Statue of Liberty, L-865, cast iron, 6½" **65.00**

Tally-Ho, L-1190, painted cast iron, 4½", EX **100.00**

Tank, W-161 ....**285.00**

Temple Bar, M-1163, japanning on cast iron, 4" **300.00**

Two-Faced Black Woman, cast iron, no paint, 4¼", $125.00

Time Safe, M-389, nickel plate, 7⅛", VG **185.00**

Treasure Chest, M-928, red- & gold-painted cast iron, worn, 2¾" **155.00**

US Mail, M-855, nickel-plated cast iron, worn, 4¼" **25.00**

Wise Pig, M-609, painted cast iron, 6¾", EX **85.00**

Yellow Cab, L-1570, cast iron, 4", VG **400.00**

3 Monkeys, M-743, gold-painted cast iron, worn, 3¼" **175.00**

Barber Shop

Though few fans of barber shop memorabilia have any personal recall of the old-time tonsorial establishments, the fancy blown glass barber bottles, tufted velvet chairs, and red, white, and blue poles that once hung at their doors kindle a spark of nostalgia among them.

See also Shaving Mugs; Razors.

Bay rum bottle, embossed basketweave with paper label, 8", $15.00.

Blade bank, barber pole form, painted metal, 7" **48.00**

Blade bank, donkey form, Listerine giveaway, EX **15.00**

Bottle, amber, melon based, blown 3-mold, rolled lip, 7" **45.00**

Bottle, amethyst, white enamel flowers, pontilled, 6¾" ..**50.00**

Bottle, Coin Spot on milk glass, melon base, rolled lip, 7½", EX **80.00**

Bottle, cut Art Nouveau decoration on clear, porcelain stopper, 7" **45.00**

Bottle, hand-painted floral, gold Sea Foam label on blue..**98.00**

Bottle, Pineapple, label under glass, gold trim, 7" **275.00**

Bottle, Wildroot Hair Tonic, colorful label, 1940s **15.00**

Cream dispenser, Fitch's Sanitary, chromed top, celluloid base, EX **90.00**

Display box, Gillette Blue Blades, 2½x12x6" **25.00**

Hair shaper, Weck, in pouch with box of blades, early, EX .**15.00**

Hair trimmer, Kristee's, directions on back, M **20.00**

Mustache set, silver brush & curling iron, ca 1780s, EX..**245.00**

Neck duster, sterling handle, 6", EX **30.00**

Pole, folk art, red & white paint, crude, old, 24½"............**100.00**

Pole, turned acorn ends, worn spiral stripes, 23" **140.00**

Shaver, Collman, electric, 1940s, EX **20.00**

Sterilizer, brass plated, Antiseptic, hinged top, 8" **35.00**

Strop, Red Imp Will Beat 'Em All..., leather, EX............**12.50**

Tool case, oak, compartments, brass hinges, 9x6½x3" ...**35.00**

Baseball Cards

The first baseball cards were issued in the late 1800s by cigarette and tobacco companies

Willie Mays, #130, 1956, Topps, $150.00.

Topps, #182, Darryl Strawberry, 1984, VG **3.50**

Topps, #186, Charlie Bishop, 1953, EX/NM **4.00**

Topps, #19, Johnny Buchia, 1952, EX/NM **42.50**

Topps, #192, Wally Westlake, 1953, VG **1.75**

Topps, #195, Ed McGhee, 1953, EX/NM **6.50**

Topps, #2, Luke Easter, 1953, EX/NM **10.00**

Topps, #21, Cal Ripken, 1982, EX/NM **10.00**

Topps, #212, Hank Aaron, 1959, EX/NM **15.00**

Topps, #213, Bob Tiefenauer, 1956, EX/NM..................**12.00**

Topps, #222, Hoot Evers, 1952, EX/NM **16.00**

Topps, #227, Casey Stengel, 1960, VG.....................................**2.75**

Topps, #227, Morrie Martin, 1953, EX/NM..........................**30.00**

Topps, #239, Bill Skowron, 1954, EX/NM..........................**25.00**

Topps, #247, Johnny Bench, 1968, EX/NM..........................**225.00**

Topps, #25, Al Kaline, 1963, EX/NM............................**12.00**

Topps, #251, Sid Hudson, 1953, EX/NM............................**30.00**

Topps, #252, Henry 'Hank' Foiles, 1953, VG **8.00**

Topps, #265, Sandy Consuegra, 1956, EX/NM **5.00**

Topps, #27, Ron Darling, 1984 Turn Back the Clock, VG . **1.25**

Topps, #275, Jim Greengrass, 1956, VG **1.35**

Topps, #297, Jack Crimian, 1957, EX/NM..........................**10.00**

Topps, #30, Willard Nixon, 1953, EX/NM..........................**10.00**

Topps, #309, Jim Busby, 1952, EX/NM..........................**35.00**

Topps, #316, Davey Williams, 1952, VG **37.50**

Topps, #320, Pete Rose, 1975, EX/NM..........................**15.00**

Topps, #327, Matty Alou, 1961, EX/NM........................... **2.50**

Topps, #330, Jim Wilson, 1957, EX/NM..........................**10.00**

Topps, #336, Haywood Sullivan, 1957, VG **2.50**

Topps, #341, Don Gross, 1957, EX/NM 10.00

Topps, #343, Sandy Koufax, 1950, VG 16.00

Topps, #395, Jake Pitler, 1952, EX/NM 135.00

Topps, #4, Don Lenhardt, 1952, EX/NM 42.50

Topps, #404, Dick Brodowski, 1952, VG 37.50

Topps, #407, Bill Freehan, 1964, EX/NM 2.25

Topps, #43, Ray Scarborough, 1952, VG 12.50

Topps, #46, Gordon Goldsberry, 1952, VG 12.50

Topps, #461, Tom Ferrick, 1960, EX/NM 3.00

Topps, #464, Ken Aspromonte, 1963, EX/NM 5.00

Topps, #467, Phil Ortega, 1963, EX/NM 5.00

Topps, #470, Tom Tresh, 1963, EX/NM 15.00

Topps, #485, Ernie Banks, 1961 Most Valuable, EX/NM ... 8.00

Topps, #485, Tim McCarver, 1967, EX/NM 2.00

Topps, #487, Tom Reynolds, 1967, EX/NM 1.50

Topps, #51, Jim Russell, 1952, EX/NM 42.50

Topps, #525, Marv Breeding, 1960, VG 1.50

Topps, #526, Rene Lachemann, 1965, VG 17.50

Topps, #532, Hector Lopez, 1965, EX/NM 2.50

Topps, #536, Kirby Puckett, 1985, EX/NM 10.00

Topps, #539, Billy Moran, 1962, EX/NM 9.00

Topps, #539, Dennis Doyle, 1970, EX/NM 3.25

Topps, #540, Jackie Jensen, 1961, EX/NM 20.00

Topps, #542, Jim Perry, 1959, EX/NM 8.00

Topps, #543, Bill Virdon, 1959, EX/NM 25.00

Topps, #543, Elio Chacon, 1960, EX/NM 6.00

Topps, #544, Duke Carmel, 1963, EX/NM 25.00

Topps, #547, Horace Clarke, 1966, EX/NM 10.00

Topps, #550, Frank Baumann, 1961, EX/NM 15.00

Topps, #552, Birdie Tebbetts, 1966, VG 3.00

Topps, #553, Mike Hegan, 1967, EX/NM 10.00

Topps, #556, Ken Hunt, 1961, EX/NM 15.00

Topps, #559, Roberto Pena, 1966, EX/NM 10.00

Topps, #569, Tom Lasorda, 1973, EX/NM 3.50

Topps, #570, Jim Palmer, 1971, EX/NM 8.00

Topps, #573, Ed Kranepool, 1971, EX/NM 1.00

Topps, #575, Dave Boswell, 1967, EX/NM 6.50

Topps, #577, Jack Lamabe, 1966, EX/NM 10.00

Topps, #579, Doyle Alexander, 1972, EX/NM 1.25

Topps, #586, Claude Raymond, 1966, VG 3.00

Topps, #593, Dave Hamilton, 1962, EX/NM 15.00

Topps, #596, Nate Colbert, 1966, EX/NM 10.00

Topps, #596, Phil Linz, 1962, EX/NM 30.00

Topps, #597, Amado Samuel, 1962, EX/NM 15.00

Topps, #599, Chris Zachary, 1976, VG 4.00

Topps, #605, Orlando Cepeda, 1971, EX/NM 2.50

Topps, #608, George Medich, 1973, EX/NM 1.00

Topps, #620, Tommy Harper, 1973, EX/NM 1.50

Topps, #650, Thurman Munson, 1976, EX/NM 4.00

Topps, #654, Boots Day, 1970, EX/NM **2.00**
Topps, #683, Vern Geishert, 1970, EX/NM **2.00**
Topps, #69, Ed Bailey, 1955, EX/NM **4.00**
Topps, #70, Harmon Killebrew, 1962, VG **3.50**
Topps, #706, Pat Corrales, 1972 In Action, EX/NM **1.75**
Topps, #707, Paul Molitor, 1978, EX/NM **27.50**
Topps, #73, Eddie Robinson, 1943, VG **2.75**
Topps, #744, Mike Witt, 1982, EX/NM **1.50**
Topps, #759, Chris Cannizzaro, 1972, EX/NM **1.75**
Topps, #80, Wally Joyner, 1987, EX/NM **1.25**
Topps, #99, John 'Boog' Powell, 1962, VG **2.25**

Baskets

Hand-crafted baskets made from 1860 until around the turn of the century are commanding good prices on today's collectibles market, and early factory-made baskets are gaining in interest. Most valued are the Nantucket Lighthouse baskets and Shaker miniatures. Those designed for specific use—cheese baskets, herb baskets, and egg baskets, for example—are preferred over the general-purpose type.

See also Indian Artifacts.

Buttocks, oak splint, 36-rib, 1900, 15x18x14", NM **165.00**
Cheese, woven splint, minor damage, 10" diameter **150.00**
Egg, bentwood handle, 11x11½", VG **80.00**
Flower, oval top, oblong bottom, 1900s, 6x6x10", EX **65.00**

Garden, oak splint, open-weave bottom, 1900s, 6x6x10" .**65.00**
Melon rib, oak splint, ca 1900, 13x13x16", EX **100.00**
Nantucket, oval, slightly weathered, early, 14" long **800.00**
Potato print, 2-color, with bentwood rim handles, 5x9" diameter................................**450.00**
Rye straw, with lid, 16x20" .**100.00**

Splint basket, kick-up bottom, 14" diameter, $120.00.

Table, twine, heavy tight weave, green paint, bowl form, 3½x11" **65.00**
Utility, woven splint, rectangular, 1800s, 4x12x7", VG......**135.00**
Willow, old green paint, handles, 16x17" long **50.00**
Wool, short feet, bentwood rim handles, 14x18x21"......**275.00**
Woven splint, dark brown, old, 7"+bentwood handle, 13" diameter, VG..................**45.00**
Woven splint, faded color, lift-out compartment, with lid, 13" high.................................**65.00**
Woven splint, original yellow, 10½" +handle, 14" diameter **195.00**
Woven splint, paint spatters, 6½"+ handle, 9x10" **55.00**
Woven splint, painted yellow band, with lid, 1850s, 12x19" diameter **110.00**

Buttocks basket with 'Eye of God' at handle, 5¾" high (plus handle), $185.00.

Woven splint, red bands, with lid, minor damage, 13x18" diameter **60.00**

Woven splint, scrubbed finish, oblong, 6"+handle, 16x13", EX **55.00**

Woven splint, scrubbed finish, 5½"+bentwood handle, 9x12", EX **45.00**

Woven splint, well-shaped handle, 5x7" dia...........................**55.00**

Woven splint, wooden handle & bottom, 12x16x18", NM .**60.00**

Woven splint, 4¾"+bentwood handle, 7½" diameter, NM .**150.00**

Woven splint & grass, good age & color, 2½"+bentwood handle, 5¼x8½"............................**40.00**

Bauer

The Bauer Company moved from Kentucky to California in 1909, producing crocks, gardenware, and vases until after the Depression when they introduced their first line of dinnerware. From 1932 until the early 1960s, they successfully marketed several lines of solid-color wares that are today very collectible. Some of their most popular lines are Ring, Plain Ware, and Monterey Modern.

Bottle, water; Ring, orange-red, open **45.00**

Bowl, fruit; Monterey, turquoise, 6"......................................**10.00**

Bowl, fruit; Monterey, white, 9".**45.00**

Bowl, mixing; Al Fresco, coffee brown, 5½x4"...................**5.00**

Bowl, mixing; plain, #4, black, 1 ½-gallon **225.00**

Bowl, mixing; Ring, #36, yellow, 1-pint **14.00**

Bowl, salad; Ring, light blue, low, 9"......................................**32.00**

Bowl, vegetable; Al Fresco, speckled, round, 9½" **12.50**

Bowl, vegetable; Contempo, any color, 9½" **13.00**

Bread & butter plate, Al Fresco, 6" **2.50**
Butter dish, Ring, turquoise, round **55.00**
Candlestick, Ring, red-brown, 2½" **25.00**
Coffeepot, plain, burgundy, 2-cup **40.00**
Coffeepot, Ring, blue or gray, 8-cup **145.00**
Creamer, Al Fresco, hemlock green **3.50**
Creamer, La Linda, light brown, new shape **8.00**
Cup, Monterey, canary..........**20.00**
Cup & saucer, El Chico **45.00**
Flowerpot, Ring, white or yellow, 2" **15.00**
Goblet, plain, blue.................**70.00**
Goblet, Ring, light blue.........**48.00**
Gravy bowl, Monterey Moderne, yellow..............................**22.00**
Jardiniere, Ring Art, speckled, 14"...................................**120.00**
Pie plate, Ring, white, 9" **24.00**
Pitcher, Al Fresco, coffee brown, 1-pint **9.00**
Pitcher, Monterey Moderne, gray, 2-quart............................**28.00**
Plate, chop; Contempo, pumpkin, 13"...................................**12.50**
Plate, Monterey Modern, dark brown, 9½" **8.50**
Platter, Monterey, turquoise, oval, 17"...................................**25.00**
Platter, Ring, orange-red, oval, 12"...................................**30.00**
Relish plate, Ring, yellow, divided...........................**45.00**
Shakers, Al Fresco, coffee brown, large, pair **8.00**
Sugar bowl, Ring, yellow, with lid, 12-ounce **28.00**
Teapot, La Linda, burgundy, 4-cup **32.00**
Teapot, Monterey, burgundy, 6-cup **40.00**
Teapot, Monterey Moderne, yellow or pink, 6-cup..........**42.50**

Tumbler, Al Fresco, gray, 12-ounce............................... **8.00**
Tumbler, La Linda, pink, 8-oz.**12.50**
Tumbler, Monterey Moderne, green or yellow...............**12.50**
Tumbler, Ring, dark blue, wood handle, 6-ounce..............**15.00**

Ringware, see listings for specific values.

Beatles

Beatles memorabilia is becoming increasingly popular with those who grew up in the '60s. Almost any item that could be produced with their pictures or logos were manufactured and sold by the thousands in department stores. Some have such a high collector value that they have been reproduced, beware!

Album, Sgt Pepper's Lonely Hearts Club Band, in original folder, M.........................**75.00**
Book, Love Letters to Beatles, 1964, original cover, EX.**25.00**
Calendar, salesman sample, 1964, 12x10"............................**45.00**
Color book, 1964, M **40.00**
Doll, inflatable, cartoon style, set of 4, M............................**85.00**
Figure with instrument, Remco, 1964, VG....................**75.00**
Nylon stockings, M in original package.........................**38.00**
Pin-back, guitar, 1964, M, set of 4 on card...........................**20.00**
Pin-back, I'm An Official Beatles Fan, 2¼"........................... **5.00**

Pin-back, Yellow Submarine, brass with enameling, 1", set of 8 ....20.00

Puzzle, group holding instruments, black & white, 20½x18½", EX 22.50

Record holder, Disk-Go-Case, 4 signatures, 1966.............55.00

Serving tray, metal, 4 pictures on front, original tag, NM ..50.00

Stamps, uncut, 1964, set of 100, M.......................................22.50

Tie tack, gold & black 12.50

Toy, Yellow Submarine, metal, pop-up figures, 5¼" 75.00

Plastic model, in original box, $35.00.

Beer Cans

The earliest beer cans, the flat tops, were introduced in 1934 and came with instructions on how to use the punch opener. Cone tops, patented in 1935, are rare today and usually bring the highest prices. From 1960 on, these were replaced by the pull-tab type which is still in use. Condition is very important. Rust, dents, scratches, or other such defects lessen the value considerably.

Blitz-Weinhard, red & tan on white, pull top, 15-oz 3.50

Buckeye, Meister Brau, red & white, flat top, 12-oz 8.00

Butte Special, red & white, cone top, 12-oz 70.00

Carling Red Cap Ale, solid green, pull top, 12-oz 2.25

Country Club Beer, red & white, cone top, 12-oz................32.00

Dawson's Extra Dry Ale, tan & green, flat top, 12-oz 48.00

Eastside Old Tap, red & white, flat top, 16-oz.................16.00

Eastside Old Tap Lager, red & white, flat top, 12-oz 8.00

Fitzgerald Ale, red & white, flat top, 12-oz 42.50

Gettelman Bock Beer, brown & white, pull top, 12-oz 12.50

Golden Glow Ale, green & yellow, flat top, 12-oz 125.00

Hapsburg Brand, red, white & blue, flat top, 12-oz 55.00

Huber, red, gold & white, flat top, 12-oz 5.50

Kingsbury Bock, yellow & brown, flat top, 12-oz.................48.00

Lubeck Premium, brown & yellow, flat top, 12-oz 25.00

South Pacific, Hawaii, $15.00.

Metz Jubilee, white letters on red, cone top, 12-oz **48.00**

Mule Malt Liquor, kicking mule, pull top, 16-oz **7.50**

Old Ranger, red bull's eye, flat top, 12-oz **65.00**

Pikes Peak Ale, red banner, pull top, 12-oz **32.00**

Ruppert Knickerbocker, man with cane, flat top, 12-oz **12.50**

Schmidt Draft, horse & colt, pull top, 16-oz **5.00**

White Cap, red & blue on white, cone top, 12-oz **50.00**

Bells

Of the many types of bells available to the collector today, perhaps the most popular are the brass figurals. School bells, sleigh bells, and dinner bells are also of interest. Bells have been made from a variety of materials–even glass and wood.

Figural lady, brass, 3¾", $50.00.

Bear figural handle, green flint glass **150.00**

Cranberry glass, swirled ribs, clear handle, 10" **120.00**

Cupid handle, silver, small ... **85.00**

Dinner, glass, brilliant cuttings, 5¾" **255.00**

Dutch girl with jug figural, bronze, 4½" **148.00**

Lady in hoop skirt holding fan figural, brass, 6" **80.00**

Lady with hoop skirt & umbrella figural, brass, 3½" **45.00**

Minute man with musket figural, silverplate, 4" **45.00**

Napoleon figural handle, embossed battle scenes, brass, 6" **68.00**

Pilgrim figural handle, silver, Udall & Ballou, 4-oz **115.00**

Queen Elizabeth figural, brass, clapper feet, 3¼" **90.00**

Sleigh, brass, 24 graduated on original leather strap .. **125.00**

Sleigh, brass, 27 on original leather strap, EX **165.00**

Sleigh, brass, 4 on arched metal strap, EX **45.00**

Sleigh, brass, 6 on leather strap, EX **100.00**

Tea, angel figural handle, silver, 800 mark **70.00**

Tea, Victorian, brass, 3½" **48.00**

Windmill figural, brass **60.00**

Witch from Hansel & Gretel figural, brass **165.00**

Big Little Books

Probably everyone who is now forty to sixty years of age owned a few Big Little Books as a child. Today these thick hand-sized adventures bring prices from $10.00 to $75.00 and upwards. The first was published in 1933 by Whitman Publishing Company. Dick Tracy was the featured character. Kids of the early fifties preferred the format of the comic book, and Big Little Books were gradually phased out. Stories about super heroes and Disney characters bring the highest prices, especially those with an early copyright.

Dick Tracy's Ghost Ship, $30.00.

Adventures of Dick Tracy, 1st story, rare, VG 100.00
Arizona Kid on the Bandit Trail, 1936, VG 14.00
Barney Google, 1935, EX......40.00
Betty Boop, Snow White, Whitman, 1934, EX 45.00
Big Chief Wahoo & the Great Gusto, 1938, EX 15.00
Blondie, Papa Knows Best, 1945, VG....................................15.00
Brad Turner, Transatlantic Flight, 1939, EX 15.00
Brer Rabbit, Song of the South, 1945-1947, EX 25.00
Bronco Peeler, The Lone Cowboy, 1937, EX.........................12.50
Buck Jones, Fighting Rangers, many illustrations, EX ..35.00
Buck Rogers, City Below the Sea, 1934, NM 50.00
Buck Rogers, Depth Men of Jupiter, 1935, VG...........55.00
Buck Rogers, Planetoid Plot, 1936, EX 55.00

Buck Rogers, War with the Planet Venus, 1938, VG............65.00
Bugs Bunny, 1943, VG.........25.00
Captain Frank Hawks, Air Ace & League of 12, 1938, EX .14.00
Charlie Chan Solves a New Mystery, 1940, EX.................25.00
Chester Gump at Silver Creek Ranch, 1933, VG............15.00
Dan Dunn & the Border Smugglers, 1938, EX 20.00
Dan Dunn & the Underworld Gorillas, 1941, EX..........18.00
Dick Tracy & the Bicycle Gang, EX....................................25.00
Dick Tracy, Wreath Kidnapping Case, 1943-45, EX..........28.00
Doctor Doom, Ghost Sub, 1939, EX....................................18.00
Don Winslow, Secret Enemy Base, 1943, EX........................18.00
Donald Duck, Ghost Morgan's Treasure, 1942, EX........30.00
Eddie Cantor, Hour with You, 1934, VG 22.50

Jackie Cooper, Movie Star of 'Skippy & Sooky,' EX, $25.00.

Flying Sky Clipper, Winsie Atkins, EX 48.00
G-Men Alien, 1939, NM 20.00
Jack Armstrong & the Ivory Treasure, 1937, EX 20.00

Jack Pearl, Baron Munchausen, Goldsmith, 1934, NM **25.00**
Jungle Jim, Vampire Woman, 1937, EX.........................**35.00**
Jungle Jim, 1935, NM **50.00**
Ken Maynard, Wheels of Destiny, 1934, EX.........................**25.00**
Kit Carson, 1933, EX.............**25.00**
Last Days of Pompeii, EX.....**25.00**
Li'l Abner Among the Millionaires, 1939, EX..............**50.00**
Little Annie Rooney, Highway to Adventure, 1936-38, G ..**12.00**
Lone Ranger, Vanishing Herd, 1936, VG **15.00**
Lone Star Martin, Texas Ranger, 1939, VG.........................**10.00**
Mickey Mouse, Bell Boy Detective, VG............................**25.00**
Mickey Mouse, Lazy Daisy Mystery, 1945, EX.................**28.00**
Mickey Mouse, World of Tomorrow, VG..........................**35.00**
Mickey Mouse Sails for Treasure Island, 1933, EX **25.00**
Napoleon, Uncle Elby & Little Mary, 1939, NM **12.50**
Paramount, Newsreel, Admiral Byrd, 1934, VG..............**25.00**
Red Ryder & Little Beaver on Hoofs of Thunder, EX **28.00**
Roy Rogers, Robin Hood of the Range, EX.......................**20.00**
Roy Rogers at Crossed Feather Ranch, 1945, EX **25.00**
Smilin' Jack, Stratosphere Ascent, 1937, VG............**20.00**
Smilin' Jack & the Jungle Pipe Line, 1941-47, EX **25.00**
Stan Kent, Varsity Man, EX.**14.00**
Story of Charlie McCarthy & Edgar Bergen, EX..........**20.00**
Tailspin Tommy, Air Racer, 1940, VG...................................**20.00**
Tailspin Tommy, Great Air Mystery, movie edition, EX ..**38.00**
Texas Kit, 1937, VG **15.00**
Three Finger Joe, 1937, EX... **8.00**
Tom Beatty, Ace of the Service, Big Brain Gang, NM......**18.00**

Tom Mix, Range War, Whitman, 1937, EX **45.00**
Tom Mix, Tony Jr, 1935, EX .**35.00**
Tom Swift, Magnetic Silencer, 1941, EX **20.00**
Uncle Don's Strange Adventure, 1936, EX........................**12.50**
Uncle Sam's Sky Defenders, movie-flip corners, G......**15.00**
Wells Fargo, 1938, VG **18.00**
West Point Five, VG.............**12.00**
Wimpy, Hamburger Eater, 1938, VG..................................**18.00**
Winged Four, 1937, EX **12.00**
Winning Point, 1936, EX......**12.00**

Black Americana

This is a wide and varied field of collector interest. Advertising, toys, banks, sheet music, kitchenware items, movie items, and even the fine arts are areas that offer Black Americana buffs many opportunities to add to their collections.

Apron, Mammy applique on pocket, polka dot ruffle, 16x20" **38.00**
Ash tray, man with beard plays piano, cast iron, 3¼x4" ..**60.00**
Ash tray, Uncle Mose, painted cast iron, Hubley, NM....**95.00**
Book, Black Boy, R Wright, Harper & Bros, 1st edition, 1945, EX **50.00**
Book, Black Mother Goose, Oliver, 1st edition, 1969, M **65.00**
Bottle, liquor; Mammy dancing, banjo player...................**75.00**
Broom holder, figural man, cast iron, Pat 1894...............**175.00**
Brush, bellhop figural wooden handle, EX paint, 8".......**24.00**
Cigarette holder, 3 children on clothesline, ceramic **20.00**
Cookie jar, Aunt Jemima's Cookies, plastic.....................**85.00**

Cookie jar, white chef's head, white hat, pottery, 1930s, EX ..**65.00**

Cookie jar, Mammy, black face, white dress, ceramic, unmarked, 11" **110.00**

Cookie jar, Mammy, National Silver, M **135.00**

Figure, Black woman waving, cast iron/lead, England **32.00**

Figure, Sprinklin' Sambo, wooden, with hose & cast iron base, 27", EX **70.00**

Figurine, boy eating melon, chalkware, 15", EX...................**85.00**

Figurine, boy eating watermelon while on pot, ceramic, Germany, 5" **90.00**

Figurine, boy seated with melon, glass, 2¾".......................**22.00**

Figurine, girl in bonnet, bisque, Germany, 1900s, 5¾" **75.00**

Film, Beware, Black exploitation, Louis Jordan, 1940s **125.00**

Game, Sambo, tin, with darts & gun, NM in box **250.00**

Note pad holder, plastic, 10", $40.00.

Game, Snake Eyes, cards, Selchow & Richter, 1945.....**75.00**

Knife, Coon Chicken Inn, stainless, 9¼"..........................**20.00**

Lawn sprinkler, Sprinklin' Sambo, metal with iron base, Dapco, 30"......................**70.00**

Lithograph, Pet Chicken, Pore Li'l Mose, 10½x14", EX **45.00**

Map, Amos 'N Andy Souvenir, Andrew H Brown, framed, EX **60.00**

Mask, exaggerated features, cardboard, USA.....................**12.50**

Matchbook, Coon Chicken Inn, 10 figural matches, EX.......**30.00**

Memo holder, Mammy, painted wood, 1940s, 11¾"..........**40.00**

Menu, Coon Chicken Inn, small, EX **35.00**

Noisemaker, minstrel caricature, tin with wooden handle, 4", EX...**22.00**

Pitcher, Black Sambo on frosted glass, chrome cap, 5¼" ..**88.00**

Planter, boy with watermelon, Interco, 5½" **38.00**

Plaque, man & lady, chalkware, EX paint details, pair ...**45.00**

Post card, Farina, Hal Roach Studios, NM **12.50**

Post card, This Am No Lemon, boy with watermelon, 1900s, EX **3.00**

Poster, He Was Ready! Are You?, Malcolm X, 22x17".........**60.00**

Pot holder caddy, Chef, googly eyes, chalkware, 6" **30.00**

Print, couple in field, Treasury of Stephen Foster, 1920s, 11x8", NM................................... **7.50**

Shakers, Chef & Maid, brown skin with gold trim, ceramic, 3¾", pair **38.00**

Shakers, Mammy & Butler, Japan, 5", pair................**45.00**

Shakers, Mammy & Chef, gold trim, ceramic, 5", with matching drip jar...........**88.00**

Shakers, minstrels, ceramic, 3½",
pair **45.00**
Shakers, Salty & Peppy, gold
names, Pearl China, 4½".**45.00**
Sheet Music, Carry Me Back to
Old Virginni **25.00**
Spice set, Black Chef, ceramic, on
wood rack, EX **95.00**
String holder, Mammy, ceramic,
6½", EX **32.00**
Syrup pitcher, Little Black Sambo
painted on glass...........**125.00**
Tablecloth, children with melons,
Mammy with pie, etc, 52x48",
EX **100.00**

Book, Mule Twins, 48-page, $30.00.

Teapot, boy on elephant, pottery,
5¼x6½".............................**65.00**
Tin can, Old Black Joe Speckled
Butter Beans, 4½" **10.00**
Toaster cover, Mammy, stuffed
head & arms, large, EX .**35.00**
Token, Am I Not a Woman & a
Sister?, chained woman, cop-
per, 1838......................**125.00**
Toothpick holder, well-dressed boy
painted on milk glass...**150.00**
Tumbler, Aunt Fanny's Cabin on
frosted glass, 7"..............**30.00**

Black Cats

This line of fancy felines was
produced mainly by the Shafford
Company, although black cat
lovers accept similarly-modeled,
shiny glazed kitties of other manufacturers into their collections as
well. Some of the more plentiful
items may be purchased for
$10.00 to $15.00, while the Napco
bank is worth around $85.00 and
the nine-piece spice set in a
wooden rack usually sells for
$75.00.

Ash tray, full body, flat, green
eyes, gold trim, 3¼x4"..... **8.00**
Ash tray, head only, open mouth,
Shafford label, 3" **18.00**
Bookends, seated on book, fluffy
look, 5½", pair **30.00**
Candy tray, face only, flat, wicker
handle, 5" **28.00**
Cookie jar, head only, green eyes,
red bow & ears, 5" **75.00**
Creamer & sugar bowl with lid,
blue eyes, with lid, Enesco,
4¼" **21.00**
Creamer & sugar bowl, stack-
ing..................................**28.00**
Cruet, seated, kitten on back as
handle, 8½" **20.00**
Decanter, seated, red polka dots,
7", with 6 cups...............**55.00**
Desk caddy, pen forms tail, spring
body for letters, 6½".......**15.00**
Figurine, arched back, on book by
vase, 3" **12.50**
Figurine, seated, emerald green
eyes, 5¾", with 2 kittens on
leash **14.50**
Napkin ring, ring forms body, 2⅜",
pair................................. **5.00**
Pincushion, crouches, cushion on
back, tongue tape measure,
2x4½"..............................**20.00**
Planter, seated, green eyes, Alco-
Japan label, 6" **12.00**

Planter, stalking panther style, 11½" long **14.00**

Shakers, seated, voice boxes in base, Japan 5", pair **21.00**

Shakers, strolling, double-ended, 10¼" long **15.00**

Shakers, voice boxes in base, Souvenir of..., 3⅛", pair........**12.00**

Sugar bowl, cat-head lid is shaker, 5⅜" **35.00**

Teapot, paw spout, 8½" **35.00**

Wall pocket, green eyes, red bow, pocket at back, 5½" **45.00**

Teapot, individual, 5", $25.00.

Blue and White Stoneware

Collectors who appreciate the 'country look' especially enjoy decorating their homes with this attractive utility ware that was made by many American potteries from around the turn of the century until the mid-thirties. Examples with good mold lines and strong color fetch the highest prices. Condition is important, but bear in mind that this ware was used daily in busy households, and signs of normal wear are to be expected.

Bean Pot, Boston Baked Beans, Swirl, diffused blue......**225.00**

Beater jar, Blue Band, diffused blue, EX.........................**25.00**

Beater jar, Blue Band, NM ..**55.00**

Bowl, berry; Flying Bird.....**125.00**

Bowl, Daisy, 5" H **135.00**

Bowl, Wedding Ring, 7" **85.00**

Butter crock, Blue Band, original lid & bail......................**110.00**

Butter crock, Colonial original lid & bowl, scarce **130.00**

Butter crock, Daisy on Waffle, original lid & bowl **110.00**

Butter crock, Eagle, original lid & bowl **475.00**

Butter crock, Vintage, unglazed rim, Robinson Clay, 3x6½" diameter **100.00**

Canister, Basketweave, Raisins, original lid.....................**175.00**

Canister, Blue Band, Pepper, with lid, small........................**75.00**

Canister, Wildflower, Farina, with lid...................................**70.00**

Chamber pot, Fleur-de-lis & Scrolls, pale blue, bail handle, 13".................................**225.00**

Coffeepot, Blue Band..........**275.00**

Coffeepot, Oval, diffused blue, blue-tipped knob, 11" ..**225.00**

Cup, Bowknot........................**65.00**

Cup, Roses, decal **65.00**

Egg crock, barrel staves, blue bands & dots, bail handle, 5½x6" **175.00**

Ice water jug, diffused blue, high handle, original cork stopper, 7"...................................**185.00**

Milk crock, blue sponging, bail handle, 4x8" diameter .**110.00**

Milk crock, stove top, bail handle, advertising **75.00**

Mug, Bands & Rivets............**75.00**

Mug, Barrel **65.00**

Mug, Bow Tie, bluebird transfer, NM................................**75.00**

Mug, Flemish tavern scene ..**95.00**

Pickle crock, Blue Band, advertising, flat knob on recessed lid, 9"...................................**125.00**

Pitcher, Cosmos, 9", $225.00.

Pie plate, Bow Tie **125.00**
Pie plate, Star Mfg..............**125.00**
Pitcher, Avenue of Trees, 8".**145.00**
Pitcher, Blue Band, tapered form, 8"....................................**85.00**
Pitcher, Butterfly, diffused blue, 9"....................................**175.00**
Pitcher, Dutch Children & Windmill................................**150.00**
Pitcher, Grape Cluster on Trellis, short & squat **120.00**
Pitcher, Grape with Leaf Band, 9", NM **150.00**
Pitcher, Grape with Rickrack on waffle ground, 8" **100.00**
Pitcher, Indian Good Luck Sign (swastika), with blue sponging, 7"...........................**150.00**
Pitcher, Morning-Glory.......**225.00**
Pitcher, Peacock, diffused blue, 7¾x6½" diameter **300.00**
Pitcher, Rose on Trellis, M..**175.00**
Pitcher, War Bonnet............**300.00**
Pitcher, Wild Rose, blue sponging on textured clay, 9" **225.00**
Refrigerator jar, diffused blue, advertising **165.00**
Roaster, Daisy **135.00**
Rolling pin, Wildflower.......**175.00**
Salt crock, Apple Blossom, original lid............................**100.00**

Salt crock, Blue Band, SALT in gold **85.00**
Salt crock, Blue Band, yellow tint, printed letters, 6x5".......**95.00**
Salt crock, Eagle **295.00**
Salt crock, Flying bird, diffused blue, with original lid .**300.00**
Salt crock, Maple Leaf, original lid **90.00**
Soap dish, Cat's Head **165.00**
Soap dish, Lion's Head **165.00**
Spittoon, Leaf & Wreath.....**125.00**
Spittoon, Peacock, brick designed base, pale blue, 9x10" diameter **250.00**
Spittoon, Shell......................**45.00**
Toothbrush holder, Bow Tie..**60.00**
Toothpick holder, Swan.........**65.00**
Vase, cemetery; Cone **195.00**
Vase, Diffused Blue.............**125.00**
Wash bowl & pitcher, Rose & Fishscale, 2-piece set ...**275.00**

Blue Ridge

One of the newest and most exciting collectibles on the scene today is American dinnerware. Some of the most attractive is Blue Ridge, produced by Southern Potteries of Erwin, Tennessee, from the late 1930s until 1956. More than four hundred patterns were hand painted on eight basic shapes. The Quimper-like peasant-decorated line is one of the most treasured and priced at double the values listed below. For the very simple lines, subtract 25% to 50%.

Ash tray, individual **10.00**
Bonbon, divided, center handle, china **38.00**
Bowl, flat soup, 8" **9.00**
Bowl, 8".................................. **9.00**
Breakfast set **250.00**
Cake lifter..............................**20.00**

Cake plate, 10½"	**18.00**
Candy box, round, with lid	**75.00**
Chocolate pot	**125.00**
Cigarette box	**45.00**
Coffeepot	**70.00**
Creamer, china	**25.00**
Cup & saucer, jumbo	**20.00**
Egg cup, double	**15.00**
Lamp, china	**88.00**
Mug, child's	**12.00**
Plate, Christmas	**55.00**

Pitcher, Milady, 8½", $85.00.

Plate, salad; bird decor, 8½"	**30.00**
Plate, 6"	**2.00**
Platter, 11"	**7.00**
Platter, 15"	**17.00**
Relish, loop handle	**45.00**
Relish, T-handle	**27.00**
Salad fork	**25.00**
Shakers, Apple, pair	**10.00**
Shakers, tall, footed, pair	**35.00**
Syrup jug, with lid	**40.00**
Teapot, china	**50.00**
Teapot, demitasse	**65.00**
Tidbit, 2-tier	**25.00**
Vase, boot, 8"	**65.00**
Vase, tapered	**75.00**

Bottle Openers

Figural bottle openers are figures designed for the sole purpose of removing a bottle cap. To qualify as an example, the cap lifter must be part of the figure itself. Among the major producers of openers of this type were Wilton Products; John Wright, Inc.; L & L Favors; and Gadzik Sales. These and advertising openers are very collectible.

Alligator with head up, cast iron with original paint, Wright, 5"	**65.00**
Baseball cap, New York Mets, cast iron, VG paint	**17.50**
Baseball pitcher, silverplated, patent 1894, EX	**50.00**
Billy Goat, cast iron, EX original paint	**25.00**
Bird dog, upheld paw, opener on chest, cast iron	**45.00**
Black man's face with huge grin, red bow tie, cast iron	**165.00**

Jolly Black Man, chrome, $50.00.

Crab, cast iron with old red paint, EX	**15.00**
Crayfish, cast iron	**40.00**
Dachshund, brass	**18.00**
Deco nude with hands behind head, brass	**50.00**
Dodo Bird, aluminum	**10.00**

Drunk at lamppost, leg out-
stretched, cast iron, worn
paint, 4", EX...................**15.00**

Drunk at palm tree, bald head,
cast iron, EX paint.........**40.00**

Duck with head up, cast iron,
worn paint, 3", EX..........**45.00**

Elephant, flat, atop square
opener, cast iron, worn paint,
3⅛" **25.00**

English Setter, cast iron **40.00**

Foundry man, aluminum **15.00**

Heinz 57, metal...................... **5.00**

Horse's behind, cast iron, original
paint, ca 1900, 5¼".........**30.00**

Indian, Iroquois Beer, brass, old,
EX **40.00**

Lamb with ewe, recumbent, cast
iron, repainted, 4"..........**30.00**

Man in top hat, chromed metal,
with corkscrew, 6" **55.00**

Man with horn, brass, EX **15.00**

Monkey seated by tree stump,
cast iron, EX paint.......**185.00**

NuGrape, in combination with
pen knife, EX..................**28.00**

Old Canada Dry, cast iron, wall
type, EX........................... **9.00**

Parrot on stand, cast iron, dated
1952, 5¾".......................**25.00**

Pelican, cast iron, white body,
orange bill, green base, 3½",
EX...................................**30.00**

Pheasant, aluminum **10.00**

Pointer, cast iron, worn original
polychrome paint, 4½" ...**25.00**

Ram, upright, cast iron, worn
original paint, 4"...........**22.00**

Rooster, cast iron, EX paint, John
Wright, 3¼" **45.00**

Shark, aluminum..................**15.00**

Squirrel, cast iron **30.00**

Toucan, oversized head, cast iron,
repainted, 3¾"................**25.00**

Trout, cast iron, minor wear on
original paint, 5" **35.00**

Turtle, cast iron, worn black
paint, Golding, Franklin MA,
3"....................................**30.00**

Turtle, pot metal, EX paint,
corkscrew tail.................**20.00**

Woman streetwalker by lamppost,
cast iron, worn paint **25.00**

4-eyed lady, cast iron, Wilton, wall
type, EX **60.00**

Bottles

Bottles have been used as
containers for commercial products since the late 1800s. Speci-
mens from as early as 1845 may
be occasionally found today
(watch for a rough pontil to indicate this early production date).
Some of the most collectible are
bitters bottles, used for 'medicine'
that was mostly alcohol, a ploy to
avoid paying the stiff tax levied
on liquor sales. Spirit flasks from
the 1800s were blown in the mold
and were often designed to convey
a historic, political, or symbolic
message. Even bottles from the
1900s are collectible, especially
beer or pop bottles and commercial containers from defunct bottlers.

**Christies Ague Balsam, aqua,
open pontil, applied mouth, 7",
$80.00; Dr. Conver's Invigorating
Cordial, aqua, open pontil,
applied mouth, 6", $120.00.**

Allen Springs Mineral Water, aqua, applied lip, paper label, 11½" 7.50

Ayer's Ague Cure Lowell, aqua, rectangular, 7" 12.50

Ayer's Restorative Bitters, aqua, rectangular, 8 " 55.00

Bear figural, amber, 1-quart.100.00

Belfast Ginger Al Co SF, light green applied lip, 7" 7.50

Bininger's Regulator, clock, yellow-amber, pontil scar, 1-pint, NM 300.00

Blatz, Old Heidelberg, amber, stubby style 42.50

Bourbon Whiskey, barrel shape, puce, square collared mouth, 8" 170.00

Brant's Indian Pulmonary Balsam, 8-sided, pontil, 7" ..34.00

Bumstead Worm Syrup, aqua, ring top, #3 on base......... 5.00

Burnett's Standard Flavoring Extracts, aqua, 5½"......... 2.75

California Natural Seltzer Water, bear on back, aqua, 7"....15.00

Carter's #1 on base, ink, cobalt, 32-ounce, 9½" 8.00

Century Liquor & Cigar Co, amber, B-8, 1-pint 8.00

Chamberlain's Cough Remedy, aqua, rectangular, 6¾" ... 4.50

Champagne Catsup, amethyst, round, screw top, 7½"...... 6.00

Chase Bros, ink, Feb 15, 1885 on base, cobalt, 9" 16.00

Chestnut flask, amber, vertical ribs, Zanesville, 4¾".....250.00

Chestnut flask, green, swirl tooled top, pontil, 5¾" 88.00

Cigar figural, amber, whiskey nipper, EX............................35.00

Cologne, blue opalescent, freeblown, England, 10¾" .120.00

Cologne, clear opalescent with gold, corseted, American, 1850s, 7"......................160.00

Cologne, sterling, violin form, cupids fishing, 4x1½"...335.00

Harrison's Columbian Ink, aqua, open pontil, rolled lip, 1¾", $65.00.

Dr Thacher's Liver & Blood Syrup, amber, rectangular, 3½".. 5.00

Flask, double eagle, Pittsburgh, citron, 1-pint 185.00

Flask, Girl for Joe, girl on bike, aqua, pint 65.00

Flask, Louis Taussig, Main Street, San Francisco, CA, amber...........................185.00

Flask, scroll, deep golden amber, ca 1850, 1-pint, EX 225.00

Flask, scroll, 1 star, aqua, smooth base, 7" 7.50

Garter's Wild Cherry Bitters, amber, 7½".....................27.50

Graduated Nursing Bottle, embossed letters, '10, 12-ounce 20.00

Guilford Mineral Spring Water, dark green with short neck, 10".................................35.00

Hagan's Magnolia Balm, white milk glass, beveled corners, 5"....................................10.00

Harvard Rye, HR monogram, clear, double-banded collar, 7½" 6.00

Hock Wine, teal blue, sheared top & ring, pontil, 14" 10.00

Holmes & Co, mineral water, aqua, sloped collared mouth, ½-pint 600.00

Holtzermann's Pat Stomach, cabin form, gold-amber, 10"...130.00

Hostetter's Stomach Bitters, amber, 8½"......................**15.00**

Hurdle Rye, clear, etched letters, 3"......................**10.00**

Ink, cobalt blue, round with pouring spout, 9⅝"..................**14.00**

J Boardman & Co Mineral Water, cobalt blue, graphite pontil, 7¼"................................ **78.00**

JA Blaffer & Co New Orleans LA, amber, squat, blob top, 6½"..................................**18.00**

JH Vangent Schiedam, brown, tapered top, 9⅜"............**20.00**

Keene Geometric Ink, amber, open pontil......................**65.00**

Lightner's White Rose Perfumes, milk glass, 6½"..............**25.00**

Ludin's Condensed Juniper-Ade, aqua, 5", M **2.50**

Miller Becker, Send Me Home When..., aqua, 11½"........ **5.00**

Mokelumne Hill Soda Works, aqua, applied lip, 6½"..... **5.00**

Not To Be Taken, cobalt blue, ribbed sides, 5½x1¾"......**20.00**

Nurser, blown, clear, curved neck, 6", NM **15.00**

Old Continental Whiskey, dark yellow-amber, embossed soldier, 9½"......................**700.00**

Owl Poison Ammonia, cobalt blue, label, 5¼", M **42.50**

Peptogenic Milk Powder, amber, machine made, tin measure top, 5¾".......................... **5.00**

Peruvian Tonic Bitters, amber, rectangular, 10¼"..........**60.00**

Pickles, Skilton Foote Bunker Hill, lighthouse form, amber, 11", NM........................**130.00**

Pomeroy Ink, Newark NJ, aqua, rings on shoulder, 2¾" **7.50**

PW Perkins, Tannersville NY, aqua, 6½", EX..................**7.50**

Queen Mary Scotch Whiskey, amber, 1-quart...............**28.00**

Rennes Magic Oil Pain Killing, aqua, 6", M **5.00**

Royal Luncheon Cheese on base milk glass, 3" **2.50**

Royal Pepsin Stomach Bitters, amber, rectangular, 9" ...**85.00**

Scroll, GIX-1, sea green, sheared mouth, 1-quart, EX **150.00**

Scroll, JR & Son, GIX-43, aqua, corseted, 1-pint, NM **375.00**

Seabury Pharmacal Laboratories, cobalt blue, 9"..................**7.50**

Stafford's Inks, cobalt, pouring spout, Made in USA, 6" .**28.00**

Star Mail Order House, amethyst, #243 on base, 12¼"........**12.50**

Star Whiskey, jug, yellow-amber, pouring spout, 8"..........**275.00**

Stoddard Umbrella Ink, amber, 8-sided, open pontil...........**55.00**

Taylor and Williams Incorporated Whiskey, amethyst, 12" .**12.50**

Tea Kettle Ink, cobalt, blue kettle form, 8-panel, 2x4"......**100.00**

Teddy's Pet, nurser, clear, 4".**20.00**

Turlington's Balsam, embossed bass fiddle form..............**25.00**

Underwood Inks, aqua, tapered, 3¼x2¼"..........................**45.00**

Ward's Eureka Tonic Bitters, clear, square, 8¾"..........**32.00**

Warner's Safe Tonic, gold-amber, collared mouth, worn label, 9½" **465.00**

Waterman's Ideal Ink, New York, amethyst, screw top, 3"..**10.00**

WE Bonney Ink, South Hanover MA, aqua, 2¼"...............**48.00**

West Bend Old Timers Lager Beer, aqua, label, 9¼" **3.50**

Whiskey, green, plain, fifth ..**10.00**

Wm Foster's, pottery, gray, cylindrical, 10¾"...................**80.00**

Woonsocket Bottling Works, medium green, embossed, 7-ounce.............................. **5.00**

Dairy

The storage and distribution of fluid milk in glass bottles

became commonplace around the turn of the century. They were replaced by paper and plastic containers in the mid-1950s. Perhaps 5% of all US dairies are still using some glass, and glass bottles are still widely used in Mexico and some Canadian provinces.

Milk-packaging and distribution plants hauled trailer loads of glass bottles to dumping grounds during the conversion to the throw-away cartons now in general use. Because of this practice, milk bottles and jars are scarce today. Most collectors search for bottles from home-town dairies; some have completed a fifty-state collection in the three popular sizes.

Bottles from 1900 to 1920 had the name of the dairy, town, and state embossed in the glass. Nearly all of the bottles produced after this period had the copy painted and then pyro-glazed onto the surface of the bottle. This enabled the dairyman to use colors, pictures of his dairy farm or cows on the bottles. Collectors have been fortunate that there have been no serious attempts at this point to reproduce a particularly rare bottle!

For further information we recommend contacting Mr. O.B. Lund, who is listed in the Directory under Arizona.

Aerl's Dairy, Waco TX, quart . **5.00**
Bear Meadow Farm, Guernsey Cream, Patented 9/17/1889, ½ -pint **10.00**
Borden's Condensed Milk Co, embossed eagle, quart ..**32.50**
Bordens Condensed Milk Co, milk glass or clear, 4½" **7.50**
Carnation's Fresh Milk, Chicago, amber, quart **3.00**

Sun Valley Dairy, Highland Park, IL, green with pyro lettering, ½ - gallon, $32.00.

Cloverdale Dairy, Chippewa Falls WI, clover front, orange, ½ -pint. **3.00**
Cottage Cheese, 10-sided, amethyst, 4½"................. **5.00**
Cream top, 1925, pint **30.00**
Dairyland Product, Cleveland, A on bottom, clear, 7" **5.00**
Gandy's Inc, Registered, clear, pint................................. **7.50**
Golden State Dairy Products, boy & mining scene on back.**30.00**
Grant's Dairy, Bangor ME, red on 2 sides, square quart....... **7.50**
Indian Hill Farm Dairy, Indian Chief on both sides.........**12.00**
Metzger's Milk, embossed baby face, clear, 5½"................**15.00**
Mountain Brook Dairy, Santa Cruz CA...........................**12.50**
Primrose Jersey Farm, Abilene TX, clear with red lettering, 5⅜" **5.00**
Whiting Milk Companies, embossed, ½ -pint............ **5.00**

Windmill Brand Dairy Products, windmill, boy & girl on both sides....................................**35.00**

Brass

Brass, a non-rusting alloy of copper and zinc, was used as far back in civilization as the first century A.D. Items most often found today are from the 19th century, although even 20th-century examples are collectible due to the simple fact that most are now obsolete. Even decorative brass from the 1950s has collector value.

Andirons, simple style with ball feet, 12½", pair..............**250.00**

Ash tray, tooled and enameled, India Benares, 3⅝x1⅞"... **7.50**

Ash tray, 12 animal relief panels at rim, 4¼" diameter **10.00**

Bed warmer, floral engraving on lid, turned wood handle, 43".**250.00**

Bed warmer, long iron handle, early, VG.........................**80.00**

Bell, hand; 3"..........................**12.00**

Bowl, embossed florals, India, 1¾x6½" diameter............**10.00**

Bowl, round with wrought iron handles, 13"....................**35.00**

Bridle rosette, 2¼" diameter on 16" strap, pair **16.00**

Bucket, apple butter; wrought iron bell handle, 10½x16" diameter **185.00**

Bucket, handmade, bail handle, 1700s, 5¼x7½"................**55.00**

Bucket, spun, Hiram W Hayden, EX, 7¼" diameter **50.00**

Candlestick, capstan, polished, 4⅝"..............................**150.00**

Candlestick, diamond-quilted details, Victorian, 12" **55.00**

Candlestick, engraved & enameled, India, 8¾" **12.00**

Candlestick, octagonal stem on square base, 6⅜" **325.00**

Candlestick, Queen Anne style, poor casting, 7¼"...........**45.00**

Candlestick, stem threads into square base, minor repair, 8½" **45.00**

Charcoal iron, turned wood handle, 8¼" **75.00**

Coaster, flowers & leaves, heavy, China, 3½" diameter....... **5.00**

Colander, starflower & flag design, wrought iron rim & handles, 10"..................**165.00**

Incense burner, foo dog on teakwood base, marked **200.00**

Incense burner, open-mouthed chick form, 2¼x2½" **15.00**

Kettle, iron bail handle, early, small............................**100.00**

Kettle, spun exterior, 10" diameter, EX............................**55.00**

Lamp, bracket; with spring-loaded candles, marked NYCS, 6¾", pair.............**95.00**

Lamp, ship's gimball, push-up socket, 11½" **475.00**

Paper clip, relief bulldog, #5267, $55.00.

Plaque, Lincoln relief, gilded, in oval frame with convex glass, 15"................................**325.00**

Sander, from desk set, minor damage, 2¼" **65.00**
Student lamp, worn nickel plating, German Student Lamp, Berlin, 21" **275.00**
Teapot, tin lined, copper rivets, gooseneck spout, 4½" **30.00**
Vase, urn shape, 1⅜" **10.00**
Wax seal, leaf design **4.00**
Wick trimmers, scissors style, marked LM, 10", with matching brass tray **250.00**

Brayton and Brayton Laguna

Located in Laguna Beach, California, this small pottery is especially noted for their amusing Disney figurines and their children's series which were made from the 1930s to the early 1950s.

Purple Cow, 7" long, $40.00.

Candle holder, sitting Blackamoor, pair **60.00**
Cookie jar, Grandma...........**195.00**
Cookie jar, puppy **125.00**
Creamer & sugar bowl, pump & bucket **28.00**
Figurine, Blackamoor holding cornucopia, with gold, 9½"..**30.00**
Figurine, Figaro, Disney **150.00**
Figurine, giraffe, red & blue polka dots on white, 10½"........**75.00**
Figurine, high-button shoe, white with black trim, 3¾x5" ..**20.00**

Figurine, hippo, turquoise, 7½x7½"............................**35.00**
Figurine, lady blues singer, long gown, necklace, 8".........**36.00**
Figurine, Miranda **35.00**
Figurine, nude seated on rock, copyright 1943, 12" **95.00**
Figurine, peasant lady with open baskets, 8" **40.00**
Figurine, Pluto, head up, Disney Ware **150.00**
Figurine, Sambo....................**50.00**
Figurine, tropical fish, orange & brown, 10¼"....................**65.00**
Flower frog, pouter pigeon, blue/white/green, incised, 5½x5¾"............................**30.00**
Lamp, Hansel & Gretel **65.00**
Planter, peasant lady with 2 baskets, 7"............................**32.00**
Shakers, Gingham Dog & Calico Cat, blue & white, pair .**30.00**
Vase, Blackamoor boy holds gold bowl-type vase, 8" **150.00**

Bread Plates

Bread Plates were very popular during the last part of the 1800s. They were produced by various companies, many of whom sold their wares at the 1876 Philadelphia Centennial Exposition. Though they were also made in earthenware and metal, the most popular with collectors are the glass plates with embossed designs that convey a historical, political, or symbolic message.

Art, triangular.....................**45.00**
Beehive, Be Industrious, deer on border **95.00**
Bishop, L-201 ....**200.00**
Carpenters Hall, 12x8½" **95.00**
Chain with Star **35.00**
Classic, James Blaine, clear & frosted, 11½" diameter ..**200.00**

53

Liberty and Freedom, Eagle and Constitution, 12½" long, $38.00.

Columbia, blue, shield shape,
11½x9½"..........................**120.00**
Constitution, L-43.................**25.00**
Delaware, green....................**50.00**
Eureka, with motto, L-103 ..**28.00**
Feather Duster.....................**22.00**
GAR, L-505, oval, 11" long....**85.00**
Golden Rule...........................**65.00**
Grant Memorial, blue, maple leaf
border, 10½" diameter....**65.00**
Horseshoe, single horseshoe han-
dles, 13x9" **55.00**
In Remembrance, 3 Presidents,
clear/frosted, 12½x10"....**85.00**
Iowa City, Be Industrious, frosted
beehive center **60.00**
Last Supper, goofus...............**50.00**
Liberty Bell, Signers **125.00**
Manhattan **20.00**
McKinley Gold Standard, oval, L-
332, 10½" long **350.00**
Nelly Bly, L-136, 12" long...**170.00**
Paneled Dogwood, green with
gold, oval **55.00**
Pleat & Panel **35.00**

Polar Bear & Ship, frosted, oval,
L-486, 16" long **150.00**
Retriever, milk glass **75.00**
Rose in Snow.........................**30.00**
Teddy Roosevelt, dancing bears,
L-357, 7¾x10¼"............**135.00**
Three Panel, amber **35.00**
Willow Oak, blue...................**22.00**

Breweriana

Beer can collectors and
antique advertising buffs as well
enjoy looking for beer-related
memorabilia such as tap knobs,
beer trays, coasters, signs, and
the like. While the smaller items
of a more recent vintage are quite
affordable, signs and trays from
defunct breweries often bring
three-digit prices. Condition is
important in evaluating early
advertising items of any type. See
also Beer Cans.

**Advertising figure, Blatz Man, 16",
$65.00.**

Ash tray, P&H Special, cast iron,
 4½x4", 4" figure at side..**55.00**
Bar, portable; Budweiser, with 2
 stools, EX......................**275.00**
Beer glass, Ask for Progress Beer,
 straight sides..................**27.00**
Beer glass, Atlantic Premium
 Beer, tapered, tall **30.00**
Beer glass, Dakota Beer, clear,
 straight sides **55.00**
Beer glass, Dick's, red circle.**12.50**
Beer glass, Enjoy Gluck's, Min-
 neapolis, straight sides..**30.00**
Beer glass, Grain Belt Beer in dia-
 mond, straight sides **37.00**
Bottle, Latrobe, PA, Rolling Rock
 Beer, 1939, M **4.00**
Bottle, Wolf's Beer, embossed
 wolf, 1920s, NM **15.00**
Bottle opener, Miller Beer, dated
 1955 ....**35.00**
Coasters, Canadian Beer & Ale,
 metal, 10 for **65.00**
Corkscrew, Anheuser Busch,
 encased, NM..................**75.00**

Foam scraper, Meister Brau, cel-
 luloid, EX **18.00**
Foam scraper, Rubsams & Hor-
 man Brewing, EX...........**16.00**
Menu Board, Reading Beer ..**35.00**
Mug, Minneapolis Brewing, Grain
 Belt Beer, M **68.00**
Plate, Krug Brewery, factory view
 & owner **95.00**
Post card, Lemp, St Louis, MO,
 Brewing Co, NM **12.00**
Sign, Falls City Beer, mallard
 duck in relief, plaster, 14x22",
 EX **65.00**
Stein, Budweiser, Chicago Skyline
 painted on glass, 1980 ...**95.00**
Stein, Budweiser Bud Man,
 painted glass figural....**250.00**
Stein, Hamm's Rathskeller
 painted on glass.............**50.00**

Brownies

The Brownie characters–The
London Bobby, The Bellhop, Uncle
Sam, and others–were strange little creatures with potbellies and
long spindle legs who emerged in
the night to do wondrous deeds
for children to delight in discover-
ing the next morning. They were
the progeny of Palmer Cox, who
in 1883 introduced them to the
world in the poem called *The
Brownies Ride*. Books, toys, napkin rings, and advertising items
are just a few of the items available to today's Brownie collectors.

Almanac, C Green Woodbury,
 illustrated by Palmer Cox
 illustrated, 1890 ....**20.00**
Ash tray, RS Germany, 1913 ..**45.00**
Basket, silverplate, Brownies
 with chocolate advertising,
 Tufts.............................**140.00**
Book, Brownies in Fairyland,
 Century Co **35.00**

Book, Queer People, Palmer Cox illustrations, VG **25.00**

Box, Log Cabin Brownies, cabin form, National Biscuit Company, 1920s....................**125.00**

Candlestick, Uncle Sam & Brownies, majolica, each **175.00**

Child's tea set, service for six in original box, $265.00.

Creamer, china, 4½" **60.00**

Cup & saucer, china..............**50.00**

Doll, stuffed **95.00**

Game, Jack Straws **65.00**

Humidor, Brownie Sailor's head form, French majolica..**150.00**

Knife & fork, child's **20.00**

Paper doll, Russian Brownie, Lion Coffee, EX......................**15.00**

Plate, silverplate, Brownies on rim, 8½" **45.00**

Sign, Howell's Root Beer, embossed Brownies on tin, EX **150.00**

Stamps, wood & rubber, original pad & box, set of 6..........**25.00**

Tin container, Brownie Ointment, 1924, M in box...............**40.00**

Butter Molds

Butter molds were once used to decorate and identify butter made by the farmer's wife who often sold her extra churnings at the market. Because the early molds were hand carved, none were exactly alike, and endless variation resulted. The ones most highly treasured today are those with animals or birds and those with unusual shapes or construction.

Cow at fence, scrubbed, rectangular, 7" long **200.00**

Daisy with two leaves with geometric border, large, EX........**95.00**

Daisy center, cross each end, rectangular, 2½x4½"..............**45.00**

Double flower sprig, scrubbed, rectangular, 4x7"............**40.00**

Double tulip, primitive, rectangular, 4½x7¼"...................**100.00**

Flower & initials, 3-part case, 11¼" long **110.00**

Fruit & F, rectangular, 5½" long, VG...............................**50.00**

Fruit & nut, 4-part, brass latches on case, 5½x6" **95.00**

Parrot, scalloped edge, Germany, early.............................**200.00**

Pears, old varnish, rectangular, 4½x7", EX **60.00**

Pineapple, dovetailed case, dark patina, rectangular, 5x6½", EX **195.00**

Rose with bud & leaves, with plunger, 4" diameter **95.00**

Sheaf & leaf, varnished, 3" diameter **85.00**

Star, eight points, machine made, very old, 3½" diameter ...**75.00**

Standing pig on grass, turned handle, cover with metal collar, 7" x 5¾", $300.00.

Stars, 4-part design, rectangular, 5¼x7½".............................**55.00**

Sunflower, primitive carving, 4½" diameter **115.00**

Swan, scrubbed, minor age cracks, 4¾" diameter **85.00**

Tulip, dovetailed case, rectangular, 5x6⅝" **185.00**

2 circles with simple flower design, machine-dovetailed case, 4x6".......................**45.00**

Butter Stamps

Butter stamps differ from molds in that the mold is dimensional while the stamp is flat and was used not to shape the butter but merely to decorate the top.

Acorn, made of maple wood, 3½" diameter **125.00**

Bird on branch, zigzag border, 1-piece, turned handle, 4" diameter **300.00**

Cow, primitive style, scrubbed finish, 4" diameter.............**145.00**

Eagle, 1-piece, turned handle, 3⅛" diameter **200.00**

Eagle & shield, starflower on back, lollipop form, 4¾" diameter................................**575.00**

Eagle with foliage & star, 1-piece, 4⅝" diameter................**450.00**

FINE in block letters, rectangular, 2¾x5⅜", EX..............**55.00**

Flower with border, 1-piece, turned handle, cracks, 4" diameter **125.00**

Flowers & ferns, birch wood, hewn handle, 3½".........**125.00**

Foliage, varnished, minor age cracks, oval, 4x6½".......**150.00**

Heart, deep cross-hatching, 1-piece, turned handle, 3¼" diameter **310.00**

Pineapple, initials carved in handle, 3⅞x4⅛" **145.00**

Pineapple, turned handle, 4" diameter, VG **65.00**

Roller, with 6 prints **195.00**

Sheaf, semicircular, turned handle: 7" long....................**295.00**

Sheaf & leaf, varnished, 3" diameter **85.00**

Sheaf with sickle & rake, lollipop form, 6¼" long..............**300.00**

Starflower center of swirled design, turned handle, 3½" diameter.......................**135.00**

Strawberry, brass hanger, 4⅛" diameter, EX **115.00**

Swan, scrubbed, minor age cracks, 4¾" diameter **85.00**

Swan, 1-piece, turned handle, 3¾" diameter **125.00**

Thistle, turned handle, minor chips, 4" diameter **75.00**

Lollipop type stamp with starflower, 8" long, $165.00.

Buttons

Beautiful buttons of the past were regarded as a symbol of status in their time, and their beauty is still appreciated by collectors today. The age of a button is an important consideration, and those made prior to 1918 are generally classifed as 'old,' while those made after 1918 are considered 'modern.' Buttons are also collected by material: fabric, metal (those of hallmarked silver being higher than some metals, with picture buttons varying in price according to rarity), glass, enamels, pearl and shell, composition, celluloid, ivory, wood, bone, horn, and rubber, to mention a few. Many collectors consider the subject matter. Animal life, plant life, pictorial objects, and miscellaneous patterns are separate classifications. There are many others. Size is another consideration. Buttons are considered large, medium, small, or diminutive.

Beware of 'carnival glass' buttons. These are most likely lustered black glass, since true carnival glass buttons are unknown. Many collectors confuse celluloid and some plastics with ivory; caution is advised. For further information, you may write the National Button Society, which is listed in the Directory under the state of Ohio.

Black glass, bat in iridescent lustre **1.50**
Black glass, chickens in a sabot, small size **2.00**
Black glass, little girl with umbrella, small size **5.00**
Black glass, ordinary design, from 10¢ up to **1.50**
Black glass, various subject matter, up to **25.00**
Bone with pin shank, minimum value **5.00**
China, calico or stencil, common type, from 5¢ up to **2.50**
China, calico or stencil, unusual pattern, up to **30.00**
Clear or colored glass, outlined glory, up to **40.00**
Clear or colored glass, painted back, up to **8.00**
Clear or colored glass, plain, can be less than **1.00**
Clear glass, radiants, dewdrops & glories, up to...................**10.00**
Colored glass, radiants, dewdrops & glories, up to..............**10.00**

Gay '90s (coat or cloak type with glass set in center), $2.00 up to **5.00**
Glass with rosette shank, from $1 up to................................. **3.00**
Imitation fabric, $1 up to....... **3.00**
Lithograph (higher with paste trim), minimum value **5.00**
Paperweight, varies on rarity & age (sulfides much more), $1.00 up to **75.00**
Pottery, Zia Indian, from $8.00 up to **15.00**
Ruby glass passementerie, minimum value......................**10.00**
Smock, plain.............................**25¢**
Steel cup, Bullfighter............. **8.00**
Steel cup, minimum value.......**75¢**
Victorian glass, varies with size, condition & rarity, minimum value ....**50¢**

Republic of Texas button, Navy, 1-piece, very scarce, $450.00.

Cambridge

Organized in 1901 in Cambridge, Ohio, the Cambridge Glass Co. initially manufactured clear glass dinnerware and accessory pieces. In the 1920s they began to concentrate on color, and soon became recognized as the largest producers of this type of glassware in the world. The company used various marks, the most common of which is the 'C in triangle.' The company closed in 1958.

Apple Blossom, colors; bowl, bonbon; handled, 5½".........**16.00**

Apple Blossom, crystal; creamer, pedestal base..................**11.50**

Apple Blossom, crystal; plate, dinner; 9½".........................**26.00**

Caprice, blue; ash tray, 5"....**18.00**

Caprice, blue; bowl, salad; pedestal base, 10".........**50.00**

Caprice, blue; pitcher, ball form, 32-oz............................**270.00**

Caprice, crystal; candlestick, 2½", each...............................**12.00**

Caprice, crystal; ice bucket...**40.00**

Chantilly, crystal; bowl, pedestal base, oval, 12"................**34.00**

Chantilly, crystal; candy box, round, with lid...............**55.00**

Chantilly, crystal; pitcher, ball form...............................**110.00**

Cleo, all colors; bowl, oval, 11½"..............................**28.00**

Compote, Farber Ware nude stem, amethyst bowl, 8", $110.00.

Cleo, all colors; candy box.....**58.50**

Cleo, all colors; decanter & stopper.....................................**75.00**

Crown Tuscan, flower block, #2899, 3".......................**35.00**

Crown Tuscan, jug, #3400/152, Doulton, 76-oz..............**600.00**

Crown Tuscan, vase, #1283, ebony foot, 8".........................**105.00**

Decagon, pastels; creamer, pedestal base..................**10.00**

Decagon, pastels; service tray, oval, 15".........................**15.00**

Decagon, pastels; tumbler, footed, 8-oz...................................**11.50**

Diane, crystal; bowl, flared, pedestal base, 10".........**36.00**

Diane, crystal; decanter, pedestal base................................**125.00**

Diane, crystal; pitcher, Doulton, water size.....................**198.00**

Elaine, crystal; candy box, round, with lid............................**52.00**

Elaine, crystal; ice bucket, chrome handle............................**58.50**

Elaine, crystal; tumbler, #1402, footed, 9-oz....................**18.00**

Elaine, crystal; tumbler, tea; #1402, 12-oz....................**20.00**

Gloria, colors; bowl, cereal; round, 6"....................................**16.00**

Gloria, colors; candy box, with lid, tab handle, 4-footed......**75.00**

Gloria, crystal; comport, low, 7".....................................**26.00**

Gloria, crystal; tumbler, #3120, footed, 5-oz.....................**13.00**

Imperial Hunt Scene, colors; bowl, 8"....................................**36.50**

Imperial Hunt Scene, colors; creamer, pedestal base...**27.00**

Imperial Hunt Scene, colors; tumbler, #1402, flat, 5-oz......**16.50**

Martha Washington, green; bowl, flared, 9".........................**20.00**

Mt Vernon, amber; ash tray, #68, 4".....................................**12.00**

Mt Vernon, crystal; bowl, #44, flared, 12½"..................**33.00**

Double keyhole candle holder, 6", $55.00.

Mt Vernon, crystal; sherbet, #2, tall, 6½-oz **9.00**

Mt Vernon, red; comport, 8" .**26.50**

Portia, crystal; cup, footed....**19.00**

Portia, crystal; vase, footed, 6".**28.00**

Rosalie, colors; candlestick, 3-lite keyhole, 6" **30.00**

Rosalie, colors; salt dip, pedestal base, 1½" **14.50**

Rose Point, crystal; ash tray, square, 2½" **37.50**

Rose Point, crystal; candy box, with lid, 7" **125.00**

Rose Point, crystal; cigarette box, #747, with lid **92.50**

Rose Point, crystal; creamer.**89.00**

Wildflower, crystal; pitcher, Doulton **138.00**

Wildflower, crystal; plate, torte; 14"...................................**38.00**

Campaign Collectibles

Pennants, buttons, posters–in general, anything related to presidential campaigns–are being sought by collectors who have an interest in the political history of our country. Most valued are items from a particularly eventful period or those things having to do with an especially colorful personality.

Book, Authentic Life of President McKinley, 1901..............**20.00**

Booklet, Theodore Roosevelt candidacy **30.00**

Bracelet, I Like Ike, brass with metal charms **20.00**

Bumper sticker, George McGovern.................................... **2.00**

Button, Bicentennial Inauguration, George to George.... **3.00**

Button, Landon for President Club, ⅞" **18.00**

Button, Lyndon Johnson, photo in center, 3½" **8.00**

Button, McCarthy Supporters for Humphrey Now, 1⅞" **9.00**

60

Button, McKinley & Roosevelt, Full Dinner Bucket........**55.00**
Button, Nixon's the One, red, white, & black, 3½"........**10.00**
Button, Parker, portrait in shield, EX....................**38.00**
Button, Reagan for Governor, photo in center, 2¼".......**45.00**
Button, Roosevelt, red, white & blue, photo center, ¾"...... **7.00**
Button, Wallace-Lamay, Let the People Speak, 1¼"........... **5.00**
Button, William J Bryan, portrait, EX **20.00**
Button, Willkie First Voter, blue & white lithograph, ⅞" ..**12.00**
Cookie cutter, Vote Republican, elephant form, ca 1952 ..**20.00**
Dice cup, Don't Gamble, Elect Willkie, 2½x3" **30.00**
Earrings, Ike, rhinestones..... **6.00**

Poster, Nixon re-election, 22x34", NM **15.00**
Poster, Roosevelt & Johnson, black & white, 18x24"....**45.00**
Poster, Warren Harding for President, sepia tones, 1920, 13x18"...........................**40.00**
Puzzle, portrait of JF Kennedy, ca 1961, 12x16"...................**45.00**
Record, JF Kennedy, Memorial Tribute, 1963, 33⅓ rpm...**15.00**
Sunglasses, I Like Ike, plastic frames...........................**18.00**
Tie tack, Jimmy Carter, enamel on brass, photo in center **7.50**
Token, Woodrow Wilson, silver metal............................**10.00**

Republican National Convention delegate's ticket, 1900, $35.00.

Candlewick

Candlewick was one of the all-time best-selling lines of The Imperial Glass Company of Bellaire, Ohio. It was produced from 1936 until the company closed in 1982. More than 741 items were made over the years; and, though many are still easy to find today, some (such as the desk calendar, the chip and dip set, and the dresser set) are a challenge to collect. Candlewick is easily identified by the beaded stems, handles, and rims characteristic of the tufted needlework of our pioneer women.

Ferrotype of Mc Clellan in center of vegetable ivory bracelet, 1⅛" diameter, $250.00.

Key chain, John F Kennedy, brass, photograph in center, 1¼" **15.00**
Match book, Nixon-Lodge jugate, 1960 ....**5.00**
Pin, Harrison, brass, 1888 ...**40.00**
Poster, Kennedy for President, 21x14" **25.00**

Divided relish, 13", $35.00.

Ash tray, heart form, 5½"	**13.00**
Basket, handled, 6½"	**27.50**
Bowl, divided, handles, 10"	**.50.00**
Bowl, square, 5"	**30.00**
Bowl, 3-toed, 10"	**85.00**
Candle holder, flat, 3½"	**13.00**
Candle holder, 2-light	**16.00**
Celery bowl, 7½"	**15.00**
Clock, round, 4"	**85.00**
Coffee cup	**7.50**
Compote, beaded stem, 8"	**65.00**
Cruet, bulbous, 6-oz	**40.00**
Finger bowl	**13.50**
Ice tub, 8" diameter	**75.00**
Mayonnaise set, heart bowl, spoon, & plate, 3-piece	**40.00**
Pitcher, Manhattan, 40-oz	**150.00**
Pitcher, plain, 80-oz	**30.00**
Plate, handles, 10"	**15.00**
Plate, with indent, 8"	**11.00**
Punch cup	**6.00**
Salad fork & spoon	**18.00**
Salt dip, 2¼"	**6.50**
Stem, brandy	**20.00**
Stem, claret	**30.00**
Stem, water, 10-oz	**16.00**
Sugar bowl, plain foot	**6.50**
Tid bit set, 3-piece	**60.00**
Tray, handles, 14"	**40.00**
Tumbler, cocktail; 3-oz	**12.00**
Tumbler, 12-oz	**14.00**
Vase, fan form, 6"	**20.00**
Vase, pitcher shape, 8½"	**100.00**

Candy Containers

From 1876 until the 1940s, figural glass candy containers of every shape and description have been manufactured for the use of candy companies who filled them with tiny colored candy beads. When the candy was gone, kids used the containers as banks or toys. While many are common, some (such as Charlie Chaplin by L. E. Smith, Barney Google by the Barrel, Felix on the Pedestal, or the Rabbit Family) are hard to find and command prices in the $450.00 to $700.00 range.

Numbers refer to a standard reference series, *An Album of Candy Containers*, Vols. 1 and 2, by Jennie Long.

Airplane, Musical Toy, #333	**.25.00**
Airplane, US Army B-51, #591	**.45.00**
Barney Google, by Smith, good paint, #79	**375.00**
Basket, grape design, #223	**...25.00**
Bear in Auto, #2	**135.00**
Bell, Liberty, #3, amber, complete, #229	**65.00**
Billiken, #82	**100.00**
Bottle, Apothecary; #62	**10.00**
Bottle, Soda Pop; #500	**50.00**
Candelabrum #202	**40.00**
Candy Pump, plastic, #240	**.125.00**
Cane, #241	**30.00**
Cash Register, #244	**375.00**
Darner, Amster, #245	**55.00**
Dog by Barrel, closure, original paint, #13	**200.00**
Donald Duck, #85	**150.00**
Duckling, closure, original paint, #30	**70.00**
Gas Pump, #316	**180.00**
Gun, Victory Glass, #149	**.45.00**
Hand Bell, wood handle, closure #494	**150.00**
Horn, Millstein's, #282	**20.00**

Submarine, $27.50.

Kettle, closure, original handle, #251 ....30.00
Lamp, Library; #207 ....400.00
Lantern, beaded trim, #180..20.00
Lantern, ruby flashed, #575 .30.00
Learned Fox, #35 ....90.00
Mug, Child's Tumbler; closure, #256 ....125.00
Owl, closure, glass eyes, complete #37 ....100.00
Play Nursing Set, #259.......130.00
Rabbit, Stough's, #54 ....20.00
Rabbit on Dome, #46..........275.00
Radio, #290 ....110.00
Rolling Pin, #267 ....185.00
Santa Claus, plastic head.....45.00
Scotty Dog, #17 ....12.00
Spark Plug, #109 ....90.00
Suitcase, clear, #217 ....30.00
Telephone, Victory Glass, #1, closure #298 ....175.00
Toy Town Dairy, #656 ....60.00
Village Buildings, no glass inserts, #76, each 20.00
Windmill, shaker top, #445..150.00
Witch's Kettle, #629 ....40.00

Carnival Chalkware

Chalkware statues of Kewpies, glamour girls, assorted dogs and horses were given to winners of carnival games from about 1910 until the 1950s. Today's collectors especially value those representing well-known personalities such as Disney characters and comic book heroes.

For further information, consult *The Carnival Chalk Prize* by Thomas G. Morris.

Abraham Lincoln Bust, marked 1940, 12"........................45.00
Bell Hop, copyrighted by June Jenkins, 1946, 13"..........25.00
Buddy Lee, hand painted, cotton cap, 1920s, 13½" 70.00
Captain Marvel, no marks, 1940s, 14½" 45.00
Donald Duck, 1934-50, 14"...45.00
Donald Duck's nephew on a barrel bank, 10½".....................25.00
Felix the Cat, Pat Sullivan, no marks, 1922, 12½"..........75.00
Hunny Bear bank, marked Walt Disney, 10½"...................35.00
I Love Me Girl, painted pink chalk, mohair wig, 11¼" 75.00
Indian boy, no marks, ca 1935-45, 9"....................................15.00
Kewpie, red devil with horns, no marks, 1925-40, 6½" 25.00
Kitten string holder, no marks, ca 1930s, 7¼" 25.00
Lone Ranger, 1938-50, 14½" .40.00

Mae West, copyrighted as May Doll by William Rainwater, 1936, 14" **50.00**

Miss America, no marks, ca 1940s, 15¾" **25.00**

Nude bust, attributed JY Jenkins, no marks, 1940, 9½".......**25.00**

Pinocchio, attributed Jenkins, no marks, 1940s, 10"...........**20.00**

Porky Pig, no marks, ca 1940s, 7½" **12.00**

Scottish Lass with bagpipes, ca 1940s, 15" **15.00**

Snow White, flat back, copyrighted by JY Jenkins, 1938, 13½" **65.00**

Superman, J Siegel & J Shuster, no marks, 1940s, 15"......**85.00**

Uncle Sam, no marks, ca 1935-45, 15" **40.00**

Baby, pink chalkware with green metallic dress, early, 8", EX, $45.00.

Carnival Glass

From about 1905 until the late 1920s, carnival glass was manufactured by several major American glass houses in hundreds of designs and patterns. Its characteristic iridescent lustre was the result of coating the pressed glassware with a sodium solution before the final firing. Marigold, blue, green, and purple are the most common colors, though pastels were also used. Because it was mass-produced at reasonable prices, much of it was given away at carnivals. As a result, it came to be known as carnival glass.

April Showers, vase, amethyst, Fenton, $55.00.

Acanthus, plate, blue, Fenton, 9" **480.00**

Acorn, compote, green, rare, Millersburg............... **1,800.00**

Acorn Burrs, punch cup, blue, Northwood......................**45.00**

Age Herald, plate, amethyst, scarce, Fenton, 10"... **1,500.00**

Apple Blossoms, bowl, amethyst, Dugan, 7½" **40.00**

Apple Tree, tumbler, marigold, Fenton **44.00**

April Showers, vase, green, Fenton....................................**60.00**

Australian Swan, bowl, amethyst, Crystal, 9".......................**95.00**

Baby's Bouquet, child's plate, marigold, scarce **90.00**

Ball & Swirl, mug, marigold.**90.00**
Balloons, cake plate, marigold, Imperial.........................**60.00**
Banded Diamonds, bowl, marigold, Crystal, 5".....**50.00**
Banded Grape, tumbler, green, Fenton **70.00**
Banded Panels, sugar bowl, open, marigold, Crystal...........**35.00**
Beaded, hatpin, amethyst.....**24.00**
Beaded Cable, candy dish, blue, Northwood **70.00**
Beaded Cable, rose bowl, marigold, Northwood.....**50.00**
Beaded Shell, butter dish, amethyst, Dugan **175.00**
Beaded Spears, tumbler, amethyst, rare, Crystal .**90.00**
Beaded Stars, bowl, marigold, Fenton **35.00**
Beaded Swirl, butter dish, marigold, English...........**60.00**
Bernheimer, bowl, blue, scarce, Millersburg, 9" **1,100.00**
Birds & Cherries, plate, blue, rare, Fenton, 10"...... **1,500.00**
Black Bottom, candy jar, marigold, Fenton **40.00**
Blackberry Spray, bonbon, green, Fenton **45.00**
Blocks & Arches, tumbler, marigold, rare, Crystal .**70.00**
Blossom & Spears, plate, marigold, 8" **45.00**
Blueberry, pitcher, marigold, scarce, Fenton **500.00**
Bo Peep, mug, marigold, scarce, Westmoreland **190.00**
Broken Arches, bowl, green, Imperial, 8½"..................**60.00**
Broken Arches, punch cup, amethyst, Imperial **30.00**
Bubbles, hatpin, amethyst ..**36.00**
Butterflies, bonbon, amethyst, Fenton **70.00**
Butterfly & Berry, tumbler, amethyst, Fenton...........**75.00**
Buzz Saw, cruet, marigold, large, rare, Cambridge, 6" **380.00**

Cane, bowl, pastel, Imperial, 10" **45.00**
Cane, pickle dish, marigold, Imperial **25.00**
Captive Rose, bonbon, blue, Fenton **55.00**
Captive Rose, bowl, green, Fenton, 8½" **48.00**
Carnival Honeycomb, bonbon, amethyst, Imperial **45.00**
Checkers, bowl, marigold, 9"..**32.00**
Cherry, bowl, amethyst, Dugan, flat, 5"..............................**40.00**
Cherry, bowl, blue, Millersburg, 4"................................**495.00**
Cherry, plate, amethyst, rare, Millersburg, 7½" **700.00**

Nu-Art Chrysanthemum, plate, amethyst, Imperial, $995.00

Cherry Blossoms, pitcher, blue, water size **95.00**
Cherry Chain, bonbon, marigold, Fenton **37.00**
Classic Arts, vase, marigold, rare, 10"..................................**200.00**
Cobblestones, bowl, amethyst, Dugan, 9".......................**70.00**
Coin Dot, plate, green, rare, Fenton, 9" **180.00**
Coin Spot, compote, blue, Dugan............................**70.00**
Constellation, compote, marigold, Dugan **40.00**

Cosmos & Cane, bowl, marigold, 10".....................................**58.00**

Country Kitchen, bowl, marigold, rare, Millersburg, 5"....**100.00**

Crab Claw, cruet, marigold, rare, Imperial..........................**650.00**

Crackle, punch cup, marigold, Imperial...........................**10.00**

Cut Arcs, compote, amethyst, Fenton **48.00**

Dahlia, creamer, marigold, Dugan.............................**75.00**

Dahlia, tumbler, amethyst, rare, Dugan.............................**135.00**

Daisy Squares, rose bowl, amethyst.......................**400.00**

Diamond Checkerboard, bowl, marigold, 5"....................**25.00**

Diamond Fountain, cruet, marigold, rare, Higbee.**675.00**

Diamond Lace, pitcher, amethyst, Imperial **265.00**

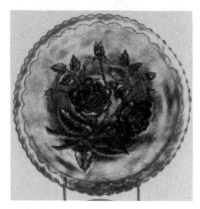

Open Rose, plate, amber, Imperial, $290.00.

Diamond Point, basket, marigold, rare **485.00**

Dotted Daisies, plate, marigold, 8"......................................**65.00**

Double Scroll, bowl, amethyst, Imperial..........................**52.00**

Double Scroll, punch cup, marigold, Imperial.........**22.00**

Dragonfly Lamp, oil lamp, pastel, rare **650.00**

Duckie, powder jar, marigold, with cover.......................**25.00**

Elks, bowl, nappy, amethyst, very rare, Dugan **2,900.00**

Emu, bowl, marigold, rare, Crystal, 10" **80.00**

Estate, mug, marigold, rare, Westmoreland **85.00**

Famous, puff box, marigold..**75.00**

Fans, pitcher, marigold, English, water size **60.00**

Fashion, pitcher, marigold, Imperial **170.00**

Feathered Serpent, bowl, amethyst, Fenton, 5" **45.00**

Fentonia, tumbler, marigold.**45.00**

Fern, bowl, green, Northwood, 9"......................................**50.00**

Fine Cut Rings, bowl, marigold, oval, English **40.00**

Fine Cut Rings, creamer, marigold, English...........**45.00**

Floral, hatpin, amber **50.00**

Flowers & Spades, bowl, green, Dugan, 5"........................**35.00**

Flute, bowl, amethyst, Northwood, 5" **27.50**

Flute, pitcher, marigold, rare, Northwood **385.00**

Forks, cracker jar, green, rare, Cambridge....................**495.00**

Formal, hatpin holder, marigold, rare, Dugan **175.00**

Four Flowers, bowl, blue, Finland, 10" **90.00**

Frosted Block, celery tray, marigold, Imperial.........**40.00**

Frosted Ribbon, pitcher, marigold, water size **80.00**

God & Home, tumbler, blue, rare, Dugan **135.00**

Golden Honeycomb, bowl, marigold, Imperial, 5"....**25.00**

Grape, pitcher, green, Imperial, water size **170.00**

Grape Leaves, bowl, green, Northwood, 9" **75.00**

Harvest Poppy, compote, amethyst........................**50.00**

Harvest Poppy, compote, marigold......................**38.00**

Heart & Vine, bowl, green, Fenton, 9" **42.00**

Heavy Prisms, celery vase, amethyst, English, 6" **90.00**

Hobstar, basket, marigold, Imperial **90.00**

Hobstar & File, pitcher, marigold, rare **1,500.00**

Holly, compote, green, Fenton, 5" **45.00**

Honeycomb & Clover, bonbon, green, Fenton **57.00**

Inverted Strawberry, bowl, marigold, 5"....................**38.00**

Jewels, candlestick, pastel, Imperial, pair **70.00**

Little Owl, hatpin, blue **165.00**

Louisa, plate, amethyst, footed, Westmoreland, 8" **150.00**

Lustre Rose, pitcher, green, Imperial **97.00**

May Basket, basket, marigold, English, 7½" **46.00**

Mayflower, compote, pastel ..**60.00**

Maypole, vase, green, 6¼" **56.00**

Melon Rib, powder jar, marigold, Imperial **35.00**

Milady, pitcher, blue, Fenton, water size **500.00**

My Lady, powder jar, marigold, with cover **87.00**

Nippon, bowl, marigold, Northwood, 8½" **48.00**

Northwood's Poppy, bowl, blue, 7" **58.00**

Octagon, vase, green, rare, Imperial **125.00**

Optic Flute, bowl, marigold, Imperial, 5" **25.00**

Orange Tree, butter dish, marigold, Fenton..........**136.00**

Orange Tree, rose bowl, white, Fenton **250.00**

Orange Tree, tumbler, marigold, Fenton **37.00**

Ostrich, compote, marigold, Australian, large **125.00**

Trout and Fly, bowl, amethyst, $650.00.

Panama, goblet, marigold, rare, US Glass.......................**120.00**

Peach, bowl, pastel, Northwood, 9"...................................**210.00**

Peacock Tail, compote, blue, Fenton....................................**48.00**

Pearl Lady, shade, white, Northwood...............................**55.00**

Puzzle, compote, amethyst, Dugan **46.00**

Question Marks, bonbon, amethyst, Dugan............**48.00**

Rococo, vase, green, Imperial, 5½" **57.00**

Sailboats, bowl, green, Fenton, 6"....................................**75.00**

Scottie, powder jar, marigold, with cover **25.00**

Singing Birds, bowl, green, Northwood, 10" **75.00**

Stream of Hearts, bowl, blue, footed, Fenton, 10" **75.00**

Sunray, compote, peach opalescent **45.00**

Twins, bowl, pastel, Imperial, 9" **42.00**

Two Row, vase, amethyst, Imperial **675.00**

Vintage, tray, marigold, Dugan, 7x11" **78.00**

Wild Berry, jar, marigold, with cover **75.00**

Windmill, pickle dish, green, Imperial..........................**45.00**

Zig Zag, bowl, green, Millersburg, 9½" **350.00**

Zipper Variant, sugar bowl, marigold, English **48.00**

Catalogs

Vintage catalogs are an excellent source of reference for collectors as well as being quite collectible in their own right. While some collectors specialize in trying to accumulate a particular company's catalogs in sequence, others prefer to look for those specializing in only one area of interest—knives, lighting fixtures, or farm machinery, for instance. Original catalogs are often hard to find, and several companies have reprinted some of their earlier editions.

Rotograph Co., NY, 1907, 32-pg., wrappers, $25.00.

Berlin Photographic Company, New York City, 1902, 600 pages, EX.......................**55.00**

Biddle & Smart Carriages, Massachusetts, 1893, 5x7¾".**65.00**

Bryant Perkins Wiring Devices, 1924, 206 pages, VG **12.50**

Butler Electro-Massage, New York, illustrated, 1889, 48 pages, EX **28.00**

Chicago Time-Piece Company, watches & jewelry, illustrated, 1885, VG.............**35.00**

Curtis Cough Compound, Indians on cover, 1889 ....**10.00**

Detroit Stove Works, Jewel stoves, illustrated, 334 pages, 1905, EX........................**50.00**

Dr Miles' Common Things, pyramids on cover, 1890s **7.50**

Electric Supply, sporting goods, 1950, EX **10.00**

Fay Manufacturing, bicycles, 1891, 6x10" illustrated folder, EX....................................**12.00**

General Electric, Schenectady NY, incandescent lamps, 1900, 110 pages **20.00**

Hartman Furniture, Chicago IL, 1916, 422 pages, EX.......**35.00**

Illinois Electric, generators & appliances, ca 1900, EX.**18.00**

James & Holmstrom Pianos, NY, ca 1911, VG **36.00**

Loubaugh, railroad supplies, 1941, VG **10.00**

Magneto Telephone Apparatus No 15, EX **35.00**

Mandel Brothers, Chicago IL, holiday gifts, 1914, 40 pages, EX **12.50**

Mine & Smelter Supply Co, NY, 1913, 6x9¼", EX.............**90.00**

Montgomery Ward, sewing machines, ca 1919, 11x14", EX **55.00**

Myrex Music, New York City, music books & sheet music, 1915, EX **6.00**

Otto Young & Company, watchmaker's/jeweler's/etc supplies, 1901, EX.............**120.00**

Public Service Electrical Supply, 1920s, VG **75.00**
Spoor's Variety, 1937 ....**20.00**
Standard Homes, illustrated homes with plans, 1925 .**12.50**
Taylor Brothers, weather instruments, 1908, 173 pages, EX **35.00**
Thresher Supply, farm supplies, illustrated, 1924, EX **15.00**
United Drug Company, sundries, illustrated, 1914, 163 pages, EX **45.00**
Wagner Manufacturing, hardware supplies, 1910, 93 pages, 6x9", EX **48.00**
Western Auto Supply, illustrated, 1929, EX **8.00**
Western Gun Works, Pittsburgh, 1888, 64 pages, EX **50.00**

Ceramic Arts Studio

Whether you're a collector of American pottery or not, chances are you'll like the distinctive styling of the figurines, salt and pepper shakers, and other novelty items made by the Ceramic Arts Studio of Madison, Wisconsin, from about 1938 until about 1952. They're among the newest collectibles on the market, and a trip to any good flea market will usually produce one or several good buys of their shelf sitters or wall-hanging pairs. They're easily spotted, once you've seen a few examples; but, if you're not sure, check for the trademark: the name of the company and its location.

Ash tray, hippo, 3½" **36.00**
Figurine, accordion boy, 5"....**35.00**
Figurine, Alice, 4½"................**65.00**
Figurine, angel praying on knees, 4¼" **25.00**

Figurines, Comedy and Tragedy, 10", $135.00 for the pair.

Figurine, Balky & Frisky, colts, 3¾", pair **35.00**
Figurine, cellist, pink, #478, 6½" **95.00**
Figurine, Lady Rowena on horseback, 8¼" **75.00**
Figurine, Little Bo Peep, 6"..**25.00**
Figurine, pekingese, 3".........**20.00**
Jug, Miss Forward, rare, 4"..**35.00**
Jug, rose motif, 2¾"...............**20.00**
Jug, Toby, 3½" **35.00**
Lamp, Flutist on base **95.00**
Plaque, Shadow Dancers, 7", pair **65.00**
Shakers, deer & doe, stylized, 3¾", pair **45.00**
Shakers, cocks, pair **28.00**
Shakers, frog & toadstool, 2" & 3", pair............................**25.00**
Shakers, mouse & cheese, 2½", pair **25.00**
Shakers, penguins, pair........**25.00**
Shakers, snuggle monkeys ...**30.00**
Shelf sitter, Fluffy & Tuffy, 4½", pair **30.00**
Shelf sitter, Mexican boy & girl, 6", pair **50.00**

Shelf sitter, puma, Cubist.....**20.00**
Vase, Becky, 5¼".................**40.00**
Vase, duck, 4¼"...................**45.00**
Vase, roses, round, 2¼" **15.00**

Character Collectibles

One of the most popular areas of collecting today and one with the most available memorabilia is the field of character collectibles. Flea markets usually yield some of the more common examples–toys, books, lunch boxes, children's dishes, and sheet music are for the most part quite readily found. Trade papers are also an excellent source. Often you will find even the rare and hard-to-find listed for sale. Disney characters, movie stars, television personalities, comic book heroes, and sports greats are the most sought after.

Addams Family, Colorform kit, NM in original box.......**132.00**
Bambi, card game, Russell Co, 1960s, M on card............**20.00**
Bambi, ceramic cup, Shaw, 3", NM................**35.00**
Bambi, Halloween mask, Ben Cooper, 1950s, VG..........**35.00**
Bashful, rubber figure, Seiberling, 5", EX..............**35.00**
Batman, action figure, Mego, 1979, 8", M in package...**40.00**
Batman, coin, plastic, 1956, M on card................**45.00**
Batman, compass, 1966, M on card................**25.00**
Batman, crazy foam.............**45.00**
Batman, lamp, vinyl Batman by Batcave, 1977, VG..........**45.00**
Batman, lantern, 1977, EX ..**75.00**
Batman, mug, milk glass......**12.00**
Batman, paint by numbers, large, M in box **15.00**

Batman, party napkins, 1960s, M in sealed package **8.00**
Batman, scope, Park Plastics, 1966, EX.........................**70.00**
Batman, space rocket, chute & launcher, Ahi, 1979, M .**28.00**
Batman, sticker book, 1966, unused, M **24.00**
Batman, talking alarm, EX..**85.00**
Batmobile, Worchester, 1966, 9", M on card.....................**125.00**
Batmobile with 2 figures, tin, battery operated, Japan, 12", M..................................**265.00**
Beatles, sneakers box, picture of singers on lid, EX...........**85.00**
Beetle Baily, board game, Milton Bradley, 1963, EX..........**40.00**
Bing Crosby, board game, Call Me Lucky, 1954, VG.............**40.00**
Bionic Woman, paint by numbers set, Craftmaster, 1976, M in box...................................**12.00**
Blade Runner, set of 4 die-cast cars, Ertl, 1982, very rare, M in box **75.00**
Bozo Clown, cloth doll, Knickerbocker, 1964, 15", EX.....**18.00**
Buck Rogers, battle cruiser, Tootsietoy, 1937, VG...........**115.00**
Buck Rogers, official utility belt, Remco, 1979, M in box ..**20.00**
Buck Rogers pocket watch, manufactured 1930s..............**175.00**
Buck Rogers, spaceman figure, lead, EX **15.00**
Buck Rogers, Tru-Vue, cards for 3-D viewer, 1953................**25.00**
Buck Rogers, 25th Century-Shaker Maker Set, Ideal, 1980, M.........................**30.00**
Bugs Bunny, ceramic planter, multi **75.00**
Captain Marvel, car, green, tin litho windup, 1947 ....**50.00**
Captain Marvel, Magic Whistle, manufactured 1948........**30.00**
Captain Marvel, Shazam paper game, scarce, 1944, M....**35.00**

Figurines, Dumbo, American Pottery Co., Los Angeles, 4" and 5½", $95.00 each

Captain Video, Secret Ray gun, with glow card & instructions, NM......................**95.00**

Casper the Ghost, Halloween display, holding balloon, 7x17", 1970, EX **15.00**

Casper the Ghost, store display, die-cut cardboard, 21x16", 1960s, EX **145.00**

Charlie McCarthy, rubber face mask **85.00**

Cinderella, Halloween costume, EX **25.00**

Clarabell, kit for stuffed doll, M in original box...................**125.00**

Columbo, detective game, 1973, VG in box........................**28.00**

Daniel Boone, poseable figure, complete with accessories, M in box **60.00**

Daniel Boone, Wilderness Scout flintlock, Marx, 12", M on card.................................**95.00**

Darth Vader, speaker phone, ATC, 1983, 14", NM in box ..**125.00**

Davy Crockett, cap rifle, 1950s, 33", EX in original cardboard case **60.00**

Davy Crockett, ceramic mug, multicolor..............................**65.00**

Davy Crockett, coon skin cap, Halco, EX........................**45.00**

Davy Crockett, costume, King of Pioneers, Wonderland, 1950s, M in box **135.00**

Davy Crockett, iron-on transfer, 1950s............................... **5.00**

Davy Crockett, powder horn, Daisy, 1950s, EX in box **36.00**

Davy Crockett, song book, Ballad of..., Disney, 1955, VG....**25.00**

Davy Crockett, western tie, 1950s, M on card **20.00**

Dennis the Menace, flashlight, with decal, 3", NM **24.00**

Dick Tracy, badge, Secret Service Patrol, brass, 1938, EX **55.00**

Dick Tracy, figural bubble bath container, 1960s, 10" **45.00**

Dick Tracy, Mugg & Tracy in color on china, 9", EX..............**65.00**

Donald Duck, Army paint book, large size, EX **20.00**

Donald Duck, ceramic cookie jar, Leeds, 14" **70.00**

Donald Duck, quartz wrist watch, Lorus Co, M in box.........**25.00**

Donald Duck, watering can, Ohio Art, 5", EX **50.00**

Donald Duck, wrist watch wall clock, Bradley, 26", EX ..**32.00**

Elvis Presley, doll, Celebrity World, Burning Love, 1984, M.................**98.00**

Elvis Presley, promotional mirror, Love Me Tender, dated 1956, NM **12.50**

Felix the Cat, Orange Dry Soda bottle cap, 1950s, EX **5.00**

Flintstones, cave house, punchout cardboard, Ideal, original box, EX **225.00**

Flintstones, finger puppets, set of 4, NM **35.00**

Flintstones, tumbler, 1962....**12.50**

Flintstones, Wilma figure, bendable, 1968, NM **36.00**

Gene Autry/Leslie Henry, 44 cap gun.................................**95.00**

Green Hornet, flasher disc, 1960s, 7½ ", M.............................**24.00**

Green Hornet, flicker ring....**12.00**

Green Hornet, playing cards, Ed-U-Card, 1966, NM **20.00**

Green Hornet, Quick Switch game, M in worn box ...**125.00**

Green Hornet, secret compartment ring, NM **450.00**

Gulliver' s Travels, tin drum, 1939 ....**65.00**

Hopalong Cassidy, cardboard gun, NM...............................**40.00**

Hopalong Cassidy, coloring book, 1951, 13x11", M..............**30.00**

Hopalong Cassidy, plate, gun drawn, on horse, WS George, VG...................................**45.00**

Hopalong Cassidy, potato chip can, complete, EX **175.00**

Hopalong Cassidy, T-shirt decal, Deputy, 1950s, NM......... **9.00**

Howdy Doody, cloth patch, Joy, 1971, 3½ " **12.00**

Howdy Doody, figural squeeze toy, 12" **125.00**

Howdy Doody, figure, plastic with movable jaw, 1950, 4", M in box **40.00**

Hopalong Cassidy clock, U.S. Time, $75.00.

Howdy Doody, Flub-a-Dub ring toss, 1950s, M.................**18.00**

Howdy Doody, football **48.00**

Howdy Doody, ice cream spoon, Kagran, M **12.50**

Howdy Doody, night light, figural, sitting, M **100.00**

Howdy Doody, teaspoon, figural, EX **45.00**

Huckleberry Hound, Huckle-Chuck target game, NM in original box....................**175.00**

Joe E Brown, badge & premium list, M.............................**48.00**

Li'l Abner, paint & crayon set, 1950s, M in box **60.00**

Little Orphan Annie, plastic mug with decal, Ovaltine **35.00**

Little Orphan Annie, Secret Society badge, brass, 1930s..**25.00**

Little Orphan Annie & Sandy, pull toy, paper litho on wood, 1930s, 9" **125.00**

Lone Ranger, coloring book, 1953, NM.................................**32.00**

Lone Ranger, neckerchief, 1930s, VG.................................**35.00**

Lone Ranger, pencil box, ca 1930s, VG **37.50**

Lone Ranger, photograph, Merita Bread, 8x10"..................**20.00**

Lone Ranger, pistol, rubber, Morton Salt, 1938 ....40.00

Lone Ranger, ring toss game, die-cut figure, Rosebud, 1946, EX in box 325.00

Mickey & Minnie Mouse, waste basket, 1930s, EX 85.00

Mickey Mouse, alarm clock, Lorus Co, M in box 30.00

Mickey Mouse, game cards, Russell Manufacturer, with box, EX 12.00

Mickey Mouse, gum card wrapper, NM 120.00

Mickey Mouse, magic slate with wooden pencil, 1930s, small, EX 35.00

Elsie the Cow, molded latex and cloth, 12", $70.00.

Mickey Mouse, night light, figural, head lights up, M ...20.00

Mickey Mouse, popcorn popper, Empire Co., 1936, EX 75.00

Mickey Mouse, push puppet, wooden, jointed, Hohner, #185, NM 125.00

Mickey Mouse, soda bottle, 1977, M 45.00

Mickey Mouse, talking telephone, Hasbro, 1974, NM 10.00

Mickey Mouse & Friends, ski jump target game, 1930s, EX in box 85.00

Mickey Mouse & Pluto, bisque toothbrush holder, 3" ...125.00

Minnie Mouse, puppet, Gund, 1960s, NM in box 30.00

Moon Mullins, bisque nodder, Germany, EX 130.00

Mork & Mindy, game, Parker Bros, 1979, M in box 12.00

Pee-Wee Herman, talking pig, M in box 48.00

Penguin, car, Corgi, 1966, M in package...........................15.00

Penguin, music box, full figure, ceramic, 8", M................78.00

Pinocchio, celluloid baby rattle, 1940s, EX 65.00

Pinocchio, figurine, pressed wood, 8" 145.00

Pinocchio, paper mask, Gillette premium, 1941, EX 32.00

Pinocchio, rubber figure, Seiberling, 1940, 5" 40.00

Pluto, ceramic cup, Patriot China, 1930s..............................40.00

Pluto the Pup, puppet, Fisher-Price, 1930s, EX.............15.00

Pogo Possum, book, Potluck Pogo, 1955, EX/NM.................25.00

Pogo Possum, plastic figure, Japan, 4".........................12.00

Pogo Possum, vinyl figure, 1969 premium, EX.................20.00

Pokey, hand puppet, Lakeside, 1965, M in package........38.00

Pokey, jack-in-the-box, Lakeside, 1965, MIB......................38.00

Popeye, application card for club, 3x6", early, EX 15.00

Popeye, figure, Gund, 17", M in box................................70.00

Popeye, mechanical pencil, dated 1929, M in box...............68.00

Popeye, refrigerator magnets, 1974, 48 piece set...........40.00

Rocky Jones Space Ranger, coloring book, 1953, NM **24.00**

Rocky Jones Space Ranger, pinback button, VG **20.00**

Roy Rogers, alarm clock, Roy Rogers riding Trigger..... **95.00**

Roy Rogers, crayon set, Standard Toycraft, 1950s, EX........ **55.00**

Roy Rogers, horseshoe set, 2 tinlitho bases/4 shoes, Ohio Art, NM................ **85.00**

Roy Rogers, pin-back button, Grape Nut Flakes premium, NM **10.00**

Six Million Dollar Man, board game, 1975, NM **11.50**

Sneezy, glass tumbler, Libbey, 1938 .... **15.00**

Dino and cave men, Kreiss Co., 7", $23.00.

Snow White, bisque figure, Disney, 2", VG **36.00**

Snow White, bookends, La Mode Studios, pair, VG............ **95.00**

Snow White, plate, Ohio Art, 1937, 4", EX................... **22.00**

Snow White & 7 Dwarfs, paint book, Disney, 1938, EX .. **32.00**

Snow White & 7 Dwarfs, safety blocks, Halsam, 1930s, set of 9, VG **30.00**

Spiderman, bicycle horn, electric, EX **32.00**

Spiderman, helicopter, Remco, 1978, M in box............... **60.00**

Spiderman, push-button telephone, Carlton, 1984, M in box **55.00**

Spiderman, Secret War figure, traditional clothes, 1st issue, M.................................... **24.00**

Spiderman, Yo-Yo, Duncan ... **25.00**

Star Wars, jigsaw puzzle, Kenner, 1978, boxed...................... **6.50**

Starsky & Hutch, Detective game, Milton Bradley, 1977, NM in box.................................. **12.00**

Steve Canyon, board game, 1959, VG.................................. **36.00**

Superman, ballpoint pen, plastic, 1978, M **6.00**

Superman, color book, ca 1960s, M.................................... **24.00**

Superman, dime bank, tin, ca 1940s, EX **225.00**

Superman, mug, glass, with fired-on color, 1970s............... **22.00**

Superman, statue, hand-painted ceramic, 13".................... **80.00**

Tarzan, coloring book, Whitman, 1966, NM........................ **17.50**

Tarzan, target set, cardboard, battery-op, Schneider, 1930s, 18x8", EX...................... **125.00**

Three Little Pigs, bisque toothbrush holder, 1920, EX .. **60.00**

Three Little Pigs, ceramic bowl, Patriot China, 1930s **35.00**

Three Little Pigs, plate, Patriot China, 1938 .... **60.00**

Three Little Pigs, toothbrush holder, figures playing instruments, 4" **65.00**

Thumper, ceramic rabbit figure, American Pottery, 4"...... **45.00**

Tom Corbett, Space Cadet tray puzzle, 1950, EX **32.00**

Tom Mix, manual, 1941, light foxing on cover **38.00**
Tom Mix, photo, Ralston premium, 1940s, framed **75.00**
Tom Mix, program, Sells-Floto circus, 1929, VG **45.00**
Tom Mix, Straight Shooters knife, Ralston premium, NM ..**32.00**
Tom Mix, telescope, Ralston premium, 1938, worn **55.00**
Wimpy, ring, Post cereal premium, M in package **20.00**
Yogi Bear, Halloween mask, Hanna Barbera, NM **15.00**
Yogi Bear, stuffed, no bow tie, 28", EX **45.00**
Zorro, magic slate, Disney, 1950s, NM **18.00**

From this century, Tales of Tarzan by Burroughs are fast becoming very collectible–*Tarzan of the Apes,* 1914, McClurg first edition, in excellent condition, is worth about $850.00.

ABC of Animals, linentex, Saalfield, 1921, VG **5.00**
Aesop's Fables, Garden City, 1939 .... **32.00**
Ali the Camel, Doubleday/Doran, 1st edition, 1931 .... **45.00**
Buccaneer Islands, Nelson, 1st edition, 1941 .... **18.00**
Cat & the Devil, Dodd/Mead, 1st edition, 1964 .... **20.00**
Circus Sights, McLoughlin, 12 color pages, 1890, G **7.50**

Fred Flintstone ash tray, black and white, Hanna Barbera, 1961, 8", $12.00.

Children's Books

Books were popular gifts for children in the latter 1800s; many were beautifully illustrated, some by notable artists such as Frances Brundage and Maxfield Parrish.

Cosey Corner, McLaughlin Brothers, 1987, VG, $15.00.

Daddy Gander Rhymes, Crowell, 1st edition, 1916............. **30.00**
Doggie Pranks, McLoughlin ..**20.00**
Donald Duck Sees South America, Heath, 1945 .... **48.00**
Dream Days, Maxfield Parrish illustrated, 1902............. **45.00**
Emerald City of Oz, O'Neill illustrated, Reilly/Lee, 1910 .**35.00**
Flip Flop Show, circus story, Donohue, 1909, EX **20.00**

Flower Children, Wise/Parslow,
1939 ....**35.00**
Glinda of Oz, Baum, Reilly/Lee,
1920 ....**30.00**
Joyce of the Secret Squadron,
Whitman, 1942................ **8.00**
Little Bears Playtime, Rand
McNally, 1922 .... **6.00**
Little Magic Horse, Macmillan,
1st edition, 1942.............**25.00**
Little Miss Ducky Daddles,
Stoll/Edwards, 1926.......**11.00**
Macaroni Tree, Hebberd, 1st edi-
tion, illustrated, 1927 ....**28.00**
Merry Jingles From Mother
Goose, McLoughlin **21.00**
Miss Hickory, Viking, 1st edition,
1946 ....**28.00**
My Automobile Book, 16 vehicles,
Gabriel, 1924..................**15.00**
National Velvet, Morrow, 1st edi-
tion, 1935.......................**32.00**
Old John, Macmillan, 1st edition,
1936 ....**34.00**
Pollyanna's Door to Happiness,
Grosset/Dunlap, 1936 ..... **5.00**
Silverlocks & the Three Bears, CE
Graham, EX **7.50**
Susanna of the Mounties, Shirley
Temple, 1936 ....**20.00**
Tarzan & the Forbidden City,
Whitman, 1952................ **7.00**
Thief in the Attic, Viking, 1st edi-
tion, 1965 ....**12.00**
Three Caballeros, Random House,
rare **95.00**
Three Little Pigs & Foolish Pig,
Rand McNally, 1918.......**15.00**
Toby's Goblin, Rand McNally, 1st
edition, 1930..................**30.00**
Told to the Little Tot, Dodge, EV
Cooke, 1906 ....**16.00**
Wee Willie Winkie, Whitman, ca
1929 ....**18.00**

Children's Dishes

In the late 1900s, glass companies introduced sets of small-
scaled pressed glass dinnerware,
many in the same pattern as their
regular lines, others designed
specifically for the little folks.
Many were of clear glass, but
milk glass, opalescent glass, and
colors were also used. Not to be
outdone, English ceramic firms
as well as American potteries
made both tea sets and fully-
accessorized dinnerware sets decorated with decals of nursery
rhymes, animals, or characters
from children' s stories. Though
popularly collected for some time,
your favorite flea market may
still yield some very nice examples of both types.

China and Pottery

Bowl, Children Fishing, Noritake,
5⅞ " **15.00**
Creamer, flowers, gold trim, Made
in Germany **20.00**
Creamer, floral medallion, Made
in Japan, 2¾ "................**10.00**
Creamer, Joseph, Mary, & the
Donkey, Germany, 3" **35.00**
Creamer, Otter Cocoa, Noritake,
2"....................................**45.00**
Cup, Bears, marked Made in
Japan, 2¼" **20.00**
Cup, flowers, Nippon, 1½ " ..**10.00**
Cup, Nursery Scene, marked Ger-
many, 2".........................**16.00**
Cup, Snow White, marked Made
in Japan, 1½ " **10.00**
Cup & saucer, Mother Goose,
Royal Doulton **55.00**
Egg cup, Old Mother Hubbard,
footed **10.00**
Mug, Deer Stalking, 2⅜".......**50.00**
Mug, Fishing Party, 2¾ " **65.00**
Plate, Blue Willow, marked Made
in Japan, 5" **25.00**
Plate, Davy Crockett, 7¼ "..... **5.00**
Plate, Little Bo Peep, Royal Doul-
ton, Schmoker, 8" **45.00**

Green and orange floral on cream, Made in Japan, 24 pieces in original box, $295.00.

Plate, Merry Christmas, pink lustre, Germany, 5⅛ " 15.00
Plate, Peter Pan, marked Occupied Japan, 3⅞ " 12.00
Platter, Charles Dickens Scenes, Ridgways, 6" 30.00
Platter, Little Orphan Annie, Made in Japan, 5" 22.00
Saucer, clown with duck & dog on ball, marked Made in Japan, 3".12.00
Saucer, Gaudy Ironstone, marked England 20.00
Sugar bowl, Nursery Rhyme, Made in Germany, 1⅜ "..18.00
Teapot, Mickey Mouse, marked Occupied Japan, 3¼ ".....35.00
Teapot, Punch & Judy, Staffordshire 70.00
Teapot, Saint Nicholas, marked Made in Germany, 5½ "..95.00

Pattern Glass

Acorn, creamer, crystal, 3⅜ " ..90.00
Austrian, spooner, crystal, 3"..95.00
Baby Thumbprint, cake stand .75.00
Block, sugar bowl, with lid, crystal, 4½ "..........................100.00
Braided Belt, creamer, white with florals, 2⅝ "..................110.00

Button Panel 44, butter dish, crystal with gold trim 95.00
Buzz Saw, spooner, crystal, Cambridge, 2⅛ " 32.00
Chimo, punch cup, crystal 20.00
Chimo, table set, 4-pc 225.00
Clear & Diamond Panels, sugar bowl, green, with lid, 3½ ".50.00
Cloud Band, butter dish, milk glass with florals, 3¾ " .165.00
Colonial, pitcher, crystal.......20.00
Colonial 2630, creamer, cobalt, Cambridge, 2⅜ " 45.00
D&M 42, honey jug, crystal..70.00
Diamond Ridge 48, spooner, crystal, 2¾ "...........................80.00
Drum, sugar bowl, crystal, with lid, 3½ "..........................100.00
Duncan & Miller 42, butter dish, crystal, 4" 100.00
Fancy Cut, tumbler, 1⅝ "......22.00
Fernland, creamer 15.00
Flute, berry set, crystal with gold trim..............................225.00
Galloway, pitcher, crystal with gold trim, 3⅞ " 35.00
Hobnail with Thumbprint 150, tray, blue, 7⅜ "................50.00
Horizontal Threads, creamer, crystal, 2¼ "....................30.00

Inverted Strawberry, punch cup, crystal, 1⅛ " **25.00**
Kittens, saucer, marigold, Fenton, 4½ " **55.00**
Lazy Daisy, berry set, crystal, 5-pc **90.00**
Liberty Bell, spooner, crystal, Gillinder & Sons, 2⅜ " . **135.00**
Long Diamond 15006, creamer, crystal, US Glass, 2⅞ " .. **55.00**
Michigan, butter dish, crystal with gold trim, US Glass Co, 3½ " **125.00**
Oval Star 300, punch set, crystal, Indiana Glass, 7-pc **125.00**
Pattee Cross, tumbler, crystal, US Glass, 1¾ " **16.00**
Pennsylvania, creamer, green, 2½ " **85.00**
Pert, creamer, 3¼ " **90.00**
Rooster 140, nappy, crystal. **120.00**
Stipple Diamond, spooner, blue, 2⅛ " **95.00**
Stippled Vine & Beads, butter dish, amber, 2⅜ " **120.00**
Sweetheart, 4-pc table set ... **85.00**
Two Band, creamer, crystal .. **35.00**
Wheat Sheaf, berry bowl, 1". **10.00**
Wheat Sheaf 500, tumbler, crystal, Cambridge, 1¾ " **25.00**
Wild Rose, punch bowl, milk glass, Greentown, 4⅛ " .. **95.00**

Colonial table set by Cambridge, cobalt, $210.00.

Children's Furnishings

Just about anything made for adults has been reduced to children' s size. Early handmade items may be as primitive or as elaborate as their creator was proficient. Even later factory-made pieces are collectible. Baby rattles, highchairs, strollers, wagons, and sleds from the 1800s are especially treasured.

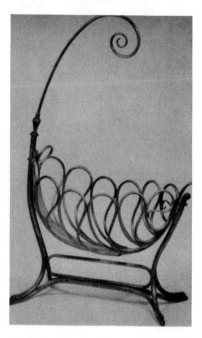

Bentwood cradle, ca 1900, 52" long, $950.00.

Armchair, turned details, 3-slat, worn black paint, splint seat, 15" **85.00**
Armchair rocker, ladderback, worn green repaint, cane seat, VG **75.00**
Armchair rocker, turned posts & finials, slat seat & back, 25", EX **125.00**
Bed, tall post, cherry, EX details, repaired, 19x13x21" **125.00**
Bed, trundle rope; short turned posts, poplar, old paint, 17x60x43" **200.00**
Chair, Windsor, bamboo turnings, paint, shaped seat with rain gutter **225.00**

Chair, wing back; pine, heart cut-out 150.00
Chest, poplar, 4-drawer, scrolled base, natural refinish, 29x29x16" 375.00
Chest, walnut/poplar/pine, cut-out bracket feet, drilled decor, 16x31x15" 200.00
Cradle, dovetailed walnut, scalloped, cut-out handles, 46" long 200.00
Drum, bentwood, brass tack design, red/white/blue paint, 13½ ", EX 50.00
Highchair, plank seat, 3-spindle back, worn red paint, 34½", EX 125.00
Highchair, primitive, green paint, turned details, 35" 200.00
Hobby horse, original paint on wood, replaced mane/tail, 33" long 550.00
Sleigh, old green paint decorated with roses, iron-tipped runners, 29" 200.00
Table & chair, hickory, primitive, splint seat, chair: 25"...250.00
Wheelbarrow, wood, John Deere, green & yellow paint, 19x34x12" 245.00
Writing stand, late George III, mahogany, tambour top, 34", EX 600.00

Christmas

No other holiday season is celebrated to the extravagant extent as Christmas, and vintage decorations provide a warmth and charm that none from today can match. Ornaments from before 1870 were imported from Dresden, Germany–usually made of cardboard and sparkled with tinsel trim. Later, blown glass ornaments were made there in literally thousands of shapes such as fruits and vegetables, clowns, Santas, angels, and animals. Kugels, heavy glass balls (though fruit and vegetable forms are found occasionally) were made from about 1820 to late in the century in sizes from very small up to 14". Early Santa figures are treasured, especially those in robes other than red. Figural bulbs from the '20s and '30s are popular, those that are character related in particular.

Bank, Santa, cast iron, Belsnickle type 300.00
Book, A Christmas Carol, 1938 edition.............................35.00
Bulb, Boy Scout.....................65.00
Bulb, cross with star, red & pink, 2½" 30.00
Bulb, dog with bandage 45.00
Bulb, grapes, NM 12.00
Bulb, Mickey Mouse..............65.00
Candle clip, Santa in blue coat, tin, 2" 160.00
Candy container, boot, papier-mache, red, 4"................25.00
Candy container, Santa, celluloid face, red suit, 6" 65.00
Candy container, Santa, plaster face, cloth coat, 7" 155.00
Candy container, snowball, composition, 7"......................50.00
Candy container, wreath, Dresden, 4¼"..........................85.00

Santa in canoe, cloth and paper, 5"

Christmas light, aqua glass, swirled ribs, folded rim, Stiegel type 165.00

79

Christmas light, cobalt glass, expanded 20-diamond....**65.00**

Father Christmas, spun glass, die-cut torso, Austria, 5".**85.00**

Feather tree, green with red berries, turned base, Germany, 17", VG **100.00**

Fence for tree, wood, green, each side: 30" **95.00**

Garland, blown glass beads, ca 1900, 132" **80.00**

Lights, pears, yellow to rose shading, Germany, early **25.00**

Mug, Father Christmas scene, ceramic, ca 1910, EX **55.00**

Ornament, angel child, diecut, on crepe-paper circle with tinsel, 4".....................................**20.00**

Ornament, banana, blown, yellow, unsilvered, 5" **95.00**

Ornament, bear, blown, gold with black features, 2½".......**110.00**

Ornament, car, blown, blue & silver, 3¼".........................**100.00**

Ornament, cat, blown, white with gold fiddle, 1920s, 3¼"...**85.00**

Ornament, cherub, Dresden, pink & blue, flat, 6" **70.00**

Ornament, clown, blown, green with red & gold, 4" **40.00**

Ornament, elk, Dresden, 3-dimensional, large..................**200.00**

Ornament, flower with girl's face, blown, flesh colored with gold, 3" **95.00**

Ornament, Kugel, ball, red, Baroque hanger, 2" **90.00**

Ornament, Kugel, grapes, green, brass hanger, 4½".........**225.00**

Ornament, Santa, blown, red & silver, 5"..........................**35.00**

Ornament, Santa on swan, scrap Santa, blown bird, 7" ..**100.00**

Print, lady with Christmas tree, Germany, 15" **70.00**

Reindeer, lead, standing, marked Germany, 2x1¼".............**30.00**

Spoon, The Madonna, Marie Henriques, pat 1916 ....**75.00**

Stocking, net with paper angel & tinsel, 1920s, 6½"..........**65.00**

Tree, cellophane, white, ca 1950, 29" **40.00**

Tree stand, cast iron stump, rough bark surface........**45.00**

Tree stand, standing Santa form, cast cement, EX paint, 11x11" **185.00**

Civil War Collectibles

Mementos from the great Civil War represent many things to many people–the downfall of the antebellum grandeur of the South, the resulting freedom of the Black race, and the conflict itself that was the most personal tragedy American has ever known. In this context, collectors of Civil War memorabilia regard their artifacts with a softness of heart perhaps not present in those whose interests lie in militaria of the 20th century.

Belt, sword; officer's, brown leather, EX **115.00**

Bit, US Cavalry...................**100.00**

Book, Civil War Battles & Leaders, 1887, VG................**375.00**

Bullet pouch, leather, oval brass 'US' plate **45.00**

Canteen, tin, Confederate, floral decor, fort on back..........**65.00**

Canteen, tin drum, old red cloth over leather strap **85.00**

Certificate, substitute volunteer enlistment, 1863 ....**35.00**

Chair, camp; folding, collapsible, carpet seat, VG..............**65.00**

Check, US Army, allotment to soldiers in 1865 ....**35.00**

Coat, frock; officer's, captain's insignia, VG **475.00**

Document, statement of Volunteer, New York, EX.........**10.00**

Fork & spoon, folding, marked
Union Knife **28.00**
Gauntlets, buff, pair **75.00**
Kepi, NY buttons, EX **215.00**
Medal, Order of Loyal Legion,
engraved gold bar **65.00**
Musket sling..........................**35.00**
Pay voucher, information on unit,
signature, witness & amount,
1865 ....**17.50**
Ribbon, Union Ex-Prisoners of
War, Andersonville, 1864,
1870s, 5", VG **38.00**
Sling, for Springfield rifle.....**25.00**
Surgeon's kit, 9 tools in mahogany
box, EX **625.00**
Syringe, medical; marked US
1862, EX **8.00**

**Sheet music, Gymnast Zouaves
Quickstep, by Charles B. Dod-
worth, 1861, $100.00.**

Cleminson

Hand-decorated Cleminson
ware is one type of the California-
made novelty pottery that collectors have recently taken an interest in. Though nearly always
marked, these items have a style
that you'll easily become

acquainted with; and their distinctive glaze colors will be easy
to spot. It was produced from the
early 1940s until 1963.

Bowl, Distlefink, 4½ x12" **20.00**
Butter dish, Distlefink, bird form,
6½ x4¾ "..........................**25.00**
Canister, cherries on a tree
branch.............................**25.00**
Cookie jar, potbellied stove, black
with flowers...................**65.00**
Gravy bowl, Distlefink, with
ladle, 6x7½ " **20.00**
Match holder, cherries on a tree
branch, wall mount........**12.50**
Mug, A Man's Home Is His Cas-
tle....................................**10.00**
Plaque, fruit **8.50**
Plaque, kitten in basket **12.00**
Plaque, Let's Pay Off the Mort-
gage................................. **8.00**
Plate, Deco fruit, red on ivory,
wall hanging **10.00**
Plate, rooster motif, hand
painted, 7".....................**25.00**
Razor blade bank, man's head
form **15.00**
Shakers, girl & boy, 6", pair ..**22.00**
Shakers, Old Salt & Hot Stuff,
pair **17.00**

**String holder, You'll always have
a pull with me, $30.00.**

Sprinkler, Oriental man **18.00**
String holder, apple with butterfly, marked......................**35.00**
Wall pocket, coffeepot, yellow with
blue decoration, 9" **30.00**
Wall pocket, row of 3 red Christmas bells, green bow......**15.00**

Clocks

Because many of the early
clocks have handmade works, condition is important when you are
considering a purchase. Repairs
may be costly. Today's collectors
prefer pendulum-regulated move-
ments from the 18th and 19th
centuries and clocks from the
larger manufacturers such as Sessions, Ithaca, Ingraham, Seth
Thomas, Ansonia, and Waterbury.

A Stowell, banjo shelf,
mahogany/brass/reverse-
painted, 20".................**325.00**
A Willard, banjo, mahogany/gilt-
wood, reverse-painted eagle,
33"..............................**880.00**
Ansonia, Cetus, crystal regulator,
brass, 11" **300.00**
Ansonia, Crystal Palace, original
oval dome, #1 Extra **800.00**
Ansonia, Lucia, crystal regulator,
EX **900.00**
Ansonia, Parisian, shelf, walnut,
8-day, time & strike **385.00**
Ansonia, Regis, crystal regulator,
EX **475.00**
Art Nouveau, digital, NM...**125.00**
Banjo, mahogany & giltwood,
reverse-painted badminton
scene, 40"................. **1,350.00**
Birge & Fuller, Empire, 8-day,
time & strike, 33" **425.00**
Blessing, novelty, space ship,
world rotates, 1970s.......**45.00**
Boston Clock Co, mantel, onyx
with bronze ormolu......**350.00**

Bradley, novelty, vampire, bat
rotates, 1978..................**45.00**
Brewster & Ingraham, gallery,
walnut, time only, NM.**325.00**
C Jerome, shelf, gilt columns,
rosewood case, 18" **150.00**
Chelsea, ship's mantel, light
mahogany case.............**325.00**
Dutch, wall, mahogany, brass
decor, Atlas finial, 19" .**100.00**
EN Welch, shelf, walnut, time &
strike, alarm **285.00**
English, carriage, brass case, time
& alarm, NM...............**325.00**

C. W. Feishtinger calendar clock,
8-day time and strike, 2 painted
zinc dials, 1895, 22", $400.00.

Forestville, shelf, weight driven,
wood dial, 8-day, 33" **425.00**
French, mantel, bronze & ivory
dancing figure, 17"... **1,000.00**
French, mantel, onyx with gilt-
bronze garlands, marked
JED, 17" **375.00**
Freres, mantel, inlaid rosewood,
1900, 9" **175.00**

German, key wind, regulator, fancy oak case, 38".......**275.00**

German, novelty, soccer players, ball turns, 1970s............**35.00**

Gilbert, #6, weight drive, wall type................**11.00**

Gilbert, Pelican, store regulator, 8-day, time & strike.....**450.00**

Gilbert, Tuscan, crystal regulator, NM................**900.00**

Ingraham, store regulator, calendar, original glass........**425.00**

Intermittent alarm, patent 1904, 2" diameter.....................**45.00**

JC Brown, steeple, etched lower glass, walnut, 8-day **325.00**

Keebler, novelty, bulldog with kitten, EX............................**30.00**

Kundo, anniversary, glass dome, miniature **65.00**

Lux, mechanical bell, digital..**50.00**

Lux, novelty, animated, clown with seals, NM.............**260.00**

Lux, novelty, animated, Shoe Shine boy, black, NM ..**140.00**

New Haven, banjo, reverse-painted ship, 29", EX...**150.00**

New Haven, shelf, walnut, 8-day, time & strike................**185.00**

New Haven, tambour, 8-day time & strike...........................**85.00**

New Haven, wall, mahogany, applied cast carving, 8-day, 1920s, 23".....................**350.00**

Novelty, animated chicken pecks ground, ceramic, 1970s .**140.00**

Seth Thomas, Adamantine, mantel, marbleized, 8-day, time & strike **225.00**

Seth Thomas, mantel, Sonora, chime, 4 rods.................**375.00**

Seth Thomas, office calendar, rosewood, 42½ "........ **2,250.00**

Seth Thomas, shelf, burl walnut, 8-day, time & strike **250.00**

Standard, master, electric, oak, 2 bell ringers **575.00**

Tiempo, novelty, horse race, horse rocks, Brazil **45.00**

Terry & Andrews steeple clock, rosewood veneer, 8-day time and strike lyre movement, EX, 20", **$475.00.**

Waterbury, Huntley, parlor shelf, walnut, silver glass......**225.00**

Waterbury, kitchen, golden oak, ornate **150.00**

Waterbury, kitchen, walnut, time & strike, alarm.............**185.00**

Waterbury, mantel, metal case, time & strike................**165.00**

Welsch, #11, wall, oak, 60". **1,500.00**

Westclox, Ironclad, cast iron, alarm **80.00**

Cloisonne

Several types of cloisonne (a method of decorating metal with enameling) have been developed since it was introduced in the 16th century–plique-a-jour (transparent enamel work); foil cloisonne; wireless cloisonne; or cloisonne on ceramic, wood, or lacquer. The type you are most likely to encounter at flea markets has the pattern outlined with fine metal wires, filled in with colored enamels. The finest examples date from 1865 until 1900, though excellent work is still being produced in China and Taiwan.

Bottle, pendant, peonies, with lid & chain, China, 1x1½"..**25.00**

Bowl, dragon, 1880, 5"..........**75.00**

Bowl, 4 butterflies on blue foil, Japan, 5"........................**50.00**

Bracelet, bangle, multicolor branches on sky blue, 1⅜" wide **65.00**

Bud vase, flowers & green mica flecks on black, Japan ...**50.00**

Charger, flying bird & lily on royal blue, 10¾" **325.00**

Charger, songbird amid mums & roses, arabesques, 12"..**200.00**

Cigarette box, overall floral on green, China, 5" **40.00**

Crumber, flowers, animals, & people, China **60.00**

Figurine, Tang-style horse, 1850, 9"...................................**275.00**

Humidor, floral on red, brass foo dog finial, 8" **225.00**

Incense burner, lion figural, ca 1800, 10"......................**400.00**

Jar, rose; floral reserves, yellow lozenges, 4½ x3½" **285.00**

Kogo, flowers & butterfly on cobalt, Japan, 2¼" dia ...**70.00**

Lamp, peacock on yellow, Japan, 7", pair...........................**300.00**

Plate, iris & arabesques, blue, black, & orchid on copper, 1800s, 12" **350.00**

Snuff bottle, floral & butterfly, multicolor on blue, pear form, 3"......................................**90.00**

Snuff box, Wall of China, 2"..**20.00**

Teapot, flying phoenix bird, mum finial, miniature...........**165.00**

Teapot, 2 phoenix birds on cobalt, bulbous, 1900, 5".........**250.00**

Vase, animals in mountains on white, ovoid, trumpet neck, 12", pair.......................**200.00**

Vase, bamboo reeds on transparent red, 5" **50.00**

Vase, dragon, 1900, 9".........**120.00**

Vase, dragon & phoenix bird on cobalt, unmarked, 12"..**385.00**

Vase, floral, silver & pink on blue foil, 2½ x1½" **60.00**

Vase, floral, 1930, 5¼"...........**60.00**

Vase, floral & butterfly reserves, goldstone, 3¾" **75.00**

Vase, mask vignettes, blue & red on light blue, gu-form, 1800s, 15"..................................**900.00**

Vase, mums, daisies, & leaves on green, 9½".....................**295.00**

Vase, peonies in pink & white, yellow duck on green, bulbous, 10" **140.00**

Vase, scrolls & florals on green foil, bulbous with stick neck, 5"......................................**95.00**

Pair of vases, stylized bats motif, 10", $450.00.

Vase, tiger lilies, orange on green, silverplated rim & base, Japan, 10"....................**600.00**

Vase, 6 windows, multicolor on black, 12" **375.00**

Clothing and Accessories

Here's one collection you can enjoy wearing, and many do! Victorian whites, vintage furs, sequined gowns, designer fashions—whatever look you prefer is yours at only a fraction of today's prices for modern copies. Alterations are possible, but unless done with tenderness and care may lessen the value. Fabrics may have become more delicate with the passing of the years, so very gentle cleaning methods are a must. Accessories are fun; and hats, fur boas, belts, and shoes from the era of your outfit finish it off with smashing authenticity.

Apron, tea; silk with lace & embroidered violets........**12.50**
Bathing suit, sateen, 1915....**25.00**
Boa, black ostrich..................**25.00**
Coat, mouton fur, full length, 1940s, EX **95.00**
Coat, Persian lamb with mink trim, walking length....**450.00**
Dress, black crepe, short sleeves, pleated skirt, 1940s **20.00**
Dress, black crepe, short sleeves, V neck, rosette, 1930s, VG .**25.00**
Dress, black lace in tiers, tea-length flapper style........**45.00**
Dress, brown polka-dot cotton, mother-of-pearl buttons, 1900, child's **35.00**
Dress, chiffon with black sequins, flapper style, EX **45.00**
Dress, metallic lace, velvet trim, flapper style, EX **75.00**
Dress, green chiffon, embroidered, tiered waist, 1900s.........**22.50**
Dress, handkerchief linen, delicate tatting, child's.........**40.00**
Dress, pink organdy, short sleeves, 1930s **10.00**
Dress, red silk, crystal beaded bodice, full skirt, 1950s .**35.00**
Dress, silk, black-lined, beads & sequins, jewel neck, 1950s, EX **135.00**
Dress, velvet, long sleeves, jewel neck, '20s, G **30.00**

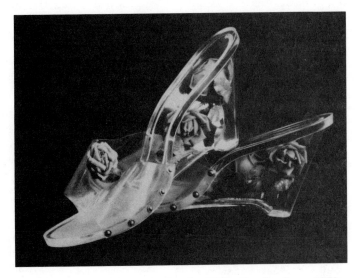

Lucite shoes, roses contained within the heel, ca 1950s, $125.00.

Dress, wedding; high neck, lace & tucking, 2-pc, Victorian, small, G **35.00**
Gloves, French kid, half-length, EX **12.00**
Gown, baby's, Victorian lace, long, EX **45.00**
Gown, christening, cutwork, hand made, 1850s, NM **125.00**
Hat, straw, cloth band, Lamson & Hubbard, NM **35.00**
Kimono, black with embroidered dragons, red-lined, VG ..**30.00**
Pantaloons, lightweight cotton, split style........................**15.00**
Pantaloons, lace trim, EX **30.00**
Pantaloons, tucked, no lace trim, EX **25.00**
Robe, man's, striped wool, 1920s, VG..................................**20.00**
Shawl, fringed wool, triangular, extra-large......................**18.00**
Skirt, blue & white pinstripe, floor length, flounce, 1890s, EX **30.00**
Sweater, bolero, lilac & gray wool, EX **17.50**
Vest, Battenburg lace, child's size, EX **75.00**

Coca-Cola

Since it was established in 1891, the Coca-Cola Company has issued a wide and varied scope of advertising memorabilia, creating what may well be the most popular field of specific product-related collectibles on today's market. Probably their best-known item is the rectangular Coke tray, issued since 1910. In excellent condition, some of the earlier examples may bring prices up to $500.00. Before 1910, trays were round or oval. The 1908 'Topless' tray is valued at $2,500.00. Most Coca-Cola buffs prefer to limit their collections to items made before 1970.

Advertising card, 1905 bathtub fold-out copy, 1978 reproduction.................................. **3.00**
Banner, 1950, cloth (possibly linen), 18½ x56", EX **125.00**
Blotter, 1904, Drink..., Deutsch & Heitmann, NM.............**100.00**
Blotter, 1916, Made To Chew, CC Pepsin gum, NM **500.00**
Blotter, 1927, couple leans at icebox, NM **35.00**
Bottle, Birmingham AL, Hutchinson script type, EX **600.00**
Bottle, dark amber, with arrows, heavy, narrow spout, reproduction...........................**10.00**
Bottle rack, 1930s, Drink...at Home, 60", EX..............**250.00**
Calendar, 1916, girl & rose basket, top only, EX...........**200.00**
Calendar, 1917, Constance with glass, 13x32", EX **900.00**
Calendar, 1933, boy fishing dog, Wyeth, NM **350.00**
Calendar, 1957, skating girl, Canada, 14x14", NM.....**30.00**
Calendar, 1976, Olympic scene, 12x9", NM........................ **7.50**
Can, 1980 Russian Olympics, rare, opened, VG............**40.00**
Can opener, Have a Coke, red paint, stamped logo, NM.. **5.00**

Clock, Sessions, copyright 1942, 15" x 15", $325.00.

Cigar band, 1940s, pictures glass, M..................................75.00

Coaster, 1939, Ice Cold, silhouette girl, NM............................ 5.00

Door lock, 1920, Kam Indore Lock, with box................35.00

Fan, 1911, paper & bamboo, geisha, edge wear.........100.00

Key chain & charm, 50th Anniversary, gold bottle . 6.00

Match striker, 1939, porcelain, French, 4-color, 4½" square, NM...............................100.00

Menu board, 1960s, tin, Sign of Good Taste, fishtail, EX.35.00

Notebook, 1903, glass/syrup-use charts, leather bound, 2¾ x5¾ ", VG 100.00

Playing cards, 1943, girl with leaves, Coke bottle, M ...90.00

Post card, 1908, bridge on Potomac, Relieves Fatigue, NM..................................15.00

Scarf, silk, centennial item, 30x30", M........................35.00

Sign, 1927, tin, Drink Coca-Cola, 10½ x31", NM...............175.00

Sign, 1930s, embossed tin, Dasco, 6x18", EX......................85.00

Sign, 1960, plastic & tin, light-up, lantern form 50.00

Sign, 1968, cardboard, Santa, Stock-up..., EX 30.00

Sign, 1970s reproduction, oval, girl with fur 10.00

Thermometer, 1938, tin, red with gold bottle, oval, NM......85.00

Thermometer, 1950s, tin, Robertson, bottle form, EX.......35.00

Tip tray, 1914, Betty, Passaic litho, 4¼x6", EX 75.00

Tray, 1921, Autumn girl, 10½ x13¼", EX.....................300.00

Tray, 1925, girl with fur, 10½x13¼", being reproduced, NM..375.00

Tray, 1933, Frances Dee, 10½ x13¼", NM....................275.00

Tray, 1941, skater girl, 10½x13¼", NM...............................110.00

Tray, 1957, birdhouse, 10½x13¼", NM 75.00

Tray, 1978, Captain Cook, 10½ x13¼", NM....................... 6.00

Watch fob, 1920s, Coke bulldogs, 1½x1", EX 100.00

Wooden nickel, 1942, Galesburg Bottlers, M...................... 5.00

Coffee Grinders

In the days before packaged ground coffee was available, coffee beans were either ground at the local grocery or in the home. Now gone the way of the pickle barrel and Grandma's washboard, coffee grinders are collected by those to whom visions of warm kitchens, rocking chairs, fresh-baked bread, and the wonderful aroma of fresh-ground coffee are treasures worth preserving.

Arcade, Favorite, lap, fancy cast iron top & hopper...........95.00

Cardboard sign, easel back, 1950s, 18", $30.00.

Arcade, Imperial, lap, wood & cast iron, 11".....................**75.00**
Canister, boy & girl decal, miniature, 5½x1½".....................**85.00**
Clevis Walton, canister, original cup, Pat 7/9/1901.............**60.00**
Common lap, wood & cast iron, unmarked, 1-lb...............**65.00**
Elgin National No 40, counter, cast iron, 2 wheels **325.00**
Enterprise, table, cast iron with brass hopper, Pat 1873, 6" wheels............................**395.00**
Grand Union Tea, canister, red, Pat 1910 ....**85.00**
Landers, Frary & Clark, Regal No 44, canister **80.00**
Lap, all cast iron, octagonal, open hopper, 4x4x4"................**75.00**
Lightning, canister, cast iron with tin hopper.......................**70.00**
National, coffee & spice, counter, 17" wheels, 28".............**425.00**
Parker, side, cast iron, adjustment on front, Pat 1876.**60.00**
Persepolis, table, cast iron & brass **155.00**
Primitive, dovetailed cherry, brass hopper, 4x4"..................**155.00**

Pyramid shape, wooden box, brass hopper, cast iron top, $90.00.

Rock Hard, Garant-Sewaarborge, lap, 4¾x4¾x5½"..............**40.00**
Royal, side, cast iron, open hopper, Pat Apr 15, 1890 ....**65.00**
Russer, canister with porcelain top...................................**55.00**
Smithy made, wall, funnel hopper, 1790s, EX..............**180.00**
Universal No 12, canister, cast iron & tin, Pat 2/4/1905.**65.00**
WW Weaver, lap, primitive, walnut, pewter hopper **155.00**

Comic Books

The 'Golden Age' is a term referring to the period from 1930 until 1950, during which today's most-prized comic books were published. First editions or those that feature the first appearance of a popular character are the most valuable and may bring prices of several hundred dollars—some even more. The original Batman comic, issued in the spring of 1940, is today worth $7,000.00 in excellent condition. Most early comics, however, are valued at less than $5.00 to $30.00. Remember—rarity, age, condition, and quality of the art work are factors to consider when determining value.

Adventure Comics, #139, DC Comics, VG **27.50**
Adventures of Bob Hope, #21, DC Comics, VG...................... **7.00**
Alice in Wonderland, #35, Marvel Classics, VG **4.00**
Aquaman, #4, Dell, G............. **4.00**
Battlestar Galactica, #3, movie story, M........................... **2.00**
Ben Bowie & His Mountain Men, #657, Dell, 4-color, VG ... **3.50**
Betty & Me, #23, Archie Publishing, EX.............................. **2.00**

Beware of the Creeper, #2, DC Comics, Ditko art, EX..... **4.50**

Black Arrow, #51, Classics Illustrated, VG........................**42.50**

Black Beauty, #167, Classics Illustrated, EX................**11.00**

Bobby Sherman, #3, Charlton, photo cover, VG................ **5.00**

Captain Atom, #79, DC Comics, Ditko cover, EX **9.00**

Captain Gallant, #195, photo cover, NM **10.00**

Creatures on the Loose, #16, Marvel, Kane art, M **4.00**

Dale Evans, 1953, NM..........**15.00**

David Cassidy, #5, photo cover, VG.................................... **2.50**

Detective Comics, #253, DC comics, G **14.00**

Donald Duck, #147, Dell, 4-color, VG...................................**95.00**

Fighting Marines, #10, Baker cover, 1952, EX................ **7.50**

Fighting Undersea Commandos, #5, 1953, VG **8.50**

Further Adventures of Indiana Jones, #21, Ditko art, M . **2.00**

Gunsmoke, #8, Dell, photo cover, VG...................................**20.00**

Huckleberry Finn, #18, Classics Illustrated, EX **50.00**

Incredible Hulk, #145, Marvel, double-size, M **5.00**

Incredible Science Fiction, #22, Wood cover & art, VG ...**20.00**

Ivanhoe, #78, Classics Illustrated, VG.................................... **6.00**

Jane Eyre, #71, Classics Illustrated, EX........................**25.00**

Julius Caesar, #165, Classics Illustrated, G.................... **6.00**

Justice League of America, #23, DC Comics, G **3.50**

Katy Keen Pinup Parade, #11, Giant, EX........................**48.00**

Legion of Super Heroes, #262, DC Comics, M **3.00**

Linda Carter Student Nurse, #5, Atlas, NM **5.00**

Lone Ranger March of Comics, #174, EX **35.00**

Lone Ranger's Silver, #12, Dell, painted cover, M **8.00**

Long John Silver & the Pirates, #23, 1956, VG **6.00**

Lorna Doone, #118, Classics Illustrated, EX.......................**15.00**

Lorna Doone, #53, Classics Illustrated, VG......................**12.00**

Machine Man, #3, Marvel, Kirby art, M **3.50**

Man in the Iron Mask, #142, Classics Illustrated, VG........**12.50**

Marvel Super Action, #3, Captain America by Kirby, M....... **2.50**

Marvel Tales, #5, early Spider-man reprint, M................ **6.00**

Marvel Two In One, #10, Black Widow, M **5.00**

Master of Kung Fu, #18, Marvel, 1st Gulacy art, M **7.00**

Mysterious Adventures, #5, bondage cover, VG..........**32.00**

Mystery in Space, #75, DC Comics, EX.....................**15.00**

Omega the Unknown, #2, Marvel, Electro, M **3.00**

Nancy and Sluggo, #178, EX, $11.00.

Planet Comics, #64, EX **50.00**
Red Badge of Courage, #10, Marvel Classics, M **6.00**
Rip Hunter Time Master, #8, DC comics, VG **10.00**
Rip Van Winkle, #118, Classics Illustrated, VG **6.00**
Robin Hood, #22, Classics Illustrated, EX **40.00**
Rod Cameron Western, #4, photo cover, G............................**12.50**
Roy Rogers, #27, EX.............**18.00**
Secret Mysteries, #18, VG ...**12.00**
Spectacular Spiderman, #3, Marvel, M **6.00**
Steve Canyon Comics, #2, Harvey Publications, VG **25.00**
Strange Adventures, #40, DC Comics, VG......................**16.00**
Strange Tales, #180, Warlock cover, M **5.50**
Superman's Pal Jimmy Olsen, #24, DC Comics, VG **10.00**
Supermouse, #22, Coo Coo Comics, VG...................... **2.50**
Supernatural Thrillers, #7, Marvel, Living Mummy, M.... **3.00**
Tarzan, #43, Dell, Lex Barker photo cover, M **26.00**
Tarzan Jungle Annual, #4, Dell, giant size, M **25.00**
Teenage Talk, #5, IW Enterprises, M....................................... **3.00**
Ten Story Love, #198, photo cover, VG **3.50**
Tommy of the Big Top, #11, King Features, 1948, VG......... **7.00**
Treasure Island, #15, Marvel Classics, M **5.50**
Unknown Worlds, #47, American Comics Group, M **8.00**
Walt Disney Comics & Stories, #14, Dell, G.....................**10.00**
Walt Disney's Comics & Stories, #202, Dell, EX **8.00**
Weird Wonder Tales, #2, Marvel, Wildey art, M **2.50**
Werewolf by Night, #5, Marvel, Ploog, M...................... **5.00**

Western Love Trails, #9, Ace Magazines, 1950, G................ **5.00**
White Rider & Super Horse, #4, LB Cole cover, NM........**18.00**
World's Finest Comics, #120, DC Comics, VG...................... **5.00**
Worlds of Fear, #10, eyeballs cover by Saunders, EX...**36.00**
2 Years Before the Mast, #30, Classics Illustrated, G ..**10.00**

Cookbooks

Advertising cookbooks, those by well-known personalities, and figural diecuts are among the more readily-available examples on today's market. Cookbooks written prior to 1874 are the most valuable; they often sell for $200.00 and up.

American Cookery, Amelia Simmons, limited edition, 1937, VG..................................**50.00**
Aunt Jenny's Spry Shortening, 1940s.............................. **7.50**
Best From the Midwest Kitchens, 284-page **4.00**
Betty Crocker's Good & Easy Cookbook, 1950s.............. **5.00**
Complete Round the World Meat, 1967, 457-page **10.00**
Continental Cookery for the English Table, 1st edition, 1915 ....**22.50**
Cook's Tour of San Francisco, 1963, 370-page **5.00**
Cooking Afloat, illustrated, 1959, 279-page **6.50**
Cross Creek Cookery, illustrated, 1942, VG........................**15.00**
Cuisine de France, 1944, 709-page **14.00**
Kerr Home Canning, 1941..... **5.00**
Ladies' Home Journal Cookbook, Truax, 1963, 728-page ...**15.00**
Luchow's German Cookbook, 1952, 224-page **4.50**

Jell-O cookbooks, Jell-O girl on front, ca late 1920s, $5.00 each.

Mary Dunbar's New Cookbook, 1933, EX **5.00**
Moody's Household Advisor & Cookbook, 1st edition, 1884, VG **36.00**
New Pennsylvania Dutch Cookbook, 1958, 240-page **5.50**
Our Favorite Recipes, by Jerome Prescott, 1930, 64-page ... **7.50**
Ryzon Baking Book, by Marion Harris Neil, 1916, VG **15.00**
Thomas Jefferson's Cookbook, 1st edition, 1949 .... **15.00**
Widdifield's New Cookbook, Philadelphia, 1856, VG .**45.00**
World of Good Cooking, 1962, 270-page **8.00**
You'll Eat It Up, 1st edition, 1943, 295-page **12.00**

Cookie Jars

The Nelson McCoy Pottery Co., Robinson Ransbottom Pottery Co., and the American Bisque Pottery Co., are three of the largest producers of cookie jars in the country. Many firms made them to a lesser extent. Today, cookie jars are one of the most popular of modern collectibles. Figural jars are the most common, made in an endless variety of subjects. Early jars from the 1920s and '30s were often decorated in 'cold paint' over the glaze. This type of color is easily removed—take care that you use very gentle cleaning methods. A damp cloth and a light touch is the safest approach.

See also McCoy.

Albert Apple, Pee Dee Co **85.00**
Baseball Boy with Bat, marked 875 USA **40.00**
Bear, eyes open, unmarked American Bisque **30.00**
Blackboard Bum, American Bisque............................**55.00**
Brownie, Robinson Ransbottom, NM..................................**45.00**
Cat on Beehive, American Bisque, NM..................................**32.00**
Chef, National Silver, M **200.00**
Chef, Pearl China **400.00**

Chicken, Twin Winton **20.00**
Churn, American Bisque **85.00**
Dog in Basket, G **25.00**
Dove, green & pink, Fapco ..**18.00**
Dutch Boy, Pottery Guild......**50.00**
Elf Bakery Tree, Keebler **38.00**
Farmer Pig, American Bisque.**30.00**
Flasher Clown, American Bisque, NM................................**70.00**
Gingerbread House **42.00**

Keystone Cop, Twin Winton, $100.00.

Kraft Bear, Regal, large......**100.00**
Mammy, National Silver.....**200.00**
Mammy, Pearl China..........**480.00**
Mickey/Minnie Mouse, Turn-about, Disney **60.00**
Monkey, Treasure Craft........**20.00**
Pig, American Bisque **35.00**
Pine Cones Coffeepot, marked USA, American Bisque .**25.00**
Poodle, behind counter, Twin Winton....................................**25.00**
Popeye, American Bisque ...**425.00**
Porky Pig, Warner Bros........**30.00**
Rabbit in Hat, American Bisque, NM................................**40.00**

Rooster, American Bisque.....**30.00**
Santa, American Bisque **60.00**
Snacks, teapot shape, marked USA, American Bisque .**15.00**
Spaceship, American Bisque..**50.00**
Train, Pfaltzgraff..................**65.00**
Train, Sierra Vista **45.00**
Umbrella Kids, American Bisque, NM................................**55.00**
Winking Farmer Pig, Robinson Ransbottom **40.00**
Wise Bird, Robinson Ransbottom, NM................................**28.00**
Wooden Soldier, American Bisque, NM................................**30.00**
Yarn Doll, American Bisque .**25.00**
Ye Olde Cookie Bucket, San Juan Capistrano, '59 ....**22.00**
1946 Bubbler Jukebox, Treasure Craft **55.00**

Santa at Workshop, Alberta's Molds, Inc., 1958, $85.00.

Coors

Though they made a line of commercial artware as well, the Coors Pottery is best represented at today's flea markets and dinnerware shows by their popular dinnerware line, Rosebud. Rosebud was made in solid colors accented only by small contrasting floral elements; the line is extensive and includes kitchen and baking ware as well as table settings.

Ash tray, Rosebud, 3½" **50.00**
Bowl, fruit; Rosebud, 5".........**7.50**
Cake knife, Rosebud, 10"......**22.50**
Cake plate, Rosebud, 11"......**16.50**
Cookie jar, hand-painted decoration, large **35.00**
Egg cup, Rosebud, 3" dia **15.00**
Jar, utility; Rosebud, 2½-pt .**15.00**
Platter, Rosebud, 12x9" **15.00**
Pudding bowl, Rosebud, 2-pt .**12.50**

Rosebud drip jar, $28.00.

Sugar shaker, Rosebud, 5½" ..**14.00**
Teapot, Rosebud, 2-cup **30.00**
Tumbler, Rosebud, low foot, 12-ounce..............................**22.00**
Underplate, Rosebud, 7"........ **7.50**

Copper

Early copper items are popular with those who enjoy primitives, and occasionally fine examples can still be found at flea markets. Check construction to help you determine the age of your piece. Dovetailed joints indicate 18th-century work; handmade seamed items are usually from the 19th century. Teakettles and small stills are especially collectible.

Baker, zinc lined, brass handles, oval, 10½" **35.00**
Baking dish, zinc lined, with lid, French, 1950s, 10" long .**90.00**
Bowl, centerpiece; hammered, animals & flowers at rim, 4¼ x15½" **55.00**
Dipper, long wrought iron handle, American, 1850s **30.00**
Planter, cauldron-shaped bowl with copper chain, 3½" diameter................................. **7.50**
Platter, rolled rim, tinned back, 1860s, 10x14" **65.00**
Skillet, brass handle, E Dehillerin, Paris, 1940s, 8".....**30.00**
Teakettle, dovetailed, gooseneck spout, 11".....................**165.00**
Teapot, hammered, Olla Monda, Switzerland, 1950s **40.00**

Teapot, Rochester, brass finial, 6", $90.00.

Teapot, tin lined, 10-sided, gooseneck spout, 4½" **28.00**
Vase, Deco florals, weighted base, footed, 12"......................**40.00**
Watering can, brass handle & spout, Chase **24.00**

Copper Lustre

Small pitchers and bowls in the copper lustre glaze made by

many of the Staffordshire potteries in the 1800s are still very much in evidence at even the smaller flea markets. They may be had for around $30.00 to $50.00 in excellent condition, often even for less. Larger items are harder to find and, depending on the type of decoration, may bring prices of $100.00 or more. Hand-painted designs and examples with historical transfers are the most valuable.

Coffeepot, ribbed & beaded, Georgian style, 10½" **375.00**
Flowerpot, painted florals on green band, handles, 5" .**85.00**
Mug, canary band with white floral reserves, 3" **100.00**
Pitcher, allegorical scenic multicolor panels, 4⅞" **75.00**

Pitcher, dancing figures relief, blue scrollwork, 6½", $65.00.

Pitcher, gold band, 3" **38.00**
Pitcher, multicolor dancing figures, ca 1800, 6⅜" **125.00**
Pitcher, multicolor roses in relief, 8½" **125.00**
Pitcher, multicolored relief spray on peach, ca 1805, 6"....**295.00**

Shaker, Toby, 4¾" **75.00**
Teapot, floral spray, blue trim, faceted sides, 7", NM ...**125.00**
Tumbler, green band, 3¼" **50.00**
Waste bowl, multicolor girl & dog, 1840, 5½" **70.00**

Cracker Jack

The sugar-coated popcorn confection created by the Ruekeim brothers in 1893 has continued to the present day to delight boys and girls with its crunchy goodness, and each 'toy inside every box' since 1916 has become a prized adult treasure. More than 10,000 different prizes have been distributed. The older ones, depending on scarcity, are usually worth in the $15.00 to $40.00 range, though some (the 2½" cast metal horse and wagon for example) may fetch as high as $110.00. Early advertising and packages are also collectible. 'CJ' in the listings indicates pieces that are marked Cracker Jack.

Baseball score counter, paper prize, CJ, 3⅜" long **45.00**
Box, store display, 1923, M...**65.00**
Boy on rocking horse, cast metal prize, 1½".......................**22.00**
Dogs, 3-D figures, plastic prize, series of 10, each............. **4.50**
Halloween mask, CJ, 10"......**12.00**
Hat, vendor cap, CJ **20.00**
Magic Game Book, erasable slate, paper, 1 of 13, each **25.00**
Pocket watch, silver or gold, tin prize, CJ, 1½" **35.00**
Post card, bear, 1907, CJ, series of 16, each **14.00**
Recipe book, Angelus, 1930s ..**22.00**
Riddle cards, CJ, series of 20, each................................. **7.00**
Stud, Me for Cracker Jack, boy & dog **18.00**

Tape measure, celluloid **38.00**
Tin can, Candy Crisp, 10-oz .**85.00**
Top, Golf Game, paper prize with
    wood center, CJ **35.00**
Watch, CJ **12.00**
Wheel of Fortune, lithograph, 2-
    part, paper prize, CJ **43.00**
Whistle, tube with animals, plas-
    tic prize, CJ **8.50**
Whistle, with litho boy, CJ ..**25.00**

Patience puzzle, glass lens, metal rim, ca 1910-14, 1½" diameter, Made in Germany, $78.00.

Cruets

Used to serve vinegar, cruets were made during the 1800s through the early 20th century in virtually every type of plain and art glass available. Nearly every early American pressed glass tableware line contained at least one style. Nice examples are still relatively easy to find, though some of the scarce art glass cruets are often valued at well over $300.00.

Alaska, blue opalescent, hand-
    painted floral................**275.00**
Amazon, amber **150.00**
Amberina, reed handle, footed,
    hollow stopper **300.00**

Amber with enameled flowers, 8½", $165.00.

Beaded Swirl with Lens, ruby
    stain..............................**110.00**
Buckingham **45.00**
Champion, amber stain **145.00**
Christmas Bead & Panel, medium
    blue...............................**300.00**
Coin Spot, blue opalescent..**200.00**
Croesus, emerald green with gold,
    4".................................**195.00**
Daisy & Button with Crossbars,
    vaseline, large **160.00**
Dice & Block, amber **100.00**
Fancy Loop, Heisey...............**70.00**
Fluted Scroll, vaseline opalescent
    with decoration **175.00**
Guttate, pink cased.............**265.00**
Herringbone, green **110.00**
Ivy Scroll, blue **135.00**
Manhattan, large **75.00**
Medallion Sprig, green **215.00**
Petticoat, vaseline, rare **275.00**
Pressed Diamond, amber....**110.00**
Ribbed Pillar, pink & white spat-
    ter **200.00**
Shoshone, ruby stain **195.00**

Stars & Bars, amber **90.00**
Strawberry Diamond & Fan,
   faceted stopper **55.00**
Swag with Brackets, blue opales-
   cent **360.00**
Tarantum's Atlanta, 1894.....**95.00**
Tiny Optic, emerald green, no dec-
   oration **60.00**
Wild Bouquet, clear opalescent,
   scarce...........................**200.00**
Wild Rose & Bow Knot, clear
   frosted **115.00**
X-Ray, green with gold........**195.00**

Cup Plates

It was the custom in the early 1800s to pour hot beverages into a deep saucer to cool. The cup plate was used under the cup in the same manner as we use coasters today. While Sandwich was the largest manufacturer, mid-western glass houses also made many styles. Condition is always an important factor; but, because of the lacy nature of the patterns, it is common to find minor edge chips. Occasionally you may find an example where the mold did not completely fill out–this was due to the primitive manufacturing methods used and the intricacy of the designs.

Collectors identify their cup plates by code numbers suggested in *American Glass Cup Plates* by Ruth Webb Lee and James A. Rose, a standard reference.

R-104, VG **34.00**
R-129, EX **45.00**
R-136-A, rare, VG **75.00**
R-158-B, scarce, VG.............**43.00**
R-174, EX **45.00**
R-226-C, VG **28.00**
R-269, VG **30.00**
R-27, VG..............................**24.00**
R-272, VG **30.00**

R-439, VG **26.00**
R-441, VG **34.00**
R-458, scarce, VG **28.00**
R-56, scarce, EX **60.00**
R-562, rare, VG **325.00**
R-570, rare, VG **100.00**
R-576, scarce, VG **55.00**
R-595, scarce, VG **47.00**
R-605-A, scarce, VG...........**135.00**
R-612-A, rare, VG **255.00**
R-624-A, VG **65.00**
R-653, rare, VG **525.00**
R-654-A, rare, EX **315.00**
R-676-C, scarce, VG..............**55.00**
R-680-B, VG **35.00**
R-79, EX **41.00**
R-80, rare, M **295.00**

R-78, New England, EX, $30.00; R-97, Eastern, NM, $45.00.

Currier and Ives by Royal

During the late 1950s, Currier and Ives dinnerware was given as premiums through A&P stores. Decorated in blue with scenes taken from prints by Currier and Ives, the line was rather extensive. In addition to the dinnerware, accessory pieces were made as well. These include glass tumblers (each size with a different scene), vinyl placemats, and a series of Fire King casseroles, baking pans, and smaller items.

Ash tray.................................**12.00**
Bowl, berry **3.00**

Bowl, cereal; scarce **10.00**
Bowl, serving; 2 sizes, each .. **15.00**
Bowl, soup **8.00**
Bowl, vegetable; oval **18.00**
Butter dish, ¼-lb **20.00**
Casserole, with lid **45.00**
Creamer & sugar, with lid **12.00**
Cup & saucer **4.00**
Gravy boat, with undertray .. **15.00**
Pie plate (baker) **10.00**
Plate, bread & butter; 6" **3.00**
Plate, dinner; 10½" **4.00**
Plate, luncheon; 7½" **6.00**
Platter, oval **18.00**
Salver or chop plate, round, 2
    sizes, each **15.00**
Shakers, pair **12.00**
Teapot **45.00**
Tumbler, iced tea **8.00**
Tumbler, juice **10.00**
Tumbler, old-fashioned **10.00**
Tumbler, regular **8.00**

Accessory Pieces by Fire King

Baker, round, handle, sm **7.00**
Baker, square, no lid, 8" **8.00**
Bowl, cereal; round **5.00**
Casserole, oval or round, with lid,
    each **15.00**
Coffee mug **5.00**
Custard, individual **4.00**
Loaf pan **8.00**

Czechoslovakian Collectibles

Items marked Czechoslovakia
are popular modern collectibles.
Pottery, glassware, jewelry, etc.,
were produced there in abundance.

Atomizer, amethyst glass with
    gold decoration, 7" **85.00**
Bottle, scent; blue stepped-form
    base, large frosted stopper,
    6¼" **235.00**

**Perfume bottle, molded
clear and frosted floral
stopper, 6¾", $75.00.**

Bottle, scent; crystal base, red fig-
    ure stopper, 5½" **95.00**
Bottle, scent; amber glass, cupid
    decoration, 6½" **125.00**
Bottle, scent; pink cut glass,
    intaglio stopper **225.00**
Bottle, scent; pink glass, frosted
    base, nude stopper, 6" .. **195.00**
Candlestick, mottled autumn-col-
    ored glass, 8½" **44.00**
Candy basket, green varicolored
    glass, 8" **100.00**
Candy basket, mottled glass, crys-
    tal thorn handle, 7" **125.00**
Candy jar, glass, applied flower
    ornament, with lid **75.00**
Mayonnaise, varicolored cased
    glass, 5½" **78.00**
Pin tray, green glass with jeweled
    ornaments, 4⅜" **38.00**
Pitcher, blue opaque glass,
    enameled exotic bird, with
    lid, 11" **110.00**
Pitcher, glass apple figural, twig
    handle, leaf spout, 8" **35.00**

Pitcher, mottled glass, cased, blue handle, 9" 65.00
Puff box, pink glass, 2⅝".....215.00
Tumbler, amber glass with yellow overlay, 4½" 30.00
Vase, mottled glass, cased, applied serpentine decoration, 9" 65.00
Vase, mottled glass, uncased, long slim neck, 8" 55.00
Vase, orange cased glass with silver decoration, classic form, 7¾" 85.00
Vase, varicolored double-cased glass, 5½" 60.00
Wine goblet, orange cased glass with silver decoration, clear stem, 3¾" 45.00

Decanters

The James Beam Distilling Company produced its first ceramic whiskey decanter in 1953 and remained the only major producer of these decanters throughout the decade. By the late 1960s, other companies such as Ezra Brooks, Lionstone, and Cyrus Noble were also becoming involved in their production. Today these fancy liquor containers are attracting many collectors.

Beam, Arizona 15.00
Beam, Baggage Car 7.50
Beam, Battery Telephone 48.00
Beam, Bluejay 10.00
Beam, Chicago Fire...............22.50
Beam, Convention Series, Showgirl, blonde 65.00
Beam, Dial Pay Telephone....48.00
Beam, Ducks Unlimited, #1, Mallard 50.00
Beam, Executive Series, Golden Jubilee 15.00
Beam, Fire Engine, Mississippi Pumper, 1867 ....100.00
Beam, Ford, 1929 Phaeton ...48.00

Beam, Ford Police Car, 1929..90.00
Beam, George Washington ...22.00
Beam, Jaguar 25.00
Beam, Trophy Series, Largemouth Bass 12.00
Beam, Martha Washington ..14.00
Beam, Mermaid 120.00
Beam, Model-T Ford, Police Car, 1982 ....60.00
Beam, Mortimer Snerd.........28.00
Beam, NY World's Fair 18.00
Beam, Paddy Wagon 68.00
Beam, Pearl Harbor 1976.....14.00
Beam, Pony Express.............10.00
Beam, Queensland................20.00
Beam, Seattle World Fair.....16.00
Beam, Shriner, Western Association................................32.50
Beam, Statue of Liberty 35.00
Beam, Thailand...................... 7.50
Beam, Tombstone.................. 9.00
Beam, Train, Coal Tender.....20.00
Beam, Train, Log Car 40.00
Beam, Viking........................15.00
Beam, Volkswagon 38.00
Beam, Wheel Series, Duesenberg Convertible...................100.00
Beam, Wheel Series, Mississippi Fire Engine 100.00
Brooks, African Lion.............30.00

Ezra Brooks, $15.00.

Brooks, Baltimore Oriole......30.00
Brooks, Bowler 7.00
Brooks, Elk...........................24.00
Brooks, Foremost Astronaut . 8.00
Brooks, Gold Prospector 10.00
Brooks, Oil Gusher...............38.00
Brooks, Raccoon 40.00
Brooks, Ski Boot...................10.00

Brooks, Snow Egret 30.00
Brooks, Snowy Owl 10.00
Brooks, Telephone 14.00
Brooks, White Shark.............. 7.50
Cyrus Noble, Burro 35.00
Cyrus Noble, Carousel Tiger ..40.00
Cyrus Noble, Mine Shaft 35.00
Famous Firsts, Butterfly, miniature 15.00
Famous Firsts, Fireman.......55.00
Famous Firsts, Kangaroos, miniature 10.00
Famous Firsts, Panda...........50.00
Famous Firsts, Tiger.............30.00
Grenadier, Arabian Horse 30.00
Grenadier, Soldier Series, MacArthur......................20.00
Grenadier, Teddy Roosevelt, miniature 20.00
Hoffman, Doe & Fawn 40.00
Hoffman, Goose That Laid the Golden Egg.....................20.00
Hoffman, Jamaica.................28.00
Hoffman, Kangaroo 40.00
Hoffman, Oklahoma Sooners .40.00
Lionstone, #8, Alarm Box 60.00
Lionstone, Betsy Ross 25.00
Lionstone, Firefighter #1, with Hose 110.00
Lionstone, Pheasant 50.00
Lionstone, Pie-Face Clown ..35.00
Lionstone, Professional #7, Helmut 70.00
McCormick, Buffalo Bill 48.00
McCormick, Elvis, Karate, miniature 45.00
McCormick, Elvis #2.............35.00
McCormick, Jefferson Davis.25.00
McCormick, Mail Car, 1969 .38.00
McCormick, Thelma Lu 18.00
McCormick, Will Rogers, miniature 10.00
Old Bardstown, Bulldog 65.00
Old Bardstown, Tiger............40.00
Old Bardstown, Trucker 32.50
Old Commonwealth, Coins of Ireland..................................25.00
Old Commonwealth, Cottontail Rabbit..............................32.00

Old Commonwealth, Firefighter #2, Nozzleman................40.00
Old Commonwealth, Miner with Shovel #1......................100.00
Old Commonwealth, Professional #5, Harmony...................50.00
Old Commonwealth, Tennessee Walking Horse 28.00
Old Commonwealth, Yankee Doodle 32.00
Old Fitzgerald, Geese 7.50
Old Fitzgerald, Lexington 2.50
Old Fitzgerald, Old Ironsides . 4.00
Old Fitzgerald, Pheasant....... 6.00
Old Fitzgerald, Tree of Life ... 5.00
Pacesetter, Corvette..............30.00
Ski Country, Black Swan, miniature 35.00
Ski Country, Bobcat & Chipmunk 55.00
Ski Country, Brown Bear......34.00
Ski Country, Cardinal 78.00
Ski Country, Fox on a Log ...80.00
Ski Country, Labrador with Pheasant......................75.00
Ski Country, Mallard Duck...40.00
Ski Country, Redtail Hawk ..60.00
Ski Country, Rocky Mountain Sheep 45.00
Ski Country, Saw-Whet Owl .40.00
Ski Country, Skunk Family .45.00
Wild Turkey, Series I, #6, striding................................24.00
Wild Turkey, Series I, #8, strutting................................37.50
Wild Turkey, Series III, #10, with coyote, miniature 40.00
Wild Turkey, Series III, #4, with eagle............................70.00
Wild Turkey, Turkey Lore Series, #2 ....42.50
Wild Turkey, Turkey Lore Series, #3 ....40.00

Decoys

Although ducks are the most commonly encountered type, nearly every species of bird has been imitated through decoys. The earliest were carved from wood by the Indians are used to lure game birds into the hunting areas. Among those most valued by collectors today are those carved by well-known artists, commercial decoys produced by factories such as Mason and Dodge, and well-carved examples or rare species.

Black Duck, EX original paint, Mason Challenge **180.00**
Black Duck, old working repaint, Dodge Co **60.00**
Black Duck, original paint, Down East Co **140.00**
Black Duck, original paint, glass eyes, Mason Standard .**175.00**
Black Duck, original paint, Pratt Mfg Co **150.00**
Black Duck, repaint, Atlantic Coast model, Wildfowler, oversize...........................**80.00**
Black Duck, repaint, Charles Perdew, Henry, IL, M ..**250.00**
Black Duck, signed Ray Schalk, miniature.......................**70.00**
Bluebill Drake, EX original paint, balsa body, Wildfowler .**100.00**
Bluebill Drake, Frank Adams, West Tisbury, MA, miniature, NM.................................**75.00**
Bluebill Drake, old working repaint, glass eyes, Mason Standard........................**80.00**
Bluebill Drake, old working repaint, Henry Holmes, Bureau, IL **100.00**
Bluebill Drake, original paint, Dodge Co **75.00**
Bluebill Drake, original paint, snaky head, Mason Challenge, EX **400.00**
Bluebill Drake, original paint, stamped Evans **150.00**
Bluebill pair, EX original paint, balsa, Wildfowler **150.00**

Bluebill pair, EX original paint, Evans Co **225.00**
Bluewinged Teal pair, repaint, Mason Challenge, EX ..**210.00**
Brant, original paint, Jay Parker, Parkertown, NJ **70.00**
Brant, original paint, Mason Challenge **350.00**
Brant, original paint, signed Charles Birdsall, Wildfowler, EX.................................**135.00**
Canada Goose, original paint, balsa body, Herters Inc .**60.00**
Canada Goose, Russell Freeman, miniature, EX **75.00**
Canvasback Drake, repaint, Mason Challenge **80.00**
Canvasback Hen, worn original paint, Evans Co..............**70.00**
Coot, original paint, 1 glass eye missing, Pratt Mfg.........**55.00**
Dove, original paint with minor wear, Herters Inc **150.00**
Golden Plover, original paint, folding tin, Strater & Sohier, EX.................................**70.00**
Goldeneye Drake, original paint, Mason Challenge **200.00**

Mason Factory, Challenge Grade Black Duck with snaky head, original stamp, NM, $2,300.00.

Goldeneye Drake, stamped George Winters, miniature, M **220.00**
Goldeneye Drake, worn original paint, Dodge Co, rare **55.00**
Goldeneye Hen, EX original paint, glass eyes, Mason Standard, EX.................................**190.00**
Gull, flying, Russ Burr, Hingham, MA, miniature, EX **50.00**

Mallard Drake, original paint, Paw Paw Factory **50.00**
Mallard Drake, original paint, Victor Animal Trap Co ..**35.00**
Mallard Drake, repaint, neck damage, Stevens Co.......**80.00**
Mallard pair, original paint, Mason Standard...........**200.00**
Pintail Drake, old working repaint, Evans Co **65.00**
Pintail Drake, paint worn to wood, Mason Premier ..**125.00**
Redhead Drake, repaint, glass eyes, Mason Standard..**110.00**
Scoter Drake, Mason-style repaint, Mason Standard, rare **120.00**
Shoveller Drake, original paint, stamped Hays #271 .....**550.00**
Swan, working repaint, Sam Barnes, Havre de Grace, MD, EX **125.00**
Widgeon Drake, balsa, branded Wildfowler, EX **175.00**
Widgeon pair, original paint, balsa, Wildfowler **325.00**

Degenhart

The 'D' in heart trademark indicates the product of the Crystal Art Glass factory, which operated in Cambridge, Ohio, from 1947 until the mid-1970s. It was operated by John and Elizabeth Degenhart who developed more than 145 distinctive colors to use in making their toothpick holders, figurines, bells, and other novelties.

Bell, Lime Ice **16.00**
Candy dish, Wildflower Pink .**25.00**
Centennial Bell, Opalescent.**15.00**
Cup plate, Heart & Lyre, Crown Tuscan **25.00**
Cup plate, Seal of Ohio, Amberina **25.00**
Dog, Bittersweet Slag **65.00**

Hand, Crown Tuscan **15.00**
Hat, Sapphire Blue **18.00**
Hen, Caramel Custard, 3" **45.00**

Dog, Tomato Red, $60.00.

Jewel Box, Light Chocolate Creme **35.00**
Owl, Antique Blue **35.00**
Owl, Persimmon....................**10.00**
Owl, Red Carnival **75.00**
Priscilla, Bittersweet Slag..**125.00**
Priscilla, Heather...............**100.00**
Skate Shoe, Cobalt Carnival..**40.00**
Tomahawk, Emerald Green..**23.00**
Toothpick holder, Beaded Oval, Bittersweet....................**35.00**
Toothpick holder, Forget-Me-Not, Amberina **15.00**
Toothpick holder, Forget-Me-Not, Crown Tuscan **20.00**
Toothpick holder, Gypsy Pot, Tomato Red....................**50.00**
Turkey, Crown Tuscan **75.00**

Depression Glass

Depression Glass, named for the era when it sold through dime stores or was given away as premiums, can be found in such varied colors as amber, green, pink, blue, red, yellow, white, and crystal. Mass-produced by many different companies in hundreds of patterns, Depression Glass is one of the most sought-after collectibles in the United States today.

Adam, bowl, cereal; pink or green, 5¾".................30.00
Adam, bowl, green, oval, 10".18.00
Adam, butter dish, with cover, green...................245.00
Adam, cake plate, green, pedestal base, 10"........................16.50
Adam, coaster, pink..............14.50
Adam, pitcher, pink, round base, 32-ounce 40.00
Adam, plate, pink, square, 9".16.50
Adam, tumbler, green, 4½"...15.00
Adam, tumbler, iced tea; green, 5½"...............................30.00
Adam, vase, pink, 7½"........160.00
American Pioneer, bowl, green, handled, 9"......................18.00
American Pioneer, bowl, green, with cover, 9"...............100.00
American Pioneer, coaster, crystal, 3½"..........................15.00
American Pioneer, goblet, wine; pink, 3-ounce, 4"............30.00
American Pioneer, ice bucket, green, 6".........................42.50
American Pioneer, lamp, crystal, tall, 8½"........................75.00
American Pioneer, sherbet, crystal, 4¾"............................18.00
American Pioneer, sugar bowl, green, 2¾"......................17.50
American Pioneer, tumbler, juice; pink, 5-ounce.................15.00
American Sweetheart, bowl, berry; pink, flat, 3".........25.00
American Sweetheart, creamer, pink, pedestal base 8.00
American Sweetheart, pitcher, pink, 80-ounce, 8"........360.00

American Sweetheart, plate, salad; monax, 8".............. 6.00
American Sweetheart, platter, pink, oval, 13"..............20.00
American Sweetheart, tumbler, pink, 5-ounce, 3".............40.00
Anniversary, bowl, berry; crystal, 4⅞"................................. 1.50
Anniversary, creamer, crystal, pedestal base.................. 3.50
Anniversary, plate, sherbet; pink, 6¼"................................. 2.00
Anniversary, wine glass, pink, 2½-ounce........................10.00
Aunt Polly, bowl, blue, oval, 8⅜" long...............................45.00
Aunt Polly, butter dish, green, with cover.....................195.00
Aunt Polly, plate, luncheon; blue, 8"....................................12.00
Aunt Polly, plate, sherbet; green, 6"..................................... 4.00
Aunt Polly, tumbler, blue, 8-ounce, 3⅝".......................18.00
Aurora, bowl, cobalt, 5⅜"....... 5.00
Aurora, tumbler, cobalt, 10-ounce, 4¾".................................12.50
Avocado, bowl, relish; pink, pedestal base, 6"............15.00
Avocado, creamer, green, pedestal base...............................27.50
Avocado, plate, cake; pink, handles, 10¼".......................25.00
Avocado, sugar bowl, green, pedestal base 27.50
Beaded Block, bowl, amber, round, flared, 7¼"........... 8.00
Beaded Block, bowl, celery; crystal, 8¼"............................ 9.50
Beaded Block, plate, amber, square, 7¾"...................... 5.00
Beaded Block, vase, bouquet; crystal, 6".....................10.00
Block Optic, bowl, cereal; green, 5¼"................................. 8.50
Block Optic, goblet, wine; pink, short, 3½".......................50.00
Block Optic, plate, sandwich; green, 10¼"....................12.50

Block Optic, whiskey, green, 2-ounce, 2¼".....................**16.00**

Bowknot, tumbler, green, 10-ounce, 5" **11.00**

Bubble, bowl, light blue, flanged, 9" **75.00**

Bubble, bowl, soup; light blue, flat, 7¾" **8.50**

Bubble, plate, dinner; ruby red, 9⅜" **5.50**

Bubble, tumbler, iced tea; ruby red, 12-ounce **8.50**

Bubble, tumbler, juice; ruby red, 6-ounce **6.00**

Cameo, bowl, berry; green, large, 8¼".....................**23.00**

Cameo, bowl, soup; green, rimmed, 9".....................**27.50**

Cameo, candlesticks, green, 4", pair **72.50**

Cameo, candy jar, pink, low, with cover, 4" **375.00**

Cameo, goblet, green, 6" **37.50**

Cameo, plate, cake; green, flat, 10½".....................**75.00**

Cameo, plate, dinner; pink, rimmed, 10¼"...............**100.00**

Cameo, platter, yellow, closed handles, 12"...................**27.50**

Cameo, tumbler, green, pedestal base, 9-ounce, 5" **19.00**

Cameo, tumbler, juice; pink, 5-ounce, 3¾".....................**65.00**

Cherry Blossom, bowl, berry; delphite, 4¾" **9.00**

Cherry Blossom, butter dish, green, with cover...........**67.50**

Cherry Blossom, plate, salad; green, 7".........................**15.00**

Cherry Blossom, platter, green, oval, 11" **22.00**

Cherry Blossom, tray, sandwich; pink, 10½" **10.00**

Circle, bowl, green or pink, flared, 5½" **5.00**

Circle, decanter, green or pink, handled...........................**27.50**

Circle, plate, luncheon; green or pink, 8¼".......................... **3.50**

Circle, tumbler, juice; green or pink, 4-ounce.................. **4.00**

Colonial Block (pink or green): Butter dish, $30.00; Bowl, 7", $12.50; Creamer and sugar bowl with lid, $23.00; Candy dish, 8½", $27.50.

Cloverleaf, bowl, salad; yellow, deep, 7" 35.00

Cloverleaf, candy dish, green, with cover 40.00

Cloverleaf, creamer, black, pedestal base, 3⅝" 12.50

Cloverleaf, tumbler, green, flat, 9-ounce, 4" 30.00

Colonial, bowl, berry; green, large, 9" 20.00

Colonial, bowl, vegetable; pink, oval, 10" 20.00

Colonial, butter dish, pink, with cover 450.00

Colonial, goblet, cordial; green, 1-ounce, 3¾" 25.00

Colonial, salt & pepper shakers, pink, pair.....................100.00

Columbia, bowl, soup; crystal, low, 8" 11.00

Columbia, butter dish, crystal, with cover.........................15.00

Columbia, plate, bread & butter; pink, 6" 5.00

Coronation, bowl, nappy, royal ruby, 6½"........................... 7.50

Coronation, pitcher, pink, 68-ounce, 7¾" 150.00

Coronation, plate, luncheon; green, 8½"........................20.00

Cube, bowl, green, 4½"........... 5.00

Cube, butter dish, green, with cover................................45.00

Cube, pitcher, pink, 8¾" 140.00

Cube, tumbler, green, 4" 40.00

Cupid, bowl, fruit; all colors, pedestal base, 9" 50.00

Cupid, creamer, all colors, pedestal base, 4½" 32.50

Cupid, tray, all colors, center handle, 10¾" 40.00

Daisy, bowl, berry; amber, deep, 7⅜" 10.00

Daisy, plate, luncheon; crystal, 8⅜" 2.00

Daisy, sherbet, amber, pedestal base............................... 7.00

Daisy, tumbler, amber, pedestal base, 9-ounce 14.00

Diamond Quilted, bowl, cream soup; black, 4¾"..............15.00

Diamond Quilted, compote, pink, with cover, 11"...............50.00

Diamond Quilted, goblet, cordial; green, 1-ounce................ 8.00

Diamond Quilted, whiskey, green, 1½-ounce.......................... 6.50

Diana, candy jar, amber, round, with cover......................25.00

Diana, plate, bread & butter; pink, 6" 1.50

Diana, salt & pepper shakers, amber, pair 75.00

Dogwood, bowl, pink, 10¼".200.00

Dogwood, platter, pink, oval, rare, 12"................................245.00

Dogwood, sherbet, green, low, pedestal base.................60.00

Dogwood, tumbler, pink, decorated, 5-ounce, 3".........200.00

Dogwood, tumbler, pink, molded band 11.00

Doric, bowl, vegetable; green, oval, 9"............................16.00

Doric (green); Creamer, 4", $8.50; Tumbler, 4½", $50.00; Cream soup, $175.00; Plate, 9", $10.00; Sherbet, $9.50; Pitcher, flat, $30.00.

Doric, candy dish, pink, with cover, 8" 25.00

Doric, pitcher, delphite, flat, 36-ounce, 6"......................750.00

Doric, plate, green, 9" 10.00

Doric, salt & pepper shakers, green, pair 27.50

Doric & Pansy, bowl, berry; teal, large, 8" 60.00
Doric & Pansy, plate, salad; green, 7" 25.00
Doric & Pansy, tumbler, teal, 9-ounce, 4½" 35.00
English Hobnail, bowl, relish; pink, oval, 12" 17.50
English Hobnail, candlesticks, pink, 8½", pair 50.00
English Hobnail, cologne bottle, turquoise 25.00
English Hobnail, lamp, amber, electric, 6¼" 50.00
English Hobnail, pitcher, turquoise, 23-ounce 125.00
Fire King, Alice, plate, luncheon jadite, 8½" 4.00
Fire King, Jane Ray, platter, jadite, 12" 5.00
Fire King, Philbe, bowl, salad; blue, 7¼" 60.00
Fire King, Philbe, plate, grill; pink, 10½" 30.00
Fire King, Square, bowl, salad; all colors, 7" 5.00
Fire King Oven Ware, baker, blue, 2-quart 10.00
Fire King Oven Ware, bowl, utility; blue, 10" 15.00
Fire King Oven Ware, bowl, vegetable; blue, 8" 9.00
Fire King Oven Ware, custard cup, blue, 5-ounce............ 3.00
Fire King Oven Ware, egg plate, blue 10.00
Fire King Oven Ware, loaf pan, blue, deep, 9" 20.00
Fire King Oven Ware, plate, blue, 10" 7.50
Floragold, bowl, cereal; iridescent, round, 5½" 20.00
Floragold, pitcher, iridescent, 64-ounce.............................25.00
Floral, bowl, cream soup; pink, 5½" 600.00

Floral, candlesticks, green, 4", pair 32.50
Floral, salt & pepper shakers, pink, flat, 6" 37.50
Floral, tumbler, green, flat, 9-ounce, 4½" 160.00
Floral & Diamond Band, bowl, berry; green, 4½" 6.00
Floral & Diamond Band, creamer, green, 4¾" 15.00
Floral & Diamond Band, tumbler, iced tea; pink, 5"............15.00
Florentine No 1, bowl, berry; pink, large, 8½" 22.50
Florentine No 1, plate, salad; yellow, 8½" 9.50
Florentine No 1, sugar bowl, crystal, ruffled 22.50
Florentine No 2, bowl, berry; crystal, large, 8".....................15.00
Florentine No 2, bowl, cream soup; yellow, 4¾" 15.00
Florentine No 2, gravy boat, yellow...................................35.00
Florentine No 2, pitcher, yellow, 48-ounce, 7"..................140.00
Florentine No 2, plate, dinner; pink, 10" 12.00
Florentine No 2, tumbler, water; blue, 9-ounce, 4"............52.50
Forest Green, pitcher, green, round, 3-quart...............20.00
Forest Green, platter, green, rectangular 18.00
Forest Green, punch bowl, green, with stand 22.50
Forest Green, sugar bowl, green, flat 4.50
Fortune, candy dish, pink, with cover, flat......................15.00
Fortune, plate, luncheon; crystal, 8" 5.00
Fortune, tumbler, water; crystal, 9-ounce, 4" 4.50
Fruits, pitcher, green, flat bottom, 7"....................................42.50

Fruits, tumbler, green, 12-ounce, 5"...40.00

Fruits, tumbler, juice; pink.... 7.00

Harp, tray, crystal, handles, rectangular 20.00

Harp, vase, crystal, 6"...........10.00

Heritage, bowl, pink, 5".........25.00

Heritage, creamer, crystal, pedestal base 15.00

Heritage, plate, sandwich; crystal, 12"...................................... 8.50

Hex & Optic, salt & pepper shakers, pink, pair..................17.50

Hex Optic, bowl, mixing; green, 7¼"................................10.00

Hex Optic, plate, luncheon; green, 8" 4.50

Hex Optic, platter, green, round, 11" 7.00

Hex Optic, whiskey, green, 1-ounce, 2" 5.00

Hobnail, pitcher, water crystal, 67-ounce 20.00

Hobnail, tumbler, iced tea; crystal, 15-ounce 6.00

Holiday, bowl, berry; pink, large, 8½" 14.50

Holiday, candlesticks, pink, 3", pair 55.00

Holiday, pitcher, milk; pink, 16-ounce, 4¾".......................45.00

Holiday, sandwich tray, pink, 10½" 9.00

Holiday, tumbler, pink, pedestal base, 4" 25.00

Homespun, bowl, cereal; crystal, 5".....................................12.50

Homespun, butter dish, pink, with cover.......................40.00

Homespun, pitcher, crystal, 96-ounce..............................30.00

Homespun, platter, crystal, closed handles, 13".................... 8.50

Homespun, tumbler, pink, pedestal base, 6" 20.00

Horseshoe, bowl, cereal; yellow, 6½" 16.50

Horseshoe, creamer, green, pedestal base.................11.50

Horseshoe, tumbler, green, pedestal base, 12-ounce..75.00

Indiana Custard, bowl, soup; ivory, flat, 7½" 25.00

Indiana Custard, plate, salad; ivory, 7½" 8.50

Indiana Custard, platter, ivory, oval, 11½" 22.50

Iris & Herringbone, bowl, soup; crystal, 7½".....................80.00

Iris & Herringbone, candy jar, crystal, with cover.........70.00

Iris & Herringbone, goblet, crystal, 8-ounce, 5"................16.00

Iris & Herringbone, plate, dinner; crystal, 9"........................30.00

Iris & Herringbone, tumbler, crystal, flat, 4"......................47.50

Jubilee, bowl, fruit; yellow, handled, 9" 45.00

Jubilee, cheese & cracker set, yellow 65.00

Jubilee, plate, sandwich; yellow, 13" 25.00

Lace Edge, bowl, ribbed; pink, 7¾" 35.00

Lace Edge, butter dish, pink, with cover.............................45.00

Lace Edge, cookie jar, pink, with cover.............................45.00

Lace Edge, plate, dinner; pink, 10½" 18.50

Lace Edge, sherbet, pink, pedestal base................................50.00

Lace Edge, vase, pink, 7" ...245.00

Lake Como, bowl, vegetable; white, 9¾" 20.00

Lake Como, creamer, white, pedestal base.................12.00

Lake Como, salt & pepper shakers, white, pair 25.00

Lake Como, sugar bowl, white, pedestal base 11.00

Laurel, bowl, berry; ivory, large, 9" 15.00

Laurel, bowl, cereal; blue, 6"..15.00

Laurel, cheese dish, green, with cover.............................40.00

Lincoln Inn, ash tray, blue....15.00

Lincoln Inn, candy dish, red, oval pedestal base..................**17.50**
Lincoln Inn, nut dish, blue, pedestal base..................**15.00**
Lincoln Inn, pitcher, red, 46-ounce, 7¼"....................**750.00**
Lincoln Inn, vase, blue, pedestal base, 12" **95.00**
Lorain, plate, luncheon; yellow, 8⅜"...................................**20.00**
Lorain, relish, crystal, 4-part, 8"..**13.50**
Lorain, sherbet, yellow, pedestal base................................**25.00**
Lorain, sugar bowl, crystal, pedestal base..................**10.00**
Madrid, ash tray, amber, square, 6"....................................**150.00**
Madrid, bowl, salad; amber, deep, 9½" **22.00**
Madrid, butter dish, amber, with cover................................**52.50**
Madrid, gravy boat & platter, amber........................ **1,000.00**
Madrid, pitcher, green, 80-ounce, 8½" **185.00**
Madrid, plate, grill; green.....**13.50**
Manhattan, bowl, pink, closed handles, 8" **13.00**
Manhattan, candy dish, crystal, with cover......................**25.00**
Manhattan, relish tray, pink, 4-part, 14" **15.00**
Manhattan, tumbler, crystal, pedestal base, 10-ounce.**10.00**
Mayfair, bowl, cream soup; pink, 5"....................................**34.00**
Mayfair, cake plate, green, pedestal base, 10" **75.00**
Mayfair, celery dish, green, divided, 9"....................**110.00**
Mayfair, goblet, cocktail; pink, 3½-ounce, 4" **57.50**
Mayfair, pitcher, green, 37-ounce, 6" **375.00**
Mayfair, plate, sherbet; pink, round, 6½" **9.00**
Mayfair, platter, pink, open handles, oval, 12" **15.00**

Mayfair, relish dish, green, 4-part, 8⅜" **100.00**
Mayfair, sherbet, yellow, pedestal base, 4¾".......................**127.50**
Mayfair, tumbler, juice; blue, 5-ounce, 3½"......................**75.00**
Mayfair, whiskey, pink, 1½-ounce, 2¼" **50.00**
Miss America, bowl, vegetable; pink, oval, 10" **16.50**
Miss America, celery dish, pink, oblong, 10½" **15.00**
Miss America, goblet, water; red, 10-ounce, 5"..................**160.00**
Miss America, pitcher, crystal, 65-ounce, 8" **40.00**
Miss America, plate, dinner; pink, 10¼" **17.00**
Miss America, platter, pink, oval, 12¼" **16.00**
Miss America, salt & pepper shakers, green, pair.....**275.00**
Miss America, tumbler, juice; pink, 5-ounce, 4"............**12.50**
Moderntone, bowl, berry; cobalt, large, 8¾"........................**25.00**
Moderntone, bowl, cream soup; cobalt, 4¾" **13.00**
Moderntone, plate, dinner; amethyst, 8⅞"................. **7.50**
Moderntone, salt & pepper shakers, cobalt, pair **27.50**
Moderntone, tumbler, amethyst, 12-ounce **40.00**
Moondrops, candy dish, red, ruffled, 8"............................**25.00**
Moondrops, goblet, wine; blue, 4-ounce, 4" **15.00**
Moondrops, platter, blue, 12".**20.00**
Moondrops, tumbler, blue, 12-ounce, 5⅛".......................**18.00**
Moonstone, bowl, relish; opalescent, divided, 7"............... **7.50**
Moonstone, creamer, opalescent, footed **6.00**
Moonstone, plate, sandwich; opalescent, 10" **16.00**
Moonstone, vase, bud; opalescent, 5½" **8.50**

Mt Pleasant, bonbon, pink, rolled-up handles, 7".................**12.50**

Mt Pleasant, plate, cobalt, handles, 12"........................**25.00**

New Century, bowl, cream soup; green, 4¾"........................ **9.00**

New Century, butter dish, green, with cover........................**47.50**

New Century, plate, dinner; crystal, 10"...........................**10.00**

New Century, salt & pepper shakers, green, pair...............**27.50**

New Century, whiskey, crystal, 1½-ounce, 2"....................**12.00**

Newport, bowl, berry; amethyst, 4¼"................................... **9.00**

Newport, tumbler, cobalt, 9-ounce, 4½"...............................**22.50**

Nora Bird, creamer, pink, round handle.............................**22.00**

Nora Bird, mayonnaise, green, with liner........................**50.00**

Nora Bird, tumbler, pink, pedestal base, 4¾".........**32.50**

Normandie, pitcher, pink, 80-ounce, 8".........................**80.00**

Normandie, plate, grill; amber, 11"...................................**10.00**

Normandie, platter, iridescent, 11¾"................................**10.00**

Old Cafe, pitcher, crystal, 36-ounce, 6".........................**50.00**

Old Cafe, plate, pink, 10".....**15.50**

Old English, bowl, amber, flat, 9½"..................................**25.00**

Old English, goblet, pink, 8-ounce, 5¾"......................**22.50**

Old English, tumbler, green, pedestal base, 5"............**25.00**

Orchid, ice bucket, cobalt, 6"..**75.00**

Orchid, vase, red, 10"............**85.00**

Oyster & Pearl, candle holder, pink, 3½", pair **15.00**

Oyster & Pearl, relish dish, pink, oblong, 10"...................... **6.00**

Parrot, bowl, soup; green.....**27.50**

Parrot, salt & pepper shakers, green, pair...................**177.50**

Parrot (green): Bowl, 5", $12.50; Bowl, 7", $25.00; Plate, 10", $45.00; Sugar bowl with lid, $115.00; Tumbler, footed, $97.50; Sherbet, $16.50.

Patrician, bowl, cream soup; pink, 4¾" 15.00

Patrician, creamer, green, pedestal base................... 9.50

Patrician, plate, sherbet; crystal, 6" 6.75

Patrician, sugar bowl, pink ... 7.00

Patrician, tumbler, green, 14-ounce, 5½".......................30.00

Patrick, bowl, fruit; yellow, handled, 9" 20.00

Patrick, goblet, water; yellow, 10-ounce, 6" 22.00

Patrick, tray, yellow, center handle, 11" 25.00

Peacock Reverse, bowl, all colors, square, 4" 22.00

Peacock Reverse, plate, sherbet; all colors, 5" 17.50

Peacock Reverse, vase, all colors, 10"...................................75.00

Petalware, bowl, cream soup; monax, 4½" 8.50

Petalware, platter, crystal, oval, 13"................................... 7.50

Pineapple & Floral, ash tray, amber, 4½".......................16.00

Pineapple & Floral, tumbler, crystal, 8-ounce, 4" 25.00

Pineapple & Floral, vase, crystal, cone-shaped...................25.00

Pretzel, bowl, crystal, 9⅜" ...10.00

Pretzel, tumbler, crystal, 5-ounce, 3½" 10.00

Princess, cake stand, green ..15.00

Princess, pitcher, amber, 37-ounce, 6" 500.00

Princess, plate, grill; green ..10.00

Princess, tumbler, juice; yellow, 5-ounce, 3" 20.00

Princess, vase, green, 8" 22.00

Pyramid, bowl, yellow, oval, 9½" long..............................45.00

Pyramid, creamer, pink 16.50

Pyramid, tumbler, green, pedestal base, 11-ounce 45.00

Queen Mary, bowl, pink, 6" ..15.00

Queen Mary, candy dish, pink, with cover..................25.00

Queen Mary, creamer, crystal, oval 4.00

Queen Mary, plate, serving tray; pink, 14" 10.00

Queen Mary, sugar bowl, crystal, oval 4.00

Radiance, bonbon, red, 6" 13.00

Radiance, punch bowl, red..135.00

Radiance, tray, red, oval 25.00

Raindrops, bowl, berry; green, 7½" 20.00

Raindrops, salt & pepper shakers, green, pair 125.00

Raindrops, whiskey, green, 1-ounce, 1⅞"....................... 4.00

Ribbon, candy dish, green, with cover 27.50

Ribbon, tumbler, green, 10-ounce, 6"....................................16.50

Ring, bowl, soup; green, 7" ...10.00

Ring, salt & pepper shakers, green, 3", pair................25.00

Rock Crystal, bowl, celery; red, oblong, 12"......................47.50

Rock Crystal, bowl, red, scalloped edge, 4½"......................22.50

Rock Crystal, candy dish, red, with cover, round 125.00

Rock Crystal, comport, crystal, 7"......................................27.50

Rock Crystal, tumbler, juice; red, 5-ounce 40.00

Rock Crystal, vase, cornucopia; crystal...........................50.00

Rose Cameo, bowl, cereal; green, 5"...................................... 8.00

Rose Cameo, plate, salad; green, 7"...................................... 5.50

Rosemary, bowl, cream soup; green, 5" 14.00

Rosemary, tumbler, pink, 9-ounce, 4¼" 25.00

Roulette, tumbler, iced tea; pink, 12-ounce, 5" 10.00

Round Robin, plate, sandwich; iridescent, 12" 6.00

Roxana, bowl, cereal; yellow.. 6.50

Roxana, tumbler, yellow, 9-ounce, 4"...................................10.00

Royal Lace, creamer, green, pedestal base **17.50**
Royal Lace, pitcher, crystal, 86-ounce, 8" **42.50**
Royal Lace, tumbler, blue, 5-ounce, 3½".......................**30.00**
Royal Ruby, bowl, popcorn; red, 5¼x9" **8.00**
Royal Ruby, punch bowl, red ..**17.50**
Royal Ruby, tumbler, iced tea; red, 13-ounce........................... **9.50**
S Pattern, bowl, berry; crystal, large, 8½"........................ **7.50**
S Pattern, tumbler, crystal, 12-ounce, 5" **7.50**
Sandwich (Hocking), bowl, salad; crystal, 7"........................ **6.50**
Sandwich (Hocking), creamer, forest green **17.50**
Sandwich (Indiana), goblet, red, 9-ounce **40.00**
Sandwich (Indiana), plate, luncheon; red, 8⅜" **15.00**
Sandwich (Indiana), sherbet, green, 3¼"......................... **5.00**
Sharon, bowl, green, 6".........**17.50**
Sharon, jam dish, pink, 7"..**100.00**
Sharon, sugar bowl, green ...**10.00**
Sharon, tumbler, pink, pedestal base, 15-ounce, 6"...........**32.50**
Sierra, bowl, vegetable; pink, oval, 9¼" **25.00**
Sierra, plate, green, 9"..........**13.00**
Sierra, platter, green, 11" **30.00**
Sierra, salt & pepper shakers, pink, pair **27.50**
Sierra, sugar bowl, pink **12.50**
Spiral, pitcher, green, 58-ounce, 7⅝".................................**22.00**
Spiral, sandwich server, pink, center handle **17.50**
Starlight, bowl, salad; crystal, 11½" **14.00**
Starlight, plate, sandwich; white, 13"..................................... **7.50**
Starlight, relish dish, crystal. **9.50**
Starlight, sherbet, white **7.50**
Strawberry, butter dish, pink, with cover **125.00**

Strawberry, pickle dish, pink, oval, 8¼" **10.00**
Sunflower, plate, green, 9"....**12.00**
Sunflower, tumbler, pink, pedestal base, 4" **15.00**
Swirl, ash tray, pink, 5⅜" **6.00**
Swirl, bowl, salad; ultramarine, rimmed, 9".....................**18.00**
Swirl, candy dish, pink, with cover...............................**55.00**
Swirl, platter, delphite, 12" ..**22.50**
Tea Room, bowl, finger bowl; green **35.00**
Tea Room, goblet, pink, footed, 9-ounce...............................**50.00**
Tea Room, ice bucket, green .**40.00**
Tea Room, tumbler, pink, flat, 8½-ounce...............................**65.00**
Tea Room, vase, green, straight, 11"......................................**70.00**
Thistle, plate, grill; pink.......**12.50**
Thistle, plate, green, 8".........**12.50**
Twisted Optic, candy jar, all colors, with cover................**17.50**
Twisted Optic, creamer, pink .. **6.00**
Twisted Optic, pitcher, all colors, 64-ounce **17.50**
Twisted Optic, tumbler, all colors, 12-ounce, 5" **6.50**
Vernon, plate, sandwich; yellow, 11"......................................**18.00**
Vernon, tumbler, green, pedestal base, 5" **25.00**
Victory, bonbon, black, 7"......**15.00**
Victory, bowl, blue, rolled edge, 11" **35.00**
Victory, goblet, amber, 5" **17.50**
Victory, sugar bowl, black.....**30.00**
Vitrock, bowl, cream soup; white, 5½" **8.00**
Vitrock, plate, soup; white, 9" . **7.00**
Vitrock, platter, white, 11½".**17.50**
Waterford, bowl, pink, 5½" ..**14.00**
Waterford, relish dish, crystal, 5-part, 13¾" **13.00**
Windsor, ash tray, green **40.00**
Windsor, bowl, pink, 8½" **85.00**
Windsor, candy jar, pink, with cover...............................**25.00**

Windsor, platter, crystal, oval, 11½" **4.50**
Windsor, tray, green 4x7" **7.50**

Doll Furniture

Every little girl has her favorite doll, and like all good mothers wants her loved one to have all the 'necessities' of life! Thus a vast array of doll-size furniture can be found, ranging from the most elaborate to those home-made items of simple design.

Armoire, wood, 2-door, opens to shelf & 2 drawers, 23" ...**65.00**
Carriage, painted basket weave, wire rim wheels, EX **95.00**
Carriage, wicker, upholstered interior, wooden wheels, 32x32", EX **65.00**
Cradle, wood, hand-painted floral bouquet on sides, 12" **35.00**
Dresser, wood, 3 drawers & mirror, 24" **65.00**
Dressing table, wood, with mirror, 15½", EX **40.00**
Highchair, maple, with lift tray, ca 1950s, 27½" **20.00**
Highchair, wood, floral decal on backrest, 21", EX............**35.00**

Rocker, painted wicker, EX...**40.00**
Settee, maple, loose cushions, 35½" long, EX.................**55.00**
Stroller, wicker, wire wheels, 25" long, EX..........................**50.00**
Table, drop leaf, wood, red paint, 16x22½", EX **45.00**
Trunk, steamer type, metal, 9x17x9¼", VG.................**20.00**
Trunk, turtle back, lift-out tray, 10x16x10", EX...............**65.00**

Dollhouse Furnishings

Collecting antique dollhouses and building new ones is a popular hobby with many today, and all who collect houses delight in furnishing them right down to the vase on the table and the scarf on the piano! Flea markets are a good source of dollhouse furnishings, especially those from the 1940s through the '60s made by Strombecker, Renwal, or the Petite Princess line by Ideal.

Baby bed, gilt trim, Adrian Cook, NM...................................**30.00**
Bathroom set, Renwal **10.00**
Bedroom set, wooden, Donna Lee, M in box..........................**15.00**

Fainting couch, 17" long, $70.00.

111

Bedroom suite, yellow cherry, Schneegass, 8-piece **175.00**
Bird cage, with bird, Adrian Cook, NM **65.00**
Chair, arm; Tootsietoy...........**12.50**
Chair, living room; gold, Tootsietoy, EX **12.50**
Chifferobe, Mattel................. **5.00**

Dining room set, Strombecker Playthings, $85.00.

Fireplace mantel & chair, Petite Princess **18.00**
High chair, Strombecker.......**25.00**
Lawn swing, Kilgore.............**22.50**
Living room, Dream House, #17, EX **45.00**
Loveseat, gilt trim, Adrian Cook, EX.................................**35.00**
Parlour set, upholstered, GA Schwartz, 5-piece.........**198.00**
Piano, Ideal, litho plastic, movable lid, mirror mounts..**25.00**
Rocker, Strombecker..............**25.00**
Stove, Mini Queen, with 5 utensils...................................**15.00**
Table, dining; Renwal, with 4 chairs, EX......................**25.00**
Vanity, Renwal **7.50**

Dolls

Doll collecting is no doubt one of the most popular fields today. Antique as well as modern dolls are treasured, and limited edition or artist's dolls often bring prices in excess of several hundred dollars. Investment potential is considered excellent in all areas. Dolls have been made from many materials—early to middle 19th-century dolls were carved of wood, poured in wax, and molded in bisque or china. Primitive cloth dolls were sewn at home for the enjoyment of little girls when fancier dolls were unavailable. In this century from 1925 to about 1945, composition was used. Made of a mixture of sawdust, clay, fiber, and a binding agent, it was tough and durable. Modern dolls are usually made of vinyl or molded plastic.

Learn to check your intended purchases for damage which could jeopardize your investment. Bisque dolls may have breaks, hairlines, or eye chips; composition dolls may sometimes become crazed or cracked. Watch for ink or crayon marks on vinyl dolls. Original clothing is important, although on bisque dolls replacement costumes are acceptable as long as they are appropriately styled.

In the listings, values are for mint or mint-in-box dolls in these categories: Madame Alexander, Mattel, and Trolls. Played-with, soiled dolls are worth from 50% to 75% less, depending on condition.

American Character

Betsy McCall, hard plastic, jointed knees, sleep eyes, 1957, 8"........................**115.00**
Betsy McCall, vinyl, original clothes, 1960, 14".........**130.00**
Chuckles, redressed, 23".....**120.00**
Dream Baby, composition with molded hair, original clothes, 11" **88.00**
Eloise, cloth with molded face, yarn hair, original clothes, 21"................................**220.00**

Girl Devil, painted features, long red hair, 18".....................**95.00**

Hedda Get Betta, 21", M **80.00**

Petite marked girl, 14".......**130.00**

Puggy, composition, Petite Doll, redressed, 12"...............**250.00**

Sally, composition, jointed neck, sleep eyes, original clothes, 16"................................**235.00**

Sally, composition, painted eyes, 1930s, redressed, 12"...**125.00**

Sampson the Strongman, with mustache & chest hair, 21", NM **90.00**

Sweet Sue, hard plastic, sleep eyes, 1955, replaced clothes, VG....................................**65.00**

Sweet Sue, hard plastic, walking mechanism, original clothes, 14" **140.00**

Sweet Sue, hard plastic, walking mechanism, replaced clothes, 23"....................................**90.00**

Tiny Tears, hard plastic & rubber, molded hair, redressed, 14", EX **80.00**

Tiny Tears, hard plastic & rubber, original clothes, 12" **100.00**

Tiny Tears, hard plastic & vinyl, open mouth, original clothes, 16"....................................**95.00**

Toni, hard plastic, original clothes, 15" **100.00**

Toodles Toddler, follow-me eyes, 22", NM **120.00**

Armand Marseille

#1775, shoulder head, kid body, redressed, 12"...............**160.00**

#233, character baby, composition, jointed, redressed, 18".**900.00**

#242, painted bisque, redressed, 14", EX.........................**250.00**

#266, socket head, jointed body, closed mouth, redressed, 6", EX................................**210.00**

#270, kid body, open mouth, redressed, 21"...............**375.00**

#300, adult lady, thin jointed limbs, redressed, 10"....**975.00**

#326, kid body, open mouth, redressed, 15"...............**245.00**

#326, toddler, composition, redressed, 10"...............**375.00**

#340, closed mouth, made for Arranbee, replaced clothes, 6"....................................**185.00**

#391, socket head, crude 5-piece body, redressed, 10" **165.00**

Alma, composition body, redressed, 14"...............**275.00**

Baby Phyllis, painted hair, closed mouth, redressed, 12"..**455.00**

Majestic, composition body, redressed, 18"...............**375.00**

Sunshine, kid or kidaleen body, redressed, 14"...............**225.00**

Character

Barry Goldwater, 1964, M **50.00**

Betty Boop, fully jointed, original clothes, 10½"....................**15.00**

Blondie & Dagwood Bumstead, vinyl, 19", each **22.50**

Ideal 'Tony,' hard plastic, marked P-90, 14", $225.00 each.

113

Charley McCarthy, composition, 12", EX..........................**125.00**
Gumby, 16" **8.00**
Julia (Diahann Carroll), leather clothes, M **50.00**
Lone Ranger or Tonto, Gabriel, M in box, each **20.00**
Mae West..............................**60.00**
Michael Jackson, vinyl, original clothes, 12½", MIB........**15.00**
Mohammad Ali, 1976, M **25.00**
Zorro, Hartland, NM............**50.00**

Effanbee

American child, closed mouth boy, composition, 15"....... **1,400.00**
American child, closed mouth girl, composition, 18"....... **1,300.00**
Baby Cuddleup, vinyl-coated cloth body & vinyl, 20"............**55.00**
Betty Brite, all composition, fur wig, 16"........................**250.00**
Brother, composition & cloth, yarn hair, 12" **150.00**
Candy Kid, all composition, black, redressed, 12" **275.00**
Charlie McCarthy, composition & cloth, 19".....................**375.00**
Crowning Glory, Limited Edition Club, 1978 ....**185.00**
Currier & Ives, plastic & vinyl, 12"................................**50.00**
Emily Ann, composition, puppet, 12", M **145.00**
Fluffy, vinyl, 10"....................**40.00**
Girl Scout, all original, 10" ..**35.00**
Historical doll, all composition, original clothes, 14" **525.00**
Honey, all composition, original clothes, 14" **225.00**
Honey, hard plastic, closed mouth, original clothes, 14" **220.00**
Lee, composition & cloth, open mouth, 18" **245.00**
Mae Star, composition, open mouth with teeth, original clothes, 26" **425.00**

Marionette, composition & wood, 14" **125.00**
Mary Jane, composition, jointed body, 1920s, 20"............**200.00**
Mickey, vinyl, molded-on hat, redressed, 11"................**65.00**
Patricia, composition, redressed, 14" **325.00**
Precious Baby, Limited Edition Club, 1975 ....**465.00**
Red Boy, Limited Edition Club, 1985 ....**125.00**
Sherlock Holmes, Limited Edition Club, 1983 ....**175.00**
WC Fields, composition & cloth, redressed, 22"..............**500.00**

Half Dolls

#A188 Germany, Empress Eugenie hat, gray curls, 4" **55.00**
#10001/13273 Germany, Madame Pompadour, 6¼" **135.00**
#104 Japan, holds fans, pink dress, fancy hair, 4" **45.00**
#1256, lady in turban, 1 arm near chest/2nd at waist, 4".....**85.00**
#13588, flapper, arms at neck, rose bodice, 3¾"..............**85.00**
#15009 MIG, nude, mohair wig over bald pate.................**75.00**
#154, flapper, fur collar, blue hat, 5"................................**250.00**
#16811 Germany, nude, arms above head, 4¼" **175.00**
#22672, maiden wearing golden crown, 3½" **125.00**
#32, composition with bisque arms, blonde hair, 3½"...**85.00**
#4367½ Germany, arms away from body, mohair wig, lace shawl, 3½" **125.00**
#5169 Germany, blonde mohair wig, red ribbon, blue eyes, 2½" **400.00**
#5670 Germany, white glaze, holds green fan, sleeveless dress, 3" **80.00**

#9093 Germany, full figure in harem pajamas, 4⅜" ...**100.00**

Hasbro

Adam, 9", M in box.................**12.50**
Aimee, plastic & vinyl, 1972, 18", M in box..........................**60.00**
Flying Nun, plastic & vinyl, 1967, 5", NM **30.00**
Monkees, 4", set of 4, M.........**95.00**
Real Baby, black vinyl & cloth, 21", M in box **55.00**
That Kid, 1967, 21", M..........**85.00**

Heubach

#10633, Dainty Dorothy, open mouth, glass eyes, redressed, 16"................................**500.00**
#6970, character child, bisque head, glass eyes, closed mouth, 18"............... **2,000.00**
#7634, crying baby, open/close eyes, redressed, 15"......**900.00**
#7845, boy, bisque shoulder head, kid body, 20"..................**700.00**
#8192, 5-piece body, open/close eyes, open mouth, 9"....**450.00**
Boy, solid dome shoulder head, molded hair, teeth, 15"..**495.00**
Dutch girl pincushion, original clothes & cushion, 7"......**65.00**
Girl, molded hair & bows, all bisque, 4½" **75.00**
Pouty baby, bisque head, open mouth, molded hair, 8"..**350.00**

Heubach-Koppelsdorf

#100 Germany, Queen Louise, socket head, 1910, 12".**300.00**
#250, 5-piece papier-mache body, paperweight eyes, redressed, 10" **175.00**
#275, jointed leather body, open/close eyes, open mouth, 20"................................**295.00**

#315 Germany 12, Queen Louise, socket head, 27" **850.00**
#342, toddler, open/close eyes, 2 teeth, redressed, 28"....**850.00**
#452, Gypsy, brown bisque, redressed, 18" **800.00**
Child, jointed composition, open mouth, sleep eyes, after 1885, 8".....................................**125.00**
Sunshine, 1910 Germany, shoulder head, 24" **525.00**

Ideal

Baby Belly Button, plastic & vinyl, 9"...........................**10.00**
Baby Crissy, 24", NM............**60.00**
Betsy Wetsy, composition/rubber body, molded hair, 14"..**120.00**
Betty Big Girl, 20" **125.00**
Betty Jane, composition, flirty eyes, redressed, 18"......**135.00**
Bizzy Lizzy, plastic & vinyl, redressed, 17".................**20.00**
Bonnie Braids, hard plastic & vinyl, redressed, 13" **40.00**
Brandi, of Crissy family, redressed, 18".................**55.00**
Child, composition, flirty original clothes, 18", NM...........**200.00**
Cinnamon, of Crissy family, Black, redressed, 12" **75.00**
Cricket, of Crissy family, redressed, 18" **45.00**
Daddy's Girl, 42", M............**800.00**
Diana Ross, plastic & vinyl, 18", M...................................**160.00**
Dina, 15", EX **50.00**
Dody, vinyl, original clothes, 9", NM **50.00**
Flexies, composition & wire, original clothes, 12".............**250.00**
Flossie Flirt, composition & cloth, flirty eyes, 22", EX.......**185.00**
Goody Two Shoes, 18" **75.00**
Jackie, 1962, 15", M.............**95.00**
Jiminy Cricket, composition & wood, 9" **245.00**

King Little, composition & wood, 14".................................**185.00**
Little Lost Baby, 3-faced doll, redressed, 22".................**45.00**
Mary Hartline, hard plastic, original clothes, 15", NM.....**200.00**
Mary Hartline, hard plastic, redressed, 18"................**100.00**
Miss Curity, hard plastic, 14", EX.................................**135.00**
Miss Ideal, multi-jointed, redressed, 25" **165.00**
Miss Revlon, 15", M............**120.00**
Patti Playpal, Black, redressed, 20".................................**175.00**
Penny Playpal, vinyl, open/close eyes, marked, 32"...........**85.00**
Pepper, freckles, marked Ideal-P9-3, 1964, 9", M............**30.00**
Pinocchio, composition & wood, redressed, 11" **135.00**
Sandy McCall, boy, 36".......**350.00**
Saralee, black vinyl & cloth, 18", NM **225.00**
Sparkle Plenty, 15"...............**45.00**
Tammy's Mom, plastic & vinyl with rooted hair, 12" **50.00**
Ted, molded hair, original clothes, 12½", NM.......................**45.00**
Tickletoes, composition & cloth, 15", M **175.00**
Tickletoes, composition & cloth, redressed, 15"................**95.00**
Tiffany Taylor, head swivels, redressed, 18"................**45.00**
Toni, hard plastic, sleep eyes, nylon wig, 14", M **225.00**
Toni, Red Cross Nurse, hard plastic, 15", M **225.00**
Tressy, of Crissy family, redressed, 18"................**45.00**

Kenner

Big Foot, hard vinyl, 13", M .**18.00**
Crumpet, plastic & vinyl, 1970, 8", M **30.00**
Erica Cover Girl, 12½", M.....**30.00**
Princess Leia, 11½", M **85.00**

R2-D2, 7½", M **88.00**
Sky, Black, 11½", M..............**25.00**

Knickerbocker

Bozo the Clown, 14", M.........**40.00**
Child, composition, right arm bends, 15", M...............**185.00**
Pinocchio, plush & cloth, 13", M.................................**135.00**
Snow White, composition, right arm bends, black wig, 15", M.................................**250.00**

Madame Alexander

Alice, hard plastic, Maggie, 1951, 18".................................**450.00**
Alice in Wonderland, composition, Wendy Ann, swivel waist, 13" **400.00**
American child, composition, Tiny Betty, 1938, 7" **200.00**
Annabelle, hard plastic, Maggie, 1952, 15"....................**425.00**
Argentine Boy, hard plastic, bend knee walker, Wendy Ann, 1965-66, 8" **525.00**
Aunt Agatha, hard plastic, Wendy Ann, 8"..................... **1,500.00**
Babs Skater, hard plastic, Margaret, 15" **450.00**
Babsie Skater (roller), Princess Elizabeth, 15"..............**550.00**
Baby Ellen (Black Sweet Tears), 1965-72, 14"..................**165.00**
Baby in Vuitton trunk with wardrobe, any year......**700.00**
Barbara Jane, cloth & vinyl, 1952, 29"......................**385.00**
Bell of the Ball, 10" **75.00**
Binny, hard plastic, Cissy, 14" **300.00**
Birthday doll, composition, Tiny Betty, 7" **225.00**
Bobby, hard plastic, Wendy Ann, 1957, 8"........................**425.00**
Bonnie Toddler, hard plastic head, vinyl limbs, 1951, 18" .**165.00**

Brenda Starr, Bride, hard plastic, 1964, 12".....................200.00
Bride, composition, Little Betty, 1936-41, 9"....................200.00
Bride, hard plastic, Margaret, 21".....................................500.00
Bridesmaid, composition, Little Betty, 9" 200.00
Bulgaria, 8" 55.00
Butch McGuffey, composition & cloth, 22" 225.00
Charity, hard plastic, Wendy Ann, Americana Group, 8". 1,700.00
Cherub baby, cloth 500.00
Cinderella, plastic & vinyl, Mary Ann, pink, 14" 145.00
Clarabell Clown, 19"...........200.00
Cuddly, cloth, 10½"..............195.00
Davy Crockett Boy, hard plastic, Wendy Ann, 8" 1,000.00
Degas Girl, plastic & vinyl, Mary Ann, 14".......................100.00
Ding Dong Dell, composition, Tiny Betty, 7".......................175.00
Dionne Quint, composition & cloth, 14".......................425.00
Dionne Quint, toddler, composition, 14" 450.00
Dressed for Opera, hard plastic, Margaret, 18" 800.00
Dutch, composition, Tiny Betty, 1935-39, 7"....................175.00
Edith the Lonely Doll, plastic & vinyl, 16" 375.00
Egypt, straight legs, 1986 to date, 8"......................................40.00
Elizabeth Monroe, President's Ladies, 1st set 150.00
Emily, cloth & felt, 1930s ...550.00
Eskimo, hard plastic, bend knee, Wendy Ann, 8" 600.00
Gene Tierney, composition, Wendy Ann, 1945, 14"...............500.00
Ginger Rogers, composition, Wendy Ann, 14" 450.00
Godey, hard plastic, Cissette, 1968, 11" 500.00
Good Fairy, hard plastic, Margaret, 14"......................550.00

Grandma Jane, plastic & vinyl, Mary Ann, 14"..............325.00
Greek Girl, hard plastic, bend knee, Wendy Ann, 8"....135.00
Guardian Angel, hard plastic, Wendy Ann, 8" 1,000.00
Hansel, hard plastic, straight leg walker, Wendy Ann, 8".750.00
Honeybea, vinyl, 12"..........225.00
Hungarian, hard plastic, walker, Wendy Ann, 8" 350.00
Irish, Cissette, 10" 55.00
Jack & Jill, composition, Tiny Betty, 7".........................175.00
Janie, plastic & vinyl, 36"...400.00
June Wedding, hard plastic, Wendy Ann, 1956, 8" ...500.00
Kathy Tears, vinyl, 11" 85.00
Kitty Baby, composition, 21".265.00
Letty Bridesmaid, composition, Tiny Betty, 7" 195.00
Little Colonel, composition, Betty, 1935, 9".......................300.00
Lucy Locket, straight legs, 1986-1989, 8" 55.00
Madame Doll, plastic & vinyl, Mary Ann, 14"..............450.00
Madelaine, composition, Wendy Ann, 1940, 14"..............350.00
Maid of Honor, composition, Wendy Ann, 18" 500.00
Marine, composition, 14"....475.00
Mary Muslin, cloth, pansy eyes, 1951, 19" 450.00
Muffin, cloth, 19"................150.00
Nina Ballerina, composition, Tiny Betty, 7".......................175.00
Orphan Annie, plastic & vinyl, Mary Ann, 14"..............400.00
Patty, plastic & vinyl, Melinda, 18"......................................475.00
Polly, Bride, plastic & vinyl, Maria, 17" 325.00
Posey Pet, cloth, 15" 400.00
Princess Elizabeth, composition, Tiny Betty, 7" 225.00
Pussy Cat, black, 14" 95.00
Red Cross Nurse, composition, Tiny Betty, 7" 175.00

Renoir Child, plastic & vinyl, Nancy Drew, 1967, 12"..**300.00**
Rozy, plastic & vinyl, Janie, 1969, 12".................................**450.00**
Scarlett O'Hara, composition, Little Betty, 7".................**225.00**

Madame Alexander 'Scarlett,' composition, 1939, 21", $1,200.00.

Sleeping Beauty, Princess Elizabeth, 15".......................**425.00**
Slumbermate, composition & cloth, 1940s, 21"............**500.00**
Switzerland, straight legs, Rosie, 8".....................................**100.00**
Tom Sawyer, hard plastic, Maggie Mixup, 8".........................**40.00**
Toulouse Lautrec, 1986-87 only, 21".....................................**325.00**
Turkey, hard plastic, bend knees, Wendy Ann, 8".............**135.00**
Virginia Dare, composition, Little Betty, 9"......................**225.00**

Mattel

Allen, Fraternity Meeting #1408, M.....................................**20.00**
Barbie, Beautiful Bride, 1st issue, M in box....................**95.00**

Barbie, Busy Barbie with Holdin' Hands, NM.....................**75.00**
Barbie, Dramatic New Living, 1971, M in box..............**78.00**
Barbie, Feelin' Groovy, M..**100.00**
Barbie, Gold Medal Skater, 1975, M in box.........................**38.00**
Barbie, Perfectly Plaid set #1193, talking, M in box..........**285.00**
Barbie, Sweet Sixteen, EX...**20.00**
Barbie, Wedding Party Gift Set #1017, M in box...........**425.00**
Brad, bendable legs, 1971, M in box................................**50.00**
Buffy & Mrs Beasley, 1968, M in box................................**65.00**
Captain Lazer, 12½", EX....**140.00**
Casey, blonde, twist 'n turn waist, M in box........................**100.00**
Clothes, Barbie in Mexico dress, with lace shawl.............**40.00**
Clothes, Barbie's, Satin 'N Rose dress, with hat..............**18.00**
Clothes, Barbie's Music Center Matinee suit, with hat, #1663, NM.....................**45.00**
Clothes, Barbie's Fashion Editor suit, with hat.................**25.00**
Clothes, Here Comes the Groom, #1426, NM.....................**75.00**
Clothes, Ken's Tuxedo, #787, M in box.................................**55.00**
Clothes, Midge's Orange Blossom dress, #987, EX.............**10.00**
Clothes, Skipper's Country Picnic dress, #1933.................**55.00**
Clothes, Skipper's Dreamtime pajamas, #1909, NM......**12.50**
Clothes, Sleeper Set, #0781, M in box................................**18.00**
Clothes, Sophisticated Lady, ball gown & long coat...........**45.00**
Clothes, Summer Job suit, #1422, NM.....................................**65.00**
Clothes, Tutti's Flower Girl dress, #3615, M.........................**20.00**
Dancerina, 24", M **45.00**
Francie, straight legs, swim suit, M in box........................**75.00**

Francie, With Growin' Pretty Hair, 1970, M in box **80.00**

Grandma Beans, 11", M **20.00**

Jamie, New 'N Wonderful, walker, 1970, M in box..............**115.00**

Kelly, Quick Curl, complete with all accessories, NM **55.00**

Ken, Arabian Nights set #074, M in box **195.00**

Ken, bendable legs, 1969, M in box.................................**55.00**

Ken, Canadian Sport Star, 1979, M in box.........................**32.00**

Ken, Live Action on Stage, 1971, M.....................................**70.00**

Ken, Play It Cool #1423, M...**25.00**

Ken, Talking, 1969, M **45.00**

Ken, 1961, M **80.00**

Kiddle Alice, in Wonderliddle case, EX **45.00**

Kiddle in baby carriage, M.**175.00**

Kiddle in ice cream cone, M..**20.00**

Kiddle Santa, M **50.00**

PJ, New 'N Groovy, talking, 1969, M in box.........................**75.00**

Ricky, Skipper's Friend, missing shoes, 1965, NM.............**55.00**

Skipper, Growing Up, original clothes, NM **35.00**

Skipper, Party Time Gift Set #1021, M in box............**185.00**

Steffie, Busy Steffie with Holdin' Hands, EX **65.00**

Tutti, Cookin' Goodies play set, M in box **135.00**

Tutti, Me & My Dog play set, M in box **165.00**

Remco

Dr John (of Little Chap Family), 14½", M...........................**50.00**

Jeannie (I Dream of), 6", M ..**15.00**

Libby (of Little Chap Family), 10½", EX........................**10.00**

Mimi, battery-operated singer, 19", M **35.00**

Tumbling Tomboy, 16, M.......**15.00**

Winking Heidi, M.................**10.00**

Shirley Temple

Bisque, Japan, 7½" **245.00**

Composition, 13", tagged dress with pin, 1930s.............**575.00**

Composition, 20", original clothes, EX **585.00**

Composition, 22", teeth, original dress, Ideal, 1934, NM .**650.00**

Composition, 27", flirty eyes, original, EX........................**900.00**

Shirley Temple baby, Ideal, composition, 1934, 16", $575.00.

Vinyl, 12", green & white dress, slip, Ideal, 1957, M **150.00**

Vinyl, 12", with 4 outfits, 1957, M in box **250.00**

Vinyl, 15", replaced clothes, Ideal, NM..............................**245.00**

Vinyl, 16", Stand Up & Cheer Dress, 1973, M in box ..**245.00**

Trolls

Bank, Dam, 7" **14.00**

Bobbin' head, Heinz, 1967 ....**50.00**

Caveman, small, M **35.00**
Cow **20.00**
Dam Things, 16" **30.00**
Dam Things, 6" **20.00**
Donkey....................................**65.00**
Giraffe.....................................**65.00**
Grandma & Grandpa, 1977, 13",
    each...............................**30.00**
Horse **65.00**
Laugh In, Sock It to Me, 6"...**55.00**
Monkey, M **55.00**
Playboy, 3" **12.50**
Santa, Bank...........................**25.00**
Tiny Tim, sitting **15.00**

Troll bank, 8", $16.00.

Turtle, Dam, 1964, 5" **55.00**
Unmarked, 12" **12.00**
Unmarked, 6" **8.00**

Uneeda

Anniversary Doll, 25", M **55.00**
Baby Dollikins, 21" **35.00**
Baby Trix, 16".......................**20.00**
Ballerina, vinyl, original clothes,
    14", NM..........................**15.00**
Ballerina, vinyl, 14" **22.50**
Bare Bottom Baby, 12" **20.00**
Blabby, 18"...........................**22.50**
Dollikins, 11" **20.00**
Fairy Princess, 32", M...........**75.00**
Freckles, 32" **70.00**

Freckles Marionette, 30" **65.00**
Lucky Lindy, 14" **275.00**
Pollyanna, 10½".....................**32.50**
Pollyanna, 17", M **45.00**
Pri-thilla, 12".........................**20.00**
Rita Hayworth, 14" **245.00**
Serenade, battery-operated talker,
    21"...................................**40.00**
Suzette, sleep eyes, 11½" **32.00**
Suzette, 10½"........................**40.00**
Tiny Teens, 5" **10.00**

Vogue

Baby Dear One, original clothes,
    NM................................**175.00**
Brickette, plastic, 2-piece, jointed
    waist, 22", M **95.00**
Ginny, Ginger of Debutante
    Series, hard plastic, all origi-
    nal, 8" **300.00**

Vogue, 'Ginny', hard plastic, #99, #100, #101, $225.00 each.

Ginny, hard plastic, sleep eyes,
    strung, redressed, 8"....**125.00**
Ginny Crib Crowd, bent leg,
    lamb's wool wig, original
    clothes, EX **500.00**

Ginny International, vinyl, all original, NM **35.00**
Ginny Toddles, composition, redressed, EX **95.00**
Jill, all original, 10" **55.00**
Lil Imp, 11", M **65.00**
Littlest Angel, plastic & vinyl, sleep eyes, all original, 15", NM **65.00**
Wee Imp, red wig, redressed, 8", EX **100.00**

Door Knockers

Figural door knockers were made in cast iron, often with painted-on colors, or brass–they're not easy to find and often bring high prices on today's market.

Parrot in oval, painted cast iron, 4", $45.00.

Cat, arched back, bronze, England, 1900, 3½" **40.00**
Cherub, cast iron with mother-of-pearl, for interior door .. **40.00**
Eagle, brass, EX **55.00**
Gargoyle, brass, large **30.00**
Grecian lady with basket of grapes on head, painted cast iron, 8" **75.00**

Indian head, brass, 7½" **125.00**
Lady's hand, brass **20.00**
Masonic emblem, brass **32.00**
Owl, painted cast iron, oval back, 4½" **125.00**
Rooster, painted cast iron, 1940s, 4¼x3" **150.00**

Doorstops

Doorstops, once called door porters, were popular from the Civil War period until after 1930. They were used to prop the doors open during the hot summer months so that the cooler air could circulate. Though some were made of brass, wood, and chalk, cast iron was by far the most preferred material, usually molded in amusing figurals–dogs, flower baskets, frogs, etc. Hubley was one of the largest producers.

Basket of Kittens, worn paint, M Rosenstein, '32, 10x7"..**250.00**
Bobby Blake, boy holds teddy, Hubley, 9½x5¼" **265.00**
Cat licking paw, Sculptured Metal Studios, 10¾"................**245.00**
Chinese Girl, cast iron with worn repaint, 7¾" **100.00**
Cosmos Vase, pastel flowers in white vase, Hubley, 18x10" **150.00**
Cricket, cast iron, Tri State Foundry, 10½" long **105.00**
Donald Duck, stop sign in hands, Disney, 8⅜x5¼" **155.00**
Elephant, trumpeting, Hubley, 8¼x12" **100.00**
Elk, wide antlers, rocky base, bronze finish, 11x10" ...**125.00**
French Bulldog, seated, cast iron with black & white porcelain finish, 7" **85.00**
George Washington, worn original paint, 12¼x6⅜" **250.00**
Gnome with Shovel, worn original paint, 9½x4½"...............**225.00**

Huckleberry Finn, worn paint, Littco, 12½x9½"............**325.00**
Jonquil, yellow flowers, Hubley #453, 7x6"...................**110.00**
Lobster, claws held high, black paint, 12½x6½ "...........**225.00**
Messenger Boy, holds bouquet, worn original paint, Hubley, 10x5⅜"..........................**225.00**
Owl, fine feather details, B&H #7797, 15½x5"..............**265.00**
Parrot on stump, old paint, glass eye, National Foundry, 10¾x6¾"......................**100.00**
Rabbit from Alice in Wonderland, original paint, 10"........**150.00**
Red Riding Hood & Wolf, worn original paint...............**290.00**
Sunbonnet Girl, billowing dress, faces left, 9x5½"..........**175.00**
Turkey, cast iron with multicolor repaint, 12".....................**65.00**
Whippet, stands, faces right, worn paint, 6¼x7½"................**65.00**
Wolfhound, cast iron, worn repaint, full figure, 15½" long ...**115.00**

Pointer Spaniel, painted cast iron, minor wear, 15" long, $115.00.

Farm Collectibles

Farming memorabilia is a specialized area of primitives that is of particular interest to those wishing to preserve the memory of farm life when horses drew the plow and steam engines ran the thrashers, when 'hands' were called to noon-time 'dinner' by the ringing of the dinner bell, and work days began at three in the morning. Today, cast iron implement seats make stools for the family room bar; and scythes, wagon wheels, and oxen yokes are almost commonplace on restaurant walls.

Barn hinge, wrought iron, rattail pintel spikes, 7", pair **27.50**
Bee smoker, copper, poor leather on bellows......................**65.00**

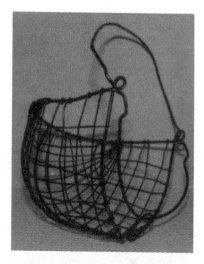

Calf muzzle, wireware restrainer, $25.00.

Corn dryer, twisted wire, 50 prongs, 1900, 37" long....**37.50**
Corn grater, curved hand-punched tin on 10x8" pine board..............................**75.00**
Corn sheller, hand held, primitive, 28" long **65.00**
Egg box, solid wood, bail handle, lid, old paint, 1900, EX..**65.00**
Gimbet, wooden hog stretcher, 28" long **40.00**
Harness hook, iron, 10" **12.50**
Implement seat, Bradley's Mower, cast iron........................**100.00**
Implement seat, Kingman, cast iron, plain **38.00**

Implement seat, McCormick, cast
iron, plain **35.00**
Implement seat, Walter A Wood,
cast iron, fancy **85.00**
Lantern, wood with tin front,
kerosene burner, 11" **150.00**
Milking stool, 3 stick legs, pegged,
hewn **55.00**
Scoop, grain; wood, 1-piece ...**80.00**
Seed dryer, chestnut frame with
pine spindles, 21x43" **75.00**
Sharpening stone, cast iron,
hand-cranked wheel, Deering
Harvester **49.00**
Winnowing tray, pine with
punched dark tin back,
18x22x5" **165.00**
Yoke, goose style, hewn hickory &
chestnut, 1830s, 12".....**130.00**
Yoke, ox; curly maple, 1-piece,
54", EX.........................**250.00**

Fast Food Collectibles

Everyone is familiar with the
glass tumblers offered by fast-food
resturants, but perhaps you didn't
realize that they are becoming
one of the new fun collectibles on
today's market. Though plentiful
today, as you may have already
noticed, plastic items are beginning to be seen more often than in
the past; and when glass items
are featured, they're seldom
free–in fact their prices are rising.
Only buy examples with bright
unfaded colors and perfectly exe-
cuted printing.

Glass, Camp Snoopy collection,
McDonald's, 1983, 6", set of 5,
ea **2.00**
Glass, Dairy Queen, Little Miss
Dairy Queen, 1970s, 5⅝". **2.50**
Glass, Dallas Cowboys/Dr Pep-
per, Burger King, 1977, 5⅝",
ea **3.50**

**Pepsi Super Series (moon set)
tumblers: Supergirl or Wonder-
woman, $10.00 each.**

Glass, Domino's Pizza, 3 Domino's
Pizza logos, frosted, 4¼". **2.50**
Glass, Endangered Species series,
Burger Chef, 1978, set of 4,
ea **6.00**
Glass, ET series, Pizza Hut, 1982,
6", set of 4, ea **2.00**
Glass, Looney Tunes series, Arby's,
1980, 6", set of 6, ea.......... **4.00**
Glass, McVote '86, McDonald's,
5⅞", set of 3, ea................ **6.00**
Glass, Norman Rockwell Winter
Scenes, Arby's, 1979, 4", set of
4, ea **3.50**
Glass, Popples, Pizza Hut, 1986,
5⅞", set of 4, ea **3.00**
Glass, Seattle Seahawks, McDon-
ald's, 1978 & 1979, set of 4,
ea..................................... **3.50**
Glass, Smurfs, Hardee's, 1982,
5⅞", set of 4, ea................ **2.00**
Glass, Star Trek III, Taco Bell,
1984, 5⅝", set of 4, ea...... **3.75**
Glass, Star Wars, Burger King,
Coca-Cola logo, 1977, set of 4,
ea..................................... **6.50**
Glass, The Chipmunks, Hardee's,
1985, 5⅞", set of 4, ea...... **3.50**
Glass, The Empire Strikes Back
series, Burger King, 1980, set
of 4, ea............................. **2.75**
Glass, Wendy's, Bicentennial,
red/white/blue, limited edi-
tion, 5" **6.00**

Glass, Ziggy, Hardee's, 1979, 6",
set of 4, ea........................ **3.50**

Mug, Arby's, green letters on
stained glass design, milk
glass, 3"........................... **2.50**

Mug, Burger Chef, Breakfast at
Burger Chef logo, milk glass,
early............................... **3.00**

Mug, McDonald's, black with
McDonald's in gold script,
ceramic, 3⅝" **7.00**

Sundae cup/glass, Dairy Queen,
flowerpot form, red logo.. **2.50**

Fenton

The Fenton glass company,
organized in 1906 in Martin's
Ferry, Ohio, is noted for their fine
art glass. Over 130 patterns of
carnival glass were made in their
earlier years (see Carnival Glass),
but even items from the past 25
years of production (Hobnail,
Burmese, and the various colored
'crest' lines) have collector value.

**Bicentennial mug, paper sticker,
6¾", $32.50.**

Aqua Crest, basket with handle,
#1924, 5" **85.00**

Aqua Crest, bowl, fruit **40.00**

Aqua Crest, cup & saucer, ca
1950s.............................**35.00**

Aqua Crest, vase, 3½"...........**32.00**

Baby Thumbprint, rose bowl,
3½ " **35.00**

Basketweave, nappy, topaz
opalescent......................**20.00**

Beaded Melon, basket, gold over-
lay, 7" **75.00**

Beaded Melon, rose bowl, rose
overlay, 4" **40.00**

Beaded Melon, vase, gold overlay,
3½"..................................**30.00**

Beaded Melon, vase, green overlay, tulip form, 9" **35.00**

Blue Overlay, pitcher, 8½" ...**42.00**

Burmese, basket, 6¾x7¾" **45.00**

Coin Dot, basket, blue opalescent,
7" **65.00**

Crystal Crest, plate, 10¼" **28.00**

Daisy & Button, bonbon, milk
glass, 5½".......................**11.00**

Daisy & Button, creamer, Colonial
blue **16.00**

Diamond Optic, pitcher, cran-
berry, 6" **75.00**

Diamond Optic, sherbet, ruby,
footed **9.00**

Dolphin, bowl, jade green, #1608,
10½" **70.00**

Dolphin, candlestick, red, 3½",
pair **35.00**

Ebony, ice bucket **75.00**

Emerald Crest, comport, footed,
3¾x7" diameter **25.00**

Emerald Crest, flowerpot **75.00**

Figurine, swan, blue **25.00**

Georgian, sugar bowl, ruby ..**14.00**

Gold Crest, vase, triangular,
#180, with label, 8" **25.00**

Hobnail, ash tray, French opalescent, 5¼" **22.00**

Hobnail, basket, topaz opalescent,
#3837, 7" **55.00**

Hobnail, bowl, blue opalescent,
10"..................................**65.00**

Hobnail, bowl, French opalescent, #389, 11".........................**60.00**

Hobnail, candy box, French opalescent, with lid........**35.00**

Hobnail, syrup jug, milk glass, 12-ounce..............................**20.00**

Hobnail, vase, cranberry opalescent, 4½"..........................**32.00**

Hobnail vase, cranberry opalescent, 10¾", $95.00.

Hobnail, vase, green opalescent, tricorn, miniature..........**20.00**

Ivy, bowl, ruby overlay, footed, #1021.............................**55.00**

Jade Green, vase, straight sides, 8"...................................**30.00**

Lilac Cased, shell bowl, #9020, 10"...................................**95.00**

Lincoln Inn, tumbler, cobalt, footed, 6"..........................**22.00**

Mandarin Red, bowl, footed, cupped, 7½"....................**45.00**

Mandarin Red, vase, flared, #621, 6"...................................**70.00**

Ming, basket, green..............**95.00**

Ming, jar, macaroon; green, reeded handle..............**125.00**

Mongolian Green, vase, fan form, 6"....................................**45.00**

Peach Crest, vase, tricorn, #187, 6"....................................**20.00**

Peach Crest, vase, tulip, #7250, 9"....................................**50.00**

Rose Crest, vase, 5"...............**22.00**

Ruby, bowl, flower form, #848, 9" diameter.........................**25.00**

San Toy, vase, etched, #898, ca 1936, 11½"......................**60.00**

Silver Crest, banana boat **20.00**

Silver Crest, cake plate, low footed, 13".......................**27.00**

Silver Crest/Spanish Lace, cake stand, footed, 11"............**40.00**

Silver Turquoise, plate, 8½"..**30.00**

Spiral Optic, bottle, bitters; cranberry opalescent...........**115.00**

Spiral Optic, vase, blue opalescent, flared, 10"..............**65.00**

Spiral Optic, vase, cranberry, 8⅜x8¾"..........................**110.00**

Spiral Optic, vase, French opalescent, 6"..........................**30.00**

Vasa Murrhina, vase, rose/green aventurine, 11"............**100.00**

Fiesta

Since it was discontinued by Homer Laughlin in 1973, Fiesta has become one of the most popular collectibles on the market. Values have continued to climb until some of the more hard to find items now sell for several hundred dollars each. In 1986, HLC re-introduced a line of new Fiesta that buyers should be aware of. To date, these colors have been used: cobalt (darker than the original), rose (a strong pink), black, white, apricot (very pale tan-peach), yellow (a light creamy tone), turquoise and a country blue they call periwinkle. When old molds were used, the mark will be the same. The ink stamp differs from the old–all the letters are upper case.

'Original color' in the listings indicate values for four of the original six colors–ivory, light green, turquoise, and yellow.

Ash tray, '50s colors **50.00**
Ash tray, red or cobalt...........**40.00**
Bowl, cream soup with handles; '50s colors **40.00**
Bowl, dessert; 6", '50s colors...**35.00**
Bowl, large footed salad; original colors............................**160.00**
Bowl, large footed salad; red or cobalt **190.00**
Bowl, fruit; shallow, 11¼", red or cobalt **140.00**
Bowl, fruit; 4¾", '50s colors ..**22.00**
Bowl, fruit; 4¾", turquoise....**18.00**
Bowl, fruit; 5½", medium green, rare **50.00**
Bowl, fruit; 5½", red **22.00**
Bowl, mixing; 10", Kitchen Kraft, light green or yellow **60.00**
Bowl, mixing; 10", Kitchen Kraft, red or cobalt **70.00**
Bowl, mixing; 6", Kitchen Kraft, light green or yellow **32.00**
Bowl, mixing; 8", Kitchen Kraft, red or cobalt **60.00**
Bowl, nappy; 8½", rose..........**35.00**
Bowl, onion soup; cobalt **270.00**
Bowl, Tom & Jerry, ivory with gold letters **120.00**
Cake plate, Kitchen Kraft, red or cobalt **40.00**
Cake server, Kitchen Kraft, red or cobalt **65.00**
Candle holder, bulb; original colors, pair **50.00**
Carafe, original colors.........**115.00**
Casserole, '50s colors **165.00**
Casserole, individual; Kitchen Kraft, red or cobalt **100.00**
Casserole, medium green ...**240.00**
Casserole, original colors......**75.00**
Casserole, 8½", Kitchen Kraft, light green or yellow **65.00**

Casserole, 8½", Kitchen Kraft, red or cobalt........................**75.00**
Coffeepot, '50s colors...........**160.00**
Coffeepot, demitasse; stick handle red or cobalt **165.00**
Compote, 12", red or cobalt...**75.00**
Covered jar, large; Kitchen Kraft, light green or yellow **160.00**
Covered jar, medium; Kitchen Kraft, light green **150.00**
Covered jar, small; Kitchen Kraft, red or cobalt **145.00**
Covered jug, red or cobalt...**165.00**
Creamer, '50s colors **20.00**
Creamer, individual; yellow..**40.00**
Creamer, medium green **35.00**
Creamer, stick handle, original colors............................**22.00**
Cup, demi; '50s colors **115.00**
Cup, demi; red or cobalt........**40.00**

Egg cup, red, $40.00.

Fork, Kitchen Kraft, light green or yellow **45.00**
Fork, Kitchen Kraft, red.......**50.00**
Gravy boat, original colors ...**28.00**
Lid, for mixing bowl #4.......**300.00**
Marmalade, original colors.**100.00**
Marmalade, red or cobalt ...**135.00**
Metal frame for platter, Kitchen Kraft **20.00**
Mixing bowl, #1 nesting, red or cobalt **75.00**

Mixing bowl, #3 nesting, red or cobalt 55.00
Mixing bowl, #4 nesting, original colors............................50.00
Mixing bowl, #4 nesting, red or cobalt 55.00
Mixing bowl, #7 nesting, original colors............................125.00
Mug, Tom & Jerry; rose 60.00
Pie plate, 10", Kitchen Kraft, light green or yellow...............35.00
Pie plate, 9", Kitchen Kraft, red or cobalt 35.00
Pitcher, disk juice; gray 600.00
Pitcher, disk water; medium green 150.00
Pitcher, disk water; red.........85.00
Pitcher, jug, 2-pt; yellow 38.00
Plate, cake; original colors..300.00
Plate, calendar; 1955, 9" 35.00
Plate, chop; 15", '50s colors ..45.00
Plate, chop; 15", yellow 25.00
Plate, compartment; 10½", original colors 20.00
Plate, deep; '50s colors.........35.00
Plate, 10", medium green 55.00
Plate, 6", red or cobalt............ 5.00
Plate, 9", medium green 30.00
Plate, 9", original colors......... 7.50
Platter, '50s colors.................32.00
Platter, original colors 20.00
Refrigerator unit, Kitchen Kraft, light green or yellow 30.00
Saucer, demi; original colors 10.00
Saucer, '50s colors 5.00
Saucer, medium green 7.50
Saucer, red or cobalt 3.50
Shakers, Kitchen Kraft, red or cobalt, pair 70.00
Shakers, medium green, pr .48.00
Spoon, Kitchen Kraft, red or cobalt 52.00
Stacking refrigerator lid, Kitchen Kraft, red or cobalt 45.00
Sugar bowl, with lid, 3¼x3½", original colors................17.00
Sugar bowl, with lid, 3¼x3½", '50s colors..............................35.00
Syrup, original colors..........165.00

Teacup, '50s colors.................28.00
Teapot, large, yellow 80.00
Teapot, medium; '50s colors150.00
Teapot, medium; red 90.00
Tray, figure-8; yellow 150.00
Tray, relish; no red 130.00

Tripod candle holders, cobalt, $225.00 for the pair.

Tumbler, juice; chartreuse, Harlequin yellow or dark green............................160.00
Tumbler, juice; red or cobalt ..28.00
Tumbler, water; ivory............35.00
Vase, bud; ivory 38.00
Vase, bud; red or cobalt........50.00
Vase, 8", original colors 265.00
Vase, 8", red or cobalt 350.00

Finch, Kay

From 1939 until 1963, Kay Finch and her husband, Braden, operated a small pottery in Corona Del Mar, California, where they produced figurines of animals, birds, and exotic couples as well as some dinnerware. Most items are marked.

Ash tray, dog's head, hand-painted details 20.00
Bank, Panda figural, 9" 35.00
Cookie Jar, Pup, pink, hand-painted details, 12¾" ..150.00
Figurine, camel, 5" 50.00
Figurine, Chanticleer, hand-painted details, 10½" ...115.00

Figurine, Godey couple, 7½", hand-painted details pair **75.00**
Figurine, Madonna with bowed head, hand-painted, 7" ..**45.00**
Figurine, owl, hand-painted details, 3¾" **20.00**
Figurine, penguin family, hand painted, set of 3 ....**85.00**
Figurine, pig, standing, pink, hand-painted details, 4" .**25.00**
Figurine, rabbit, hand-painted details, 2½x4" **30.00**
Wall mask, Grecian man & lady, pink lustre with gold, 10", pair................................**115.00**

Fire Fighting Collectibles

Fire fighting squads from the early 19th century were made up of volunteers; their only pay was reward money donated by the homeowner whose property they had saved. By 1860, cities began to organize municipal fire departments. Much pomp and ceremony was displayed by the brigade during parade festivities. Fancy belts, silver trumpets, and brightly-colored jackets were the uniform of the day. Today these are treasured by collectors who also search for fire marks, posters, photographs of engines and water wagons, and equipment of all types.

Alarm bell, Edwards, with cast iron box, electric **190.00**
Alarm bell, gong style, Gamewell, in oak case, 6" **575.00**
Alarm bell, Western Electric, double **65.00**
Alarm box, Gamewell, Telegraph Station, 1880s **75.00**
Badge, sterling, fireman with ladder, hook, & hydrant......**50.00**

Badge, Veteran Fireman Association of Westerly, RI, EX .**30.00**
Baton, wood shaft with nickel & brass top, 52"................**150.00**
Book, American Fire Marks, illustrated, 1933, 133-page...**16.00**
Book, The Salem Fire, Arthur B Jones, 1914, 137-page....**20.00**
Booklet, An Analysis of Firefighting, 1945, 16-page, EX.... **6.00**
Booklet, Constitution & By-Laws of Cumberland Fire Co, 26-page................................. **9.00**
Bucket, 1st-Church Chancy-Place 1821, leather, repaint ..**125.00**
Calendar, Sun Fire Office of London, US Branch, 1888....**28.00**
Card, fire equipment in color on white, 1880s, 2x4", VG.... **7.50**
Chemical fire cart, from factory, with 25" hose & brass nozzle, EX **650.00**
Coloring book, Fire Engines, Trucks, & Trains, EX **18.50**
Extinguisher, Acme Dry Chemical Fire Extinguisher, 22" ...**25.00**
Grenade, glass in original metal holder, EX......................**35.00**
Hatchet, wooden handle with nickel-plated head, hooks, & base **120.00**
Helmet, Engine I, MFD, red leather, brass shield, Cairn & Bros, EX **195.00**
Lantern, brass, Dietz King, original bracket, M..............**500.00**
Lantern, Dietz King, tin & copper with clear globe..............**45.00**
Mirror, Liberty Fire Co No 5, Reading, PA, fire station in color **47.50**
Nozzle, double handle, Akron Brass Mfg, 16"..............**135.00**
Nozzle, fog; nickel-plated, marked 4A Fog Noz, 7½" **17.50**
Photograph, member of Mansfield Fire Dept in uniform......**18.00**
Print, Rescue of John Wesley, framed, 29x37"............**400.00**

Program, 3rd Annual Ball, Washington Fire Dept, 1887...**26.00**
Puzzle, engine with steamer in color, framed, 9½x8½"....**26.00**
Sheet music, The Fireman's Polka, by Dressler **32.00**

Wristlet candle lantern, red paint on tin, 4 glass panels, VG, $200.00.

Fireplace Accessories

From the primitive cooking utensils of the early years of our country to the elegant Federal brass andirons, fireplace accessories (while rarely collected in that particular context) are purchased for reasons as varied as the items themselves. Screens, fire fenders, bellows, and the like may be needed to furnish a period room, while simple items such as gypsy pots, trivets, and firebacks may be put to a decorative use for which they were never intended.

Andirons, cast iron figurals, early 20th century, 16½", $1,200.00.

Andirons, bell metal, cylindrical with arch spur legs, 1820s, pair **250.00**
Andirons, brass, EX detail, 1820s, 20½", pair **465.00**
Andirons, fitted with mug holders, swivel arm, wrought, 1950s, 32".....................**300.00**
Bellows, fruit/leaves on mustard leather, 1810, EX **245.00**
Broiler, wrought iron, rotating, 12" diameter with long handle **180.00**
Fender, brass, paw feet, grillwork sides, 9½ x47"..............**165.00**
Fender, brass, pierced decoration, late 1800s, 46"..............**165.00**
Hearth broom, turned handle with black paint, red & gold foliage, 22" **135.00**
Hearth brush, horsehair, painted wooden handle, 23"........**40.00**
Kettle shelf, cast iron, pierced top, 10x18".............................**65.00**
Toaster, heavy wire, 2 large loops, wooden handle **55.00**
Toaster, rotating, wrought iron with 4 arches, flat handle, 1700s, EX **260.00**
Trammel, wrought iron, sawtooth, PA, 1700s, 30" **95.00**

Fishing Collectibles

Very much in evidence at flea markets these days, old fishing gear is becoming a popular collectible. Because the hobby is newly established, there are some very good buys to be found. Early 20th-century plugs were almost entirely carved from wood, sprayed with several layers of enamel, and finished off with glass eyes. Molded plastics were of a later origin. Some of the more collectible manufacturers are James Heddon, Shakespeare, Rhodes, and Pfueger.

Book, The Angler's Handy Book, by Lake Brooks, 1912 ..... **5.00**
Book, Travel Diary of an Angler, by Van Dyke, 1929 ....**70.00**
Button, pin-back; New York Hunting, Trapping, & Fishing, 1939 .... **6.00**
Button, pin-back; Pennsylvania, 1943, 1¼" **6.50**
Catalog, Creek Chub 1942....**40.00**

Catalog, Pfleuger, 1928........**35.00**
Fly rod, bamboo, 2 tips, M in original case..........................**75.00**
Lure, Creek Chub, 1925 Midget Pikie, 1 glass eye............. **5.00**
Lure, Creek Chub Baby Pikie Minnow, glass eyes.......... **8.00**
Lure, Creek Chub Darter, painted eyes, wood........................ **5.00**
Lure, Creek Chub Sucker, glass eyes, wood **150.00**
Lure, Heddon's Coast Minnow #630, crackle back, hook missing **200.00**
Lure, Heddon's Dowagiac Minnow #100, yellow with black & red stripes.............................**85.00**
Lure, K&K Minnowette, jointed body, metal tail, 3½" **325.00**
Lure, Pfleuger Monarch, green crackle back, 1 eye, 3-hook model **20.00**
Lure, Pfleuger Monarch Minnow, glass eyes, 3-hook model, 3½"..**35.00**
Lure, Pfleuger Portage Reflex, yellow, 1907-type, 3⅝" ...**12.50**
Lure, Shakespeare, Evolution, ca 1910, 3" **50.00**

John Dineen's 1911 Spinning Minnow, copper, 3⅜", in original box, $275.00.

Lure, Shakespeare, frog skin bait, glass eyes, 3¾" **65.00**
Lure, Winchester, glass eyes, 2-hook model **150.00**
Magazine, Fisherman's Journal, 1932, May 20, Oakland, California **6.50**
Painting, Two Hanging Fish, by Lasse, oil on canvas, 1919, 16x24" **90.00**
Poster, US Line Co, 2 men fishing from boat, 26x14"..........**35.00**
Reel, Ambassadeur Bait Caster #6000, level wind, free spool, EX...............................**60.00**
Reel, Pflueger Sal-Trout #1555, EX **9.00**
Reel, Shakespeare Tru-Art #1836, automatic....................... **7.50**
Reel, South Bend #1110, 3½". **6.50**
Reel, Winchester #1235, black finish over brass, 2⅝".........**50.00**
Rod, Heddon Black Beauty, bamboo, 9-foot **75.00**
Rod, Orvis-Impregnated, 2-piece, maroon wraps, 7-foot **40.00**
Rod, Heddon, 3-piece, 2 tips, maroon wraps, 8½-foot .**70.00**
Tackle box, Kennedy, metal..**15.00**

Florence Ceramics

Produced in California during the 1940s and '50s, these lovely figurines of beautiful ladies and handsome men have recently become items of much collector interest. Boxes, lamps, planters, and plaques were also made. Values are based on size, rarity, and intricacy of design.

Abigail **95.00**
Adeline...................................**125.00**
Amelia...................................**95.00**
Angel **45.00**
Ann **30.00**
Bea, planter...........................**55.00**
Camille **85.00**

Camile, 8½", $85.00; With applied lace and flowers, add approximately $20.00.

Charmaine **95.00**
Charmaine, with bow & lace on umbrella **110.00**
Clarissa................................**75.00**
David **80.00**
Delia **70.00**
Delores.................................**95.00**
Grace **115.00**
Kay **75.00**
Lantern Boy **40.00**
Matilda **85.00**
Melanie.................................**75.00**
Mikey **60.00**
Molly, planter **40.00**
Roberta **125.00**
Sarah **95.00**

Fostoria

Fostoria has been called the largest producer of handmade glassware in the world. One of their most famous lines was their American pattern, which was introduced in 1915 and continued in production until the plant closed in 1986. They also produced lamps and figures of animals and birds.

American, ash tray, crystal, square, 5".........................25.00
American, bottle, water; crystal, 44-oz, 9".......................275.00
American, bowl, fruit; crystal, 3-footed, 10" 15.00
American, hair receiver, crystal, 3x3"..............................100.00
Baroque, bowl, punch; crystal, footed 250.00
Baroque, mayonnaise, blue, with liner, 5½" 35.00
Baroque, plate, torte; yellow, 14" diameter 25.00
Baroque, vase, yellow, 7" 38.00
Century, basket, crystal, wicker handled, 10x7" 55.00
Century, comport, crystal, footed, 4" 14.00
Century, ice bucket, crystal ..45.00

Coin Glass candy jar, ruby, 13",
$110.00.

Colony, ash tray, crystal, 3" .10.00
Colony, bowl, salad; crystal, 8" diameter 20.00
Colony, comport, crystal, with lid, 6½" 30.00
Fairfax, bowl, bonbon; blue ..13.00
Fairfax, sauce boat, blue 30.00
Fairfax, sugar pail, orchid 40.00
Fairfax, whipped cream pail, green 28.00
June, ash tray, blue..............45.00
June, bowl, finger; topaz, with liner 45.00
June, comport, blue, 7" 65.00
June, grapefruit liner, blue...50.00
June, ice bucket, rose...........75.00
June, vase, blue, 8" 165.00
Kashmir, bowl, cream soup; yellow 22.00
Kashmir, ice bucket, green ...65.00
Kashmir, plate, green, 10"....35.00
Kashmir, salt & pepper shakers, yellow, pr 90.00
Navarre, pickle dish, crystal, #2440, 8½" 22.00
Navarre, plate, cracker; crystal, #2496, 11" 40.00
Navarre, relish, crystal, #2419, 5-part, 13¼" 35.00
Royal, bowl, nappy, amber, #2350, 9" 30.00
Royal, candlestick, amber, #2324, 4" 14.00
Royal, egg cup, green, #2350..18.00
Trojan, ash tray, topaz, sm ...23.00
Trojan, candlestick, rose, 5" .20.00
Trojan, goblet, wine; topaz, 3-oz, 5½ " 40.00
Trojan, mayonnaise, rose, with liner 30.00
Trojan, sugar pail, rose.........95.00
Versailles, bonbon; blue........20.00
Versailles, candlestick, blue, 5", pr 60.00
Versailles, comport, blue, 8" ...75.00
Versailles, ice bucket, yellow..75.00
Versailles, plate, luncheon; blue, 8¾" 10.00
Versailles, vase, blue, 8" 150.00

American, double-arm candle holder, $30.00.

Versailles, whipped cream pail, green 85.00
Vesper, comport, blue, 8" 50.00
Vesper, platter, green, 12".....35.00
Vesper, sugar bowl, amber, with lid 125.00
Vesper, vase, blue, 8" 110.00

Fountain Pens

Fountain pens have been manufactured commercially since the 1880s. Today's collectors value those made by well-known companies such as Waterman, Parker, and Sheaffer's, or those made of gold or set with jewels. Various types of pumping mechanisms were employed.

Chilton, 1926, green jade marble, touchdown filler, EX 72.50
Conklin, Glider, 1940, gold/silver marble, EX 45.00
Eberhard Faber, 1945, black, NM................................... 5.00
Eclipse, 1927, gold-filled metal & trim, lever filler, G 70.00

Moore, L-92, 1925, black chased hard rubber, EX 47.50
Moore, 1934, black, gold-filled trim, lever filler, EX.......95.00
Nardi, Tri-Color, 1927, magenta, NM................................50.00
Parker, Deluxe, 1937, black, nickeled trim, M 60.00
Parker, Vacumatic desk, 1936, nickeled trim, EX...........78.00
Parker, VS, 1947, blue with Lustralow cap, back filler 45.00
Parker, 51 Special, 1950, blue with chrome cap, aeromatic filler, M 62.00
Sheaffer's, Lifetime, 1928, jade green marble, EX 65.00
Sheaffer's, Lifetime Vigilant 500, 1942, gold pearl stripe ...70.00
Sheaffer's, Lifetime 875, 1939, black, EX 60.00
Sheaffer's, Statesman Snorkel, 1955, green, touchdown filler, NM................................47.50
Sheaffer's, Triumph, 1951, black, touchdown filler, EX 70.00
Sheaffer's, Triumph Lifetime, 1942, golden pearl, lever filler, EX 90.00

Sheaffer's, Tuckaway, 1947, brown, gold-filled trim ...**50.00**
Sheaffer's, White Dot Statesman Tuckaway, 1948, black ...**50.00**
Sheaffer's, White Dot Triumph, 1949, touchdown filler ..**60.00**
Sheaffer's, White Dot Tuckaway, 1948, black, EX **50.00**
Sheaffer's, 3-25, 1923, black chased hard rubber, EX.**50.00**
Sheaffer's, 350, 1934, gold pearl stripe, EX **36.00**
Wahl-Eversharp, Skyline, 1946, brown, EX......................**50.00**
Wahl-Eversharp, 1931, green jade marble, EX **60.00**
Waterman, 1945, silver pearl marble, EX **40.00**
Waterman Ideal, #52, 1922, black chased hard rubber, lever filler, G..........................**60.00**
Waterman Ideal, #52½V, 1918, chased hard rubber, nickeled trim, G **26.00**
Waterman Ideal, 1925, red ripple hard rubber, EX **40.00**

Franciscan

Dinnerware has been made by Gladding McBean and Company from 1934 until the present day. Their earlier lines have become popular collectibles, especially Coronado (Swirl) which was made in more than sixty shapes and fifteen solid colors; and Apple, the ivory line with the red apple on the branch whose design was purchased from the Weller Pottery. During the 1930s the ware was marked with a large 'F' in a double-walled square; a two-line mark was used in the 1940s, and after 1947 a circular mark identified their product.

Apple, ash tray, individual ...**10.00**
Apple, bowl, lug handle, sm..**14.00**

Apple, casserole, stick handle, 12-oz.....................................**20.00**
Apple, coaster, 3¾" **15.00**
Apple, compote, lg **25.00**
Coronado, bowl, vegetable; serving, oval **25.00**
Coronado, bowl, vegetable; serving, round **13.00**
Coronado, cigarette box **35.00**
Coronado, creamer & sugar bowl, with cover **28.00**
Coronado, plate, chop; 14" **20.00**
Coronado, plate, 8½" **10.00**
Coronado, platter, 15½" **28.00**
Coronado, saucer for cream soup bowl................................ **6.00**
Coronado, sherbet **9.00**
Desert Rose, bowl, batter **35.00**

Desert Rose, tea canister, ca 1982, $50.00; Round box, ca 1982, $27.50.

Desert Rose, bowl, soup **14.00**
Desert Rose, bowl, vegetable; with cover................................**35.00**
Desert Rose, coffeepot...........**45.00**
Desert Rose, pickle dish, 10"..**28.00**
Desert Rose, plate, chop; 14" .**50.00**
Desert Rose, platter, 12½" ...**30.00**
El Patio, bowl, cereal **10.00**
El Patio, bowl, fruit **9.00**
El Patio, bowl, salad; 3-qt.....**22.00**
El Patio, butter dish **28.00**
El Patio, creamer **8.00**
El Patio, cup **8.00**
El Patio, gravy boat, attached underplate **24.00**
El Patio, plate, 10½" **12.00**
El Patio, saucer, jumbo **6.00**

El Patio, sherbet **9.00**
El Patio, sugar bowl **15.00**
El Patio, teapot, 6-cup **35.00**
Fine China, bowl, vegetable; serving, oval **45.00**
Fine China, plate, bread & butter, 6½" **15.00**
Fine China, plate, salad **18.00**

Frankoma

Since 1933, the Frankoma Pottery Company has been producing dinnerware, novelty items, vases, etc. In 1965 they became the first American company to produce a line of collector plates. The body of the ware prior to 1954 was a honey tan color. A brick red clay was used from then on, and this and the colors of the glazes help determine the period of production.

Ash tray, black, #30...............**30.00**
Ash tray, cigar; #455, 1934-1957, 5" **18.00**
Bookend, Bucking Bronco, #423, 5½", pair **135.00**
Bookend, Leopard, Ada clay, #421, 1934-1942, 5x9" **100.00**
Bookend, Walking Ocelot, #424, each **200.00**
Bowl, ball form, pedestal footed, #42, 6½" **20.00**
Bowl, Texas, Ada clay, 1957..**20.00**

Button, non-production item, rare **15.00**
Candle holder, square, #307, 1942, pair **30.00**
Christmas card, 1944.........**100.00**
Christmas card, 1950-1951 .**70.00**
Christmas card, 1955-1956 .**70.00**
Christmas card, 1957...........**65.00**
Christmas card, 1969-1971 .**30.00**
Creamer & sugar bowl, #87-A & #87-B, 1942-1953 ....**15.00**
Donkey mug, Centennial Red, 1976 ....**20.00**
Elephant mug, Prairie Green, 1972 ....**38.00**
Grease jar, with lid, #46, 1938, 3¾" **18.00**
Lamp base, from Wagon Wheel sugar bowl **45.00**
Pitcher, Autumn Yellow, 2-qt .**10.00**
Pitcher, Snail, Old Gold, miniature **10.00**
Planter, Madonna of Grace, #231-B, 6" **35.00**
Plaque, Buffalo.....................**35.00**
Plaque, Will Rogers, with border, Prairie Green, Ada clay .**25.00**
Rose jar, with lid, #32, 1934-1938, 5¼" **95.00**
Sculpture, Bull, #166, 2" **40.00**
Sculpture, Dreamer Girl, Sorghum **85.00**
Sculpture, Fawns, #100-#101, 8", pair **30.00**
Sculpture, Pekingese Dog, #112, 7¾" **175.00**

Figure of a greyhound, ivory, 14" long, $50.00.

135

Shakers, Gracetone, Cinnamon, egg form, 3½", pair........**25.00**
Shakers, Pumas, #165-H, 3", pair **45.00**
Swan, #228, open tail, 7½" ...**25.00**
Trivet, American Eagle, #AETR, 1976-1978 .... **5.00**
Tumbler, juice; #90-C, 1938-1965, 3-oz, 2½" **3.00**
Vase, #505, 1950-1951, 2¾" .**15.00**
Vase, collector; V-1, Prairie Green, 1969, 15" **45.00**
Vase, collector; V-12, 1980 ....**35.00**
Vase, flat, #40, 6"...................**35.00**
Vase, Frank Potteries, #501 .**150.00**
Vase, Modeled, #74, 9" **35.00**
Vase, Swan, #168, 3".............**55.00**
Wall pocket, Acorn, Ada clay, #190, 6"...........................**20.00**
Wall pocket, Leaf, #197, 9" ...**35.00**
Wall pocket, Negro, late 1930s, 2½" **85.00**
Wall pocket, Phoebe, Prairie Green, Ada clay, #730 ....**75.00**
Wall pocket, Wagon Wheel, Prairie Green **15.00**

Fruit Jars

Some of the earliest glass jars used for food preservation were blown, and corks were used for seals. During the 19th century, hundreds of manufacturers designed over 4,000 styles of fruit jars. Lids were held in place either by a wax seal, wire bail, or the later screw-on band. Jars were usually made in aqua or clear, though other colors were also used. Amber jars are popular with collectors, milk glass jars are rare, and cobalt and black glass jars often bring $3,000.00 and up if they can be found! Condition, age, scarcity and unusual features are also to be considered when evaluating old fruit jars.

Acme (on shield with stars & stripes), clear, pint **1.00**
Atlas E-Z Seal, green with aqua lid, quart.........................**5.00**
Ball Ideal, clear, half-pint...... **2.00**
Ball Improved, blue, quart **4.00**
Ball Perfect Mason, Italic & Block letters, quart **8.00**
Ball Refrigerator & Freezer jar, clear, 16-ounce................. **2.00**
Crystal Jar, clear, midget **38.00**
Dexter (circled by fruits & vegetables), aqua, quart...........**58.00**
Dolittle (script), clear, pint ...**43.00**
Double Safety, narrow mouth, clear, quart **2.00**
Drey Improved Everseal, clear, half-gallon **6.00**
Eagle, aqua, half-gallon......**125.00**
Electric (world globe) Fruit Jar, aqua, quart **78.00**
Franklin No 1 Fruit Jar, aqua, quart..............................**55.00**
Fruit Common Wealth Jar, clear, half-gallon **123.00**
Globe, amber, pint.................**73.00**
Hero, name above cross, aqua, quart..............................**53.00**
J&B (in octagon) Fruit Jar, Patd July 14 1898, aqua, pint .**48.00**
Kerr Mason, self sealing, amber, quart..............................**18.00**
King (on banner below crown), clear, quart **9.00**
Knowlton Vacuum (star) Fruit Jar, aqua, half-gallon.....**33.00**
Mason, Ball Perfect, clear, ribbed, half-pint **4.00**
Mason Jar 1872, aqua, quart..**33.00**
Mason's #2, Patd Nov 30 1858, aqua, midget..................**30.00**
Mason's BCCo Improved, aqua, half-gallon **58.00**
Mason's KBGCo Patent Nov 30th 1858, aqua, quart...........**12.00**
Millville (WTCo Mono) Improved, aqua, quart.....................**53.00**
Moore's, Patd Dec 3rd 1861, aqua, quart..............................**78.00**

The Valve Jar Co., Philadelphia, Patent March 10th, 1868, aqua quart, $225.00; Whitney Glass Works, Glassboro, N.J., deep aqua quart, glass lid with zinc band, rare, $450.00.

Mrs Chapins Mayonnaise, Boston Mass, clear, pint.............. **3.00**

Protector, arched, aqua, quart, rare **50.00**

Queen, reverse: CFJCo, aqua, half-gallon **28.00**

Queensland (Pineapple) Fruit Jar, green, quart..................**123.00**

Simplex (in diamond on lid), clear, half-pint **5.00**

Smalley Self Sealer, widemouth, clear, pint.......................... **4.00**

Trademark Keystone Registered, clear, pint.......................... **7.00**

Woodbury, aqua, pint.............**43.00**

Worchester, aqua, quart **148.00**

Furniture

Golden oak continues to be a favorite of furniture collectors; Victorian, Country, and Mission Oak are also popular, and flea markets are a good source for all these styles. After the industrial revolution, mail-order furniture companies began to favor the lighter weight oak over the massive rosewood and walnut pieces, simply because shipping oak was less costly. This type of furniture retained its popularity throughout several decades of the 20th century. Mission was a style developed during the Arts and Crafts movement of the late 1900s. It was squarely built of heavy oak, with extremely simple lines. Two of its leading designers were Elbert Hubbard and Gustav Stickley. Country furniture is simply styled, often handmade, and generally primitive in nature. Recently, good examples have been featured in magazine articles on home decorating.

Armchair, painted and decorated Windsor thumb-back, ca 1820, 34",$800.00.

Armchair, Adironack willow twig, ca 1915, EX 550.00

Armchair, mahogany with inlay, Sheraton style 95.00

Armchair, walnut, Queen Anne style, early 1900s.........125.00

Armchair, 4-slat back, turned legs, original black paint, New England 1,000.00

Bench, bucket; poplar, worn gray paint, 25x28"................190.00

Bench, chapel; oak with worn finish, shelf under seat, 58½" long...............................200.00

Bench, deacon's; maple legs, pine seat, refinished, 1860s, 60" long...............................600.00

Bench, poplar, bootjack ends, 15x54"............................65.00

Bench, water; pine, gray paint, 2-shelf, bootjack feet, 33" .300.00

Bench, water; poplar, worn blue paint over gray & black, 40" long 350.00

Bookcase desk, oak, much carving, drop front, square mirror, restored **785.00**

Bureau, mahogany with swell front and rope carved posts, early 19th century, 37" wide, $700.00.

Cabinet, china; mahogany veneer, bow front, 1930s, 71"...500.00

Cabinet, china; oak country style, bow front, restored... 1,200.00

Cabinet, corner; oak, spindled top, ball feet, restored..... 1,500.00

Candlestand, mahogany, Chippendale style, tilt top 275.00

Cedar chest, mohair upholstery, 1930s, 36x20x19" 225.00

Cedar chest, waterfall walnut veneer with satinwood, 1930s, 46".....................185.00

Chair, child's rocker; oak, pressed back, turned legs 165.00

Chair, child's rocker; oak, 2-slat back, woven seat............90.00

Chair, corner; country, curved rail, shaped arms.........225.00

Chair, desk; walnut veneer splat, cane seat, French legs, 1920s, 37"...................................50.00

Chair, rocker; quarter-sawn oak, Mission style 200.00

Chair, rocker; quarter-sawn oak, spindle arms 165.00

Chair, rocker; twig art, blue paint, ca 1890s, EX 550.00

Chair, sewing rocker; oak, padded seat, side extension......**165.00**

Chair, side; banister back, turned legs & posts, repaint....**875.00**

Chair, side; curly maple, Country Sheraton, turned legs ..**250.00**

Chair, side; maple country style, painted finish, 1870s ...**125.00**

Chair, side; refinished curly maple, sabre leg, replaced cane seat.......................**200.00**

Chair, side; Windsor, saddle seat, 7-spindle back, repaint.**250.00**

Chest, blanket; cherry, dovetailed, turned feet, 23x28" **425.00**

Chest, blanket; cherry, dovetailed case & bracket feet, miniature **250.00**

Chest, blanket; European pine, wrought iron handles, 56½ x22½".............................**300.00**

Chest, blanket; pine, original blue paint, applied base, 40¾" long **375.00**

Chest, blanket; poplar, red stripes, refinished, 44".**245.00**

Chest, blanket; poplar with original brown graining, 48½" long **400.00**

Chest, curly maple, bird's eye veneer top drawer, scroll feet, 45x45" **400.00**

Chest, mule; poplar, scrolled base, dovetailed drawer, 38".**275.00**

Chiffonier, quarter-sawn oak, 2 small drawers over 5, oval mirror **325.00**

Cupboard, corner; Colonial, 9-pane door over panel door, ca 1890s **1,750.00**

Cupboard, corner; walnut Biedermeir, 1825, 40x35" **225.00**

Cupboard, jelly; pine, old blue-green paint, original hardware, 60x53"................**800.00**

Cupboard, oak, 4 flat panel doors, 2 drawers, tall, EX.......**575.00**

Desk, lap; mahogany, brass bound, drawers & compartments, 17x20"...............**150.00**

Curio side-by-side, oak, bowed glass door, mirror, carved feet, 75", $1,100.00.

Desk, lap; mahogany, white metal mounts, 13x11".............**165.00**

Desk, oak, Queen Anne style, restored **375.00**

Desk, oak, 3 side drawers, simple style, small **175.00**

Desk, oak waterfall roll top, 8 drawers, restored **1,750.00**

Desk, quarter-sawn oak, drop front, 4 drawers, square legs, restored **450.00**

Dresser, oak, bow front, 4 drawers, tall mirror **350.00**

Dresser, oak, 4 drawers, large square hinged mirror, restored **350.00**

Dry sink, curly maple with poplar door panels, 55"........ **2,200.00**

Dry sink, pine, cut-out feet, rebuilt, 29x43" **250.00**

Footstool, Moravian, chip-carved, 3 whittled legs, repaint..**55.00**

Footstool, pine, cut-out legs motised through top.......**75.00**

Footstool, walnut, scalloped legs & apron, 8x8x16" **85.00**

Hall tree, oak, much carving, tall rectangular mirror... **1,000.00**

Highchair, oak, spindle back & arms, turned legs.........**225.00**

Ice box, oak, raised panel door, original hardware, medium size................**550.00**
Ice box, pine, on bracket base, ca 1890, restored **650.00**
Magazine rack, gum veneer finished walnut, 2-pocket, 1940s, 21x18x14" **25.00**
Pie safe, poplar, 3 punched-tin panels, refinished.........**650.00**
Pie safe, 6 punched-tin panels, drawer, 1890s factory made, restored **500.00**
Shelf, walnut, 3-tier, 1900, 35x25" **400.00**
Smoking stand, walnut veneer, flower stencil, 1930s, 30x13x9" **75.00**
Stand, cherry, tripod base with snake feet, 27" high **375.00**
Stand, cherry, 16½" dish-turn walnut top, snake feet **375.00**
Stand, cherry with dark finish, Country Hepplewhite .**525.00**
Stand, mahogany, drop leaf, Empire style, 1900s **150.00**
Stand, refinished cherry, Country Hepplewhite, 28½".......**500.00**
Stand, refinished cherry, turned legs, 1 drawer, 29" **350.00**
Stand, walnut, dovetailed drawer, 18x24" top.....................**175.00**
Stool, lady's shoe; pine, turned legs, 1860s...................**125.00**
Stool, 2-step, original blue paint, ca 1900........................**185.00**
Table, card; mahogany, Sheraton, reeded legs, New England, 1820s **450.00**
Table, dressing; pine, poplar, & maple, Country Sheraton, 34x17"...........................**450.00**
Table, drop leaf, walnut with band inlay, Hepplewhite......**250.00**
Table, quarter-sawn oak, pedestal base with 4 claw & ball feet, NM...............................**650.00**
Table, sofa; maple, Biedermeier style, 65".......................**275.00**

Table, tea; birch with dark finish, tilt top, 29" diameter ...**375.00**
Table, trestle; oak, shoe feet, 29x59½".........................**550.00**
Table, walnut, country style, tripod base with scimitar legs, 29½" **300.00**
Table desk, bleached mahogany, birch base, 1 drawer, 1940s, 30x36x18" **25.00**
Table desk, walnut veneer top, antique white base, 1940s, 30x48x24"....................**375.00**

Table, William and Mary, oak, replaced foot, restoration, $650.00.

Washstand, birch & pine, Country Sheraton, 25¾" high **300.00**
Washstand, pine, red repaint, dovetailed gallery & base drawer **200.00**

Gambling Devices

Though Lady Luck still attracts her share of eager partakers at the games of chance, today those interested in vintage gambling devices can be confident of gaining rather than losing by making wise selections on their investments. Especially valued are cheating devices, layouts, and items that can be authenticated as having been used in the 'Floating Palace' riverboats or in the early days of the famous casinos of the West.

Book, Practical Poker, Foster, 1905, 253-page, EX **18.00**
Book, Sucker's Progress, hard back, Asbury, 1938, 490-page, EX **35.00**
Card press, wood, turned screws & handles, 9x4", EX.......**85.00**
Cash box, wood, 4-section, 3½x8x23½ " **28.00**
Chip, ivory, floral scrimshaw, red dye, 1½" dia **18.00**
Dice, Made in Austria, 1½x1½", EX **12.50**
Dice cage, wire, with 3 dice, silver paint, 12½ x5", NM **55.00**
Dice cup, leather, with cover, El Paso Saddlery.................**75.00**
Dice drop, wood & glass, with 6 red & white celluloid dice, 11x6" **50.00**
Game, El Sapo, toss coin into frog's mouth..................**265.00**
Photograph, 2 man playing cards on a barrel.....................**20.00**
Poker chip, embossed speedboat, 6 for **5.00**
Poker chip, ivory with scrimshaw, all different, 10 for.......**200.00**
Rack, wood with cover, base turns, +300 multicolor celluloid chips **80.00**
Roulette game, Bestmaid, EX in box with instructions **40.00**
Shot glass, 12-sided, base cavity holds dice, 3", NM **165.00**
Wheel, roulette; Bakelite, cast steel center, unmarked, 14" dia **60.00**
Wheel, wood, colorful, complete with hardware, wall mount, 24" dia..............................**95.00**
Whist marker, rules on back, DeLaRue, ca 1890, pair .. **5.00**

Games

Before the turn of the century, several large companies began to produce parlor games; among them were Milton Bradley and Parker Brothers, both of whom still exist and continue to distribute games that delight young and old alike. These early games make wonderful collectibles; especially valuable are those dealing with a popular character, transportation theme, Black theme, or other areas of special interest. Condition of both game pieces and the box is important.

Across the Continent, dice game, Parker Bros, VG.............**45.00**
Aerospace, race game, Wolverine, VG **35.00**
Annie, 1981, NM **18.00**
Art Linkletter's People Are Funny, 1954, complete ..**15.00**
Astro Launch, space game, tin, Ohio Art.........................**25.00**
Beat the Clock, 1954, EX......**22.00**
Branded, board game, M **27.50**
Calling All Cars, Parker Bros, VG in box **32.00**
Close Encounter of the 3rd Kind, Parker Bros, 1978, EX...**10.00**
Comic Cards, Milton Bradley, 1972, VG **10.00**
Dating Game, 2nd edition, complete, EX.........................**17.50**
Dodging Donkey, target game, Parker Bros, 1924, EX...**35.00**
Easy Money, Milton Bradley .**20.00**
Incredible Hulk, 1978 ....**24.00**
Legend of the Lone Ranger, 1980, M in box **20.00**
McDonald's Farm, Sel-Right, 1965, M......................**22.50**
Mother Goose, cards, 1900s, EX, missing box....................**18.00**

Playtime Pop-Up Library, Platt & Munk, 1963, EX **18.00**
Rin Tin Tin, EX **25.00**
Space 1999, Milton Bradley, 1978, M **32.00**
Steeplechase, McLoughlin, early, EX **130.00**

Steeple Chase, Edgar O. Clark, 1905, $160.00.

SWAT, Milton Bradley, 1976, EX in box **12.00**
Tell It to the Judge, Eddie Cantor, NM **28.00**
The Frog Who Would a Wooing Go, Parker, EX **65.00**
Touring, cards, 1947.............**16.00**
Uncle Wiggily, 1954...............**15.00**

Gas Globes and Panels

Globes that once crowned gasoline pumps are today being collected as a unique form of advertising memorabilia. There are basically four types: plastic frames with glass inserts from the 1940s and '50s; glass frames with glass inserts from the '30s and '40s; metal frames with glass inserts from the '20s and '30s; and one-piece glass globes (no inserts) with the oil company name etched, raised, or enameled onto the face from 1914 to 1931. There are variations.

American, glass frame, glass inserts, 1926-1940s......**185.00**

Champlin, plastic body, glass inserts, 1931-1950s **100.00**
Derby, glass frame, glass inserts, 1926-1940s **165.00**
DX Ethyl, plastic body, glass inserts, 1931-1950s **85.00**
Esso, glass frame, glass inserts, 1926-1940s, 13", pr **150.00**
Good Gulf, 1-piece glass, 1914-1931 ....**500.00**
Koolmotor, clover shape, glass frame, glass inserts, 1926-1940s **350.00**
Marathon, no runner, plastic body, glass inserts, 1931-1950s............................**70.00**
Red Crown, round, etched, 1-piece glass, 1914-1931 ...... **1,800.00**
Shamrock, oval, plastic body, glass inserts, 1931-1950s......**125.00**
Sinclair Pennant, glass frame glass frame & insert, 1926-1940s **225.00**
Skelly, 1-piece, 1914-1931...**600.00**
Skelly Powermax, glass frame & insert, 1926-1940s........**175.00**
Spartan, glass frame, glass inserts, 1926-1940s......**210.00**
Spur, plastic body, glass inserts, 1931-1950s **75.00**
Standard Blue Crown, glass frame, glass inserts, 1926-1940s **300.00**
Super Shell, round, etched, 1-piece, 1914-1931....... **1,200.00**
Tidex, metal frame, glass inserts, 1915-1930s, 16"...........**250.00**
Tydol, metal frame, glass inserts, 1915-1930s, 17"...........**300.00**
White Flash, gill body, glass frame, glass insert, 1926-1940s **185.00**
WNAX, glass frame, glass inserts, 1926-1940s **200.00**
Wood River, plastic body, glass inserts, 1931-1950s......**110.00**
66 Flite Fuel, Phillips, plastic body, glass inserts, 1931-1950s **120.00**

Geisha Girl China

More than sixty-five different patterns of tea services were exported from Japan around the turn of the century, each depicting geishas going about the everyday activities of Japanese life. Mt. Fuji is often featured in the background. The generic term for these sets is 'Geisha Girl China.'

Hatpin holder, Flower Garden Bench, 4", $25.00.

Ash tray, Mother & Son C, red with gold, oval, Japanese mark **16.00**

Bowl, Porcelain Bench, red-orange with gold buds, Japan, 8".**28.00**

Bowl, Servant with Sacks, red-orange with gold, 10".....**55.00**

Cocoa pot, Lesson, waved cobalt with gold lacing, fluted, Japan..............................**65.00**

Cocoa pot, Origami, red-orange with gold buds, fluted, Made in Japan..........................**45.00**

Cookie jar, Checkerboard, cobalt blue, 3-footed.................**85.00**

Cookie jar, Temple Vase, cobalt with gold & red, Japanese mark **75.00**

Creamer, Porch, cobalt blue with gold, Nippon **20.00**

Cup & saucer, Waterboy, pine green.............................**10.00**

Eggcup, Garden Bench D, red-orange, Kisoke mark......**12.00**

Hair Receiver, Geisha in Sampan A, grass green **20.00**

Jug, Cherry Blossoms, red-orange edge, 6½ " **35.00**

Mustard jar, Rendevous, apple green with gold **30.00**

Nappy, Lantern Gateway, cobalt blue with gold, 6-lobed, handled **25.00**

Pin tray, Kakemono, blue-green, free-form shape with cut-out handle...........................**20.00**

Pitcher, Grape Arbor, red with gold lines & slashes, 6"..**28.00**

Plate, Butterfly Dancers, red with gold, 7"...........................**25.00**

Plate, Duck Watching A, gold, Kanji mark, 7"...............**14.00**

Plate, Flag Day, red with yellow lacing, 6⅛" **15.00**

Plate, Processional, gold border, 6"...................................... **8.00**

Teapot, Bamboo Tree, marked Japan..............................**20.00**

Teapot, Flute & Koto, red **25.00**

Trivet, Prayer Ribbon, red, Cherry Blossom mark....**15.00**

Goofus Glass

Produced in the early part of the 20th century, 'goofus' glassware was pressed with designs in very high relief and painted on the reverse with metallic lustres. Lamps, pickle jars, vases, and trays are easy to find. Flea markets are often a good source, but watch for flaking paint. Careful cleaning is a must to prevent paint loss.

Bowl, butterfly, 6-crimp, original paint, 4x8", EX..............45.00
Bowl, dahlia, scalloped, gold, ornate, 10x4"..................45.00
Bowl, dogwood, original paint, 3x10", EX.......................45.00
Bowl, reindeer in center, EX.18.00
Cake plate, acorn & leaf, amethyst, 12"................20.00
Lamp, oil; cabbage rose, milk glass, miniature, 9".......50.00
Nut dish, cherries, original paint, scalloped rim, 7" 40.00
Pin tray, basketweave, gold with red rose, original paint, 4½", long................................25.00
Plate, cake; carnation border, elk center, 13"......................50.00
Plate, cake; carnations, red on gold, 12" 30.00
Plate, monk drinks from tankard, rose rim, 7" 40.00
Plate, roses in center, 9" 20.00

Powder box, puffy rose, original paint, 3x4"....................45.00
Shakers, poppy, EX original paint, 3", pr 35.00
Tray, basketweave & rose, original paint, 7x10"..............30.00
Tray, dresser; cabbage rose, square, 6"......................30.00
Tray, fruit; square with serrated rim, original paint, 9" .125.00
Tumbler, grapes, gold on crackle, original paint, 4"...........40.00
Vase, cabbage rose, squatty, original paint, 6"...................22.00
Vase, chrysanthemums, original paint, 8", EX.................35.00
Vase, dogwood blossom cluster, original paint, 15".........50.00
Vase, grapes on basketweave, original paint, 10".........25.00
Vase, irises, original paint, 12", EX 65.00
Vase, mixed fruit, repainted gold on clear, 10"...................35.00
Vase, morning-glory, pink or amethyst, 2" 30.00

Bowl, Grape and Cable, original paint, 2" x 9" dia, $40.00.

144

Vase, poppy, milk glass, no paint,
5" **20.00**
Vase, Tree Rose, original paint,
12", M **50.00**

Graniteware

A collectible very much in demand by those who enjoy the 'Country' look in antiques, graniteware (also called enameled ware) comes in a variety of colors, and color is one of the most important considerations when it comes to evaluating worth. Purple, brown, or green swirl pieces are generally higher than gray, white, or blue–though blues and blue-swirled examples are popular. Decorated pieces are unusual, as are salesman's samples and miniatures; and these also bring top prices.

Baby bath, gray, small **45.00**
Batter jug, gray, with lid & tin
spout cap, rare, large ...**275.00**
Bedpan, blue swirl **90.00**
Biscuit sheet, blue, rectangular,
large............................**395.00**
Bowl, blue, 11½" **15.00**
Bowl, soup; gray....................**18.00**
Bread box, white **35.00**
Bread riser, blue swirl, tin lid,
NM..............................**395.00**
Bucket, berry; blue swirl **75.00**
Bucket, berry; sky blue, tin lid,
bail handle, M **45.00**
Butter dish, white...............**125.00**
Can, milk; gray, granite lid, 1-gal-
lon **55.00**
Can, milk; white, Dutch girl in
blue **75.00**
Candlestick, dark green........**95.00**
Canister set, light green, alu-
minum lids, 6"..............**135.00**
Casserole, blue swirl, with lid,
EX **75.00**

Coffeepot, speckled brown, wood finial and handle, 10", $195.00.

Chamber pot, turquoise swirl,
with bail & lid, tall, EX .**95.00**
Chamberstick, yellow or green,
each **40.00**
Coffee urn, gray mottle & brass
spout, 5-gal, NM **245.00**
Coffeepot, brown swirl, large,
EX **250.00**
Coffeepot, cream & green, match-
ing lid, 8" **85.00**
Coffeepot, gray with pewter trim,
copper bottom...............**250.00**
Coffeepot, light blue speckled,
NM **295.00**
Coffeepot, red swirl, gooseneck
spout, NM **300.00**
Colander, blue swirl..............**75.00**
Colander, gray, teardrop form,
hanging ring, VG **215.00**
Cuspidor, solid brown, 2-pc...**25.00**
Dipper, gray mottle...............**23.00**
Dish, vegetable; cream & green,
oblong **15.00**
Dish pan, white, miniature ..**35.00**
Double boiler, black & white large
swirl, 3-pc, rare............**295.00**
Egg poacher, blue, white interior,
EX **125.00**
Fish poacher, gray mottle, lid &
handle insert, NM........**215.00**
Flask, cobalt, porcelain stopper,
M **165.00**

Foot tub, blue with blue mottle, oval, rare, NM..............**165.00**
Funnel, canning; dark gray mottle, NM..........................**23.00**
Grater, sky blue, curved, oblong, open loop handle, M....**125.00**
Invalid feeder, white............**22.00**
Jelly roll pan, medium blue swirl, round, EX......................**65.00**
Ladle, gray bowl with long cobalt handle, EX......................**22.00**
Ladle, white, pierced, EX.....**65.00**
Mug, mush; blue & white mottle, 7½ x6", VG....................**115.00**
Pail, lunch; gray, 3-pc.........**125.00**
Pail, water; cobalt & white swirl, large, EX......................**175.00**
Pan, milk; gray mottle, 11"..**25.00**
Pan, pudding; gray mottle, 9", EX..............................**20.00**
Pan, white with red trim, advertising Knight Pickles.....**75.00**
Pitcher, sky blue, white interior, small, G........................**70.00**

Graduated set of measuring pitchers, largest: 1-gallon, $250.00 for the set.

Plate, luncheon; gray, M.......**25.00**
Plate, soup; blue & white......**30.00**
Potty, cobalt swirl, M..........**180.00**
Rack, utensil; white............**125.00**
Roaster, blue, Savory, 9x18x12", M....................................**45.00**
Roaster, emerald green swirl, large, EX......................**225.00**
Roaster, green & white spatter, round, with lid...............**40.00**
Roaster, turquoise & white speckled, large....................**35.00**
Salt box, azure blue, M.......**110.00**
Saucer, gray........................**16.00**

Scoop, grocer's, gray............**95.00**
Skillet, gray, 8½"................**65.00**
Skillet, medium dark blue & white speckled, 2x8"......**42.00**
Soap dish, solid brown, white interior, flat, Elite.........**35.00**
Spittoon, cobalt & white swirl, 2-pc, large......................**145.00**
Stove, kerosene, solid blue, 1-burner...........................**185.00**
Syrup, medium blue, M.....**145.00**
Tea steeper, gray, with granite lid, NM................................**85.00**
Tea strainer, white...............**35.00**
Teakettle, blue & white swirl, large, EX........................**55.00**
Teakettle, gray with red wooden handle, squatty, small....**85.00**
Teapot, cobalt mottle..........**125.00**
Teapot, turquoise swirl.........**95.00**
Thermometer, oven; white with green base, Taylor..........**35.00**
Tray, cobalt, oval, shell shaped, 2x10x9"..........................**50.00**
Tumbler, azure blue, with label, VG..................................**135.00**
Wash basin, emerald green & white swirl, 3x11".........**65.00**
Washboard, blue & white.....**85.00**
Washboard, cobalt, National Washboard Co #421, Made in USA...............................**80.00**

Green and Ivory

Green and ivory stoneware is identical in design to the more familiar blue and white ware. It was produced from about 1910 until 1935 by many manufacturers, though it is never marked.

Bowl, Daisy & Waffle, 10"....**45.00**
Bowl, Reverse Pyramid & Picket Fence, set of 4...............**175.00**
Butter crock, Apricots & Honeycomb, with lid & bail......**85.00**
Milk crock, Apricots, bail handle, 10"..................................**65.00**

Mug, Grape...........................**40.00**
Pitcher, Cow, EX color & detail, 7½"................................**125.00**
Pitcher, Cow, graduated set of 3, NM..............................**325.00**
Pitcher, Flying Birds, top & bottom green **150.00**
Pitcher, Grape Cluster in Shield, arrow bands, 9" **85.00**
Pitcher, Rose on Trellis.........**95.00**
Spittoon, Grape......................**55.00**
Spittoon, Waffle & Grape, salesman's sample, 2"....**75.00**
Umbrella stand, Iris, 20"....**250.00**

Griswold

During the latter part of the 19th century, the Griswold company began to manufacture the finest cast iron kitchenware items available at that time. Soon after they became established, they introduced a line of lightweight, cast aluminum ware that revolutionized the industry. The company enjoyed many prosperous years until its closing in the late 1950s. Look for these marks: Seldon Griswold, Griswold Mfg. Co., and Erie.

Ash tray #0, round **58.00**
Bread pan #22 ....**35.00**
Brownie pan #9 ....**75.00**
Cake mold, lamb **95.00**
Cake mold, rabbit **225.00**
Corn stick pan #252, miniature, EX **40.00**
Danish pan #32 ....**36.00**
Drip pan #00..........................**18.00**
Dutch oven #8, Tite-Top........**38.00**
Griddle #10, oval **50.00**
Griddle #18............................**20.00**
Griddle #6...............................**48.00**
Griddle #9, 10½ " **48.00**
Kettle #3 ....**85.00**
Meat loaf pan, large emblem ..**65.00**
Muffin pan, heart & star **130.00**

Platter #861, well & tree **35.00**
Rack, Dutch oven **150.00**
Roll pan #950 ....**55.00**
Skillet, breakfast; #666.........**45.00**
Skillet, poaching; 7-egg.........**65.00**
Skillet #3, large emblem, no smoke ring......................**25.00**
Skillet #4, large emblem.......**40.00**
Skillet rack **100.00**
Trivet, 5-leg, for coffeepot **75.00**
Waffle iron #11, high stand, metal handles **50.00**
Waffle iron #8, American, early version **120.00**

Corn stick pan #954, $30.00

Hall

Most famous for their extensive lines of teapots and colorful dinnerwares, the Hall China Company still operates in East Liverpool, Ohio, where they were established in 1903. For listings of their most popular dinnerware line, see Autumn Leaf.

Acacia, bean pot, New England, #4 ....**75.00**
Acacia, casserole, Medallion.**34.00**
Arlington, platter, oval, 15" .**13.00**
Blue Blossom, canister, Radiance, with lid **100.00**
Blue Blossom, cookie jar, Sundial, with lid **180.00**
Blue Blossom, teapot, Streamline, with lid **120.00**
Blue Bouquet, gravy boat **21.00**
Blue Bouquet, platter, 11¼"..**15.00**
Blue Garden, batter jug, Sundial, with lid **100.00**

Blue Garden, canister, Radiance, with lid **95.00**
Blue Willow, finger bowl **13.00**
Blue Willow, teapot, Boston, 6-cup, with lid...................**75.00**
Bouquet, butter dish.............**27.00**
Bouquet, jug, 1¼-qt **11.00**
Bouquet, vinegar bottle **15.00**
Cactus, jug, 5-Band, 2-qt **43.00**
Cactus, teapot, French..........**50.00**
Cameo Rose, platter, 11¼ " ...**13.00**
Cameo Rose, sugar bowl.......**13.00**
Caprice, teapot, 6-cup...........**23.00**
Crocus, bowl, vegetable; round, 9¼ " **19.00**
Crocus, tidbit, 3-tier..............**35.00**
Fantasy, ball jug, #1 ....**45.00**
Fantasy, bean pot, New England, #4 ....**65.00**
Fantasy, coffeepot, 6-cup.......**19.00**
Fantasy, egg cup....................**13.00**
Fantasy, gravy boat................ **9.00**
Fantasy, teapot, Streamline, with lid..................................**165.00**
Flamingo, bowl, 5-Band, 7"...**11.00**
Flamingo, canister, Radiance, with lid **70.00**
Frost Flowers, bowl, 5¾"........ **3.00**
Frost Flowers, casserole, 2-qt, with lid **15.00**
Heather Rose, cake plate.....**11.00**
Heather Rose, jug, Rayed **11.00**

Monticello, pickle dish, 9"...... **4.00**
Monticello, platter, oval, 13"..**11.00**
Morning Glory, bowl, Thick Rim, 7½ " **13.00**
Morning Glory, teapot, Aladdin, with lid **40.00**
Mt Vernon, platter, 11" **10.00**
Mums, bowl, round, 9¼" **15.00**
Mums, bowl, salad; 9" **11.00**
Orange Poppy, bowl, soup; flat, 8½" **9.00**
Orange Poppy, cake plate **11.00**
Orange Poppy, casserole, round, #76 ....**23.00**
Orange Poppy, pie baker.......**19.00**
Orange Poppy, platter, 13¼"..**17.00**
Pastel Morning Glory, platter, 13¼ " **17.00**
Pinecone, tidbit, 3-tier **19.00**
Primrose, sugar bowl **7.00**
Red Poppy, bowl, round, 9"...**17.00**
Red Poppy, cake safe, metal .**19.00**
Red Poppy, gravy boat **19.00**
Red Poppy, platter, 13¼ " **17.00**
Red Poppy, teapot, New York, with lid **40.00**
Richmond, bowl, vegetable; with lid....................................**20.00**
Richmond, teapot, Aladdin ..**37.00**
Rose Parade, bean pot, tab-handled **37.00**
Royal Rose, ball jug, #3........**29.00**

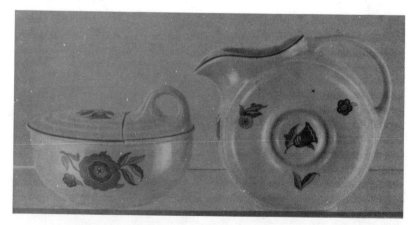

Fantasy leftover with loop handle, $40.00; Donut jug, $90.00.

Royal Rose, custard, straight-
sided................................ **8.00**
Serenade, coffeepot, Terrace .**25.00**
Serenade, teapot, New York .**30.00**
Shaggy Tulip, pretzel jar **80.00**
Shaggy Tulip, stacking set, Radi-
ance **50.00**
Silhouette, gravy boat...........**20.00**
Silhouette, platter, 11¼" **13.00**
Springtime, bowl, oval **13.00**
Springtime, coffeepot, Washing-
ton...................................**25.00**
Springtime, platter, 15" **17.00**
Sundial, coffee server..........**140.00**
Sundial, teapot, 6-cup **60.00**
Sunglow, butter dish.............**22.00**
Sunglow, relish, 4-part..........**11.00**
Sunglow, teapot, 6-cup..........**23.00**
Teapot, Adele, maroon **65.00**
Teapot, Aladdin, Chinese red, oval
infuser **65.00**
Teapot, Aladdin, pink, swag, gold
label **38.00**
Teapot, Baltimore, gold trim ..**35.00**

**Basketball teapot, ultramarine,
$300.00.**

Teapot, Bamboo Tree, #19.....**20.00**
Teapot, Cleveland, warm yellow
with gold.........................**32.00**
Teapot, Globe, cobalt with gold
decoration.......................**75.00**
Teapot, Hollywood, marine blue
with gold.........................**38.00**
Teapot, Kansas, emerald green
with gold........................**175.00**
Teapot, Philadelphia, cobalt with
gold, 4-cup **35.00**

Teapot, Star, cobalt with gold dec-
oration **85.00**
Teapot, Surfside, green **45.00**
Tulip, bowl, round, 9".............**15.00**
Tulip, casserole, Thick Rim ..**27.00**
Tulip, platter, 13¼ "..............**15.00**
Tulip, sugar bowl, with lid, mod-
ern style **11.00**
Wild Poppy, baker, oval.........**17.00**
Wild Poppy, onion soup, individ-
ual...................................**27.00**
Wildfire, bowl, Thick Rim, 8½"
diameter **17.00**
Wildfire, coffee dispenser, metal,
NM **11.00**
Wildfire, gravy boat **17.00**
Wildfire, jug, Pert, 5" **27.00**
Wildfire, teapot, Aladdin **35.00**
Yellow Rose, bowl, salad; 9"..**11.00**
Yellow Rose, bowl, vegetable;
round, 9¼" **13.00**

Halloween

Halloween items are fast
becoming the most popular holi-
day-related collectibles among
today's collectors. Although originally linked to pagan rituals and
superstitions, Halloween has long
since evolved into a fun-filled
event; and the masks, noisemak-
ers, and jack-o'-lanterns of earlier
years are great fun to look for.

Bank, cat, seated, yellow pottery,
4" **100.00**
Book, Halloween Party, colorful
cover, 1931, EX...............**18.00**
Candy container, black cat, glass
eyes, Germany, 6"...........**95.00**
Candy container, goblin on candy
box, composition, Germany,
3".....................................**95.00**
Costume, jester, orange & black,
brass bells, 1930s...........**65.00**
Costume, Uncle Sam, cloth, Col-
legeville Costumes, original
box..................................**55.00**

Candle lantern, paper in eyes and mouth intact, $70.00.

Decoration, black cat, papier-
mache, 4" **85.00**
Decoration, owl, papier-mache,
orange, 3½" **45.00**
Decoration, witch, diecut cardboard, 16" **50.00**
Fan, cat face, paper with crepe-
paper trim, 12½" **65.00**
Jack-o'-lantern, papier-mache,
crepe-paper trim, 6½" ..**120.00**
Jack-o'-lantern, papier-mache, printed
tissue eyes & mouth, 4"..**65.00**
Jack-o'-lantern, tin litho, owl,
moon, & bats, 5x6".........**45.00**
Mask, man's head, molded wire
mesh, painted face, 8"....**70.00**
Noisemaker, orange & black tin
litho, Chein, 5½ " dia **40.00**
Noisemaker, tin litho, Mr Pumpkin head smoking cigarette,
4½ " **66.00**
Ornament, black cat in moon,
glass, 10" **22.00**
Ornament, pumpkin face, glass,
10"...................................**18.00**
Post card, A Merry Halloween,
black cat in center of pump-
kins **16.00**
Rattle, pumpkin face with witch
on reverse, Germany, 3"..**90.00**
Rattle, witches & cats on tin litho,
Gotham, 6x4" dia **35.00**

Harker

One of the oldest potteries in the East Liverpool, Ohio, area, the Harker company produced many lines of dinnerware through the late 1920s until it closed around 1970.

Amy, bean pot, individual **4.00**
Amy, bowl, utility; 9".............**10.00**
Apple & Pear, plate, 11"........**10.00**
Calico Tulip, rolling pin **45.00**
Cameo, plate, blue, 6" **3.50**

Cameo: Drip jar, $15.00; Shaker, $6.00; Cup and saucer, $8.50.

Chesterton, cup & saucer **5.00**
Deco Dahlia, bowl, 5½" **2.50**
Deco Dahlia, casserole **15.00**
Orange Tulip with Wheat,
creamer & sugar bowl, with
lid **12.50**
Orange Tulip with Wheat, rolling
pin....................................**75.00**
Orange Tulip with Wheat, teapot
with lid **15.00**
Petit Point, cake server **10.00**
Petit Point, rolling pin **45.00**
Petit Point II, platter, 12"...... **8.00**
Priscilla, bowl, cream soup.... **9.00**
Rose Spray, cup & saucer....... **2.50**
Ruffled Tulip, pitcher............**18.00**
Tulip, batter set **45.00**

Harlequin

Made by the Homer Laughlin China Company who also pro-duced the popular Fiesta, Harlequin was a lightweight dinnerware line made in several solid glaze colors. It was introduced in 1938 and was marketed mainly through Woolworth stores. During the early forties, the company made a line of Harlequin animals: a fish, lamb, cat, duck, penguin, and donkey. Values designated 'low' in the listings that follow are for these colors: mauve blue, turquoise, and yellow. 'High' values are for maroon, gray, medium green, spruce green, chartreuse, dark green, rose, red, and light green.

Ash tray, regular, high **42.00**
Bowl, nappy; low, 9" **14.00**

Candle holders, $125.00-150.00 for the pair (low range).

Casserole, high **80.00**
Creamer, individual, high **14.00**
Egg cup, double, high **16.00**
Egg cup, single, high **20.00**
Marmalade, in any color.....**100.00**
Nut dish, basketweave, high . **8.00**
Perfume bottle, in any color .**60.00**
Pitcher, jug; low, 22-oz **22.00**
Pitcher, service water; high ..**42.00**
Plate, high, 6" **4.00**
Plate, high, 9" **10.00**
Platter, high, 13" **20.00**
Salt & pepper shakers, high, pair **14.00**
Sauce boat, low......................**12.00**
Saucer, demitasse, high **9.00**
Sugar bowl, with lid, high **15.00**
Syrup, in any color..............**150.00**
Teacup, low **7.00**
Teapot, low............................**50.00**
Tray, relish; mixed colors....**175.00**

Tumbler, high **40.00**
Tumbler, with car decal, high ..**42.00**

Cream soup bowl, $12.00-$15.00.

Hatpin Holders

Made from many materials, hatpin holders are most often encountered in china decorated by hand painting or floral decals. Glass hatpin holders are rare, especially those of slag or carnival glass.

Adams Jasperware, white shield & designs on blue, 5" ...**225.00**
Bavaria, multicolor roses, artist signed **65.00**
Carnival glass, Grape & Cable, marigold, 7" **200.00**
Devon Ware, Torquay, various sayings, 4¾" **65.00**
Flow Blue, signed Shung, Wood & Sons, #d, 5" **145.00**
Germany, floral, with attached pin tray **45.00**
Ivorine, closed top with pin holes, rare **85.00**
Ivorine, open top, weighted base **35.00**
Limoges, hand-painted floral, rare, 9"........................**350.00**
MZ Austria, floral, stickpin holder & ring tree on tray.......**325.00**
Rosenthal, green china with silver overlay.........................**225.00**
Royal Bayreuth, musicians, signed Dixon.................**295.00**
Royal Bayreuth, red poppy figural, blue mark **350.00**

Royal Bayreuth, roses, yellow on green, with tray, mark.**175.00**

Schafer & Vater, cameo on urn form, 5¼" **135.00**

Suhl Prussia, florals, gold border, 5"..................................**80.00**

Unmarked china, King & Queen, 2-faced figural **265.00**

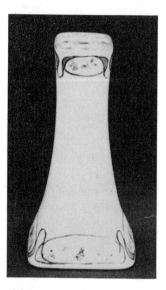

Ribbons and florals on white, Limoges, 5", $80.00.

Hatpins

Hatpins range in length from about 4" to as long as 12", depending upon the fashion of the day. The longer type was required to secure the large bonnets that were in style from 1890 to 1914. Many beautiful examples exist— some with genuine or manufactured stones, some in silver or brass with relief-molded Art Nouveau motifs, others of hand-painted porcelains, and 'nodder' types.

Art Deco, long ivorine wand.**28.00**

Black jet stone on 1¼" domed top, twist-wire caging............**40.00**

Carnival glass, butterfly, green iridescent.........................**75.00**

Filigree, 1½" rhinestone & red stones.............................**75.00**

Ivory, figural bear dancing on solid ball **150.00**

Porcelain ball, hand-painted figure, silver overlay, large, 1½" dia................................**250.00**

Porcelain ball, hand-painted lady's head, 1½" dia **175.00**

Rhinestones, prong set, on domed 1¼" brass filigree top **55.00**

Rhinestones with large central amethyst and three more on sides, 11" pin, $85.00.

Satsuma, floral, 1" dia, 9½" long pin.................................**195.00**

Sterling, amethyst thistle, signed Charles Horner **150.00**

Sterling, cherub, ¾" dia **50.00**

Sterling, Nouveau lady.........**85.00**

Sterling, owl **90.00**

Sterling, 4-leaf clover form, marked, 1" wide **40.00**

Head Vases

Many of them Japanese imports, head vases were made primarily for the florist trade. They were styled as children, teenagers, clowns, and famous people. There are heads of religious figures, Blacks, Orientals, and even some animals. One of the most common types are ladies wearing pearl earrings and necklaces.

Baby boy holding his bottle, Sampson, #313A, 5½ " ...**10.00**
Baby boy sucking his finger, Relpo, #459B, 5" **10.00**
Baby girl, blanket over head, holding a bear, Enesco, 5".....**12.50**
Benjamin Franklin, 6".........**35.00**
Child winking, blue hat with pink rose, Japan, 4½" **8.50**
Clown, face painted white, Inarco, #E5071, 4½".................... **8.50**
Girl, blond hair, holding red telephone, Nancy Pew, 6" **10.00**
Girl, braided hair, pearl earrings, Rubens, #4135, 6" **10.00**
Girl, cap & gown, holding diploma, gilt trim, Napco, #C4072G, 6" **10.00**

Napcoware, #C-7498, 11", $65.00.

Girl, floral hat & dress, Lefton's, #1343B, 6" **12.50**
Girl, long blond hair, pearl earrings, Napcoware, #C8495, 8½" **25.00**
Jackie Onassis, white scarf Inarco, #1852, 5½ ".........**65.00**
Lady, bow at neck, holding a poodle, unmarked, 6" **18.50**
Lady, eyes closed, hand toward chin, Inarco, #E2104, 7"..**15.00**
Lady, flat hat, raised collar, brush eye lashes, Napco, #C3815B, 6"....................................**15.00**
Lady, hands folded under chin, Relpo, #K1175L, 6½" **20.00**
Lady, pink hat, high collar, gilt trim, unmarked, 4½"....... **6.50**
Lady, pink hat with blue bow, Nancy Pew (paper label), #2260, 7".........................**18.50**
Lady, rose in hair, hand to cheek, Inarco, #E193/S, 4½"....... **7.50**
Lady, ruffled collar, hand to face, Sampson Import, 6".......**15.00**
Lady, short blond hair, head turned, Napcoware, #C7471, 4½" **7.00**
Lady, short brown hair, green dress trimmed in sequins, unmarked......................**15.00**
Mary & Child, Napcoware (paper label), #R7076, 6½" **12.50**
Oriental lady, holding fan, gilt trim, unmarked, 4¾"....... **8.00**
Soldier boy, eyes closed, Inarco, #E3250, 6" **10.00**
Uncle Sam, McCoy, 7½" **30.00**

Heisey

The Heisey glassware company operated in Ohio from 1896 until 1957, producing many fine dinnerware lines, many of which were made in lovely colors and etched with intricate floral motifs. They also made animal and bird figures, some of which sell for more than $500.00 each. They signed their ware with an H in a diamond mark or with a paper label.

Plug horse, $85.00.

Animal, Airdale...................**450.00**
Animal, Clydesdale.............**425.00**
Animal, colt, rearing **195.00**
Animal, dolphin, candlestick, #110 ....**185.00**
Animal, donkey **235.00**
Animal, elephant, small **195.00**
Animal, fish, bookend **100.00**
Animal, fish, match holder.**130.00**
Animal, frog, flamingo, cheese plate, #1210..................**125.00**
Animal, frog, moongleam, cheese plate **240.00**
Animal, giraffe, head turned to side **175.00**
Animal, show horse............**550.00**
Bird, duck, hawthorne, flower block............................**240.00**
Bird, goose, wings up **95.00**
Bird, Kingfisher, flamingo, flower block............................**225.00**
Bird, Ringneck Pheasant....**135.00**
Bird, rooster, stem cocktail...**40.00**
Bird, Wood Duck **500.00**

Dinnerware

Adam, goblet, flamingo, #3376, 11-oz.............................**50.00**

Biltmore, sherbet, crystal, #3316, 5½-oz.............................**10.00**
Comet Leaf, goblet, sahara, #1306, 9-oz **100.00**
Course Rib, pickle tray, moongleam, #407, 6".............**25.00**
Course Rib, tumbler, crystal, #406, 8-oz......................**15.00**
Diamond Rose, pilsner, crystal, #3386, 12-oz...................**35.00**
Empress, bonbon, sahara, #1401, 6"...............................**25.00**
Fairacre, cordial, crystal, #3555, 1-oz..............................**60.00**
Fern, plate, sandwich; zircon, #1495, 13" **100.00**
Gayoso, sherbet, marigold, #3312, 5½-oz.............................**35.00**
Kohinoor, bowl, fruit; zircon, #1488, 15½" **150.00**
Octagon, basket, moongleam, #500, 5"......................**130.00**
Old Glory, claret, hawthorne, #3333, 4½-oz **50.00**
Pleat & Panel, platter, crystal, #1170, oval, 12" **20.00**
Pleat & Panel, vase, flamingo, #1170, 8".........................**45.00**
Portsmouth, goblet, flamingo, #3440, 9-oz **25.00**
Pyramid, goblet, moongleam, #3379, 10-oz...................**80.00**
Quaker, bowl, nappy, crystal, #1463, 8".........................**25.00**
Ridgeleigh, ash tray, zircon, #1469, square................**50.00**
Ridgeleigh, celery tray, crystal, #1469, 12".....................**25.00**
Rococo, plate, salad; sahara, #1447, 7".........................**40.00**
Saturn, bowl, fruit; zircon, #1485, 12"...............................**65.00**
Saturn, parfait, zircon, #1485, 5-oz **60.00**
Saxony, cordial, sahara, #3394, 1-oz **200.00**
Stanhope, bowl, salad; crystal, #1483, 11"......................**40.00**
Stanhope, oil bottle, crystal, #1483, 3-oz....................**65.00**

Stanhope: Plate, 7", $7.00; Cup and saucer, $18.00; Creamer and sugar bowl, $35.00.

Tudor, goblet, crystal, #412, 7½-oz...................................**20.00**

Tudor, plate, luncheon; crystal, #411, 8"...........................**10.00**

Twist, oil bottle, moongleam, #1252, 4-oz **75.00**

Victorian, bowl, nappy, cobalt, #1425, 8" **200.00**

Victorian, plate, salad; cobalt, #1425, 7"........................**70.00**

Yeoman, celery tray, moongleam, #1184, 13" **25.00**

Homer Laughlin

Founded in 1871, the Homer Laughlin China Company continues today to be a leader in producing quality tablewares. Some of their earlier lines were produced in large quantity and are well marked with the company name or HLC logo; collectors find them fun to use as well as to collect, since none are as yet very expen-sive. See also Fiesta; Harlequin; Riviera.

Max-I-Cana (Fiesta molds): Cup and saucer, $30.00; Platter, $40.00; Fruit bowl, $28.00.

Amberstone, ash tray............**16.00**

Amberstone, casserole **28.00**

Amberstone, jam jar **30.00**

Amberstone, plate, 10"........... **5.00**

Americana, cup & saucer....... **5.50**

Americana, sugar bowl **9.00**

Casualstone, creamer **4.00**

Casualstone, pie plate...........**18.00**

Casualstone, platter, 13" **9.00**

Conchita, creamer **7.00**

Conchita, plate, deep, 8" 10.00
Epicure, bowl, nappy, 8"........ 8.50
Epicure, platter, large........... 9.00
Hacienda, creamer 9.00
Hacienda, teapot 75.00
Jubilee, chop plate 15.00
Jubilee, creamer.....................7.50
Mexicana, butter dish, ½-lb .80.00
Mexicana, egg cup, footed, rolled
    edge.................................25.00
Mexicana, platter, 10"...........15.00
Priscilla, sauce boat, 8½" 10.00
Priscilla, teapot, tall 30.00
Rhythm, bowl, fruit; 5½"........ 4.50
Rhythm, plate, 10"................12.00
Serenade, bowl, nappy, 9" 9.00
Serenade, casserole...............40.00
Serenade, sugar bowl........... 10.00
Tango, cup & saucer.............. 7.50
Tango, platter, 11¼" 11.00
Virginia Rose, cake server 30.00
Virginia Rose, plate, 10½" 15.00
Virginia Rose, gravy liner.....12.00
Wells Art Glaze, plate, 10" ...10.00
Wells Art Glaze, platter, oval,
    15½"..................................14.00
Wells Art Glaze, gravy liner, with
    handles, 9".................... 10.00

Hull

Established in Zanesville,
Ohio, in 1905, Hull manufactured
stoneware, florist ware, art pottery, and tile until about 1935,
when they began to produce the
lines of pastel matt-glazed artware which is today very collectible. The pottery was
destroyed by flood and fire in
1950. The factory was rebuilt and
equipped with the most modern
machinery which they soon dis-
covered was not geared to dupli-
cate the matt glazes. As a result,
new lines–Parchment and Pine,
and Ebb Tide, for example–were
introduced in a glossy finish. During the forties and into the fifties,

their Red Riding Hood kitchenware and novelty line was very
successful. Collectors of character
memorabilia, Hull collectors, and
kitchenware collectors alike vie to
own these endearing figural
charmers–match safes, banks,
canisters, salt and pepper shakers, etc.–dressed in the traditional
red cape and hood and carrying a
basket to Grandma's house.

Blossomflite, basket, T-9, with
    handle, 10" 65.00
Blossomflite, ewer, T-3, 8½"..45.00
Bow Knot, basket, B-25, with
    handle, 6½".................115.00
Bow Knot, bowl, console; B-16,
    13½"..............................165.00
Bow Knot, teapot, B-20, 6" .225.00
Calla Lily, bowl, #500/32, 10"
    diameter 95.00
Calla Lily, ewer, #506, 10"..150.00
Calla Lily, vase, #540/33, 6" .48.00
Camellia, creamer, #111, 5"..32.00
Camellia, ewer, #128, 4¾".....38.00
Camellia, vase, #123, 6½".....40.00
Dogwood, ewer, #520, 4¾".....48.00
Dogwood, jardiniere, 4" 42.00
Dogwood, vase, #517, 4¾".....35.00
Early Utility, bowl, #106, H in cir-
    cle, green, 5" 15.00
Early Utility, pretzel jar, H in cir-
    cle, 9½"............................180.00
Ebb Tide, basket, E-11, 16"...95.00
Iris, jardiniere, #413, 5½".....60.00
Iris, vase, #406, 4¾"..............36.00
Magnolia, glossy; candle holder,
    H-24, pink floral, 4" 20.00
Magnolia, glossy; vase, H-16,
    salesman's sample sticker,
    12½" 95.00
Magnolia, matt; console bowl,
    #26, 12"..........................85.00
Magnolia, matt; double cornu-
    copia, #6, 12" 95.00
Magnolia, matt; ewer, 4¾" ...32.00
Magnolia, matt; sugar bowl, #25,
    open, 3¾" 32.00

Magnolia, matt; vase, 4¾" ...**28.00**

Magnolia, matt; vase, #3, with handles, 8½"..................**60.00**

Magnolia, matt; vase, 10½" .**80.00**

Novelty, dancing girl, #955...**16.00**

Novelty, vase, #110, 9¼"........**18.00**

Orchid, jardiniere, #310, 6"..**90.00**

Orchid, vase, #303, 4¾".........**42.00**

Poppy, basket, #601, 12".....**300.00**

Poppy, vase, #606, 10½"......**160.00**

Red Riding Hood, bank.......**175.00**

Red Riding Hood, butter dish, with lid.........................**150.00**

Red Riding Hood, canister, salt; with lid.........................**325.00**

Red Riding Hood, creamer, tab handle...........................**55.00**

Red Riding Hood, match box, wall hanging........................**300.00**

Red Riding Hood, pitcher, side pour, 7"..........................**95.00**

Red Riding Hood, shakers, small, pair **25.00**

Red Riding Hood, sugar bowl, open **35.00**

Red Riding Hood, wall pocket/planter..............**195.00**

Serenade, ewer, S-21, pink with gold, 10½" **60.00**

Serenade, teapot, S-17, 5".....**80.00**

Serenade, vase, S-4, 5¼".......**35.00**

Thistle, vase, #52, 6½"..........**30.00**

Tokay, cornucopia, #10, shaded background, 11".............**32.00**

Tokay, vase, #8, shaded background, 10"....................**40.00**

Water Lily, cornucopia, L-7...**45.00**

Water Lily, jardiniere, L-23..**55.00**

Water Lily, lamp base, W-17, 12½"...........................**145.00**

Water Lily, vase, #17, 12½".**110.00**

Water Lily, vase, 10½".........**100.00**

Water Lily, vase, L-8, 8½" **60.00**

Water Lily, vase, W-1, 5½" ...**28.00**

Water Lily, vase, W-9, 8½" ...**60.00**

Wildflower, bowl, console; W-21, 12"................................**85.00**

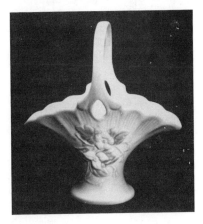

Wildflower basket, W-16, 10½", $135.00.

Wildflower, cornucopia, W-7.**45.00**

Wildflower, vase, 12½"........**110.00**

Wildflower, vase, W-9, 8½" ...**60.00**

Woodland, glossy; cornucopia, W-2, 5½" **22.00**

Woodland, glossy; jardiniere, W-7, 5½" **35.00**

Woodland, glossy; vase, 6½" .**24.00**

Figure of St. Francis, ivory matt with gold trim, 12", $18.00.

Woodland, matt; bowl, console; W-29, 14".........................**120.00**
Woodland, matt; creamer, W-27, 3½" **40.00**
Woodland, matt; jardiniere, W-7, 5½" **70.00**
Woodland, matt; vase, 6½" ...**42.00**

Hummel

Figurines, plates, and plaques produced since 1935 by Franz Goebel of West Germany are today highly collectible, often bringing prices several times that of their original retail value. They can generally be dated by their marks, each variation of which can be attributed a production period: Crown mark, 1935-1950; Full Bee mark, 1950-1959; Stylized Bee mark with variations, 1957-1970; Three-Line mark, 1964-1972; Goebel Bee mark 1972-1979; and Current mark, no bee, 1979 to the present.

Adoration, Full Bee mark, #23/I, 6¼"................................**340.00**
Adoration, Stylized Bee mark, #23/I, 6¼".......................**300.00**
Angel Cloud, font, Stylized Bee mark, #206, 2x5".........**250.00**
Apple Tree Boy, Full Bee mark, #142/3/0, 4"...................**120.00**
Apple Tree Boy, Stylized Bee mark, #142/3/0, 4"..........**80.00**
Bookworm, Full Bee mark, #8, 4"..................................**200.00**
Bookworms, bookends, 3-Line mark, #14A&B, 5½".....**275.00**
Boy with Toothache, Full Bee mark, #217, 5½" **155.00**
Chick Girl, candy box, Full Bee mark, #III/57, 5¼" **325.00**
Chick Girl, Full Bee mark, #57/I, 4¼"...............................**230.00**
Child Jesus, font, Full Bee mark, #26/0, 1½x5" **40.00**

Child with Flowers, Full Bee mark, #36/0, 2¾x4" **50.00**
Chimney Sweep, Crown mark, #12/I, 5½".....................**350.00**

Chimney Sweep, #12/I, 3-line mark, 5½", $110.00.

Christ Child, Crown mark, #18, 2x6"...............................**260.00**
Christ Child, Stylized Bee mark, #18, 2x6"........................**90.00**
Culprits, Stylized Bee mark, #44/A, 9½" **290.00**
Doll Mother, Stylized Bee mark, #67, 4¾" **140.00**
Farm Boy, Full Bee mark, #66, 5¼" **200.00**
Flower Madonna, Crown mark, #10/I, (color), 9½".........**400.00**
Flower Madonna, Crown mark, #10/I, (white), 9½".......**375.00**
Going to Grandma's, Stylized Bee mark, #52/0, 4¾".........**150.00**
Goose Girl, Stylized Bee mark, #47/3/0, 4"......................**100.00**
Happy Pastime, candy box, Stylized Bee, #III/69, 6" **200.00**
Joyful, ash tray, Stylized Bee mark, #33, 3½x6"...........**95.00**

Confidentially (with bow tie), #314, 3-line mark, 1972, 5½", $165.00.

Joyful, candy box, 3-Line mark, #III/53, 6¼"...................125.00
Joyous News, 3-Line mark, #27/III, 4¼x4¾"............400.00
Little Fiddler, 3-Line mark, #2/0, 6"...................140.00
Little Gabriel, 3-Line mark, #32/1, 5"..........................80.00
Little Guardian, Full Bee mark, #145, 3¾"......................125.00
Lullaby, candle holder, 3-Line mark, #24/I, 3¼x5".......125.00
Madonna, plaque, Full Bee mark, #48/0, 3x4"....................100.00
Madonna Without Halo, Crown Mark, #46/0, 10¼"........225.00
Madonna Without Halo, Full Bee mark, #46/0, 10¼".........85.00
Merry Wanderer, Crown mark, #11/2/0, 4¼"..................295.00
Merry Wanderer, Stylized Bee mark, #11/2/0, 4¼".........85.00
Mischief Maker, 3-Line mark, #342, 5".....................165.00
Out of Danger, 3-Line mark, #56/B, 6¼"...................150.00

Prayer Before Battle, 3-Line mark, #20, 4¼"............115.00
Puppy Love, Stylized Bee mark, #1, 5"...........................120.00
Retreat to Safety, Full Bee mark, #201/2/0, 4"...................140.00
Retreat to Safety, Stylized Bee mark, #20½/0, 4".........115.00
Sensitive Hunter, Full Bee mark, #6/0, 4¾"......................150.00
Signs of Spring, Full Bee mark, #203/I, 5"....................200.00
Signs of Spring, Stylized Bee mark, #203/I, 5"..........145.00
Silent Night, candle holder, 3-Line mark, #54, 5x6"...150.00
St George, Crown mark, #55, 6¾"...............................900.00
St George, 3-Line mark, #55, 6¾"...............................225.00
Village Boy, Full Bee mark, #51/3/0, 4"......................85.00
Volunteers, Crown mark, #50/0, 5½"...............................700.00
Volunteers, Full Bee mark, #50/0, 5½"...............................275.00
Wayside Devotion, 3-Line mark, #28/II, 7½"...................250.00
Weary Wanderer, Crown mark, #204, 6"........................500.00
Weary Wanderer, Full Bee mark, #204, 6"........................225.00

Imperial Glass

The Imperial Glass Company became a well-known fixture in the glassmaking business in 1910, due to the large quantities of carnival glass they produced. During the next decade they employed the lustre process in the manufacture of another successful product, Imperial Jewels, today called stretch glass. In 1958 Imperial bought the old Heisey and Cambridge molds and reproduced some of their original lines; Imperial marked these items with the 'I' superimposed over a 'G' logo.

Animal, dog, Airdale, cobalt .**35.00**
Bird, swan, caramel slag, marked, 9¼" **95.00**
Bird, duck, caramel slag **28.00**
Bookends, Cathay, concubine, satin, pair.....................**285.00**
Bowl, Beaded Block, green, deep, 6" **8.50**
Bowl, Twisted Optic, pink or green, 7"........................... **6.00**
Cake stand, Cape Cod, 11" ..**42.00**
Candy dish, Ipswich, amethyst, with lid, Heisey mark **40.00**
Claret, Cape Cod.................... **8.00**
Cruet, Cape Cod, #160/119, with stopper, 4-oz **20.00**
Cup, Hazen, pink **6.00**
Cup, Laced Edge, blue with opalescent rim **17.50**
Decanter, Cape Cod, 24-oz ...**50.00**

Donkey, caramel slag, 6½", $50.00.

Epergne, 2-piece, rare.........**165.00**
Goblet, Cape Cod, 7-oz........... **7.00**
Martini mixer, Big Shot Series, red....................................**85.00**
Pitcher, Cape Cod, 60-oz.......**65.00**
Pitcher, Old Williamsburg, yellow, 32-oz..............................**25.00**
Plate, Cape Cod, 10" **30.00**

Old Williamsburg (amber): Pitcher, $75.00; Goblet, $11.00; Wine, $9.00.

Plate, Laced Edge, blue with opalescent rim, 8" **15.00**
Punch set, Cape Cod, bowl & cups, 15-piece **200.00**
Sandwich server, Twisted Optic, pink, green, or amber, center handle............................**15.00**
Sugar bowl, Beaded Block, pink or amber **12.50**
Tray, windmill scene, milk glass, oval, 9½" **15.00**
Tumbler, Big Shot Series, ruby, 16-oz **20.00**
Vase, free-hand, black with applied amber threading, 9" ...**150.00**
Vase, free-hand, hearts on cobalt, paper label, 10" **250.00**
Vase, Laced Edge, green with opalescent rim, 5½"........**40.00**
Water set, frosted windmills, marigold, 5-piece..........**145.00**

Imperial Porcelain

From 1947 through 1960, the Imperial Porcelain Company of Zanesville, Ohio, produced a line of figurines, trays, bottles, etc., called Blue Ridge Mountain Boys, designed by Paul Webb. It is for this series that they are best known, although they also produced others: the Al Capp Dogpatch series and American Folklore miniatures, a line of twenty-three animals measuring one inch or less.

American Folklore miniature, cow, 1¾" **35.00**
American Folklore miniature, plaque, store ad, 4½" ...**300.00**
Ash tray, #101, man with jug & snake **75.00**
Box, cigarette; #98, dog atop, baby at door, square..............**115.00**
Decanter, #104, Ma by stump, with baby & skunk........**95.00**
Figurine, #101, man leans against tree trunk, 5"..................**75.00**

**Figurine, man on hands & knees, 3",
$80.00**

Figurine, cat in high-heeled shoe, 5½" long...........................**40.00**
Figure of Mammy, 3"..............**58.00**
Hot pad, Dutch boy with tulips, round, IP mark...............**30.00**
Jug, #101, Willie & snake **75.00**
Mug, #94, double baby handle, 4¼" **95.00**
Mug, #94, man with blue pants handle, 4¼"......................**75.00**
Mug, #99, Target Practice, boy on goat, farmer, 6"..............**85.00**
Planter, #104, Ma by stump, with baby & skunk **95.00**
Planter, #105, man with chicken on knee, washtub **110.00**
Planter, #27, man, jug & barrel, signed Paul Webb **25.00**

Shakers, Ma & Old Doc, figural, pair **95.00**

Indian Artifacts

Anything made by or related to the American Indian is of interest to collectors, whether it be a simple utilitarian tool or an object of art. Often each tribe exhibited certain characteristics in their work which help collectors determine the origin of their treasures. Some of the tribes are best known for their expertise in a particular craft. For instance, Navahos were weavers of rugs and blankets, the Zuni excelled in petit-point and inlay jewelry, and the Hopi made beautiful kachina dolls. Ceremonial items, fine beaded clothing and bags, and antique rugs are among the most valuable examples of Indian art.

Arrowhead, Autauga, Alabama, tan, 1¾" **6.00**
Awl case, Plains, with bone-handle awl & knife, tin cone dangles, 9" **45.00**
Basket, Hopi, coiled, Kachina mask design, miniature, 1¾x2" dia.......................**85.00**

Basket, Hopi, coiled, 5-color, 6" x 8½", $200.00.

161

Basket, Papagos, wire, for baking, 2x11" diameter **65.00**
Bowl, Mississippian, fish effigy pottery, 3½x6½", EX.....**225.00**
Celt, Mississippian, Illinois, dark gray, 7¾" **110.00**
Celt, Ohio, gray ground stone, good polish, 7" **125.00**
Container, Algonquin, birchbark with remnants of varnish, 4¾x9½x11"......................**15.00**
Drill, wine striped stone, miniature, 1⅛"........................**12.00**
Jar, Acoma, linear design, ochre on buff, red ochre base, 1900s, 8" **475.00**

Jar, Acoma, polychrome, 7" x 9", $200.00.

Knife, Archaic, black flint, deeply notched, 2½"...................**75.00**
Knife, Mississippian, late Woodland, gray & tan, 5x1½" ..**20.00**
Moccasins, Blackfoot, well-tanned elkhide, beadwork, 10" ..**65.00**
Moccasins, Sioux, red & white quills on purple quill ground, 1930s **150.00**
Olla, Paiute, some rim stitches missing, 15x18"............**225.00**
Pin, Navajo, silver with 9 turquoise, 4"...................**35.00**
Pipe, Mound Builder, squirrel effigy, pottery, pre-historic, 3½"................................**250.00**

Pipe, Plains, black stone with pewter inlay, puzzle stem, 5" elbow.............................**175.00**
Pipe, stone, common Southeastern style, 3x8½", EX.......**50.00**
Point, Clovis, gray, 1¾", M....**65.00**
Point, Dalton, Arkansas, off-white, well made, 3½" ...**75.00**
Pouch, Blackfoot, quilled & beaded, muslin back, early, 10x11", EX....................**125.00**
Quirt, Sioux, multicolor beadwork, red dyed horsehair end, 31", EX............................**45.00**
Quiver, parfleche, red ochre stained elkhide, dtd 1885, 30", EX..........................**600.00**
Spear point, Adena, light pink, 5½", M **285.00**
Spear point, Dalton, Arkansas, tan & red, thin, 3½" **135.00**
Spear point, Greenbriar Dalton, tan, 3⅛", EX **45.00**
Spear point, Hardin, off-white, 4½", EX......................**90.00**
Spear point, Hemphill, Missouri, tan color, 4½" **185.00**
Spear point, Osceola, Ohio, gray, 4½", M **165.00**
Spear point, Snyder, Illinois, tan with rose, 4" **145.00**
Storage jar, Hopi, pottery, 1850s, 17½" **300.00**
Tobacco bag, Iroquois, beadwork with fringe on buckskin, 32" long **25.00**
Trade beads, oval green chevrons, 1820s, 28" **60.00**
Tray, Athebascan, basketry with brown arrow designs, 17" diameter **95.00**
Tray, Salishan, basketry, imbricated, 12x21", EX...........**35.00**
Vessel, Hopi, umber & red ochre on buff, ca 1900, 12x8½", EX...............................**200.00**
War bonnet, Plains style, flannel cap, dyed feathers, beaded band **50.00**

War club head, effigy of mountain sheep, stone, 5½".........**185.00**
Whistle, Arapaho, bone, used in Sun Dance, 1920, 15".....**65.00**

Moccasins, Eastern Woodlands, quilled leather and tradecloth, $385.00.

Inkwells

Since about 1835 when ink was refined, there has been a market for inkwells. Today collectors appreciate them for their beauty, ingenuity, rarity, and styling. They are found in abundance in art glass of all types, brass, bronze, cast iron, wood with glass liners, natural stones, pottery, and pewter.

Basalt, turned sides, 3 quill holes, marked, 1700s, 1¾x2¼".**90.00**
Blown, cobalt, funnel opening, tooled, 2½" **40.00**
Brass, Bradley & Hubbard logo, 2"......................................**20.00**
Brass, Egyptian head, glass insert, EX **125.00**
Brass, mandolin & sheet music figural, EX **110.00**
Bronze, bird & chick, cold paint, Austria, 1900, 3"..........**250.00**
Bronze, mottled finish, marked Silvercrest **85.00**
Bronze, Victorian boy at well figural **295.00**
Bronze, walrus head figural, 1880, 4½" **600.00**

Cast iron, marked TA & Sons, bottle marked Higgins...**40.00**
Cast metal, camel figural, saddled, 6"............................**75.00**
Cloisonne, lady & child in scene, signed, 10"....................**525.00**
Crystal, hexagonal panels, sterling lid, 2⅛" **45.00**
Cut glass, repousse sterling top with roses, 3½".............**100.00**
Glass, amber, paneled pyramid form, 2⅜" **65.00**
Glass, yellow, embossed swirl, hinged top.....................**125.00**
Glass, snail, in cast iron stand, revolves, 3x5x2" **160.00**

Wedgwood Jasper, light blue and white, 6", $225.00.

Keene, Diamond Point pattern, olive green, 1¾x2½" **175.00**
Leather & brass, traveler's, violin case shape **165.00**
Lignum vitae, traveler's, barrel form, ca 1850.................**75.00**
Pewter, round, with quill holes, unmarked, 3½x5".........**150.00**
Porcelain, floral, attached tray, Dresden **125.00**
Porcelain, floral, box form, handle, 2¼x4" **80.00**
Porcelain, 2 boys with bird's nest, double, 6x9¼".............**145.00**
Staffordshire, cavalier & boy, double baskets form wells, 9x7".**250.00**

Staffordshire, monk peeks at sleeping lady, 3x5" **225.00**

Stoneware, 1⅞x3⅜" diameter, EX **65.00**

Wood, bulldog's head, glass eyes, English, 1800s, 3", EX .**300.00**

Wood, owl, glass eyes, hinged head, 6" base **45.00**

Insulators

After the telegraph was invented in 1844, insulators were used to attach the transmission wires to the poles. With the coming of the telephone, their usefullness increased, and it is estimated that over 3,000 types were developed. Collectors today value some of them very highly–the threadless type, for example, often brings prices of several hundred dollars. Color, rarity, and age are all important factors to consider when evaluating insulators. In the 1960s, N.R. Woodward developed a standard system of identification using numbers with a 'C.D.' prefix.

CD, #102, BGM Company, smooth base, purple **18.00**

CD, #102, California, smooth base, blue........................**15.00**

CD, #102.2, Westinghouse, smooth base, blue.........**130.00**

CD, #121, Diamond, smooth base, purple, foreign................**15.00**

CD, #138, Kerr, smooth base, clear **4.00**

CD, #141, No Name (Hot Cross Bun), smooth base, emerald green **9.00**

CD, #145, Hemingray, sharp drip points, blue...................... **1.00**

CD, #162, SS & Company, smooth base, lime green **75.00**

CD, #168, Hemingray, smooth base, carnival **25.00**

CD, #263, Hemingray, smooth base, blue........................**80.00**

CD, #270, No Name, smooth base, green **150.00**

CD, #317, Chambers, smooth base, lime green **150.00**

CD, #320, Pyrex, smooth base, clear **9.00**

CD, #731, McKee, smooth base, aqua, threadless...........**130.00**

Hemingray 60, Mickey Mouse, clear, $15.00.

Irons

The iron gradually evolved from the smithy-made flatiron to the improved patented models of the 1870s (all of which had to be heated on the stove) to box irons (which held heated slugs), charcoal irons, gas irons, and finally to electric models. Fluting irons, pleating irons, and tailor's irons did little to make ironing day easier but nevertheless performed specialized jobs efficiently.

Baby Betsy Ross, electric, in original box **20.00**

Charcoal, cast iron, figural lion finial, 7¼" **50.00**

Charcoal, cast iron, figural dolphin uprights, 9"..........**65.00**
Charcoal, man's head forms latch, 8"....................**70.00**
Child's, Sandy Andy #22, sadiron, 4"....................**30.00**
Child's, swan figural, cast iron, 2½"..........................**55.00**
Fluter, Crown Pat Nov 2, 1875, heater slugs, 6" roller ..**125.00**
Hatter's, rope curl shackle, hinged..........................**200.00**
Pleater, cast iron & brass **95.00**
Polisher, Gleason's Pat Jan 22, 1870, 5"........................**110.00**
Sadiron, Le Parisien #6, coat-of-arms in relief, 6½"..........**75.00**
Sadiron, Sensible #4, cast iron, 5¼"....................**40.00**
Sadiron, Sensible #90, Pat May 5, 1908, 6½"........................**40.00**
Sleeve, Ober Co, Chagrin Falls 801, corn cob grip, 6¾" ..**90.00**

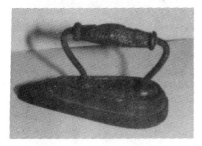

Sleeve iron, 6" long, $25.00.

Sleeve, rope handle, 5½".......**40.00**
Sleeve, Sensible #5, 8"..........**60.00**
Tie Press, faux marquetry on top, 4x8⅞"..............................**40.00**
Wintenberger, plain face, PW mark, 2⅞".....................**80.00**

Ironstone

There are many types of decorated ironstone available today, but the most sought-after is the simple white dinnerware some-times decorated in relief with fruit, grains, and foliage, ribbing and scallops. It was made by many English potters from the last quarter of the 18th century until well into the 1900s.

Baker, Hebe, oval, open, Alcock, 9⅜x7⅛".........................**60.00**
Baker, Wheat, JF, small **55.00**
Bowl, sauce; Baltic, with cover & ladle, T Hulmes **135.00**
Bowl, sauce; Ceres, with cover, Elsmore & Forster **120.00**
Bowl, sauce; Fish Hook, with cover, Meakin................**95.00**
Bowl, sauce; Leaf Fan, with cover, Alcock, 7⅞" **95.00**
Casserole, Plain Square, with cover, Wedgwood...........**35.00**
Casserole, Wheat & Clover, with cover, Turner & Goddard, large................................**75.00**
Compote, Arched Forget-Me-Not, on standard **110.00**
Compote, Gothic, tall pedestal, Edwards, 1850s..............**75.00**
Creamer, Double Sydenham.**55.00**
Creamer, Grenade.................**60.00**
Cup, handleless coffee; Wheat in Meadow **22.00**
Cup, hot toddy; Columbia.....**25.00**
Cup, hot toddy; 1851 Octagon, T&R Boote....................**30.00**
Cup & saucer, handleless; Chinese shape, Shaw **40.00**
Cup & saucer, handleless; Columbia **35.00**
Cup & saucer, Paris, Alcock .**30.00**
Gravy boat, Ceres, Elsmore & Forster, 1859 ....**55.00**
Gravy boat, Fuchsia, bulbous, 1860s, 5¼" **35.00**
Ladle, plain with fleur-de-lis on handle............................**40.00**
Nappy, Mocho, T&R Boote....**12.00**
Nappy, Vintage, Challinor ...**12.00**
Pitcher, milk; Ceres, Elsmore & Forster, 8½"................**125.00**

Pitcher, milk; Sydenham, T&R
Boote, 7⅞" **185.00**
Pitcher, syrup; Panelled
Columbia, 1850s **135.00**
Plate, Bell Flower, Edwards, din-
ner size **18.00**
Plate, Fluted Pearl, Wedgwood,
1847, 9½" **18.00**
Plate, soup; Paris, Alcock **30.00**
Platter, Sydenham, oval, T&R
Boote, 16x11¾" **50.00**
Punch bowl, Berry Cluster, with
handles, Furnival **145.00**
Relish, Fish Hook, Meakin ..**20.00**
Relish, Wheat, J&G Meakin .**30.00**
Sugar bowl, Ceres, with lid,
miniature......................... **75.00**
Sugar bowl, Fish Hook, Meakin,
small **55.00**
Teapot, Ceres, Elsmore & Forster,
9¾" **225.00**
Teapot, Sydenham, Boote **65.00**
Teapot, Trent, Alcock **125.00**
Waste bowl, Shaw's 1856 Fan,
large............................... **65.00**

of other animals. Teeth of the
sperm whale are also considered
ivory. Much of what we are familiar with are Oriental carvings,
but this substance was often used
for more utilitarian objects by
carvers in other parts of the world
as well.

Apple corer, ca 1820 .... **155.00**
Apple with leaf & stem, village
scene, 3¼" **150.00**
Bird trainer, bird on cord, with
basket, Japan, 9"..........**450.00**
Christ at Pillory, Renaissance
style, 14" **2,100.00**
Cigarette holder, bird claw ...**25.00**
Crocodile, open mouth with
carved teeth, 17" **175.00**
Dice shaker, ornate carving, ca
1820 .... **125.00**
Dr's lady, nude Oriental lady,
1800s, 7½" **150.00**

Teapot, #38 incised on base, Meakin, 9", $135.00.

Ivory

Ivory, though primarily
thought of as the material com-
posing the elephant's tusk, may
also be from the tusks and teeth

Japanese group: man with a young boy and a monkey under umbrella, signed, 8½", $350.00.

Elder with trained monkey, signed, Japan, 1900, 6" **180.00**
Farmer carrying basket of seed, Japan, 9½" **450.00**
Fisherman, pole/fish/basket, terrain base, signed, 6" **150.00**
Fisherman stands with fish & basket, Japan, 9½" **400.00**
Foo lion, fierce expression, China, 5", pair **325.00**
Game markers, 4 in round ivory box, ca 1800 ....**65.00**
Girl with instrument, seated, set of 4, 4" **350.00**
Ink sander, ca 1820 ....**95.00**
Jar, foo dog form, 4" **230.00**
Lady gardener with rake, artist signed, Japan, 6¼" **95.00**
Nutmeg grater, egg shaped, ca 1800 ....**245.00**
Warrior in chain mail with sword & shield, 8" **160.00**
Whistle, age cracks, 2⅝" **85.00**

Japanese Lusterware

Imported from Japan during the 1920s, novelty tableware items, vases, ash trays, etc. often in blue, tan, and mother-of-pearl lustre glazes were sold through five-and-dime stores or given as premiums for selling magazine subscriptions. You'll find several nice examples at nearly any large flea market you attend this summer, and they may be purchased at reasonable prices.

Condiment, 2 cruets, shakers, mustard jar, blue & tan .**28.00**
Shakers, ball-form faces **10.00**
Shakers, bulbous, on tray with center handle, 4" long **8.00**
Shakers, yellow chick in shell, handle, 1929 ....**10.00**
Tea set, bluebird decor, child's size, 13-piece, serves 4 ..**45.00**

Toothpick holder, grotesque bird with wings wide, open mouth, 5" **10.00**

Jewelry

Today, anyone interested in buying gems will soon find out that the antique stones are the best values. Not only are prices from ⅓ to ½ less than on comparable new jewelry, but the craftsmanship and styling of modern-day pieces are lacking in comparison. Costume jewelry from all periods is popular, especially Art Nouveau and Art Deco examples. Signed pieces are particularly good, such as those by Miriam Haskell, Georg Jensen, David Anderson, and other well-known artists.

Bracelet, Eisenberg, rhodium & rhinestones, individually linked...........................**115.00**
Bracelet, Renoir, copper links, Art Moderne.........................**60.00**
Bracelet, Weiss, emerald-cut rhinestones in rhodium, flexible **85.00**
Brooch, Eisenberg, sterling butterfly with faux gemstones, 1930 ....**475.00**
Brooch, Kramer, rhinestones & aurora borealis stones form butterfly.........................**60.00**
Brooch, Miriam Haskell, filigree fretwork in goldtone with seed pearls **88.00**
Brooch, Trifari, crown design, multicolor faux gems & rhinestones **80.00**
Brooch & earrings, Emmons, antiqued goldtone & aurora borealis stones **70.00**
Earrings, Charel, foiled & faceted aurora borealis, 1950 .....**18.00**

Earrings, Eisenberg, rhinestone & rhodium drops.................75.00

Earrings, Emmons, faux pearls in rhodium, clip style.........12.50

Earrings, Hobe, faceted & bezel set gemstones, leaf design, 1¾x1".............................85.00

Earrings, Mosell, shell design, hand-painted gold electroplate.................................30.00

Earrings, Napier, rope design, gold-plated.....................20.00

Earrings, Nettie Rosenstine, gold-plated flower with rhinestones.............................30.00

Necklace, Danecraft, sterling cast design, choker style.......58.00

Necklace, DeMario, multicolor blue beads, 3-strand......85.00

Necklace, Monet, dog collar style, 15½" chain....................150.00

Necklace, Monet, heavy cast linkage, goldtone, 1945........68.00

Necklace, Napier, flexible links, silver finish, Art Moderne, 1960................................75.00

Necklace, Sarah Coventry, rhodium chain, 1960.....12.50

Necklace, Weiss, rhodium & rhinestones, hand cut....95.00

Pendant, JJ, pewter, rabbit with spectacles, 1950..............30.00

Pendant, Trifari, amber bezel set cabochon, gold-plated choker collar.............................85.00

Scottish pin, agate set in sterling, 2¼", $100.00.

Pin, Castlecliff, gold electroplate with faux baroque pearl mount, 1960 ....45.00

Pin, Emmons, scarecrow, goldtone with faux pearl...............30.00

Pin, Park Lane, horse, 2-tone florentine finish..................32.00

Pin, Sarah Coventry, goldtone flower, rhinestones, & amber glass, 1950 ....75.00

Pin, Trifari, elephant form with rhinestone accents.........90.00

Pin, Trifari, goldtone feather, for scarf 12.50

Pin, unmarked, bird in flight, wood & plastic, Art Moderne, 1935................................50.00

Pin, Weiss, Christmas tree, multicolor stones 50.00

Pin & earrings, Emmons, Blue Bud, faceted glass in burnished rhodium..............25.00

Plastic

Bracelet, Bakelite, bangle, black, narrow, no carving 35.00

Bracelet, Bakelite, bangle, mottled plastic, set of 5........40.00

Bracelet, Bakelite, black, cutwork medallion, hinged..........80.00

Bracelet, Bakelite, strawberries & leaves hang on gold-colored chain.............................100.00

Bracelet, Catalin, apple-juice clear, floral carving 100.00

Bracelet, Catalin, figural, animal or novelty applique, clamp style 200.00

Bracelet, Catalin, inlaid rhinestones, clamp style.........30.00

Bracelet, Catalin, multicolor, uncarved, stretch type with original elastic 30.00

Bracelet, Catalin, 3-color stripes, bangle style 50.00

Bracelet, red & white beads on elastic cord 35.00

Dress clip, Catalin, novelty, figural, animal or vegetable.25.00

Earrings, Catalin, stylized floral carving.............................. 6.00

Earrings, floral design with rhinestones, pair......................**22.00**

Earrings, Weiss, rhinestone decorations, marked Weiss, pair.**35.00**

Necklace, Bakelite, amber & brown square beads on clear link chain **60.00**

Necklace, Bakelite, cherries on plastic chain, metal links to fruit................................**150.00**

Necklace, Catalin, animal figurals on plastic chain **110.00**

Pin, Bakelite, Scotty dog, brown with green bow...............**65.00**

Polished wood and plastic pin, ca 1935, $60.00.

Pin, Casein with applied celluloid in cameo style, ca 1930..**55.00**

Pin, Catalin, animal or vegetable, 1-color, small **30.00**

Pin, Catalin, multicolor Art Deco design, large....................**40.00**

Pin, Catalin, novelty or patriotic figural, 1-color, large......**80.00**

Pin, Catalin, with danglers, geometric form, multicolor..**45.00**

Pin, Celluloid, bunch of bananas, large...............................**22.50**

Pin, Celluloid, flying bird, blue & white **40.00**

Pin, Celluloid, red leaves in bouquet form **45.00**

Pin, Lucite, fruit form, clear with painted background **100.00**

Keen Kutter

Watch for items marked Keen Kutter, a brand name used before the mid-1930s by E.C. Simmons Hardware Company. Not only are their products (household items, tools of all types, knives, etc.) collectible, but so are the advertising materials they distributed.

Apple peeler...........................**85.00**
Bit, countersink; KK-113....... **7.50**
Calipers **22.00**
Corkscrew **20.00**
Food grinder, KK-21.............**25.00**
Grinder, bench; hand type ...**45.00**
Hammer, KK-411, 20-oz **15.00**

Fan, floral design on back, $45.00.

Manicure set..........................**22.00**
Matchbook **8.00**
Plane, block; KK-17, 7".........**20.00**
Plane, block; KK-220, 7½" **18.00**
Plane, circular; KK-115, 10".**165.00**
Pliers, slim nose; KK-25 ....**12.00**
Punch, revolving, KK-44.......**17.50**
Rule, steel, KK-312, 12"........**15.00**
Saw, crosscut; KK-3002, EX.**35.00**
Saw, meat cutting; KK-106 ..**18.00**
Screwdriver, 20" **12.50**
Waffle iron **95.00**

Kentucky Derby Glasses

Souvenir glasses commemorating the Kentucky Derby have

been produced since the 1940s. These have become popular collectibles, especially among race fans.

1940s, aluminum	**150.00**
1940s, plastic Beetleware	**275.00**
1945, short	**375.00**
1945, tall	**150.00**
1948	**48.00**
1949, He Has Seen. . .All	**48.00**
1950	**155.00**
1951	**150.00**
1952, Gold Cup	**45.00**
1953	**38.00**
1954	**35.00**
1955	**30.00**
1956	**30.00**
1957	**28.00**
1958, Gold Bar	**30.00**
1958, Iron Liege	**42.00**
1959-1960, ea	**24.00**

1960, $24.00.

1961	**20.00**
1962-1963, ea	**18.00**
1964-1965, ea	**18.00**
1966	**15.00**
1967-1968, ea	**14.00**

1969	**13.00**
1970	**10.00**
1971	**9.00**
1972	**9.00**
1973	**7.00**
1974	**6.00**
1975	**5.00**
1976	**4.50**
1977-1978, ea	**4.00**
1979-1980, ea	**3.50**
1981-1982, ea	**3.00**
1983	**2.50**
1984-1986, ea	**2.00**
1987-1988, ea	**2.00**

Kewpies

Since first introduced through the pages of *The Ladies' Home Journal,* Rose O'Neill's Kewpies have continued to work their charms on us all. Collectors today treasure dolls with the original O'Neill label. Anything decorated with Kewpies is considered very collectible.

Ad, They Wanted Jell-O, 1919, EX/NM	**12.00**
Bank, composition, Kewpie, nude, sits with arms around knees, 12"	**48.00**
Book, Brownie Primer, O'Neill illustration, 1905	**25.00**
Book, Kewpies' Health Book, 1929, EX	**75.00**
Book, Little Kewpie Book, O'Neill illustration	**10.00**
Bride & Groom, vinyl, Cameo by Jesco, 16", pair	**85.00**
Candy container, Kewpies, Borgfeldt, NM	**160.00**
Charm, Kewpie sterling	**20.00**
Cup & saucer, with Kewpies, signed, Germany	**55.00**
Doctor & Nurse, vinyl, Cameo by Jesco, 12", each	**27.50**
Door knocker, brass, Kewpie figural	**60.00**

Kewpie, bisque, in basket with flowers, 3½" **600.00**
Kewpie, bisque, jointed hips & shoulders, 4" **465.00**
Kewpie, bisque, jointed hips & shoulders, 9" **850.00**
Kewpie, bisque, 1-piece body, jointed shoulders, 1½"....**95.00**
Kewpie, bisque, 1-piece body, jointed shoulders, 2½"..**115.00**
Kewpie, bisque, 1-piece body, jointed shoulders, 4-5" .**145.00**
Kewpie, bisque, 1-piece body, jointed shoulders, 6" **185.00**
Kewpie, Bride & Groom, bisque, 4" **465.00**
Kewpie, celluloid, Black, 5"..**100.00**

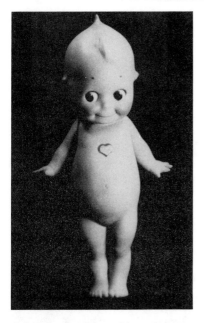

Jointed shoulders, bisque, paper label, 6", $185.00.

Kewpie, celluloid, 12"..........**250.00**
Kewpie, celluloid, 2" **40.00**
Kewpie, celluloid, 2-piece body, jointed shoulders, 3" **60.00**
Kewpie, celluloid, 2-piece body, jointed shoulders, 5" **95.00**
Kewpie, celluloid, 5" **85.00**

Kewpie, cloth, mask face, Kreuger, 12", NM........**175.00**
Kewpie, Confederate Soldier, bisque, 6" **775.00**
Kewpie, shoulder-head on cloth body, 6" **600.00**
Lamp, Kewpie decor, metal, Ronson, 1920s.....................**150.00**
Magazine page, Harper's Bazaar, with O'Neill illustration, 1909..............................**10.00**
Paper dolls, uncut, 1967 ....**60.00**
Pincushion, bisque, Kewpie half-doll, signed, 2¾"..........**325.00**
Pincushion, silverplated, Kewpie on each side **200.00**
Pitcher, 7 Kewpies on blue, signed, Germany, 2½"..**200.00**
Place-card holder, bisque, Kewpie on back, Germany........**110.00**
Plaque, blue jasper, 3 Kewpies on bench, triangular, 4½".**265.00**
Plate, Kewpies, 1973, 8".......**25.00**
Post card, Kewpies at play ...**40.00**
Poster, Kewpies, signed Rose O'Neill, large.................**25.00**
Powder box, Kewpies, marked Germany......................**125.00**
Shakers, Kewpies on tummies, old Japan, pair...............**40.00**
Sunbonnet Kewpie, vinyl, Cameo by Jesco, 11½"................**45.00**
Tea set, Kewpies, Rose O'Neill, Germany, 23-piece **650.00**
Teapot, lustre, signed O'Neill, tray marked Germany.**135.00**
Thimble, metal, marked **35.00**
Toothpick holder, glass, standing Kewpie, marked.............**45.00**
Tray, 8 Kewpies, signed O'Neill, Rudolstadt, 10" **295.00**
Vase, white on blue jasper, Kewpies, signed 4" **350.00**
Whistle, brass Kewpie **20.00**

Kitchen Collectibles

From the early patented apple peelers, cherry pitters, and

food choppers to the gadgets of the twenties and the thirties, many collectors find special appeal in kitchen tools.

Apple peeler, cast iron, Goodell, May 28, 1898 ....80.00
Apple peeler, cast iron, Little Star, pat June 9, 1885....90.00
Apple peeler, Lockey Howland, cast iron, 1856 ....60.00
Apple peeler, Shaker table model, maple, EX.....................265.00
Apple peeler, straddle type, walnut with iron prong, 1850s, EX 115.00
Bean slicer/pea sheller, Vaugn's, cast iron, clamps to table, EX 40.00
Bowl, mixing; pink, Hazel Atlas, 11⅝" 18.00
Bread knife, primitive, wheat carved on handle, 11½"..32.50
Butter dish, Crisscross, green, 1-lb 28.50
Butter dish, crystal, embossed Butter 19.00
Cake plate, pink, embossed snowflake........................18.00
Can opener, Columbia, cast iron, EX 7.50
Canister, McKee, custard, with lid, 48-oz 25.00
Cherry seeder, double, cast iron clamp-on, Goodell Co, Antrim NH, EX 32.00

Cherry seeder, New Standard No 50, ca 1900, 10" 35.00
Churn, Dazey, 1-quart, original paper label...................875.00
Cookie jar, green, barrel form, with lid 45.00
Egg poacher, tin, 4-egg..........24.00
Food grinder, Chipaway, cast iron, screw clamps, EX...........20.00
Food, Griswold #11, cast iron.25.00
Grater, brass half-cylinder with iron handle, ca 1820s, 14" long 90.00
Grater, nutmeg; Acme, tin, sliding lid, EX.............................45.00
Grater, nutmeg; carved wood with ivory lid, 1800s, small....40.00
Griddle, Griswold #10, oval..50.00
Ice bucket, Fry, pink 70.00
Knife, chopping; wrought iron with wood handle, 1850s, 8x9" long........................32.50
Ladle, Cambridge, amber 13.00
Lemon reamer, turned & carved wood, ca 1870s, 7" long .20.00
Measuring cup, delphite blue, 2-cup 48.00
Measuring set, Jeannette, ultramarine, 4-pc 100.00
Mug, pink, Adam's Rib 14.00
Pitcher, milk; cobalt 45.00
Pretzel jar, Hocking, green, fine ribbed..............................55.00
Salt bowl, crystal, wood lid ..15.00
Sausage stuffer, cast iron, Russell & Irwin, Aug 17, 1886 ...35.00

Cookie press, tin with wooden plunger, $30.00.

Sausage stuffer, tin cone, cast iron base, 1880s, EX **25.00**

Shakers, Hocking, green clam-broth, 8-oz, pr **25.00**

Shakers, Red Tulip, pr **5.00**

Sharpener, knife; Eversharp, iron with wooden handle, EX. **5.00**

Sieve, pierced tin, shallow pan form, ca 1880s, EX **12.50**

Sifter, Standard, tin with side crank, pat'd, October 15, 1918, 7" **10.00**

Skillet, heavy metal, Grand Union Tea Co, 10½" **30.00**

Tumbler, Hazel Atlas, white opaque, 8-oz **5.00**

Waffle iron, Foxhall, with bail, Pat 1869 .... **20.00**

Tin egg poacher, marked Kreamer, $55.00.

Knives

Collectors of pocket knives look for those with bone handles in mint, unsharpened condition; those with pearl handles; Case doctor's knives; and large display models.

Case, #R1048, marked Tested XX, candy striped handle, 1 blade, 4⅛" **265.00**

Case, #R1098, marked Tested XX, candy striped handle, 1 blade, 6" **315.00**

Case, #1116SP, marked 10 Dot, bud walnut handle, 1 blade, 3½" **45.00**

Case, #2109B, USA, slick black handle, 1 blade, 3¼" **125.00**

Case, #2136B, marked XX, black handle, 1 blade, 4⅛" **125.00**

Case, #22001R, marked Tested XX, slick black hdl, 2 blades, 3" **115.00**

Case, #5172, marked USA, stag handle, 1 blade, 5½" **145.00**

Case, #61011, marked USA, bone stag handle, 1 blade **30.00**

Case, #61048SP, USA, delrin handle, 1 blade, 4⅛" **30.00**

Case, #6111½, marked XX bone handle, 1 blade, 4⅜" **365.00**

Case, #6185, marked XX bone handle, 1 blade, 3⅝" **115.00**

Case, #6200, marked Tested XX, green bone handle, 2 blades, 4" **570.00**

Case, #6278, white bone handle, 2 blades, 3½" **250.00**

Case, #64047PU, 10-dot, bone handle, 4 blades, 4" **35.00**

Primble, #4983, waterfall handle with slant bolsters, 2 blades, 4". **75.00**

Primble, #5264, bone handle, 3 blades, 3⅝" **35.00**

Primble, #5373, bone handle, 3 blades, 3⅜" **35.00**

Primble, #5517, imitation bone handle, 4 blades, 4⅛" **30.00**

Primble, #5763, bone handle with tip bolsters, 2 blades, 3". **20.00**

Primble, #702, Rogers bone handle, 2 blades, 3¼" **25.00**

Primble, #732, imitation pearl handle, 4 blades, 3¼" **38.00**

Primble, #909, peachseed bone handle, 2 blades, 3" **40.00**

Primble, #921, peachseed bone handle, 3 blades, 2¾" **35.00**

Queen, #11, winterbottom bone handle, 1 blade, 4⅛" **30.00**

Queen, #15, winterbottom bone handle, 2 blades, 3½" **30.00**

Queen, #22, brown bone handle, 2 blades, 3½" **48.00**
Queen, #4, pearl handle, 2 blades, 3⅜" **38.00**
Queen, #46, winterbottom bone handle, 2 blades, 5"........**35.00**
Queen, #6, smoked pearl handle, 2 blades, 2½" **25.00**
Queen, #60, winterbottom bone handle, 1 blade, 3½" **38.00**
Queen, #8420, genuine stag handle, 2 blades....................**35.00**
Remington, #R105B, pyremite handle, 3 blades, 3¼" ...**120.00**
Remington, #R1092, black handle, 2 blades, 3⅜" **50.00**
Remington, #R151, redwood handle, 3 blades..................**115.00**

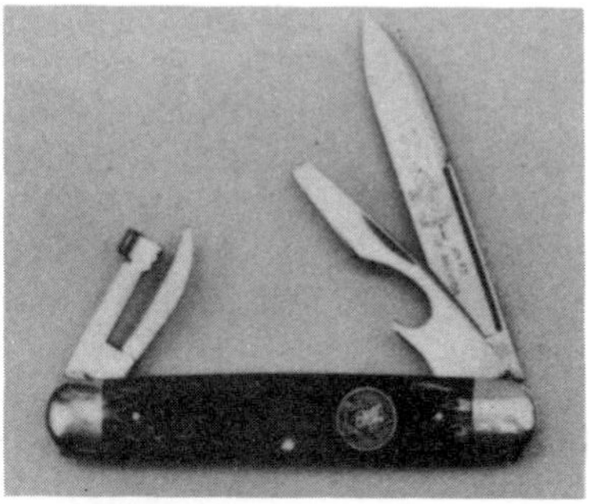

Remington RS-4773 Scout knife, brown bone, 3⅜", $175.00.

Remington, #R1905, pyremite handle, 2 blades **85.00**
Remington, #R212, black handle, 2 blades, 3⅝" **150.00**
Remington, #R3113, bone handle, 3 blades, 4" **185.00**
Remington, #R3500BU, buffalo horn handle, 3 blades ..**200.00**
Remington, #R4144, pearl handle, 3 blades **240.00**
Remington, #R488, cocobolo handle, 2 blades, 3½" **150.00**
Remington, #R595, pyremite handle, 2 blades, 3¼" **145.00**
Remington, #R6105, pyremite handle, 2 blades, 3"......**125.00**
Remington, #R6448, cocobolo handle, 3 blades....................**55.00**
Remington, #R679, metal handle, 2 blades, 3" **150.00**
Remington, #R874, pearl handle, 1 blade, 3⅛" **115.00**
Schrade Cutlery, #S7706B, mother-of-pearl handle, 2 blades, 3" **48.00**
Schrade Cutlery, #2014S, ivory celluloid handle, 2 blades, 3⅝" **80.00**
Schrade Cutlery, #2073¾, ebony handle, 2 blades, 3⅝" **75.00**
Schrade Cutlery, #7114, horn pyralin handle, 2 blades, 3⅜" **50.00**
Winchester, #1621, cocobolo handle, 1 blade, 3⅜" **85.00**
Winchester, #1905, stag handle, 1 blade, 4½" **150.00**
Winchester, #2377, pearl handle, 2 blades, 2⅝" **155.00**
Winchester, #2666, ebony handle, 2 blades, 3⅜" **75.00**
Winchester, #2868, stag handle, 2 blades, 3¾" **230.00**
Winchester, #2911, stag handle, 2 blades, 3½" **160.00**
Winchester, #3019, red celluloid handle, 3 blades, 3½" ..**280.00**
Winchester, #3907, stag handle, 3 blades, 4" **325.00**
Winchester, #3916, brown bone handle, 3 blades, 3½" ...**225.00**
Winchester, #4340, pearl handle, 3 blades, 3¼" **300.00**

Labels

The colorful lithographed labels that were once used on wooden packing crates are being collected for their artwork and advertising. Clever association between company name or location and depicted themes are common; particularly good examples of this are usually most desirable. For instance, Santa Paula lemon labels show a jolly Santa Claus, and Red Cat oranges have a cat mascot.

Snowboy apples, 1930s, 11" x 9", $3.50.

Airport Bourbon Whiskey, ca 1934, 3x5" **6.00**

America's Delight Apples, stone lithograph, 1920 .... **4.00**

Brewer's Best Beer, ca 1950s-1960s, 3x4" **1.00**

California Dream Oranges, gold peacock, 1920 ....**17.00**

Chekola Pears, stone lithograph of orchard, 1915 ....**18.00**

Frisco Vegetables, Art Deco building, 1930 .... **3.00**

Glendora Vegetables, stone lithograph of vegetables, 1930. **3.50**

Golden State Lemons, map of California & lemons, 1930 ... **3.00**

Hatchet Brand Vegetables, stone lithograph of ear of corn, 1906 ....**19.00**

Hill Choice, orchard scene, purple mountains **2.00**

Irish Singer Cigars, ca 1920s, 4½x4½" **4.00**

Locust Grove Tomatoes, view of lane **9.00**

Loot of Ventura County, bright yellow, blue, & white **2.00**

Lucky Strike Apples, hunter shooting buck, 1920 .... **8.00**

Marvel Coffee, ca 1900-1920s, 11x4" **3.00**

Navajo, fruit crate, proud Indian brave, stitched leather ... **5.00**

Our Family Tomatoes, mother, father, & 2 children **7.00**

Pride of the River Asparagus, river boat, 1930 .... **7.50**

Queen Beauty Brand Soap, embossed printing, 1906 ..... **8.00**

Snoboy Cigars, snowman holding apple, ca 1930s, 11x9" **5.00**

Star, big gold & white star in center of green **2.00**

Tom Mix Cigars, famous cowboy, ca 1930s, 6x10" **22.00**

Uncle Sam Cigars, ca 1900s, 4x4½" **15.00**

Up N' Atom Vegetables, rabbit wearing boxing gloves..... **3.00**

US Seal Cigars, 1890s, 4x4"...**15.00**

Woodlake Gold, lake & mountains, fruit crate, 1930 ... **6.00**

Yema Cigars, Art Nouveau, woman in cigar smoke ...**15.00**

7-Up (Slenderizes & Settles the Stomach), 1930 .... **1.50**

I Grow These Myself, citrus, $8.00.

Lace, Linens and Needlework

Crocheted and tatted lace are varieties of handwork most often encountered at flea markets today; and collectors can still appreciate the tedium, expertise, and eyestrain that went into their making. If your treasured laces are yellowed or stained, an instant tea bath can be used to obtain a natural ecru look and is far less damaging to the old threads than using bleach to whiten them. Doilies are often framed and hung in groupings on bedroom walls or used to top throw pillows. From remnants of lace trims, you can create your own Victorian 'waist'–either trim a ready-made or sew one up using a basic pattern. Machine washing is not recommended.

Back splash, linen, embroidered, pullwork, 23x17" **25.00**
Bolster cover, linen, embroidered birds, 34x70" **55.00**
Centerpiece, Battenburg scalloped border, 12" diameter **45.00**
Chair set, crochet, Butterfly pattern, 3-piece....................**30.00**
Chair set, crochet filet, American eagle, 3-piece, large........**20.00**
Curtains, ecru machine lace, 48x60", pair **20.00**
Doily, Battenburg lace, drawn center, 30" square **50.00**
Doily, Battenburg lace, Grape & Leaf, 10" diameter, EX...**24.00**
Doily, Battenburg lace, solid center, 18" diameter **25.00**
Doily, crochet, Bread in center, 4½x11" **15.00**
Doily, crochet, rooster in center, 10x13" **24.00**
Doily, embroidery on linen, not old, 32" square................**45.00**
Doily, hairpin lace, linen center, 13x18", EX **45.00**
Pillowcase, cotton, double-row tatting insert, 32x21", pair.**35.00**
Runner, Battenburg lace, drawn insert centers, 20x46" ...**65.00**
Runner, linen, cut & crochet flower border, 20x38".....**35.00**
Sham, linen, blue, white scallop trim **15.00**
Table runner, crochet, God Bless Our Home, 12x20"..........**25.00**
Table runner, crochet, scalloped border, 11x29".................**35.00**
Tablecloth, Battenburg lace, 72" diameter, EX **220.00**

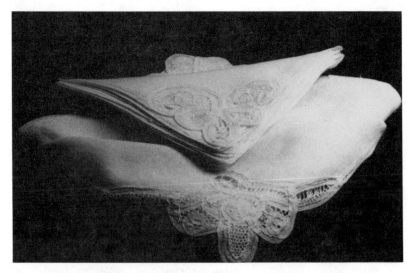

Tablecloth, small, with four napkins, 12" square, $25.00.

Tablecloth, Battenburg lace, 8-pointed star center, 29" square, EX....................**165.00**

Tablecloth, floral machine lace, scalloped border, oval, 60x108", EX....................**65.00**

Tablecloth, hand-tied flowers on chenille, Victorian, 45". **185.00**

Tablecloth, homespun, red cross-stitch initials, EX...........**85.00**

Lamps

From the primitive rush light holder and Betty lamp to Tiffany's elaborate stained glass lamps, lighting devices have evolved with the style of the times and the development of better lighting methods. Depending on the taste of the collector, there are many types that are especially desirable. Miniature figural and art glass lamps are popular and often bring prices of several hundred dollars.

Fairy lamps, Gone-with-the-Wind lamps, and pattern glass lamps of many types are also treasured. Aladdin lamps are the most popular kerosene lamps; they have been made since 1908 by the Mantle Lamps Company of America in over eighteen models and more than one hundred styles. Emeralite lamps, recognized by their green cased glass shades, are also highly collectible. They were made from about 1909 into the forties by the H.G. McFaddin Company in a variety of styles.

Alacite, M-251, modified kerosene, electric, NM...**65.00**

Aladdin, #2305-SS, whip-o-lite fluted & flocked, EX **145.00**

Aladdin, Alacite, G-44, electric, EX..............................**35.00**

Aladdin, B-112, Cathedral, rose moonstone, NM **135.00**

Aladdin, B-52, Washington Drape, amber crystal, filigree stem, NM **68.00**

Aladdin, B-77, Tall Lincoln Drape, ruby crystal, old, NM...**400.00**

Aladdin, B-92, Vertique, green moonstone, EX.............**125.00**

Aladdin, G-212, Alacite, table lamp, EX........................**25.00**

Aladdin, G-223, Alacite, electric, M....................................**50.00**

Aladdin, G-314, Alacite, Bolero, illuminated base, electric, NM................................**75.00**

Aladdin, G-375, Dancing Ladies Urn, electric, M............**685.00**

Aladdin, G-77, Susie figurine, electric, EX...................**585.00**

Aladdin, M-458, ceramic, iron base, electric.................**25.00**

Aladdin, P-55, ceramic, electric, EX **25.00**

Banquet, Grape & Leaf, red satin, 29" **650.00**

Candle lantern, tin, punched cylinder, cone top, hinged door, 14" **100.00**

Miniature lamps: Amber with embossed flowers on orange-skin texture, 8", EX, $275.00; Embossed brass with jeweled shade and green beaded fringe, replaced burner, 8", $200.00.

Candle lantern, tin, 3-corner shade with turret top, 18½", VG.................210.00

Colonial Lady figural, small black base, Tiffin...................120.00

Desk, Emeralite, dome-shaped green cased shade, adjusts, 13", EX.........................255.00

Fairy, blue & white nailsea, ruffled, 6x6½"....................485.00

Fairy, blue opaque, stippled with embossed beads, Clarke base, 5"...................88.00

Fairy, blue verre moire, ruffled Clarke base, 5½".........425.00

Fairy, burmese, clear Clarke base, 4x3"............................165.00

Fairy, Cleveland, blue & white satin stripes, 6¼".........650.00

Fairy, green overlay, white lined, dome shade, Clarke base, 4¼x4".........................115.00

Fairy, rose Diamond Quilt mother-of-pearl, Clarke base, 3½x3"...........................145.00

Fairy, ruby Diamond Quilt, clear Clarke base, 3½x3"........95.00

Fairy, white opalescent overshot, crown figural, Clarke base, 4½"...................175.00

Hall, clear & frosted acid-etched crown-top shade, brass foot, hanging.........................165.00

Hanging, blown, brass candle holder, side arms, smoke bell, 11"................................375.00

Kerosene, Acanthus, pink & white, miniature..........295.00

Kerosene, Daisy & Cube, amber, nutmeg burner, miniature, 7½", EX.........................350.00

Kerosene, emerald green, Olmstead-style wick, applied handle, 7⅜".........................225.00

Kerosene, Glow, ruby, melon ribs, 4⅝", EX..........................80.00

Kerosene, Inverted Thumbprint, green, finger lamp, complete, 6¼".................................75.00

Kerosene burner with Shelley pattern font, gilded octagonal iron base, 10", $150.00.

Kerosene, Log Cabin, clear figural, complete, miniature, 3½", NM.......................355.00

Kerosene, Sweetheart, crystal, Findlay, miniature 140.00

Night light, covered wagon, frosted crystal..............135.00

Night light, Sunbonnet Girl figural, frosted crystal..........25.00

Pattern glass, Bull's Eye, green, footed, finger lamp 175.00

Pattern glass, Coin Cot, French opalescent, Fenton, metal base, tall........................50.00

Pattern glass, Daisy, milk glass, 9¼"................................195.00

Pattern glass, Emblem, fluid burner, 6¾", EX............100.00

Pattern glass, Emblem, hand lamp, Lindsey-63, 10" .100.00

Pattern glass, Heart, custard, finger lamp **215.00**

Pattern glass, Princess Feather, #2 burner........................**88.00**

Pattern glass, Ribbed Panel, custard, Rayo base, oil burner, 18½"...........................**245.00**

Pattern glass, Riverside Rib Band, table lamp, 8" **50.00**

Peg, pink satin half shade, fancy silvered-brass candlestick, 18", EX **450.00**

Perfume, crystal with prisms, Czechoslovakia, 5¼".......**80.00**

Perfume, graceful nude figures, round, DeVilbiss, 12" ..**225.00**

Slag glass, reticulated motif, Nouveau bronze std, 24".....**525.00**

Southern belle figural, fired-on pink, clip-on shade **35.00**

Student, Manhattan, milk glass shade, brass, dtd Dec 25 '77, 20½"...........................**400.00**

Westmoreland, Dolphin, pink, #1049/1 ....**80.00**

Westmoreland, English Hobnail, pink, #555/1, 6¼"...........**70.00**

Whale oil, Harp, flint, Sandwich, 8", NM **150.00**

Letter Openers

Made from wood, ivory, glass, and metals, letter openers are fun to collect without being expensive. Generally the most valuable are advertising openers and figurals made of brass, bronze, copper or iron.

Century of Progress Chicago 1934, Art Deco design, brass, 8", NM...........................**18.00**

Dixogen Chemical Co, celluloid handle, early **10.00**

Durant, enameled emblem on brass, 9"........................**65.00**

General Motors Trucks & United State Tires, brass, EX ...**24.00**

Keystone Spring Works, Philadelphia, brass, 1870-1920 ..**38.00**

Nabisco Boy, metal, VG **55.00**

Neel-Cadillac, enameled logo on brass, 9", NM **95.00**

Rickenbacker-Berks Motors, enamel on brass, Metal Arts, 9"................................**125.00**

Rifle figural, cast iron........... **4.00**

License Plates

Early porcelain license plates are treasured by collectors, and those in good shape often sell for more than $100 for the pair when found in excellent condition.

Arizona, 1971, EX **6.00**

California, 1942....................**12.50**

Connecticut, 1955, M **18.00**

Hawaii, 1932, VG...............**145.00**

Illinois, motorcycle, 1952, M .**48.00**

Illinois, 1913, EX................**155.00**

Iowa, 1912, VG, pair **38.00**

Iowa, 1913, VG, pair **32.00**

Iowa dealer, 1916, pair, VG ..**75.00**

Maine, brass, 1949, VG.........**35.00**

Nebraska, 1934 ....**40.00**

New Hampshire, porcelain, 1918, VG, pair **20.00**

New York, 1922, EX **48.00**

Tennessee, 1923, EX **75.00**

Wisconsin Dealer, 1949, EX..**16.00**

Wisconsin Fair, 1915, EX......**10.00**

Wyoming, 1953, VG **10.00**

Wyoming, 1974 .... **8.00**

Limited Edition Plates, Ornaments, and Figurines

Many companies have joined the ranks of Bing and Grondahl, Royal Copenhagen, and Hummel in producing Christmas and Mother's Day plates, and there are many that issue limited editon figurines, prints, and ornaments. Some have been known to appreciate in value considerably over issue price, especially those that are first in a series.

The Secret, Norman Rockwell, 1979, 5¼", $110.00.

American Greetings

Ornament, 1980, Holly Hobbie, acrylic disc, dated **3.50**
Ornament, 1981, Ziggy & Friends Christmas Spirit **4.50**
Ornament, 1983, Friendship, acrylic disc, dated............ **6.50**
Ornament, 1983, Our First Christmas Together, acrylic disc................................... **6.00**
Ornament, 1984, Baby's First Christmas, musical.......**21.00**
Ornament, 1985, Baby's First Christmas, dated **9.00**
Ornament, 1986, Out with the Old..., Ziggy, dated **6.50**
Ornament, 1986, Special Friend, acrylic disc, dated............ **4.75**
Ornament, 1987, rocking horse, wooden, dated.................. **4.75**

Anri

Figurine, 1979, First Blossom, Boy & Girl series, 6" **158.00**

Figurine, 1979, Prayer Changes Things **80.00**
Figurine, 1980, Friends, Boy & Girl series, 6" **175.00**
Figurine, 1983, God Sent His Son...................................**57.00**
Figurine, 1983, Morning Chores, 1½" **100.00**
Figurine, 1984, Friendly Faces, Boy & Girl series, 3" ...**100.00**
Figurine, 1986, Sharing Our Christmas Together **44.00**
Plate, 1975, Alpine Stroll, Mother's Day series **62.00**
Plate, 1976, Knitting, Mother's Day series.......................**62.00**
Plate, 1976, Sailing, Father's Day series **88.00**
Plate, 1977, Legend of Heilgenblut, Christmas series ...**78.00**
Plate, 1980, Wintry Churchgoing, Christmas series **159.00**

Bing and Grondahl

Ornament, 1986, Christmas Eve in Williamsburg **80.00**
Ornament, 1987, Christmas Eve at the White House........**15.00**
Plate, 1975, Horses Enjoying Meal, Jubilee..................**46.00**
Plate, 1979, Christmas **66.00**
Plate, 1980, WoodpeckerYoung, Mother's Day..................**38.50**
Plate, 1984, Home Is Best, Moments of Truth **33.00**
Plate, 1985, The Magical Tea Party, Children's Day **24.00**
Plate, 1986, A Joyful Flight, Children's Day.......................**28.00**
Plate, 1986, Elephant with Calf, Mother's Day..................**41.00**
Plate, 1986, Unfair Competition, Moments of Truth **30.00**

Edwin M. Knowles

Plate, 1980, Melanie, Gone with the Wind........................**63.00**

Plate, 1980, The Grand Finale, Wizard of Oz **50.00**
Plate, 1985, Fire, The Four Ancient Elements **43.00**
Plate, 1986, Annie, Lily, & Rooster **40.00**
Plate, 1986, I Cain't Say No, Oklahoma **27.00**
Plate, 1986, The Home Run, Csatari Grandparent **36.00**
Plate, 1987, Inauguration, Lincoln, Man of America **37.00**

Enesco

Ornament, 1981, Baby's First Christmas **27.00**
Ornament, 1982, First Noel .**37.00**
Ornament, 1985, Happiness Is the Lord **19.00**
Ornament, 1986, It's a Perfect Boy **23.00**
Ornament, 1986, Serve with a Smile **15.00**
Ornament, 1987, I'm a Possibility **18.00**
Plate, 1983, Jesus Loves Me.**45.00**
Plate, 1984, The Wonder of Christmas **59.00**
Plate, 1987, My Peace I Give Unto Thee **52.00**

Goebel

Figurine, 1982, Garden Fancier, Fashions on Parade **45.00**
Figurine, 1983, Bride & Groom, Fashions on Parade **90.00**
Figurine, 1983, Reflections, Fashions on Parade **45.00**
Figurine, 1985, Afternoon Tea, Fashions on Parade **45.00**
Figurine, 1985, Joseph **62.00**
Ornament, 1978, Angel with Harp, pink **30.00**
Ornament, 1980, Angel with Tree, glass **9.00**
Ornament, 1981, Mrs Santa, glass................................ **9.00**

Ornament, 1982, Angel with French Horn, red **30.00**
Ornament, 1984, Angel with Drum, green **30.00**
Plate, 1976, Apple Tree Girl, Annual **90.00**
Plate, 1978, Happy Pastime, Annual **82.00**
Plate, 1984, Little Fiddler, Little Music Makers................**58.00**
Plate, 1985, Serenade, Little Music Makers **54.00**
Plate, 1986, Soloist, Little Music Maker **50.00**
Plate, 1987, Valentine Joy, Celebration **100.00**

Gorham

Figurine, 1976, Disastrous Daring, Me & My Pal series, Rockwell **200.00**
Figurine, 1976, Saying Grace, Rockwell **100.00**
Figurine, 1978, Shear Agony, Going on Sixteen series, Rockwell **150.00**
Figurine, 1980, Swatter's Right, Helping Hand series, Rockwell **150.00**
Figurine, 1981, Day in the Life, Boy II, Rockwell.............**77.00**
Ornament, 1977, snowflake, sterling **49.00**
Ornament, 1978, snowflake, sterling **49.00**
Ornament, 1980, snowflake, silverplated **40.00**
Plate, 1977, The Scoutmaster, Boy Scout series, Rockwell ...**54.00**
Plate, 1977, Yuletide Reckoning, Rockwell, Annual **27.50**
Plate, 1978, Campfire Story, Boy Scout series, Rockwell ...**22.00**
Plate, 1978, Spring Tonic, Tender Years Four Seasons.......**65.00**
Plate, 1979, Santa's Helpers, Rockwell, Annual...........**38.50**

Plate, 1981, Santa Plans His
Visit, Rockwell, Annual .**30.00**

Hallmark

Ornament, 1976, Betsey Clark,
set of 3 ....**46.00**
Ornament, 1977, Baby's First
Christmas......................**30.00**
Ornament, 1978, For Your New
Home **36.00**
Ornament, 1978, Mrs Claus, Yarn
series..............................**13.00**
Ornament, 1978, Peanuts.....**41.50**
Ornament, 1979, Baby's First
Christmas......................**10.50**
Ornament, 1979, Snoopy &
Friends **100.00**
Ornament, 1980, Beauty of
Friendship.....................**13.50**
Ornament, 1980, Christmas at
Home **13.50**
Ornament, 1980, Merry Redbird,
Little Trimmers series ..**48.50**
Ornament, 1981, The Friendly
Fiddler...........................**26.00**
Ornament, 1982, Moments of
Love **9.00**
Ornament, 1983, First Christmas
Together.........................**10.50**
Ornament, 1985, Twelve Days of
Christmas, 2nd ed..........**38.50**
Ornament, 1986, Ten Years
Together.........................**19.50**
Ornament, 1987, Baby's Second
Christmas......................**13.50**

Lenox

Ornament, 1982, Annual **80.00**
Ornament, 1983, Annual **70.00**
Ornament, 1984, ball, crystal,
deep cut **45.00**
Ornament, 1987, Partridge, Days
of Christmas series........**22.00**
Plate, 1977, Robins, Boehm Birds
series..............................**82.00**
Plate, 1978, Mockingbirds, Boehm
Birds series **72.00**

Plate, 1979, Golden-Crowned
Kinglets **95.00**
Plate, 1982, Massachusetts, Colo-
nial Christmas Wreath ..**76.00**
Plate, 1983, Maryland, Colonial
Christmas Wreath **73.00**

Reed and Barton

Ornament, 1977, Christmas
Cross, sterling silver......**49.00**
Ornament, 1978, Christmas
Cross, 24kt gold over sterling
silver **45.00**
Ornament, 1980, Christmas
Cross, sterling silver......**40.00**
Ornament, 1983, Turtle Doves, 12
Days of Christmas **20.00**
Ornament, 1984, Calling Birds,
12 Days of Christmas **20.00**

River Shore-Rockwell

Figurine, 1981, Looking Out To
Sea **130.00**
Figurine, 1982, Grandpa's
Guardian **125.00**
Plate, 1976, Brown's Lincoln,
Famous Americans **45.00**
Plate, 1977, Rockwell's Triple
Self-Portrait **50.00**
Plate, 1979, Spring Flowers.**130.00**

Rockwell Society

Plate, 1978, Bedtime, Mother's
Day series **49.00**
Plate, 1979, Reflections, Mother's
Day series **28.00**
Plate, 1980, Ship Builder, Her-
itage series **37.50**
Plate, 1985, A Young Girl's
Dream, American Dream
series..............................**29.00**
Plate, 1986, Sitting Pretty, A
Mind of Her Own **26.50**
Plate, 1986, The Musician's
Magic, American Dream
series..............................**24.00**

Plate, 1987, Shadow Artist, Heritage series **49.00**

Royal Copenhagen

Plate, 1976, Danish Watermill, Christmas series **31.00**
Plate, 1977, Immervad Bridge, Christmas series **34.00**
Plate, 1986, Dog & Puppies, Motherhood series **40.00**
Plate, 1987, Goat & Kid, Motherhood series **46.00**

Schmid

Ornament, 1983, mailbox, Lowell Davis...............................**53.00**
Ornament, 1985, pig in trough, Lowell Davis Country Christmas **21.00**
Ornament, 1985, Snow Biz, Disney **18.00**
Ornament, 1986, Christmas at Red Oak, Davis, glass **8.00**
Ornament, 1986, church, Lowell Davis...............................**21.00**
Ornament, 1986, Tree for Two, Disney............................**10.50**
Ornament, 1987, Blossom's Gift, Lowell Davis, glass **10.00**
Plate, 1976, Linus & Snoopy, Mother's Day series **29.00**
Plate, 1977, Dear Mom, Peanuts Mother's Day series **27.00**
Plate, 1978, Heavenly Bliss, Peanuts Valentine's Day series..............................**27.50**
Plate, 1979, Special Letter, Peanuts Mother's Day series **20.00**
Plate, 1979, Love Match, Peanuts Valentine's Day series....**24.50**

Little Golden Books

Little Golden Books (a registered trademark of Western Publishing Company, Inc.), introduced in October of 1942, were an overnight success. First published with a blue paper spine, the later spines were of gold foil. Parents and grandparents born in the '40s, '50s, and '60s are now trying to find the titles they had as children.

From 1942 to the early 1970s, the books were numbered from 1 to 600, while books published later had no numerical order. Depending on where you find the book, prices could vary from 25¢ to $30 plus. The most expensive books are those with dust jackets from the early '40s, or books with paper dolls and activities. The three primary series of books are the Regular (1-600), Disney (1-140), and Activity (1-52).

Television influence became apparent in the '50s with stories like the Lone Ranger, Howdy Doody, Hopalong Cassidy, Gene Autry, and Rootie Kazootie. The '60s brought us Yogi Bear, Huckleberry Hound, Magilla Gorilla, and Quick Draw McGraw to name a few.

A TV Western title from the '50s is worth around $12 to $15. A Disney from 1942 to early '60s will go for $8 to $15 (reprinted titles would be lower). Cartoon titles from the '60s would range from $6 to $12. Books with the blue spine or gold paper spine (not foil) can bring from $8 to $15. If you are lucky enough to own a book with a dust jacket, the jacket alone is worth $20 and up. Paper doll books are worth around $30 to $36. These values are meant only to give an idea of value and are for 1st editions in mint condition. Condition is very important when purchasing a book. You normally won't want to purchase a book with large tears, crayon or ink marks, or missing pages.

As with any collectible, a 1st edition is always going to bring the higher price. To determine what edition you have on the 25¢ and 29¢ cover price books, look on the title page or the last page of the book. If it is not on the title page there will be a letter of the alphabet on the bottom right corner of the last page. A is for a 1st edition; Z will refer to the twenty-sixth printing.

To find out more about Little Golden Books we recommend *Collecting Little Golden Books,* a most informative book by Steve Santi, who is listed in the Directory under California.

A Day at the Playground, #119, 1951, M............................ **8.00**
Betsy McCall, #559, 1965 .....**25.00**
Big Red, #D102, 1962, M **8.00**
Brave Cowboy Bill, #93, '50..**10.00**
Busy Timmy, #50, 1948, M ...**12.00**
Chip 'N Dale at the Zoo, #D38, 1954, M............................**10.00**
Davy Crockett, #D45, '55......**10.00**
Dog Stamps, #A9, 1955, M ...**10.00**
Duck & His Friends, #81, '49.. **8.00**
Gordon's Jet Flight, #A48, 1961, M....................................**15.00**
Gunsmoke, #320, 1958, M **10.00**
Hopalong Cassidy & the Bar-20 Cowboy, #147, 1952, M .**15.00**
Howdy Doody's Circus, #99, 1950, M....................................**15.00**
Jack's Adventure, #308, 1958, M..................................... **6.00**
Jamie Looks, #522, 1963, M .. **6.00**
Lion's Paw, #367, 1959, M **8.00**
Little Black Sambo, #57, 42 pages, 1948, M **75.00**
Little Lulu & Her Magic Tricks, #203, 1954, M.................**20.00**
Little Red Riding Hood, #42, with puzzle, 1950, M **25.00**

Madeline, #186, 1954, M........ **8.00**
Mary Poppins, #D113, '64...... **6.00**
Merry Shipwreck, The; #170, 1953, M............................ **6.00**
My Baby Brother, #279, '56 ... **8.00**
My Christmas Book, #298, '57. **8.00**
My Snuggly Bunny, #250, '56, M. **6.00**
Nursery Songs, #7 (with dust jacket), 1942, M **35.00**
Our Flag, #388, 1960, M........ **5.00**
Pick Up Sticks, #461, '62 ...... **5.00**
Play Ball, #325, 1958, M........ **6.00**
Quick Draw McGraw, #398, 1960, M.................................... **8.00**
Road to Oz, #144, 1951, M....**15.00**
Robin Hood, #D126, 1973, M. **4.00**
Sky, The; #270, 1956, M......... **5.00**
Sleeping Beauty (paper doll), #A33, 1959, M **30.00**
Sly Little Bear, #411, '60........ **6.00**
Smokey the Bear, #224, '55 ..**15.00**
Words (activity book), #A1, 1955, M....................................**10.00**
Zorro, #D68, 1958, M **10.00**

The Night Before Christmas, by Watson, illustrated by Wilkin.

Locks

Among the most collectible locks on the market today are those made by Yale, Sargent,

Winchester, and Keen Kutter. When evaluating the value of locks consider construction, condition, and rarity. Generally, brass and bronze locks outsell those made of steel or iron. Some railroad locks are included here, also see section on Railroadiana.

Adlake, 3½" x 3", $17.00.

Burglar Stop, Scandinavian jail type, EX 24.00
Columbus, 3-lever, square shape, small, EX 6.00
Corbin, Hercules, ward lock .. 4.00
Corbin, Made in USA, brass, iron shackle, regular size 3.00
Defiance, 3-lever, EX 7.00
Delamater Rustless, 8-lever .12.50
Eagle, Coop Padlock, wafer lock, EX 5.50
Eagle, 2-lever, small, EX 7.00
English VR, wrought iron, ward lock.................................35.00
Fraim, brass body, iron shackle, large, EX......................... 5.00
Fraim, Western Union, 4-lever, EX 32.00
Fraim-Slaymaker, ward lock. 4.50
Fraim-Slaymaker Victory, ward lock, EX 12.50
Master Lock, Milwaukee Wis, Master in lion's mouth, iron case, large....................... 4.00
Miller, Simmons Quality, 6-lever, EX 7.50
Miller Champion, 6-lever pancake push key, EX 20.00

Miller Climax, all brass, fancy, EX................................... 5.50
Miller Protector, 3-lever, EX . 7.50
Shapleigh, ward lock, EX....... 6.00
Simmons Preparedness, ward lock, NM 8.00
Slaymaker, Made in USA, S on back side, iron, EX......... 1.50
Star, Scandinavian jail type, EX.35.00
US Mail, 2-lever, EX.............12.50
Wilson Bohannon, 3-lever, small, EX...................................28.00
Yale, Jr Vulcan, ward lock 7.50
Yale, 2-lever, oval shape 17.50
Yale, 3-lever, regular size.....15.00

Lu Ray Pastels

Introduced in the 1940s by Taylor, Smith, and Taylor of East Liverpool, Ohio, Lu Ray Pastels is a line that has become popular with today's collectors of American dinnerware. It was made in solid colors: Windsor Blue, Gray, Persian Cream, and Sharon Pink.

Bowl, cream soup 24.00
Bowl, fruit; 5½".................... 5.00
Bowl, mixing; large 45.00
Bowl, vegetable; oval 10.00
Coffeepot, demitasse; ovoid, with cover.............................50.00
Creamer, demitasse; ovoid ...20.00
Creamer, demitasse; straight sides..............................40.00
Egg cup, Chatham Gray, rare color 15.00
Epergne 50.00
Muffin cover on 8" plate........65.00
Pitcher, juice; ovoid 75.00
Plate, cake 25.00
Plate, Chatham Gray, rare color, 7"..................................... 6.00
Plate, grill............................12.00
Plate, serving; tab handle.....25.00
Platter, oval, 13"...................10.00
Sauce pitcher 15.00

Plates: Grill, $12.00; Calendar, $20.00.

Saucer, cream soup **13.00**	
Sugar bowl, with cover, demitasse; ovoid **20.00**	
Teapot, curved spout.............**35.00**	
Teapot, flat-top spout............**45.00**	
Tumbler, water **37.50**	

Lunch Boxes

In the early years of this century, tobacco companies often packaged their products in tins that could later be used for lunch boxes. By the 1930s oval lunch boxes designed to appeal to school children were produced. The rectangular shape that is now popular was preferred in the 1950s. Character lunch boxes decorated with the faces of TV personalities, super heroes, and Disney and cartoon characters are especially sought after by collectors today.

Adam 12, EX **24.00**
Addams Family, 1974, NM ...**55.00**

Astronaut, dome top, 1960 ...**65.00**
Astronauts, Chein, mini, EX..**27.50**
Beverly Hillbillies, '63, NM ..**65.00**
Bobby Sherman, EX **35.00**
Buck Rogers, 1979, with thermos **32.00**
Fat Albert & Cosby Kids, with thermos, 1973, M **45.00**
Fox & Hound, EX **16.00**
Garfield, with thermos, EX ..**18.00**
Gremlins, with thermos, EX.**16.00**
Hardy Boys, with thermos, 1977, M **24.00**
Hee Haw, with thermos, 1969, NM **68.00**
Kiss, with thermos, 1970s ...**48.00**
Knight Rider, EX...................**15.00**
McDonald's, with thermos & tag, 1982, M...........................**25.00**
Pony Express, 1960s, EX......**78.00**
Popeye, 1964, NM **55.00**
Scooby Doo, with thermos, 1970s, NM **30.00**
Star Treck (movie), VG **22.00**
Welcome Back Kotter, 1977 .**32.50**
Zorro, 1958, EX **85.00**

Pac Man, with thermos, $12.00.

Maddux of California

In opperation since the late 1930s, Maddux made dinnerware accessories, figurines, TV lamps, cookie jars, etc., that are today becoming items of collector interest. The company is located in Los Angeles and continues today to produce and market their own products as well as contracted merchandise for various other companies.

**Basset hound TV lamp, #896, 12",
$35.00.**

Bull, red, head up/head down, 11" long, pair **30.00**
Chinese pheasant, air-brushed colors, 11", pair...............**25.00**
Ducklings, 3 on grassy base.**15.00**
Planter, flamingo, #515, 11" .**25.00**
Planter, swan, black, 11" **18.00**
Rooster, #932, tall **25.00**
Stag, standing, natural colors, #914, 12½" **15.00**
TV lamp, prairie schooner (covered wagon), 11".............**30.00**
TV lamp, stallion, prancing, on base, 12" **35.00**
TV lamp, swan, #828P, 12" ...**35.00**
Vase, swan, #221, 12"............**20.00**

Magazines

Magazines are collected for both their contents and their covers, often signed by well-known illustrators. Their values hinge on the type and quality of the advertising they contain, their cover illustrations, age, rarity, and condition.

Amazing Stories, P Nowlan, 1929, March, EX **30.00**
Amazing Stories, 1928, August, HG Wells, EX **30.00**
American Heritage, 1968, April, Mickey Mouse cover.......**25.00**
Arizona Educator, 1896, October 5, Indian relics cover......**11.00**
Army Laughs, 1944, December, military & girlie humor, 64-page **10.00**
Art Lover's Weekly, 1890s, full page sepia prints, EX.....**12.00**
Beacon, 1843, May 13, many articles on religion, politics, & science **12.00**
Black Cat, 1905, April, large black cat cover................**10.00**
Burr McIntosh Monthly, 1909, November, Taos Indian..**50.00**

Christian Herald, 1908, January 8, Teddy Roosevelt cover. **7.50**

Collier's, 1911, June 3, Hearst cover, EX **12.00**

Collier's, 1911, June 3, Randolph Hearst on cover +article, 34-page, VG **10.00**

Collier's, 1917, April 7, Doughboy cover, Leyendecker **18.00**

Collier's, 1942, October 3, boy in Sailor's uniform, EX **15.00**

Collier's, 1945, Disney's 3 Caballeros cover, EX......**20.00**

Cosmopolitan, 1893, Dec **35.00**

Dorcas-Woman's Magazine of Handiwork, 1885, VG....**10.00**

Down Beat, 1978, August 10, Lionel Hampton cover **5.00**

Family Circle, 1933, December 29, Eleanor Roosevelt cover, EX **10.00**

Family Circle, 1944, March 3, WWII theme cover, Cooper article, EX **10.00**

Farmer's Wife, 1935, June, household articles, Dizzy Dean Comics **15.00**

Gay Parisienne, 1938, July, pinup cover, EX **18.00**

Godey's Lady's Book, 8 color fashion plates, 1842 ....**75.00**

Harper's Weekly, 1858, July 24, Hudson Bay gold fields article, EX.............................**30.00**

Ideals, 1951, Christmas issue, 100-page **15.00**

Life, 1927, February 3, comic strip theme, EX **27.50**

Life, 1929, October 4, girl & football player cover.............**20.00**

Life, 1938, July 25, Elizabeth, Queen of England cover.**20.00**

Life, 1939, July 17, Lord Halifax cover, Wizard of Oz article, EX **20.00**

Life, 1943, March 29, Stalin cover, EX..................................**15.00**

Life, 1958, February 3, Shirley Temple cover, NM **14.00**

Life, 1964, February 21, Lee Oswald cover.................**12.50**

Life, 1964, March 6, Cassius Clay cover & story, NM **14.00**

Life, 1966, April 15, Louis Armstrong cover +article......**15.00**

Life, 1969, February 14, Barbara Streisand cover **10.00**

Life, 1972, December 29, Vietnam & space articles, EX **12.50**

Literary Digest, 1931, August 4, Walt Disney article **9.00**

Mayflower, 1896, August, article on plants at 1893 Chicago Fair **9.00**

McCall's, 1926, January, paper doll sheet of twins **12.50**

Mentor, 1918, May 1, Lewis & Clark Expedition article +5 prints **10.00**

Mentor, 1927, August, Boy Scout article by Dan Beard, illustrated **12.50**

Modern Screen, 1939, Deanna Durbin cover, EX............**35.00**

Modern Screen, 1952, November, Ava Gardner cover **17.50**

Movieland, 1943, June, Rosalind Russell cover, 68-page....**27.50**

Movieland, 1945, June, John Hodiak cover **17.50**

Peterson's, 1882, June, hand-colored fashion print, EX ...**30.00**

Photoplay, 1938, July, Clark Gable cover, 92-page **27.50**

Photoplay, 1939, August, Alice Faye cover **25.00**

Photoplay, 1939, June, Bette Davis cover, 92-page **27.50**

Pictorial Review, 1931, Dolly Dingle doll cutout, EX..........**25.00**

Police Gazette, 1942, October, Dagmar on cover +article, 16-page **15.00**

Ramparts, 1965, March, Charlie Chaplin cover, EX **10.00**

Ramparts, 1967, October, John Lennon cover, Vietnam articles, EX..............................**12.00**

Ramparts, 1973, October, Watergate article **10.00**
Rexall, 1944, August, Eisenhower cover & article, 16-page.. **9.00**
Rolling Stone, 1973, November, Dan Ellsberg & Grateful Dead articles **8.00**
Rolling Stone, 1974, June, James Dean, Pointer Sisters, etc on cover................................**12.50**
Saturday Evening Post, 1934, Rockwell cover, EX.......... **4.50**

The Saturday Evening Post **July 9, 1921, Rockwell cover, EX, $60.00.**

Saturday Evening Post, 1963, December, JF Kennedy memorial edition............**20.00**
Silver Screen, 1932, Garbo cover, EX **15.00**
Silver Screen, 1943, February, M Monroe cover, EX **35.00**
Song Fan, Volume 1, #1, Rita Hayworth cover, EX.......**15.00**
System, 1925, July, memoirs of Harvey Firestone **11.00**
Time, 1940, August 21, Eleanor Holm swimsuit cover **10.00**
True, 1971, July, John Wayne cover, EX......................... **7.50**

Wisdom, 1956, April, Winston Churchill cover..............**12.50**
Wisdom, 1956, February, Albert Schweitzer cover............**12.50**
Wisdom, 1956, November, Helen Keller cover +article **12.50**
Youth's Companion, 1920 ...... **5.00**

Majolica

The type of majolica earthenware most often encountered was made during the 1880s, reaching the height of its popularity in the Victorian period. It was produced abroad and in this country as well. It is usually vividly colored, and nature themes are the most common decorative devices. Animal and bird handles and finials and dimensional figures in high relief were used extensively.

Bowl, Bird & Fan, Shorter & Boulton, 5"....................**125.00**
Bowl, bird on lily pad at rim, cobalt interior, Wedgwood, 7"....................................**400.00**
Bowl, lilies in center, multicolored, footed, large **185.00**
Bowl, water lilies, Nouveau style, oval, 9x5" **85.00**
Box, sardine; fish in relief on lid, square, 6"......................**500.00**
Box, sardine; Seaweed, cobalt, 6x6½x5" **350.00**
Butter dish, Bamboo & Basketweave, Banks & Thorley with lid **175.00**
Butter pat, green leaf, Copeland, 3 for..............................**110.00**
Cake stand, strawberries & blossoms on light blue, Zell..**85.00**
Charger, cherub clutches large white flying crane, marked, 12½" **300.00**
Compote, Begonia Leaf, rolled edge, round, 3" **225.00**
Compote, flowers & leaves, bark pedestal, 5x10".............**210.00**

Compote, Overlapping Begonia
Leaves, Etruscan, 5"....**225.00**

Creamer, Albino Shell & Sea-
weed, small......................**65.00**

Creamer, Wild Rose, Etruscan,
4½"..................................**85.00**

Creamer & sugar bowl, Bird &
Fan................................**185.00**

Cup & saucer, Dainty Cream,
strawberries & vines ...**165.00**

Cup & saucer, Pineapple, lavender interior...................**155.00**

Cuspidor, lady's, Wild Rose,
7½x7½", M....................**225.00**

Humidor, Black Boy...........**150.00**

Humidor, Scotsman bust, blue
tam, gray hair..............**155.00**

Jardiniere, pink flowers on dark
Green, St Clement mark,
7½x6½"........................**175.00**

Match strike, mottled green-
brown, 4", NM **90.00**

Mug, brown with pink flowers &
green leaves...................**85.00**

Mug, flower in vase within panel,
overall decor, 4" **100.00**

Mug, Picket Fence, pink flowers
on aqua..........................**85.00**

Pitcher, barrel shape, lavender
interior, 4½"..................**125.00**

Pitcher, Begonia Leaf on Bark,
7½" **95.00**

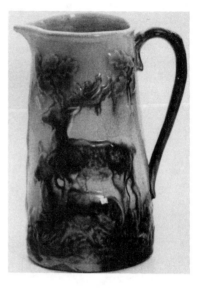

Pitcher, stag and doe, 7", $150.00.

Pitcher, bulldog with open mouth,
Frie Onnaing, 8½"........**295.00**

Pitcher, children scenes, satyr on
lip, France, 8½"............**150.00**

Pitcher, hunt scene, dog figural
handle, Wedgwood **295.00**

Pitcher, multicolor floral on brown
tree bark, 7" **110.00**

Pitcher, roly poly monk, brown
robe, hat spout **225.00**

Pitcher, shell figural, Fielding, 8",
NM...............................**335.00**

Pitcher, steer's head on each side,
5"....................................**85.00**

Planter, Picket Fence & Rasp-
berry, 8" **275.00**

Plate, Bamboo, 7" **75.00**

Plate, Begonia Leaf, 7½".......**40.00**

Plate, Blackberry, 8" **85.00**

Plate, Grape Leaf, fruit & flower,
Wedgwood, 8½" **125.00**

**Mustard pot, figural lady with
spoon and melon, $75.00.**

Plate, Pond Lily, white on green, 8".....................................**85.00**

Plate, Strawberry, ribbed ground, Clifton Avalon, 11" **110.00**

Platter, Fish & Seaweed, angular shape, England, 14".....**245.00**

Platter, Strawberry, raised rim, English mark, 15"........**400.00**

Relish dish, leaf shape, open handle, Morley, 7½x8"........**110.00**

Spooner, Shell & Seaweed, Albino, Etruscan.........................**95.00**

Syrup, floral frieze, footed, pewter lid, Wedgwood, 7½".......**550.00**

Teapot, Bamboo, Griffin, Smith, & Hill, 6"...........................**175.00**

Teapot, Cauliflower.............**330.00**

Tray, bread; Wheat & Basketweave, with inscription, 13½".............................**225.00**

Vase, pink flowers on blue & green, handles, 6"..........**35.00**

Vase, vines & scrolls, double-column handles, ovoid, Copeland, 11½".............**200.00**

Match Holders

Because early matches were easily combustible, they were stored in match holders, usually wall-hanging or table-top models. Though the safety match was invented in 1855, the habit was firmly entrenched, and match holders remained popular well into the 20th century.

Acorn figural, cast iron, dated 1862, EX.........................**68.00**

Bicycle, high wheel; silverplate, Tufts, 1880s...................**400.00**

Castle, enameled, 4-sided striker, 1894, 3¼".........................**75.00**

Cat figural, wood, tail is hanger, 10½"...............................**48.00**

Hat figural, cranberry opalescent rib, 3x4".........................**100.00**

Indian's head, silver, 2½" **75.00**

Kangaroo figural, brass, pouch holds matches.................**22.50**

Man holding barrel figural, bisque, Germany............**50.00**

Pipes & florals, unmarked RS Prussia, double.............**135.00**

Silverplated spinning wheel and basket, #2613 on bottom, 4" x 3" x 5¾", $55.00.

Match Safes

Before cigarette lighters were invented, matches were carried in pocket-size match safes, as simple or elaborate as the owner's financial status and flair for fashion dictated.

Sterling, embossed Art Nouveau lady, 2½", $90.00.

Advertising, Coleman's Mustard, football scene, sterling.**375.00**

Butterfly/flowers bright cut on silverplate, marked............**55.00**

Chicago World's Fair, 1893, silver-
plate, EX..........................**50.00**
Cigars in bundle figural, silver-
plate **85.00**
Columbia (lady's head), clear
glass, hanging, with striker,
4½"..............................**75.00**
Doctor's bag, sterling.........**275.00**
Dog with whistle, silverplated fig-
ural **185.00**
Fish figural, brass..............**145.00**
Golfer figural, sterling........**275.00**
Horse figural, silverplate &
enamel............................**90.00**
King of Hearts, silverplated, with
scorer **85.00**
L&F Kammerer, metal & cellu-
loid, EX..........................**35.00**
Man's head, brass, 1½x2"....**110.00**
Punch figural, silverplate, base
with striker opens, 2⅜" .**135.00**
Repousse florals on silverplate,
marked **45.00**
Repousse tulips & monogram on
sterling **75.00**
Walnut, silverplated, top opens,
striker on back, 2x2"......**75.00**

McCoy

A popular collectible with
flea market goers, McCoy pottery
has been made in Roseville, Ohio,
since 1910. They are most famous
for their extensive line of figural
cookie jars, more than two hundred in all. They also made amusing figural planters, etc., as well
as dinnerware, and vases and
pots for the florist trade. Though
some pieces are unmarked, most
bear one of several McCoy trade-
marks.

Bookends, birds, pair **12.00**
Bookends, lilies, pair.............**30.00**
Cookie jar, American Eagle ..**20.00**
Cookie jar, Basket of Eggs, #274,
1977-79 ....**40.00**

Cookie jar, Basket of Eggs, late
1970s, $40.00.

Cookie jar, Bear & Beehive,
brown bear hugging beehive,
#0143, 1988 ....**25.00**
Cookie jar, Black Kettle........**25.00**
Cookie jar, Bobby the Baker,
#183, 1974-79 ....**40.00**
Cookie jar, Burlap Bag, half circle
finial, #158, 1973-77 .....**35.00**
Cookie jar, Caboose.............**105.00**
Cookie jar, Canister, floral design,
#F166, 1989....................**25.00**
Cookie jar, Canister, pink & blue
stripes, #S166, 1989.......**25.00**
Cookie jar, Chillie Willie the Pen-
guin, #0155, 1988..........**40.00**
Cookie jar, Chinese Lantern.**40.00**
Cookie jar, Circus Horse **115.00**
Cookie jar, Clown Bust **70.00**
Cookie jar, Coke Can, 1988 ..**25.00**
Cookie jar, Coke Jug, reproduc-
tion of old Coca-Cola label,
#1004, 1988 ....**25.00**
Cookie jar, Cookie Churn, #266,
1977-87 ....**25.00**
Cookie jar, Cookie Jug, Sahara
coloring, #213, 1978-79..**15.00**
Cookie jar, Cow-Reclining, large
black & white cow, #8166,
1988 ....**25.00**

Cookie jar, Dog, blue with satin finish, #1501, 1988........**25.00**
Cookie jar, Dog on Basketweave bottom...........................**45.00**
Cookie jar, Drum..................**50.00**
Cookie jar, Forbidden Fruit..**50.00**
Cookie jar, Gingerbread Boy.**22.00**
Cookie jar, Goodie Goose, white, #0166, 1989....................**25.00**
Cookie jar, Granny, 1972 .....**50.00**
Cookie jar, Happy Face, yellow with Have a Happy Face in black, #235.....................**30.00**
Cookie jar, Hen on Nest........**70.00**
Cookie jar, Hobby Horse.......**90.00**
Cookie jar, Hot Air Balloon, #353, 1985-86...........................**25.00**

Cookie jar, Bugs Bunny, $125.00.

Cookie jar, Ice Cream Cone, #159, 1978-87 ....**35.00**
Cookie jar, Keebler Treehouse, #0350, 1988....................**25.00**
Cookie jar, Kookie Kettle, black with brass trim handle, #171, 1960-77.........................**25.00**
Cookie jar, Lamb on Basketweave Bottom...........................**45.00**
Cookie jar, Love Birds, kissing penguins........................**50.00**

Cookie jar, Lunch Bucket, #357, 1978 ....**25.00**
Cookie jar, Mother Goose......**95.00**
Cookie jar, New Strawberry, #263, 1972 ....**32.00**
Cookie jar, Oaken Bucket, copper trim bail, 1961-71 ....**25.00**
Cookie jar, Picnic Basket **50.00**
Cookie jar, Quaker Oats **200.00**
Cookie jar, Rooster...............**75.00**
Cookie jar, Rooster, white jar, #4257, 1988....................**25.00**
Cookie jar, Snow Bear **40.00**
Cookie jar, Stoplight, good paint, #351, 1978 ....**28.00**
Cookie jar, Strawberry-Tilted on It's Side #4097................**35.00**
Cookie jar, Tepee **185.00**
Cookie jar, Thinking Puppy, #272, 1977 ....**30.00**
Cookie jar, Timmy Tortoise, #271, 1977-80 ....**40.00**
Cookie jar, Wishing Well.......**30.00**
Cookie jar, Wren House **70.00**
Cookie jar, Yosemite Sam ...**110.00**
Creamer, embossed, Water Lily motif................................**14.00**
Creamer, Grecian.................**10.00**
Decanter, Astronaut..............**38.00**
Decanter, Missile **20.00**
Flower frog, Zuniart, 1923....**22.00**
Jardiniere, flying birds, 7½".**24.00**
Mug, grape motif..................**11.00**
Mug, Robin Hood..................**14.00**
Pitcher, duck's neck handle ..**32.00**
Pitcher, embossed, angel fish motif................................**16.00**
Planter, convertible..............**12.00**
Planter, dog with cart **8.00**
Planter, fawn **8.00**
Planter, Humpty Dumpty.....**10.00**
Planter, lamb **10.00**
Planter, pink cradle **6.00**
Planter, poodle.....................**11.00**
Planter, rooster....................**10.00**
Teapot, Grecian **24.00**
Teapot, cat **28.00**
Vase, lizard handles.............**16.00**
Vase, matt white, 1940s........**12.00**

Vase, Uncle Sam....................**20.00**
Wall pocket, bird bath............**15.00**
Wall pocket, pear **14.00**
Wall pocket, violin..................**12.00**

Planter, banana boat, 11" long, $35.00.

Metlox

Since the 1940s, the Metlox company of California has been producing dinnerware lines, cookie jars, and decorative items which today have become popular collectibles.

Antique Grape, cup & saucer.. **7.00**
California Ivy, coaster............ **4.00**
California Provincial, bowl, round, 10"......................**25.00**
California Provincial, bowl, vegetable; divided, oblong ...**25.00**
California Provincial, bowl, 2-part, with handles..........**25.00**
California Provincial, casserole, with lid **45.00**
California Provincial, chop plate, 12"....................................**25.00**
California Provincial, plate, dinner....................................**10.00**
California Provincial, plate, salad; 7½" **8.00**
California Provincial, shakers, pair **12.00**
Cookie jar, dog's head, Cockapoo, Poppy Trail **25.00**
Cookie jar, rose.....................**35.00**
Cookie jar, squirrel on stump .**24.00**
Homestead Provincial, bowl, stick handle.............................**15.00**

Cookie jars: Lamb's Head, Cat's Head, $40.00 each.

Homestead Provincial, box, rectangular, with lid.............**25.00**
Homestead Provincial, match holder..............................**18.00**
Homestead Provincial, mustard, part of cruet set.............**18.00**
Homestead Provincial, sugar bowl, with lid................... **9.00**
Red Rooster Provincial, bowl, salad; 11½" **20.00**
Red Rooster Provincial, chop plate, 13½".......................**15.00**
Red Rooster Provincial, plate, dinner; 10" **9.00**

Bowl, figural frog perched on side, aqua matt, 11" wide, $35.00.

Red Rooster Provincial, platter, oval, 11" **10.00**
Red Rooster Provincial, tureen, soup; with ladle, rare...**100.00**
Romanelli artware, figure of cowgirl, 9½" **75.00**
Romanelli artware, sea horse vase, 9¼" **45.00**
Romanelli artware, swordfish vase, 9" **45.00**
Romanelli artware, waterbearer bud vase, 9¼" **60.00**

Sculptured Grape, bowl, fruit; 6¼" **5.00**
Strawberry, platter, 13" **10.00**

Milk Glass

Milk glass has been used since the 1700s to make tableware, lamps, and novelty items such as covered figural dishes and decorative wall plaques. Early examples were made with cryolite and ring with a clear bell tone when tapped.

Bottle, dresser; Actress, cut stopper **39.00**
Bowl, Basketweave, Atterbury, dated 1874, large **80.00**
Bowl, Drunken Sailor, lattice rim, Atterbury, 3x9x7½" **50.00**
Bowl, fruit; Daisy, hand-painted decoration **75.00**
Card case holder, heart marker on side...................................**20.00**
Compote, Atlas, scalloped rim, Atterbury......................**105.00**
Creamer & sugar bowl, Blackberry, with cover & tray.**60.00**
Creamer, Paneled Wheat......**45.00**
Creamer & sugar bowl, Pheasant, with cover **55.00**

Dish, covered; battleship, 2-funnel, 8"...............................**50.00**
Dish, covered; Moses in the Bullrushes, 5½" **130.00**
Dish, covered; sleigh, large...**90.00**
Jar, Flaccus, elk head, original insert, no band **200.00**
Jar, fruit; owl, screw-on cap, Atterbury......................**110.00**
Jar, mustard; bull's head, with ladle **150.00**
Match holder, minstrel boy...**40.00**
Mug, Gooseberry, 1⅞" **30.00**
Novelty, cat emerging from boot, lacy base **40.00**
Novelty, hatchet, 6"...............**12.00**
Paperweight, setter, recumbent on platform...................**225.00**
Pitcher, Block Daisy, 7".........**55.00**
Pitcher, fish, Atterbury, 7"..**200.00**
Pitcher, owl, yellow glass eyes, 7½", NM.......................**145.00**
Plate, An Easter Lay **68.00**
Plate, Anchor & Belaying, painted decoration......................**25.00**
Plate, Angel with Harp.........**38.00**
Plate, Easter Ducks, 6".........**25.00**
Plate, Fleur-de-Lis **12.50**
Plate, He's All Right **140.00**
Plate, Niagara Falls, openwork leaf border **35.00**
Plate, Owl Lovers, 7" **40.00**

Inkwell with enameled flowers, 7" wide, $32.50.

Plate, WJ Bryan, flag & star border..................................**120.00**
Plate, Yacht & Anchor **25.00**
Plate, 3 puppies with squirrel, with wall hanger............**95.00**

Plate, three gold owls, hand-painted florals, 7½", $40.00.

Platter, fish, pat 1872, 10"....**28.00**
Shaker, basketweave base, bulbous, sterling top **20.00**
Shakers, rabbits & chickens reliefs, 3", pr..................**135.00**
Sugar bowl, Roman Cross.....**10.00**
Sugar bowl, Wild Iris, EX gold trim, with lid **55.00**
Tray, dresser; floral sprays in center, loop hdls, 11x7"........**18.00**
Vase, embossed Dutch boy with wagon, 6" **15.00**
Vase, Mephistopheles, 2" horns, pointed ears, 8½"............**55.00**

Molds

The two most popular types of molds with collectors are chocolate molds and ice cream molds. Chocolate molds are often quite detailed and are usually made of tin or copper. While some are flat backed, others make three-dimensional shapes. Baskets, Santas, rabbits, and those with holiday themes are abundant. Ice cream molds are usually made of pewter and come in a wide variety of shapes and styles.

Chocolate

Baby, sitting, medium **65.00**
Basket, tin, 3x6½" **45.00**
Bugs Bunny, tin, 2x5¼" **14.00**
Bunny, fat, hinged, 7x8½".....**40.00**
Christmas wreath, tin, 1½" ... **7.00**
Circus elephant, wearing a cap, 1½x3¾"............................**35.00**
Cradle, 3-part, K-344 ....**40.00**
Davy Crockett **75.00**
Duck, 5x5" **48.00**
Egg, cherub decor, small.......**40.00**
Frogs, each: 1½x2½" on 9¾x22" tray **50.00**
George Washington, 2½".......**15.00**
Heart with roses, tin, 2x2¼".. **8.00**
Hen, sitting, medium............**65.00**
Horse, running, 4x3".............**38.00**
Indian head, tin, 1½x1¾"......**10.00**
Jack-o'-lantern, tin, 2¾x2¾" .**25.00**

Chocolate mold, Three monkeys, 7" long, $85.00.

Owl, 4½x3" **38.00**
Rabbit, sitting, 6" **18.00**
Rabbit pulls Easter egg cart, 2-part clamps, #192, 7x3½" **50.00**
Rabbits, 1 small on 1 larger, tin, 2-part, 6½x5½" **50.00**
Rabbits pull carts, hinged, 6x11½" long **70.00**
Santa with candy cane, 2-part, 3½x2" **15.00**
Scotty dog, large **95.00**
Swan, large..........................**195.00**

Teddy bear, medium............**170.00**
Turtle, tin, 1½x2¼" **9.00**

Food

Cast iron, fish, 3-footed, PA, ca
    1890, 13x5½" **100.00**
Copper, geometric with cylinder
    center, 5" dia...................**85.00**
Copper, jumping fish, 10" ...**115.00**
Copper & tin, abstract swirls,
    dovetailed, 4x7x5" **150.00**

Cookie mold, nickeled tin, $45.00.

Copper & tin, fish, 3½"..........**45.00**
Copper & tin, fruit design, scal-
    loped sides, 12x14".......**165.00**
Copper & tin, lion, recumbent,
    oval, 5x7x5" **150.00**
Copper & tin, pear, 5" **55.00**
Copper & tin, pineapple, 6" ..**65.00**
Copper & tin, roses & 3 leaves,
    oval, 7"...........................**85.00**
Copper & tin, seashell, curved,
    scalloped, 5" **45.00**
Pewter, 8 designs, wood back,
    springerle **225.00**
Tin, fish, 11½"........................**95.00**
Tin, squirrel, 3x12x10" **36.00**

Ice Cream

Apple, #238, medium **20.00**
Apples, K-102 ....**30.00**
Apricot, CC-0018...................**28.00**
Arctic explorer, S-510, rare.**110.00**
Asparagus spear, E-223, 8"...**42.00**
Banjo, S-545 ....**50.00**

Basket, #471..........................**45.00**
Basket, fancy scrolls, #203 ...**25.00**
Billy goat, grazing.................**30.00**
Bride with long flowing veil, E-
    1148 ....**58.00**
Camel, E-681.........................**78.00**
Cat, sitting, S-170 ....**70.00**
Cradle, 3-part, K-344 ....**40.00**
Cupids crack eggs, E-1082 ...**66.00**
Duck, nesting, #622, 4".........**30.00**
Duck egg, K-188 ....**14.00**
Egg, raised yolk, CC, 3"........**25.00**
Elk's head, 3-part, K-493......**66.00**
Fisherman sitting, #951, 5"..**70.00**
Football player, K-491 ....**70.00**
Goat, rearing, S-346..............**78.00**
Grape cluster, #278, 5".........**35.00**
Halloween cat, E-644 ....**55.00**
Horse, rearing, E-639 ....**56.00**
Indian, K-458, dated 1896 ...**75.00**

**Ice cream mold, lady's shoe, S &
Co., #570, 3", $45.00.**

Lettuce leaf, #1143, 4" **20.00**
Lion's head, turned, CC, 3"...**30.00**
Morning-glory, E-297............**34.00**
Mother Hubbard, E-981, dated
    1890 ....**75.00**
Napoleon, S-426 ....**60.00**
Piece of pie, E-1097..............**40.00**
Pineapple, CC815, 3" **22.00**
Ring, wedding; K-608............**35.00**
Santa with pack, 7" **50.00**
Slipper, 3-part, #570 ....**35.00**
Thimble, K-372......................**75.00**
Truck, 1¼x2¾" **25.00**
Valentine in envelope, E-1046,
    dated 1896 ....**60.00**
Wishbone, K-322 ....**50.00**

Mortens Studios

Animal models sold by Mortens Studios of Arizona during the 1940s are among today's most interesting collectibles, especially with animal lovers. Hundreds of breeds of dogs, cats, and horses were produced from a plaster-type composition material constructed over a wire framework. They range in size from 2" up to about 7" and most are marked.

Beagle, ivory, tan, & black, standing, 6" **65.00**
Boston Terrier, #725..............**50.00**

Bulldog, 6" long, $45.00.

Cocker Spaniel, 7" **50.00**
Collie, tan & ivory, 6x7" **75.00**
Dalmation, 3" **35.00**
Doberman, black with tan, recumbent, 4x8", M **85.00**
French Poodle, 5" **75.00**
Irish Setter, rust, standing, 6x7", NM..............................**65.00**
Pomeranian, paper label, 4" .**50.00**
Springer Spaniel, ivory & black, 5x5½", M........................**65.00**
St Bernard, large **75.00**
Whippet, 6½" long.................**72.00**

Movie Memorabilia

Anything connected with the silver screen and movie stars in general is collected by movie buffs today. Posters, lobby cards, movie magazines, promotional photos, souvenir booklets, and stills are their treasures. Especially valuable are items from the twenties and thirties that have to do with such popular stars as Jean Harlow, Bella Lugosi, Carol Lumbard, and Gary Cooper. Elvis Presley and Marilyn Monroe have devoted fans who often limit their collections to them exclusively.

Book, If I Had Million, R Andrews, Paramount, 1931, 280-page **18.00**
Display card, Jack & Beanstalk, Abbott & Costello, 1952, 22x28".............................**35.00**
Display card, Egg & I, Claudette Colbert, 22x28"...............**24.00**
Display card, The Robe, Richard Burton, 22x28", EX........**10.00**
Film clip, Coming to America, promotional **15.00**
Film clip, Gorillas in the Mist, promotional **15.00**
Handbill, Roar of the Crowd, Joe Louis, boxing pose, 6x12". **8.00**
Insert card, Inside Straight, Arlene Dahl, 1951..........**15.00**
Lobby card, Baby Doll, Caroll Baker, 1957, 11x14", EX .. **8.00**
Lobby card, Come to the Stable, Loretta Young, 1949, 11x14", NM................................**15.00**
Lobby card, Command Decision, Gable, 1948, 11x14" **15.00**
Lobby card, Easter Parade, Garland & Astaire, 1948, 11x14", EX **40.00**
Lobby card, Man from Black Hills, Johnny Mack Brown, 1952, 11x14", EX **20.00**
Lobby card, Rebel Without a Cause, James Dean, 11x14", EX **50.00**
Poster, Baby the Rain Must Fall, Steve McQueen, 1965, 1-sheet **25.00**
Poster, It's Only Money, Jerry Lewis, 1962, 3-sheet **15.00**

Poster, My Pal Trigger, Roy Rogers, Dale Evans, Gabby Hayes, and others, 1940s, 20" x 25", $75.00.

Poster card, Wild One, Marlon Brando on motorcycle, 1953, 5x8", EX **6.00**

Press photo, Fatty Arbuckle & Minta Durfe, 1921, EX ..**22.50**

Pressbook, Coogan's Bluff, Clint Eastwood, 1968, 20 pages, NM **8.75**

Pressbook, Double Trouble, Elvis, 1967, EX **15.00**

Pressbook, Gypsy, Rosalind Russell & Natalie Wood, 1962, EX **15.00**

Pressbook, Love Has Many Faces, Lana Turner, EX **5.00**

Pressbook, St Valentine's Day Massacre, Robards, 1967 ...... **8.00**

Souvenir book, Beau Geste, Ronald Colman & William Powell **50.00**

Still, Little Giant, Edward G Robinson, 1933 .... **7.50**

Still, That Hamilton Woman, Olivier & Leigh, 1941 .... **5.00**

Still, Three Stooges in Orbit, 1962, NM **4.00**

Still, Till We Meet Again, Oberon & Brent, 1940.................**12.00**

Still, When Tomorrow Comes, Dunne & Boyer, 1939.....**10.00**

Trailer, Ole Yeller, McGuire & Parker, 1956, 33mm **7.00**

Trailer, Seven Women, Anne Bancroft, 1966, 35mm **5.00**

Napkin Rings

Figural silverplated napkin rings were popular in the late 1880s, and today's collectors enjoy finding hundreds of different designs. Among the companies best known for their manufacture are Meriden, Wm. Rogers, Reed and Barton, and Pairpoint (who made some of the finest). Kate Greenaway figurals, those with Kewpies or Brownies, and styles with wheels that turn are especially treasured.

Baby, crawling, supports ring on back **150.00**

Bird, fledgling atop nest, mouth open for feeding **65.00**

Bird, fork-tailed, tiered rectangular base, Derby #346....**150.00**

Bird, wings/tail out, on leaf base, Toronto #1142 ....**135.00**

Boy, kneeling, body forms ring, Meriden #224 ....**175.00**

Sailor boy with anchor, Reed & Barton #1346, 3½", $285.00.

199

Boy in work clothes rolls ring, Meriden #161 ....**175.00**

Boy with cookie, dog begging, Meriden **185.00**

Branches form chair, ring rests on seat **125.00**

Butterfly on leaf, Tufts **78.00**

Cat, large, contemplative, Meriden #232 ....**200.00**

Cat pushing ring with paws, no base................................**75.00**

Cat sits by ring, 3" **90.00**

Chair, low ladderback, ring on seat **95.00**

Cherub atop ring holds swan by leash, Wilcox, EX **285.00**

Cherub sits on ring, holds dog by leash, Tufts #1543........**250.00**

Cherubs, two naked twins with scrolled ring on base, Tufts #1544 ....**150.00**

Cherubs aside ring, tiered base, Reed & Barton #1320 ..**295.00**

Chick on end of wishbone, Rococo base, ring elevated.........**65.00**

Cockatoos perch on embossed dome-shaped footed base, Meriden **225.00**

Conquistador leans on rifle & ring, footed base, Toronto #1337 ....**175.00**

Crocodile carries ring on back, Meriden #0202 ....**125.00**

Cut glass, triangle shape, amber, 2½" **38.00**

Deer sits on platform under fretwork ring................**275.00**

Dog, large, holds ring on back, rope in mouth...............**175.00**

Dog crouches with ring on back, large **95.00**

Dog rests forepaws on lattice ring, square footed base **100.00**

Dog sits by keg, ring on circular base, Tufts #1531 ....**150.00**

Dolphins, two hold ring between tails **295.00**

Fans (2 Oriental) form ring, flowers/hummingbirds **75.00**

Girl, barefoot, sits by ring, book on lap, Simpson, Hall & Miller **150.00**

Girl on stomach with ring on back, oval base, Wilcox #01548 ....**250.00**

Girl with pigtails pushes ring, Rogers #280..................**185.00**

Greenaway boy holds drumstick, drum formed by ring, Hartford #30 ....**195.00**

Greenaway boy with baseball bat & ball **235.00**

Greenaway girl leads goat with rein, Meriden #0236 ....**250.00**

Greenaway girl with hands on ring, Barbour Bros.......**175.00**

Jack & Jill climb up hill-shaped ring, Tufts #1667..........**375.00**

Knight in armor with upraised torch stands by ring.....**145.00**

Lady stands behind ring, 6-leafed base, Tufts #3405 ....**200.00**

Lion stands beside ring, rectangular base **150.00**

Monkey dressed in man's clothes, Tufts...............................**295.00**

Owl, glass eyes, ring forms body, log-type base **175.00**

Owl sits on ring, log base, Rogers #248 ....**95.00**

Parrot on wheels, Simpson, Hall & Miller **175.00**

Peacock sits on ring, round base, Meriden #234 ....**150.00**

Pheasant leans on limb that holds ring, Meriden #246 ......**150.00**

Pig stands beside ring on round base...............................**125.00**

Rabbit crouches on log-type base, holds ring with ears.....**150.00**

Robin, wings out, ring in mouth, Meriden #247 ....**60.00**

Sphinx holds up ring with bud vase atop, Aurora #45..**150.00**

Sphinx with ring on back, Meriden #165 ....**150.00**

Sunflower base, octagonal, Meriden #37 ....**65.00**

Tennis racquet & ball beside ring,
Pairpoint **100.00**
Turkish dancers on rectangular
footed base....................**125.00**
Turtle, head up, ring on back,
Meriden #193 ....**150.00**
Water lily pad holds ring, Meri-
den #166 ....**65.00**
Wheelbarrow holds ring, flat
shield-type base, Tufts .**125.00**

Napkin Rings, Catalin

For a less formal setting,
Catalin napkin rings can add a
cheerful bit of color to the table.
Often found in delightful animal
shapes and comic character
forms, these whimsical accessories are becoming very collectible. Red and orange rings are
most often in demand, with blue a
second favorite. Dark green, ivory,
salmon pink, light green, yellow,
and mottled butterscotch can also
be found. Buyers beware! Many of
these are being reproduced and
sold for the 'old' prices.

Angelfish **25.00**
Chicken or bird.....................**15.00**
Cottontail rabbit **20.00**
Donald Duck..........................**55.00**
Duck.......................................**20.00**
Elephant #1 ....**23.00**
Mickey Mouse.......................**55.00**
New York World's Fair, trylon &
perisphere......................**45.00**
Penguin..................................**40.00**
Popeye....................................**85.00**
Rabbit **18.00**
Rocking Horse **40.00**
Schnauzer dog **20.00**
Scotty dog..............................**18.00**

Nazi Collectibles

An area of militaria attracting a growing following today,

Nazi collectibles are anything
related to the Nazi rise and German participation in World War
II. There are many facets to this
field; among the items hunted
most enthusiastically are daggers,
medals, badges, patches, uni-
forms, and toys with a Nazi German theme.

Arm band, WWII, Nazi SS,
swastika on red wool **50.00**
Badge, General Assault, silver,
1940 ....**30.00**
Badge, Hitler Youth Honor, enam-
eled with gold border, EX.**75.00**
Badge, Karpathenkorps, silver
metal, 2-prong back, M..**40.00**
Badge, Kriegsmarine Destroyer,
gold & gray emblem, navy
cloth **20.00**
Badge, Luftwaffe Ground Com-
bat, bullion embroidered,
eagle & wreath...............**60.00**
Badge, Luftwaffe pilot, riveted 2-
piece, hallmark **175.00**
Badge, WWII, Coast Artillery,
gold-colored wreath **70.00**
Badge, WWII, Luftwaffe Flak, silver finish **70.00**

Buckle, medical insignia, $85.00.

Book, Redemption of Democracy,
H Rauschning, 1941 ......**10.00**
Cap, Luftwaffe, M-43, summer,
embroidered trapezoid, 1944,
EX **50.00**
Collartabs, red with doubletress,
gilt with black border **15.00**

Flag, battle; with rope, lg **85.00**
Gloves, Paratrooper, leather.**42.50**
Gloves, Waffen & Army motorcycle rider, gray leather & cloth, EX **30.00**
Helmet, pith; Luftwaffe Tropics, tan canvas cover, 1940...**85.00**
Helmet, Luftwaffe M-40, single decal, combat style, EX..**80.00**
Hood, for Luftwaffe overcoat, blue-gray with drawstring, NM **12.00**
Magazine, Obersaltzberg, Hitler & Braun, 106-page **15.00**
Patch, WWII, German, Seamen Radio Telegraphists **7.00**
Tunic, M-16, field gray, hidden buttons, slash pockets ...**80.00**
Utensil set, aluminum, folding fork & spoon, EX.............**12.00**
Watch fob, Iron Cross commemorative, white metal, 1914-15, NM **22.00**

New Martinsville

Operating in New Martinsville, West Virginia, from 1901 until 1944 when it was purchased by the Viking Company, this company produced not only dinnerware lines but beautiful glass animal models, all of which are highly collectible.

Bonbon, Prelude, with handles, 6½" **20.00**
Bookend, sailing ship, each ..**40.00**
Bookend, starfish, each.........**65.00**
Bookends, fish, pair **30.00**
Bottle, cat form, crystal **10.00**
Bowl, Radiance, red, 10".......**27.50**
Box, Martha Washington, pink satin.............................**95.00**
Candlestick, Florentine, double, pair **20.00**
Candy dish, black amethyst, footed, fan finial.............**35.00**

Cheese server, Janice **40.00**
Cocktail, Carlton **12.50**
Comport, Radiance, ice blue or amber, 6", each...............**15.00**
Creamer & sugar, Prelude ...**30.00**
Cruet, Prelude, with stopper, 4-ounce **35.00**
Cup, Prelude.........................**10.00**
Cup & saucer, Kay, #34.........**15.00**
Figurine, baby chick **25.00**
Figurine, police dog...............**55.00**
Figurine, rooster, green, tall.**22.00**
Figurine, seal with ball, 7" ...**65.00**
Goblet, Carlton......................**12.50**
Shakers, Radiance, red, pair..**60.00**
Sugar bowl, Kay, amber, #34 . **7.50**
Vase, Radiance, ruby, 10" **55.00**

Seal with ball, 7", $65.00.

Niloak

Produced in Arkansas by Charles Dean Hyten from the early 1900s until the mid-1940s, Niloak (the backward spelling of kaolin, a type of clay) takes many forms—figural planters, vases in both matt and glossy glazes, and novelty items of many types. The company's most famous product and their most collectible is their swirl or Mission Ware line. Clay in colors of brown, blue, cream, red, and buff are swirled within the mold, the finished product left unglazed on the outside to preserve the natural hues. Small vases are common; large pieces or unusual shapes and those with exceptional coloration are the most valuable.

Ash tray, Mission Ware, with metal contoured cap.......**75.00**
Bowl, pink, scalloped, 5" **12.00**
Creamer, pelican with orange beak, 5" **20.00**
Creamer, stylized florals in relief, light blue, 3½" **12.00**
Ewer, blue, small **15.00**
Ewer, high gloss, 12" **19.00**
Figurine, deer, pink................**12.00**
Figurine, elephant on circus tub, 6"....................................**22.50**
Figurine, parrot on pleated basket, 6"..............................**22.50**
Mug, floral mold, light gray... **8.00**

Vase, Mission Ware, 9", $100.00.

Mug, Mission Ware, 4½" **45.00**
Mug, pink gloss, 3½" **8.00**
Pitcher, blue, 5½" **10.00**
Planter, canoe, white, 11" **28.00**
Planter, squirrel, brown, original label, 6".............................**25.00**
Vase, Grecian style, maroon matt, 7".....................................**17.50**
Vase, Mission Ware, flared neck, 3½" **30.00**
Vase, Mission Ware, 6"..........**60.00**
Vase, Mission Ware, rose bowl shape with pedestal feet, 4½x6" **55.00**
Vase, Mission Ware, teardrop form, 5½" **35.00**
Wall pocket, geometric design, yellow matt, 4x5½".........**35.00**

Nippon

In complying with American importation regulations, from 1891 to 1921 Japanese manufacturers marked their wares 'Nippon,' meaning Japan, to indicate country of origin. The term is today used to refer to the highly decorated porcelain vases, bowls, chocolate pots, etc., that bear this term within their trademark. Many variations were used. In the following listings marks are indicated by numbers: #1, China E-OH; #2, M in wreath; #3, Rising Sun; and #4, Maple Leaf.

Ash tray, moose in center, nuts at rim, hexagonal, #2 mark, 6"...................................**110.00**
Bottle, scent; gold floral overlay, blue #7 mark, 6"...........**165.00**
Bowl, fruit; man on camel, handles, #2 mark, 12" **325.00**
Bowl, gold floral overlay on cobalt, #7 mark, 7½" **80.00**
Bowl, nut & pine cones, clover shape, 3 handles, green #2 mark, 6½" **85.00**

Bowl, pastoral scene with lake, green #2 mark, 8½"......**225.00**

Coaster, Dutchman smokes pipe at water's edge **30.00**

Coffeepot, pink & white roses on cream, gold overlay, #7 mark, 5¼" **465.00**

Cookie jar, gold overlay florals & beads, handles, footed, #7 mark, 7" **325.00**

Vase, florals, green M in wreath mark, 8", $125.00.

Cup & saucer, apples, gold beaded border, #7 mark **40.00**

Ferner, moriage, peony & pussy willows, marked, 8"......**285.00**

Ferner, silhouettes, 6-sided, green #2 mark, 6¼" **165.00**

Hair receiver, roses with gold beads & trim, marked....**95.00**

Humidor, Indian in canoe, hexagonal, 5½x6½" **325.00**

Humidor, playing cards, green #2 mark, 4½" **325.00**

Pitcher, tankard; berries on tan, Imperial mark, 12" **325.00**

Plaque, hunt scene, Greek Key border, #2 mark, 10" **325.00**

Plaque, moriage sailboat with 2 fishermen, 11"..............**285.00**

Plate, deer scene, fancy gold on cobalt, #2 mark, 10" **300.00**

Plate, gooseberries, brown border with black rim, 9"...........**25.00**

Plate, souvenir of Washington DC, gold overlay rim, #7 mark, 8"........................**155.00**

Shakers, butterflies, green with gold trim, pair...............**30.00**

Syrup, floral border on yellow, underplate, #7 mark......**55.00**

Tea strainer, multicolor roses on ivory, squat form............**95.00**

Toothpick holder, river scene, earth tones with gold, #2 mark, 2" **75.00**

Urn, roses, applied gold legs, 12" **155.00**

Vase, floral reserves with gold, angle handles, green #2 mark, 10"......................**150.00**

Vase, garden scene on black, gold trim and handles, green M in wreath mark, 10", $250.00.

Vase, people in wide band, gold
beads & handles, #2 mark,
8".............................**300.00**
Vase, roses tapestry, gold trim,
bulbous, #7 mark, 5" ...**525.00**
Vase, storks with young, bulbous,
gold handles, green #7 mark,
8" **225.00**

Noritake

Since the early 1900s the
Noritake China Company has
been producing fine dinnerware,
occasional pieces, and figural
items decorated by hand in delicate florals, scenics, and wildlife
studies. One of their most popular
dinnerware lines, Azalea, is listed
in the category by that name.

Numbers indicate specific
marks: #1, Komaru; #2, M in
wreath; #3, N in wreath.

Bottle, scent; flower basket on
cream, #2 mark, 6".......**100.00**
Bowl, bird decoration, square,
handles, 8½"...................**40.00**
Cake plate, Tree in Meadow,
pierced handles..............**35.00**
Candlestick, man on camel scene,
cobalt with gold, #1 mark,
5¾"...............................**165.00**
Candy dish, orange/pearl lustre
with black trim, green mark,
15" diameter...................**40.00**
Chamberstick, orange lustre,
black trim, ring handles, #2
mark, 5".........................**75.00**
Cigarette holder, bell form, bird
finial, #2 mark, 5" **125.00**
Compote, man on camel scene,
cobalt with gold, #1 mark,
4x9"..............................**185.00**
Humidor, blown-out bulldog
smoking pipe.................**495.00**
Inkwell, clown figural, #2 mark,
4"...................................**250.00**
Match holder, Deco-style lady
smoking, #2 mark, 1¾" ..**70.00**

Lemon dish, red mark, 5¾" diameter, $30.00.

Napkin ring, Deco man & woman,
pair **100.00**
Plaque, elk at water's edge,
earth tones, #2 mark,
10½" **450.00**
Plate, Tree in Meadow, 7½" .**12.50**
Serving dish, etched gold floral,
red #2 mark, 7" long **70.00**
Shakers, river scene, earth tones,
#2 mark, 2½", pair **27.50**
Spooner, figural birds atop han-
dles.................................**75.00**
Sugar shaker, floral band on
white, lustre top, #2 mark,
6½"..............................**35.00**
Tea set, camel & rider on dark
red, #2 mark, 15-pc......**325.00**
Teapot, Tree in Meadow........**60.00**
Toothpick holder, dancer with fan,
3 handles, green #2 mark,
2¼"................................**45.00**
Vase, red with gold handle & interior, basket form, #2 mark,
5½"..............................**100.00**
Vase, swan on river reserve, gold
trim & handles, #2 mark,
7½" **100.00**
Vase, Tree in Meadow, 8½" ...**55.00**
Wall pocket, butterflies, jack-in-
the-pulpit form, #2 mark,
9"..................................**115.00**
Wall pocket, sailing ship scene,
Art Deco style, tall **60.00**

Nutcrackers

Of most interest to collectors are nutcrackers marked with patent information or those made in the form of an animal or bird. Many manufacturers chose the squirrel as a model for their nutcrackers; dogs were also popular. Cast iron examples are most often encountered; but brass, steel, even wood was also used.

Alligator, brass, 7½"..............**35.00**
Alligator, cast iron, 13½"......**45.00**
Clamp-on, cast iron, mechanical, Patent 1914....................**26.00**
Dog, marked LA Athoff, Laporte IN **48.00**

Dog, cast iron, Ideal Foundry, 12" long, $65.00.

Dog, St Bernard, bronze **50.00**
Dog, St Bernard, nickel-plated cast iron, 11" long...........**45.00**
Dome shape, cast iron, fits over knee, ca 1870..................**65.00**
Fagin & Sikes, brass figural, early, 5"..........................**55.00**
Mythological bird, for betel nuts, brass, old **48.00**
Nude, carved wood, full bodied, 13"....................................**20.00**
Punch & Judy, brass figural .**65.00**
Reed's Rocket, cast iron, rocket shape on wood base, adjusts, MIB **20.00**
Sailor & lady kiss when handle is squeezed, brass, 6" **65.00**
Squirrel, cast iron, on walnut block, ca 1850s, EX **95.00**

Wood, threaded screw device, 2-piece, early, EX..............**25.00**

Occupied Japan

Items with the 'Occupied Japan' mark were made during the period from the end of World War II until April, 1952. Porcelains, novelties, paper items, lamps, silverplate, lacquer ware, and dolls are some of the areas of exported goods that may bear this stamp. Because the Japanese were naturally resentful of the occupation, it is felt that only a small percentage of their wares were thus marked. Although you may find identical items marked simply 'Japan,' only those with the 'Occupied Japan' stamp are being collected.

Ash tray, horse pulling wagon, white, 3¼"........................ **7.00**
Ash tray, roses in center, metal, set of 4 ....**12.00**
Ash tray, Wedgwood............... **5.00**
Atomizer, blue glass..............**30.00**
Bookends, girl knitting, boy in rain gear, pair **28.00**
Candlestick, metal, 5", pair..**24.00**
Cigarette box, pink floral with 4 ash trays, 4x3" **21.00**
Cup & saucer, blue floral, marked Gold China **14.00**
Cup & saucer, children's Blue Willow, 2¾x3½"....................**10.00**
Cup & saucer, demitasse; tree relief, NM **6.00**
Cup & saucer, floral medallions on yellow, gold handle....**12.00**
Doll, celluloid, pink crocheted dress, 6" **35.00**
Figurine, accordion player, 4".. **7.00**
Figurine, angel with horn, bisque, 5" **25.00**
Figurine, boy sits with broken sprinkler, 4½" **20.00**

Figurine, bride & groom, bisque, 5", pair 25.00
Figurine, Chinese man & woman, 3½", pair 20.00
Figurine, Colonial man & woman with flowers, 7", pair 70.00
Figurine, couple with lambs, bisque, 9x10", pair 250.00
Figurine, dog begging, 2½" ... 5.00
Figurine, Dutch man & woman, 3½", pair 25.00
Figurine, flower gatherers, bisque, 10¼", pair 175.00
Figurine, Indian in canoe with plastic flowers 19.00
Figurine, man with flower, bisque, 10¼" 50.00
Figurine, musketeer, 5" 9.00
Figurine, Oriental man & woman pray, 7⅝", pair 65.00
Figurine, poodle, 3" 12.00
Incense burner, Indian..........18.00
Jewel box, wooden 14.00
Lamp, Colonial couple arm in arm, metal base, 10½" ..30.00
Lemon dish, hand-painted poppies on porcelain 18.00
Lighter, Indian, metal 9.00
Lighter, with tray, metal 22.00
Match holder, bisque, wall hanging, 6⅞x5"......................75.00
Mug, barrel form, man in red shirt as handle, 4¾" 30.00
Mug, clown face, bird handle .24.00
Mug, elephant, seated, brown, trunk as handle, 4¾"......32.00

Planter with embossed flowers and figural bird, $50.00; Planter, figural bird, $10.00.

Planter, bird on branch, 3" ...10.00
Planter, cupid with gold rings & lady with lyre, bisque, 8¼x9¼" 200.00
Planter, Donald Duck 13.00
Planter, mallard, wings hide opening, 4x5"..................15.00
Planter, Oriental girl with fan, 6" 13.00
Planter, Shoe House, rooster on the toe of shoe, 5x5" 15.00
Plaque, Colonial man standing, oval, bisque, 7x5", pair .50.00
Plaque, Dutch girl, 6¼x4".....22.00
Salt & pepper shakers, Donald Duck, 3⅜" 18.00
Salt & pepper shakers, frog, pair.................................10.00
Salt & pepper shakers, frogs on lily pad, 2½x4", pair.......25.00
Salt & pepper shakers, Geisha girls, pair 21.00
Salt & pepper shakers, Humpty Dumpty, pair 30.00
Salt & pepper shakers, Indians in canoe, pair 20.00
Shelf sitter, boy holds paint can & brush, 4¼" 15.00
Shelf sitter, boy with straw hat, 3"............................10.00
Shelf sitter, couple fishes from bench, bisque, 4"...........15.00
Stein, dog handle 22.00
Stein, figural handle 18.00
Sugar bowl, small floral transfer, gold trim.........................15.00
Teapot, tomato form, 5½"......45.00
Teapot, windmill form, 5" 38.00
Toby jug, man with gray hair, blue hat & vest, full figure, 2" 10.00
Toby mug, man's head, black hat & red bow tie, 4¾" 32.00
Toothpick holder, nude girl sits beside floral vase, 3" 12.00
Tray, Niagara Falls & Rainbow Bridge, metal.................. 7.00
Vase, bud; dancing girl on front, 4"...................................12.00

Vase, dragon, 2½" **7.50**
Vase, floral relief, white, side handles, 3½" **6.00**
Vase, fruit relief, cobalt on black with gold, 3¾" **12.00**
Vase, Oriental man, 2½" **7.50**

Old McDonald's Farm

Made by the Regal China Co., items from this line of novelty ware designed with characters and animals from Old McDonald's farm can often be found at flea markets and dinnerware shows.

Creamer and covered sugar bowl, $145.00 for the set.

Butter dish, cow's head.........**75.00**
Canister, large.....................**175.00**
Canister, medium.................**95.00**
Canister, spice; small............**55.00**
Creamer, rooster **50.00**
Grease jar, pig figural.........**100.00**
Pitcher, cow's head, tankard form, milk size **200.00**
Shakers, churn shape, pair ..**25.00**
Shakers, feed sacks with sheep's head, pair **100.00**
Shakers, figural heads, pair .**35.00**
Sugar bowl...........................**95.00**
Teapot, duck's head.............**150.00**

Old Sleepy Eye

Both the Sleepy Eye Milling Company and the Minnesota town where it was located took their name from the Sioux Indian

Chief who was born there in 1789, Old Sleepy Eye. In the early 1900s, the milling company contracted with the Weir Pottery Co. to make four pieces of blue and gray stoneware – a salt bowl, butter crock, vase, and stein – each decorated with the likeness of the old chief. One of these pieces was given as a premium inside each barrel of their flour. Weir was one of six companies that in 1906 merged to form the Western Stoneware Company. There the line was produced in blue and white, and several more items were added. These early pieces, along with advertising items such as pillow tops, post cards, match holders, signs, labels, etc., are today highly collectible.

Butter crock, Flemish **500.00**
Cookbook, loaf of bread shape, NM **250.00**
Dough scraper, tin/wood, To Be Sure, EX **350.00**
Fan, Indian chief, die-cut cardboard, 1900...................**175.00**
Ink blotter **100.00**
Label, barrel end; Indian portrait, 16", NM **125.00**
Label, egg crate **25.00**
Letter opener, bronze **850.00**
Paperweight, bronzed company trademark **450.00**
Pillow cover, trademark center 22", NM **600.00**
Pitcher, #1 ....**150.00**
Pitcher, #5 ....**350.00**
Post card **90.00**
Ruler, wooden **400.00**
Spoon, Indian-head handle .**100.00**
Stein, blue & white, 7¾" **500.00**
Stein, brown & yellow, Western Stoneware....................**900.00**
Sugar bowl, blue & white ...**600.00**
Tumbler, etched, 1979 commemorative **25.00**

Vase, blue & white **425.00**
Vase, brown on yellow, rare .**800.00**
Vase, Indian & cattails, Flemish,
8½" **375.00**
Watch fob, Sleepy Eye Mills,
Indian, M........................**50.00**

Calendar, 1904, partial pad, $350.00.

Paden City

Located in Paden City, West Virginia, this glass company operated from 1916 until it closed in 1951. They produced many lines of clear and colored dinnerware as well as glass animals.

Bookends, pouter pigeons, 6½",
pair **75.00**
Bowl, Far East, 5½" **2.50**
Bowl, Orchid, green, amber, or
pink, 2 handles, 8½".......**22.50**
Bowl, Peacock & Wild Rose, any
color, footed, 9½" **37.50**
Cake plate, roses with gold trim,
with server **25.00**
Candlestick, Bridal Bouquet,
crystal, 2-light, pair.......**35.00**
Candlestick, Cupid, any color, 5"
wide, pair.......................**50.00**
Candlestick, Nora Bird, pink or
green, pair.....................**40.00**
Candy dish, Peacock Reverse, any
color, square, 6½" **65.00**

Candy dish, Springtime, pink,
with lid **55.00**
Comport, Peacock & Wild Rose,
any color, 6¼" **20.00**
Console set, ruby red, bowl & pair
of candlesticks................**80.00**
Creamer & sugar bowl, Crow's
Foot, silver florals **55.00**
Creamer & sugar bowl, Flying
Peacock, pink **55.00**
Creamer & sugar bowl, Minion
shape, burgundy **22.50**
Cup, demitasse; Ivy...............**18.00**
Cup & saucer, Ivy **17.50**
Cup & saucer, Watta Line......**5.00**
Figurine, pouter pigeon **70.00**
Goblet, water; Lotus etched..**12.00**
Ice tub, Nora Bird, pink or green,
6" **65.00**
Lamp, Cupid, silver overlay, any
color **150.00**
Plate, American Rose, 6" **12.00**
Plate, Far East, 10½"............. **5.00**
Plate, Peacock Reverse, any color,
8½" **25.00**
Sandwich server, Orchid, cobalt or
red, center handle **50.00**
Server, Black Forest, green ..**40.00**
Shakers, Party Line, ruby red,
pair **45.00**
Sherbet, Gothic Garden etched,
amber.............................**18.00**
Sugar bowl, Nora Bird, pink,
round handles **25.00**
Tumbler, Nora Bird, pink or
green, 4" **27.50**
Vase, Cupid, elliptical, any color,
8¼" **100.00**
Vase, Orchid, pink, green, or
amber, 10".......................**40.00**
Vase, Peacock & Wild Rose, any
color, 10" **67.50**

Paper Dolls

Though the history of paper dolls can be traced even farther back, by the late 1700s they were being mass produced. A century later, paper dolls were being used as an advertising medium by retail companies wishing to promote sales. The type most often encountered are in book form – the dolls on the cardboard covers, their wardrobe on the inside pages, published since the 1920s. Those representing famous people or characters are popular; condition is very important. Those in original, uncut folders are most valuable.

American Colotype Co., Billy Bob and Georgie, 1927, $175.00.

Alice in Wonderland, stand-up dolls, 1934, EX **225.00**
All My Dollies, Samuel Gabriel, #D138 ....**25.00**
Ann & Pam, Warren Paper Products, #33 .... **6.00**
Babyland-Bobby, Samuel Gabriel, #D121, 1921 ....**25.00**
Barbie's Friendship, 1923, some cut, complete **5.00**
Barney Bear, advertising, with baseball uniform **25.00**
Betsy Ballerina, DeJournette Manufacturing..............**25.00**
Betsy McCall Dress 'N Play, McCall Publishing, #801, 1963 ....**12.00**
Betty & Peggy, Platt & Munk, #230B, 1937.....................**8.00**
Betty Ann & Audrey, Platt & Munk, #210A..................**30.00**

Big Sister, Londy Card Corporation, #5J, 1932 .... **5.00**
Billy Bob & Georgie, American Colortype, #27, 1927 ......**18.00**
Bright Eyes, DeJournette Manufacturing, #85 .... **5.00**
Brother Bob, Samuel Gabriel, #D90 ....**25.00**
Captain Marvel Flying Family, unpunched, NM **20.00**
Charles Our Negro Friend, Friendship Press............**25.00**
Charmin' Chatty, Whitman, 1964, NM............................**15.00**
Chatty Baby, with book-style holder............................**35.00**
Claire, DeJournette Manufacturing, #72 ....**10.00**
Cleopatra, Blaise Publishing, #1000, 1963 ....**15.00**
Corinne, American Colortype Company, #703, with outfit, 13"..................................**30.00**
Cutie Paper Dolls, Milton Bradley, #4053 complete, with clothes **15.00**
Dainty Dollies, Samuel Gabriel, #876, 1919 ....**30.00**
Dearie Dolls, Charles E Graham, #0212 ....**15.00**
Debbie Reynolds, Whitman, 1962, uncut, M **65.00**
Debby Dolls, Jaymar Specialty, #980 ....**12.00**
Debutantes, Samuel Gabriel, #D135 ....**35.00**
Dennison Dolls & Dresses, Dennison Manufacturing, #37 .**30.00**
Design-A-Doll, Dennison Manufacturing, #11, 1950 .... **8.00**
Dollie Dimple, complete in original envelope, ca 1894 ..**125.00**
Dollies a la Mode, Samuel Gabriel, #896..................**30.00**
Dolly Jean, Saalfield, 1932, doll, furniture & clothes, all cut, EX **35.00**
Dollyland, Samuel Gabriel, #D119, 1920..................**30.00**

Dottie Dress-Up, Dot & Peg Productions, 1950 ....10.00
Dresses Worn by First Ladies of the White House, cut 25.00
Fairy Favorite, MA Donohue, #671, 1913 ....30.00
Fancy Dress Dolls, Samuel Gabriel, #896.................30.00
Fashion Art Dolls, Art Award, #6000 .... 4.00
Fashion Model, Samuel Gabriel, #D116............................15.00
Freckles & Sniffles, uncut book, 1972, NM 6.00
Gay Dolls, Platt & Munk, #225A, 1942................................ 6.00
Gina, DeJournette Manufacturing, #R80 .... 5.00
Glendora, DeJournette Manufacturing, #1000.................10.00
Glenn, Janex Corporation, #2002, 1971 .....·......................... 5.00
Hedy Lamarr, 1951 ....100.00
Heidi, DeJournette Manufacturing, #200 .... 8.00
Ivy, Janex Corporation, #2000, 1971 .... 5.00
Jane Russell, 1955 ....25.00
Janet Leigh, 1958 ....35.00
Jill, DeJournette Manufacturing, #711 ....12.00
Jimmy & Jack, American Colortype, #103, 1927..........18.00
Lace-Me-Ups, Current, #3204, 1979 .... 5.00
Let's Build Our Camp, Samuel Gabriel, #D144, 1930 ....20.00
Little Audrey, Samuel Gabriel, #250 ....15.00
Little Miss Up-To-Date, American Colortype, #625 ....25.00
Little Nurse, Reuben H Lilja, #909 ....12.00
Littlest Darling, DeJournette Manufacturing, #222 ..... 8.00
Lovey & Dovey Magic Dolls, Parker Bros, 1951 ....15.00
Lula-Bye-Bye, Charles E Graham, #0237 ....25.00

Make a Model, 1964 World's Fair, NM..................................35.00
Mardi Gras, Einson Freeman, #432, 1935 ....35.00
Mark Antony, Blaise Publishing, #1001, 1963 ....15.00
Martha Ann, Winthrop-Atkins, #6310 ....10.00
Mary Alice, Samuel Gabriel, #D108 ....20.00
Mary Miles Minter, Percy Reeves, 1920 ....45.00

Milton Bradley, Magic Mary, 1955, $7.00.

Miss America Magic Doll, Parker Bros, ca 1953 ....18.00
Miss Holly Day, DeJournette Manufacturing, #2201 ...18.00
My Baby Dress-Up Kit, Colorforms, #176, 1964........... 6.00
My Fair Lady, Avalon, #401..18.00
National Velvet 35.00
Nursery Favorite, MA Donohue, #672, 1913 ....30.00
Old Fashioned Doll, Colorforms, #525, 1970 .... 3.00
Our Happy Family, Samuel Gabriel, #D141, 1929 ....20.00
Pam & Jeff, Transogram Toy, #4102, 1963 ....10.00
Paper Dolls To Cut Out, babies, early, EX 12.00
Patsy, Children's Press, #3002, 1946 ....15.00
Patty's Party, Stephens Publishing, #175 .... 6.00
Playmate, DeJournette Manufacturing, #800 ....15.00

Playtime Pals, Current, #5607, 1982 .... **4.00**

Poky-Hontas, DeJournette Manufacturing **10.00**

Princess Elizabeth Magic Doll, Parker Bros **25.00**

Rag Doll Sue, Harter Publishing, #H100, 1931 ....**30.00**

Raggedy Ann & Andy, uncut book, 1974, NM **5.00**

Ricky Nelson, Whitman, complete & uncut, M **30.00**

Roy Rogers, 1948..................**75.00**

Sally & Janet, American Colortype, #101, 1927 ....**18.00**

School Mates, Samuel Gabriel, #D100 ....**18.00**

Shirley Temple Play Kit, Saalfield, EX...........................**85.00**

Smile Dress-Up Set, Colorforms, #581, 1971 .... **3.00**

Snuggly Dolls, Charles E Graham, #0225....................**25.00**

Sparkle Plenty, Saalfield, 1948, EX **40.00**

Susie, Judy, Laura, & Annie; Aldon Industries **7.00**

Suzie Sweet, Samuel Gabriel, #D94 ....**10.00**

Teddy Bear Paper Doll, J Ottmann Lithograph **75.00**

Teena the Teenager, Avalon, #701-2 .... **4.00**

Tiny Twinkle, Charles E Graham, #0221 ....**18.00**

Toddler Twins, Samuel Gabriel, #D134 ....**25.00**

Tubby Twinkle, Charles E Graham, #0221....................**18.00**

Vicki Velcro, Samuel Gabriel, #130 ....**10.00**

Wedding Bells, Dot & Peg Productions, 1945......................**15.00**

Wedding Party, Samuel Gabriel, #D132 ....**30.00**

Wendy Walks, Merry Manufacturing, #6504, 1965 ....**10.00**

When I Grow Up, Current, #3216, 1980 .... **5.00**

William, American Colortype, #622 .... **8.00**

Winky Winnie, Jaymar Specialty, #994 ....**12.00**

Wishniks, Whitman, 1965 ....**12.50**

Your Own Quintuplets, Burton Playthings, #275, 1935 ..**25.00**

Paperback Books

Though published to some extent before the forties, most paperback book collectors prefer those printed from around 1940 until the late 1950s, and most organize their collections around a particular author, genre, publisher, or illustrator. Remember – (as is true with any type of ephemera) condition is extremely important.

Asimov, Isaac; Naked Sun, Lancer, 1954, VG............. **3.00**

Biggers, Earl Derr; Black Camel, Pocket, 1942, VG **14.00**

Cohen, Octavus Roy; Corpse That Walked, Gold Medal, 1957, EX.................................. **4.50**

Collins, Michael; Brass Rainbow, Bantam, 1970, EX **2.50**

Creasy, John; Figure in the Dusk, Avon, 1959, EX............... **4.00**

Cushman, Dan; Jewel of the Java Sea, Gold Medal, 1951, EX . **8.00**

Davis, Mildred; Room Upstairs, Avon, 1970, EX **3.00**

Dicks, Terrance; Doctor Who, Unearthly Child, 1984, 4th edition, EX....................... **4.50**

Dixon, H Vernor; Something for Nothing, Bantam, 1952, EX **4.00**

Farmer, Philip Jose; Alley God, Ballantine, 1962, EX....... **8.00**

Fleming, Ian; Casino Royal, Signet, 1962, 2nd edition, EX **4.00**

Fleming, Ian; Diamonds Are For-
ever, Bantam, 1971, NM. **7.00**
Francis, Dick; In the Frame, Pan,
1978, NM **5.00**
Grave, Andrew; No Tears for
Hilda, Dell, 1953, EX **4.50**
Grey, Zane; Heritage of Desert,
Grosset & Dunlap, movie edi-
tion, EX............................ **8.00**
Harrison, Harry; Planet of
the Damned, Bantam, 1962,
EX **5.50**
Howard, Robert E; Conan the
Avenger, Sphere, 1977, 4th
edition, EX....................... **4.50**
London, Jack; Call of the Wild,
Pocket, 1961, 4th edition,
EX **4.00**
Maine, Charles Eric, Timeliner,
Bantam, 1956, VG........... **4.00**
Mundy, Talbot; On the Secret of
Ahbor Valley, Avon, 1967,
EX **4.00**
Norman, John; Captive of Gor,
Tandem, 1973, VG **4.00**
Orwell, George; Animal Farm,
Signet, 1962, VG **4.00**
Owen, Betty M; 11 Great Horror
Stories, Scholastic, 1959,
EX.................................... **4.00**
Schmitz, James H; Demon Breed,
Ace, 1958, NM **5.00**
Sturgeon, Theodore; More Than
Human, Ballantine, 1953,
VG **4.50**
Tucker, Wilson; Warlock, Avon,
1959, NM **4.50**
Wilde, Oscar; Picture of Dorian
Gray, Dell, 1953, EX **5.00**

Pattern Glass

As early as 1820 glassware
was being pressed into patterned
molds to produce tablewares and
accessories. The process was per-
fected, and by the latter part of
the century, dozens of glass
houses were making hundreds of
patterns. This type of glassware
retained its popularity until about
1915. Two types of glass were
used: flint, the early type made
with lead to produce a good clear
color and resonance; and non-
flint, the later type containing
soda lime. Generally, flint glass is
the more expensive.

Actress, pitcher, $250.00.

Actress, bowl, 9½" **68.00**
Actress, cheese dish **245.00**
Actress, marmalade jar **125.00**
Almond Thumbprint, champagne,
non-flint..........................**40.00**
Amazon, champagne **30.00**
Amazon, goblet, 6" **34.00**
Amazon, salt cellar, master ..**12.00**
Arabesque, goblet **25.00**
Arched Grape, creamer **60.00**
Argus, creamer......................**90.00**
Art, sauce dish, flat, 4" **16.00**
Ashburton, compote, open, low
standard, flint, 8" **64.00**
Ashburton, goblet, flint........**30.00**
Ashburton, mug, flint, 5" **70.00**
Ashburton, wine....................**30.00**
Atlas, toothpick holder..........**15.00**
Aurora, decanter, ruby stained,
original stopper............**150.00**

Austrian, cordial **45.00**
Austrian, vase, 8" **45.00**
Ball & Swirl, creamer **23.00**
Baltimore Pear, cake stand, high
   standard **50.00**
Banded Portland, vase, 9" ...**40.00**
Banner, butter dish..............**95.00**
Barberry, tumbler, footed **22.00**
Barley, bowl, oval, 9½x6¾" ...**20.00**
Barley, celery vase................**35.00**
Barred Forget-Me-Not, pitcher,
   water..............................**45.00**
Barred Oval, pitcher, water; ruby
   stained, etched **250.00**
Basket Weave, goblet, knop stem,
   canary...........................**33.00**
Basket Weave, pitcher, milk;
   green.............................**70.00**
Beaded Grape, bowl, flat, square,
   green, 5¼".......................**20.00**
Beaded Grape Medallion, goblet.**30.00**
Beaded Loop, relish,8x4" **10.00**
Beaded Medallion, bottle, castor;
   oil, original stopper........**26.00**
Beaded Medallion, egg cup ..**18.00**
Beaded Tulip, plate, 6"..........**22.00**
Beaded Tulip, wine **28.00**
Bellflower, bowl, flat, 7½" **95.00**
Bellflower, celery vase **145.00**
Bellflower, decanter, double vine,
   12"...............................**375.00**
Bellflower, egg cup, single vine,
   flint **40.00**
Bellflower, honey dish, 3" **25.00**
Bellflower, lamp, fluid; 7", NM,
   pair **350.00**
Bellflower, sherry, flint **175.00**
Bethlehem Star, creamer......**25.00**
Bigler, tumbler, short stem...**57.00**
Bigler, wine...........................**70.00**
Bird & Strawberry, sauce dish,
   footed, 4" **18.00**
Blackberry, egg cup, double..**35.00**
Bleeding Heart, butter dish..**60.00**
Bleeding Heart, compote, open,
   6¼x7¼"............................**25.00**
Block, wine, ruby stained **35.00**
Block & Double Bar, pitcher,
   tankard; ruby stained..**135.00**

Block & Fan, ice tub **45.00**
Bow Tie, compote, 10x6" **65.00**
Bow Tie, jam jar, with lid **45.00**
Bow Tie, pitcher, 9"..............**85.00**
Bow Tie, sauce dish, flat **15.00**
Broken Column, pitcher, water;
   ruby stained **225.00**
Broken Column, tumbler **40.00**
Buckle, butter dish, acorn finial,
   flint **60.00**
Buckle, goblet, flint **42.00**
Buckle, spooner, flint **40.00**
Bull's Eye & Fan, creamer....**15.00**
Bull's Eye & Fan, sauce dish, flat,
   5¼" **11.00**
Bull's Eye with Diamond Point,
   bottle, bar; quart **85.00**
Bull's Eye with Diamond Point,
   honey dish, 4" **20.00**
Bull's Eye with Fleur-de-lis, gob-
   let...................................**80.00**
Button Arches, pitcher, water
   tankard; 11".................**125.00**
Cabbage Rose, creamer **55.00**

Cabbage   Rose,
goblet, $45.00

Cabbage Rose, tumbler **45.00**
Cable, bottle, bar; quart **125.00**
Canadian, pitcher, water......**95.00**
Cane, goblet, blue.................**38.00**
Cane & Rosette, celery vase .**30.00**
Cane & Rosette, compote, open,
   6¾x6" **20.00**

Cardinal Bird, sauce dish **13.00**
Cathedral, relish tray, fish shape, ruby stained **55.00**
Chain, butter dish.................**32.00**
Chain, wine or goblet, each ..**18.00**
Champion, tumbler **16.00**
Chandelier, cake stand, 10 diameter" **65.00**
Chandelier, tumbler..............**35.00**
Checkerboard, sugar bowl, with lid...................................**30.00**
Classic, sauce dish, footed **25.00**
Clear Diagonal Band, shakers, pair **35.00**
Colonial, goblet, knob stem ..**57.00**
Colonial, salt cellar, master..**18.00**
Colorado, dish, tricorner **8.00**
Columbian Coin, butter dish, frosted coins **165.00**
Comet, goblet, flint **100.00**
Cord Drapery, butter dish, footed, with flange **70.00**
Cord Drapery, tumbler **32.00**
Croesus, pitcher, water; green with gold......................**265.00**
Croesus, plate, purple, 7" ...**300.00**
Crystal Wedding, banana bowl, footed **95.00**
Currier & Ives, wine **20.00**
Curtain Tie-Back, spooner ...**30.00**
Cut Log, goblet.......................**60.00**
Dahlia, bread tray, oval **40.00**
Dahlia, plate, handles, 9" **17.00**
Daisy & Button, canoe, scalloped edge, amethyst, 12"........**60.00**
Daisy & Button, powder jar, amber **28.00**
Daisy & Button, waste bowl.**25.00**
Daisy & Button with Crossbar, pitcher, water; amber.....**70.00**
Dakota, cake stand, etched, 10" diameter **75.00**
Dakota, compote, jelly; etched, with lid, 6" **60.00**
Dakota, creamer, etched **68.00**
Dakota, goblet **20.00**
Deer & Dog, spooner **60.00**
Deer & Pine Tree, creamer, apple green **90.00**

Deer & Pine Tree, goblet.......**50.00**
Delaware, butter dish, green with gold **125.00**
Dew & Raindrop, punch cup . **8.00**

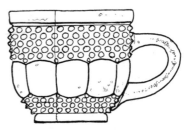

Dew and Raindrop, cup, $15.00.

Dew & Raindrop, wine..........**17.00**
Dewey, bowl, footed, 8" **45.00**
Diamond Point, bottle, bar; flint, quart..............................**58.00**
Diamond Point, sauce dish, flint, 5¼" **15.00**
Diamond Thumbprint, creamer, applied handle..............**135.00**
Drapery, butter dish..............**45.00**
Drum, creamer **50.00**
Early Excelsior, wine, flint ...**70.00**
Egyptian, plate, with handles, 10" **48.00**
Empress, tumbler, green with gold **50.00**
Esther, sauce bowl, footed, green with gold........................**15.00**
Eureka, egg cup....................**16.00**
Eyewinker, butter dish **70.00**
Feather, wine **38.00**
Festoon, cake stand, high standard, 10" **49.00**
Festoon, sauce dish, flat **8.00**
Fine Cut, butter dish **47.00**
Fine Cut, plate, amber, 10"...**18.00**
Fine Cut & Block, compote, open, yellow blocks, 4x8".........**48.00**
Fine Cut & Panel, spooner ..**32.00**
Fine Cut & Panel, tray, water; amber...............................**60.00**
Fine Rib, goblet, 6¼" **75.00**
Fine Rib, salt cellar, master .**25.00**

Flamingo Habitat, goblet......**25.00**
Flamingo Habitat, spooner ..**23.00**
Flat Diamond & Panel, honey
dish, flint, 3¼"..............**10.00**
Florida, celery vase, flat **18.00**
Flute with Bull's Eye, wine ..**25.00**
Frosted Circle, goblet............**28.00**
Frosted Leaf, sauce dish, 4"..**20.00**
Frosted Lion, compote, with lid,
high standard, 8" **75.00**
Frosted Stork, platter, 12" ...**45.00**
Galloway, pitcher, water; ruby
stained, water size.......**175.00**
Galloway, toothpick holder ...**30.00**
Galloway, wine **50.00**
Garden of Eden, bowl, oval...**10.00**
Garfield Drape, tumbler **30.00**
Grand, wine.........................**32.00**
Grape & Festoon, goblet, stippled
leaf.................................**25.00**
Hairpin, goblet **35.00**
Hamilton, cake stand..........**150.00**
Hamilton with Leaf, tumbler,
whiskey; flint................**110.00**
Hand, goblet..........................**42.00**
Hawaiian Lei, compote, jelly..**13.00**
Hawaiian Lei, wine...............**25.00**
Heart with Thumbprint, punch
cup **20.00**
Heart with Thumbprint, tray,
card; folded edge **20.00**
Hexagon Block, tray, water; han-
dles..................................**40.00**
Hickman, compote, open.......**20.00**
Hickman, punch cup **8.00**
Hidalgo, pitcher, water **50.00**
Holly, goblet **95.00**
Holly, sauce dish, flat............**20.00**
Honeycomb with Flower Rim,
creamer, green, 4" **40.00**
Hops Band, wine **20.00**
Horn of Plenty, decanter, faceted
stopper, 1-quart.............**100.00**
Horn of Plenty, plate, 6"........**68.00**
Horseshoe, cake stand, 7¼" .**50.00**
Horseshoe, compote, with lid,
8x8"...............................**78.00**
Horseshoe, relish bowl, 9x5".**13.00**
Huber, egg cup, 10-panel **20.00**

Illinois, plate, square, 7".......**20.00**
Illinois, vase, square, 8"........**20.00**

Illinois, pitcher, $80.00.

Inverted Fern, egg cup..........**30.00**
Inverted Fern, honey dish ...**15.00**
Iris with Meander, pitcher, water;
blue with gold **165.00**
Iris with Meander, tumbler,
water; blue with gold **42.00**
Jacob's Ladder, creamer.......**35.00**
Jacob's Ladder, sauce dish, footed,
4½" **15.00**
Jewel with Dewdrop, cake stand,
9"....................................**50.00**
Jewelled Moon & Star, cruet.**20.00**
Jewelled Moon & Star, wine.**20.00**
Jumbo, powder jar, with lid,
frosted...........................**155.00**
Kentucky, punch cup, green .**15.00**
Kentucky, shakers, pair........**30.00**
Kentucky, spooner **35.00**
King's Crown, wine...............**34.00**
Klondike, relish, frosted with
amber stain, 2x9x4".....**125.00**
Kokomo, syrup **58.00**
Lacy Daisy, bowl, shallow **25.00**
Late Block, rose bowl, ruby
stained, 4"......................**58.00**
Leaf & Dart, spooner **30.00**
Leaf & Flower, creamer, amber
stained **38.00**

Liberty Bell, goblet **45.00**
Liberty Bell, platter, 9½x13"..**80.00**
Lincoln Drape, spill...............**45.00**
Lincoln Drape with Tassel, goblet,
    water; flint.....................**125.00**
Loop & Dart, egg cup, flint ...**32.00**
Loop & Dart, goblet...............**25.00**
Maine, compote, jelly **25.00**
Maine, wine, green...............**50.00**
Manting, champagne, flint ..**45.00**
Maryland, goblet...................**28.00**
Mascotte, compote, 7x5" **30.00**
Massachusetts, cordial **60.00**
Massachusetts, punch cup, clear
    with gold **15.00**
Michigan, pickle dish **14.00**
Michigan, tumbler, water **20.00**
Minerva, goblet **88.00**
Minnesota, flower frog, green, 2-
    piece................................**48.00**
Mioton, sugar bowl, open......**20.00**
Mirror, spill, flint **37.00**
Missouri, sauce dish, green ..**14.00**
Missouri, wine, green **45.00**
Monkey, mug **85.00**

**Monkey, butter dish,
$185.00.**

Nail, sauce dish, footed, 3½".**12.00**
Nailhead, wine **20.00**
New Hampshire, bowl, 8" **16.00**
New Hampshire, punch cup .. **9.00**
New Jersey, compote, jelly....**20.00**
New Jersey, goblet, clear with
    gold **35.00**
New Jersey, plate, 8" **13.00**
Oak Leaf Band, bowl, 8x4" ...**10.00**

Oak Leaf Band, mug.............**40.00**
Open Rose, butter dish **50.00**
Oregon, tumbler, water.........**30.00**
Oval Mitre, goblet, flint **36.00**
Palmette, cake stand **55.00**
Panelled Daisy, celery vase ..**30.00**
Panelled Forget-Me-Not, compote,
    open, 7x7" **35.00**
Panelled Nightshade, wine ..**20.00**
Panelled Ovals, goblet, flint .**53.00**
Pathfinder, tumbler, water ...**10.00**
Pavonia, salt cellar, master ..**20.00**
Pavonia, spooner **40.00**
Pavonia, wine **30.00**
Peerless, butter dish **35.00**
Pennsylvania, creamer **37.00**
Pennsylvania, decanter, original
    stopper............................**80.00**
Pennsylvania, wine, green ...**40.00**
Pentagon, decanter, original stop-
    per, ruby stained............**95.00**
Pillar, claret, flint **58.00**
Pillow Encircled, tray, green,
    9½x5½".............................**20.00**
Pittsburgh Daisy, wine **20.00**
Plume, bowl, 6"......................**26.00**
Plume, butter dish, etched ...**48.00**
Plume, creamer **30.00**
Popcorn, butter dish..............**65.00**
Portland, bowl, with lid, shallow,
    small **20.00**
Portland, celery vase, flat.....**20.00**
Portland, cruet **40.00**
Powder & Shot, egg cup **48.00**
Powder & Shot, goblet, flint .**56.00**
Pressed Leaf, egg cup, flint ..**24.00**
Princess Feather, salt cellar, mas-
    ter **30.00**
Prism with Diamond Points, gob-
    let **18.00**
Prism with Diamond Points, tum-
    bler, flint **45.00**
Queen, goblet, blue **40.00**
Raindrop, cake plate **30.00**
Recessed Ovals, wine............**18.00**
Red Block, creamer **60.00**
Reverse Torpedo, bowl, shallow,
    ruffled, 10½"...................**80.00**
Ribbed Palm, celery vase......**75.00**

Ribbon Candy, creamer **25.00**
Ripple, spooner......................**20.00**
Ripple, wine...........................**33.00**
Roanoke, waste bowl, ruby
  stained, etched, 4" **32.00**
Roman Key, wine, frosted **65.00**
Roman Rosette, spooner **24.00**
Rope Bands, tumbler **18.00**
Rose in Snow, creamer **35.00**
Rose Sprig, boat, relish.........**20.00**
Rosette, celery vase, footed...**20.00**
Sawtooth, celery vase, knop stem,
  flint **58.00**
Scroll, spooner......................**25.00**
Scroll, tumbler, water; blue
  opaque **35.00**
Sequoia, tray, 12x7½" **20.00**
Sheraton, creamer, amber **28.00**
Sheraton, goblet....................**25.00**
Shoshone, cake stand, green .**60.00**
Skilton, creamer....................**30.00**
Snail, bowl, flat, 9x3"............**38.00**
Spearpoint Band, bowl, flat, flint,
  7".....................................**70.00**
Star Band, creamer...............**18.00**
Stippled Chain, goblet, flint ..**25.00**
Stippled Medallion, egg cup .**30.00**
Stork, celery vase, frosted **65.00**
Strawberry, spooner..............**35.00**
Sunk Daisy, cake stand, 8" ...**32.00**
Sunk Honeycomb, salt cellar. **8.00**
Swan, creamer **45.00**
Swan, goblet..........................**42.00**
Tape Measure, goblet............**20.00**
Teardrop & Tassel, bowl, 7"..**40.00**
Teardrop & Tassel, sauce dish, 4" .**10.00**
Texas, pitcher, water **125.00**
Thousand Eye, mug, amber..**20.00**
Thousand Eye, tumbler, water;
  light amber **25.00**
Three Face, cake plate........**275.00**
Three Face, compote, 10"....**250.00**
Torpedo, bowl, flat, 9x3" **16.00**
Torpedo, celery vase.............**45.00**
Tree of Life, finger bowl **15.00**
Tree of Life, sugar bowl, open,
  Portland...........................**28.00**
Triple Triangle, mug **25.00**
Tulip, ale glass, flint **58.00**

Tulip, lamp, whale oil; 9"....**130.00**
Tulip, tumbler, ale; flint........**56.00**
Tulip with Sawtooth, wine....**60.00**
Two Panel, goblet **25.00**
US Coin, cake plate, frosted coins,
  7"...................................**485.00**
US Coin, epergne, frosted coins,
  rare **1,100.00**
US Coin, syrup, frosted **500.00**
Valencia Waffle, creamer **35.00**
Vermont, vase **18.00**
Viking, celery vase **50.00**
Waffle, creamer, flint **137.00**
Waffle, salt cellar, master.....**30.00**
Washington, egg cup.............**80.00**
Wedding Bells, tray, celery;
  maiden's blush **30.00**
Westward Ho, sugar bowl, with
  lid **150.00**
Wildflower, celery vase **35.00**
Wildflower, pitcher, water.....**58.00**
Willow Oak, tumbler, water .**30.00**
Wisconsin, cake stand, 8" **38.00**
Wisconsin, plate, ...**18.00**
Wooden Pail, pail, bail handle,
  amber **25.00**
Zig Zag, goblet......................**18.00**
Zipper Slash, champagne **30.00**
Zippered Block, tumbler, water;
  ruby stained **40.00**

Pennsbury

From the 1950s through the
1970s, dinnerware and novelty
wares produced by the Pennsbury
company was sold through tourist
gift shops along the Pennsylvania
turnpike. Much of their ware is
decorated in an Amish theme.
Barber shop singers were also
popular, and a line of bird figures
was made, very similar to
Stangl's.

Ash tray, Hex, scalloped, 8"..**20.00**
Ash tray, Western & Atlantic RR,
  oval **45.00**
Bowl, pretzel; Eagle **35.00**

**Bowl, various Amish sayings, 9",
$35.00.**

Butter dish, Red Rooster **30.00**
Candy dish, Red Rooster, heart-
shaped **20.00**
Canister, coffee; Folkart, wooden
lid, 4½x6½" **60.00**
Casserole, Red Rooster, with
cover, 9" **42.00**
Cigarette box, Eagle, 4½" **18.00**
Coaster, Quartet, 4" **15.00**
Compote, Red Rooster, 5"......**30.00**
Dutch oven, Red Rooster **165.00**
Egg cup, Red Rooster............**18.00**
Figurine, chickadee...............**68.00**
Mug, Davy Crockett, 4½"......**65.00**
Pitcher, Eagle, 6".................**25.00**
Plaque, Reading RR, Iron Horse
Ramble, 1960, 6x8" **45.00**
Plate, Christmas, 1970, 8" ...**30.00**
Platter, Hex, oval, 8x11" **30.00**
Shakers, Amish, figural head,
pair **24.00**
Teapot, Red Rooster, 4-cup ...**32.00**

Peters and Reed

Peters and Reed founded a
pottery in Zanesville, Ohio,
around the turn of the century. By
1922, the firm became known as
Zane Pottery. Several lines of artware were produced which are
today attracting the interest of
pottery collectors: High Glaze
Brown Ware, decorated with in-
mold relief; Moss Aztec, relief
designs molded from red clay with
a green-washed exterior; Chromal, with realistic or suggested
scenics done in soft matt colors;
Landsun; Shadow Ware; and
Wilse Blue.

Bookends, Pereco, Arts & Crafts,
square, raised on square
base, 5" **75.00**
Bowl, Moss Aztec, pine cone,
signed Ferrell, 3x6¼".....**35.00**
Bowl, Pereco, nail-head decoration, recessed band, 5"...**30.00**
Candlesticks, Mirror Black, 10",
pair **50.00**
Flower frog, turtle form, Pereco,
unmarked, 1x5".............**45.00**
Jardiniere, Chromal, landscape,
6x7"...............................**175.00**
Jug, Brown Ware, lion's head,
leaves, 5½".....................**75.00**
Jug, Brown Ware, man with hat,
bulbous, 7".....................**85.00**
Jug, Brown Ware, sprigged garlands, 5½" **55.00**
Planter, Brown Ware, wreath,
handle across top, 6x8"..**55.00**
Vase, Brown Ware, lion's heads &
floral garlands, 12" **155.00**

**Vase, Brown Ware, cameo of Dick-
ens-type character, 5½", $80.00.**

Vase, Landsun, pale blue, ivory, & brown, #9 shape, 7x7"....**75.00**
Vase, Landsun, 5" **45.00**
Vase, Shadow Ware, black with green drip, 9"..................**75.00**
Vase, yellow/green random splotches on brown gloss, 6-sided, 9"..........................**50.00**
Vase, 4 hand-painted trees on yellow matt, 8" **75.00**
Wall pocket, Egyptian, green with profile relief **95.00**

Phoenix Bird China

Since early in the 1900s, Japan potteries have been producing a line of blue and white china decorated with the Japanese bird of paradise and vines of Chinese grass. The design will vary slightly, and newer ware is whiter than the old, with a more vivid blue.

Bowl, serving; scalloped, 9" ..**40.00**
Bowl, vegetable; scalloped corners, square, 9" **35.00**
Bowl, 5"................................... **8.00**
Chocolate pot **90.00**
Coaster, 3" **18.00**
Cup & saucer, AD..................**14.00**
Cup & saucer, Japan..............**18.00**
Egg cup, single, 2¼" **15.00**
Ginger jar, 6" **20.00**
Pitcher, milk; 4⅝" **30.00**
Plate, breakfast; 8¼"............**35.00**

Platter, 12" x 8", $40.00.

Platter, oval, 15"...................**75.00**
Platter, 12¼x8½" **35.00**
Shakers, hexagonal, 3", pair.**24.00**
Sugar bowl, with lid, 4" **20.00**
Teapot, 2¾" **60.00**
Teapot, 4½" **50.00**
Tray, relish; handles, 10" **30.00**

Phoenix Glass

Sculptured artware vases made during the 1930s and 1940s by the Phoenix Glass Company of Monaca, Pennsylvania, are very similar to a line made by the Consolidated Company of nearby Corapolis. It is very difficult to distinguish between the two. Though there are exceptions, as a general rule Phoenix added color to the background, while Consolidated left the background plain and added color to the raised design.

Aster, vase, bright yellow on white, 7".........................**55.00**
Candy box, violets, white on crystal, 6½"............................**48.00**
Cigarette box, floral, pearl on white, gray ground, 5" ...**45.00**
Dancing Nymph, plate, white on crystal, 8".......................**32.00**
Diving Girl, bowl, amber on crystal, 14" **150.00**
Fern, vase, white fronds, lavender ground, 7" **65.00**
Figured, vase, green on white, 6" **55.00**
Lace Dewdrop, bowl, milk glass, with lid, large, 9"...........**30.00**
Lace Dewdrop, spoon holder, slate blue on white..................**25.00**
Philodendron, lamp, tan on white, pearl leaves **135.00**
Philodendron, vase, dark green, 11"......................................**65.00**
Starflower, vase, white on white, round, 7" **65.00**

Wild Geese, vase, white on brown, 12" **140.00**
Wild Rose, vase, amber, 11"..**65.00**
Wild Rose, vase, cedar rose on crystal, 10½ " **120.00**

**Vase, Madonna, white on blue, 10",
$140.00.**

Photographica

Early cameras and the images they produced are today becoming popular collectors' items. The earliest type of image was the daguerreotype, made with the use of a copper plate and silver salts; ambrotypes followed, produced by the wet-plate process on glass negatives. Tintypes were from the same era as the ambrotype but were developed on japanned iron and were much more durable. Size, subject matter, aesthetics, and condition help determine value. Stereo cards, viewing devices, albums, photographs, and advertising memorabilia featuring camera equipment are included in this area of collecting.

Album, brass overlay cover, containing many tintypes, 11x8½", VG **25.00**
Albumen photo, General Chester A Arthur, cabinet size....**45.00**
Albumen photo, Pueblo Indians in village, Hillers, 9x7" **150.00**
Albumen photo, 2 soldiers with NY Regimental flags, 3x2¾", EX **75.00**
Ambrotype, 6th plate, post mortem of baby in pink gown, EX **65.00**
Ambrotype, 9th plate, Confederate soldier, well dressed, clear image **90.00**
Cabinet photo, attractive Hawaiian lady, 1890s, 7x5" **15.00**
Cabinet photo, Edwin Booth, brother of John Wilkes, Rockwood, EX.........................**65.00**
Cabinet photo, Horvath Midgets, Smallest People in World, ca 1880 ....**35.00**
Cabinet photo, priest in robe with cross holds book, EX **20.00**
Camera, Canon, Demi II, half-frame, ca 1965, NM........**45.00**
Camera, Folding Hawk-Eye No 4, nickel trim, 1905, EX.....**35.00**
Camera, Graflex Graphic 35 Electric, 35mm, inoperable motor, 1959 ....**40.00**
Camera, Hamilton Super-Flex, Bakelite, 1947, EX.......... **8.00**
Camera, Kodak Autographic Special #1, ca 1920, EX **40.00**
Camera, Kodak Brownie 44A, box style, ca 1960s, NM........**10.00**
Camera, Kodak Junior II, 1950s, EX...............................**12.50**
Camera, Minolta AL-2, 1960s, NM..............................**38.00**
Camera, Olympus Chrome Six V, lever advance, 1955 ......**85.00**
Camera, Polaroid Highlander 80, gray metal body, EX.......**12.00**
Camera, Polaroid Big Shot, 1970s, USA model **15.00**

Camera, Univex, Mercury II Model CX, 1940s, $50.00.

Camera, Shur-Shot Jr, box style, metal faceplate, 1948 ..... **8.00**
Camera, Utility Falcon, cast-metal Deco body **12.50**
Carte de visite, armed soldier, pistol at side, Boston **20.00**
Carte de visite, full-figure pose of Union soldier, EX...........**30.00**
Carte de visite, Lt Charles Whittle, MA Infantry Volunteers, EX......................................**55.00**
Carte de visite, seated Union officer in military backdrop.**25.00**
Carte de visite, 6th IL Calvary soldier in ¾ standing pose, EX **40.00**
Carte de visite albumen photo, Gen US Grant, 1868 .....**15.00**
Case, 6th plate, thermoplastic, beehive with grain border, VG **60.00**
Case, 6th plate, thermoplastic, church window with diapered center, EX.......................**45.00**
Case, 6th plate, thermoplastic, huntress & falcon, VG **35.00**
Daguerreotype, 4th plate, lady with musical instrument, in case, EX..........................**85.00**
Daguerreotype, 6th plate, well-dressed girl, white pantaloons, EX **45.00**
Sepia tone, Flathead Indians, village scene, 1890s, 4x5"..**15.00**
Stanhope, cross with rosary beads, ivory, 1 view........**75.00**

Stanhope, pipe, carved wood, 6 Port Erin views, 1", EX..**48.00**
Stanhope, scent bottle, brass, with neck chain, 6 views, EX.................................**150.00**
Stanhope, tape measure, barrel form with ivory finial, 1 view, EX **65.00**
Stereoscopic view, Alamo, closeup, HA Doerr, 5 for .**45.00**
Stereoscopic view, Blacks Pick Cotton with Splint Baskets, Havens, NM **12.50**
Stereoscopic view, Crow Indian village, Calfee, 4 for **65.00**
Stereoscopic view, Eastern Bound Tea Train at Blue Canyon, Reilly **22.50**

Daguerreotype, lady, child, and dog, sixth plate, EX $120.00.

Stereoscopic view, Eskimos with Summer Tents, Keystone. **5.50**
Stereoscopic view, Grand Hotel #1397, horse-drawn street car, carriage...................**19.50**
Stereoscopic view, Great Boston Fire, Smith, VG, 8 for ...**30.00**
Stereoscopic view, Paiute Indians, small family, Lawrence & Houseworth **28.50**

Stereoscopic view, Russian Hill, San Francisco, Kilburn... **9.50**

Stereoscopic view, Starr King's Church #457, Houseworth, EX **22.50**

Stereoscopic view, View of CT Sampson's Shoe Mfg, Chinese Shoemakers **19.50**

Stereoscopic view, Working for Peace, Roosevelt, Mikado, on Mayflower **6.50**

Stereoscopic viewer, Brewster, ebonized eye pieces, mirrored flap, EX **175.00**

Tintype, 6th plate, full-figured carpenter, EX **35.00**

Tintype, 6th plate, sailer in typical jersey & mariner's cap, EX **45.00**

Tintype, 6th plate, Union Cavalry officer, in case **125.00**

Carmen, clear, 8-sided; scrolled silverplated holder, with tongs **125.00**

Carmen, Fostoria; silverplated holder, with tongs, EX .. **95.00**

Clear, ornate Pairpoint holder with grasshopper finial, footed **200.00**

Cranberry, enameled iris; Reed & Barton holder, tongs **350.00**

Cranberry, etched decor; ornate footed holder **225.00**

Daisy & Button, sapphire blue, double; ornate silverplated holder **350.00**

Frosted Criss-Cross Diamonds; fancy holder, tongs **150.00**

King's Crown, grape etched; silverplated holder, VG.... **135.00**

Pigeon blood; original Forbes holder with braid handle, footed **295.00**

Pineapple & Fan, Holbrook; silverplated holder, tongs ..**65.00**

Photograph, albumen, titled Canyon of the Rio Las Animas, in the style of W.H. Jackson, 17"x20", EX, $100.00.

Pickle Casters

Popular table accessories during the Victorian era, pickle castors consist of a fancy silverplated frame with a glass insert, either pressed pattern glass or art glass, and tongs or a pickle fork.

Alabama, green; silverplated holder, rare **200.00**

Block Variant; Pairpoint holder with griffins **85.00**

Ruby-cut-to-clear, silverplated frame with tongs, 12", $150.00.

Pink & opal ribbed; original holder, Pairpoint #688 .**350.00**

Sculptured art glass, enameled flowers; Wilcox holder with pickles...........................**600.00**

Van Dyke, vaseline; ornate Hartford holder with birds in handle **250.00**

Vertical Optic, rubena; original Pairpoint holder **450.00**

Yellow, enameled floral; 2" cherubs hold refinished Meriden holder.....................**395.00**

Yellow Diamond Quilt, silver-plated owl ornament in holder, with tongs **350.00**

Pin-Back Buttons

Most of the advertising buttons prior to the 1920s were made of celluloid and so are called 'cellos.' Many were issued in sets on related topics. Some buttons had paper inserts on the back that identified the company or the product they were advertising. After the 1920s, lithographed metal buttons were produced; these are referred to as 'lithos.' Political buttons are listed in the section called Campaign Collectibles.

Admiral Chester W Nimitz, portrait, red, white & blue... **6.00**

Audubon Society **12.50**

Billy Graham Crusade, green & white, 1950s, M **4.00**

Bond Bread, Another New High, 1930s, NM **5.00**

Boy Scout Hosiery, scout kneeling, multicolor, ca 1920, M **8.00**

Captain Marvel, portrait, multicolor, 1940s, EX..............**20.00**

Captain Marvel Club, Shazam, red & yellow, 1¼" **25.00**

Chief Seattle memorial, black & white portrait, EX **5.00**

Boy Scouts of America Committee, $2.50

Colt Firearms Factory Guard, Tiffany NY, 1900 .... **8.00**

Deanna Durbin, She's a Doll!, portrait, 1930s, NM **27.50**

Gimme Jimmy! The Candidate, Durante portrait, EX...... **7.50**

Hopalong Cassidy, Country Club Dairy, portrait, NM **17.50**

Hudson-Fulton Celebration .**42.50**

James Dean, portrait, multicolor, 1950s, large, M...............**27.50**

JI Case, Eagle **16.00**

Paragon Beer, East St Louis, black & white, 1¼".......... **8.00**

Remember the Maine, Dewey, blue lettering, $10.00.

Penney's Back to School Days with Popeye, multicolor, 1930s, EX **15.00**

Randall's Grape Juice, child's portrait, ca 1915, EX...........**10.00**

Roy Rogers, portrait, black & white, 1940s, EX 60.00
Saturday Evening Post, Did You Get Your Post This Week? 1930s, EX 2.50
Snow White Jingle Club Member, red, white & blue 20.00
Tea Keeps You Cool, blue & white, 1940s, M 5.00
Wear Puritan Hosiery, lady shows leg, multicolor, ca 1900 .45.00

Pink Pigs

Made in Germany, these amusing pigs and piglets are portrayed driving a roadster, sitting in a suitcase, bowling, beside the feeding trough, or typing on a typewriter. While some figurines are easy to find, others are scarce and may bring prices in excess of $100.00.

One pig beside green drum, wall-mount match holder 60.00
One pig in Japanese submarine, Japan impressed on both sides...............125.00
One pig on horseshoe-shaped dish with 4-leaf clover...........65.00
One pig on shoulder of green ink bottle..............................65.00
One pig riding train, 4½ "...125.00
Three pigs, one on large slipper playing banjo, two dancing on side................................115.00
Three pigs dressed up on edge of dish 70.00
Three pigs with baby carriage, father & 2 babies, Wheeling His Own..........................75.00
Three pigs with carriage, mother & 2 babies, Germany 85.00
Three pigs with coach, More the Merrier 85.00
Two pigs by eggshell 80.00
Two pigs on basket, head raising lid, plaque on front 80.00

Two pigs on binoculars 115.00
Two pigs on green tray..........50.00
Two pigs on top hat...............95.00

Planters Peanuts

Since 1916, Mr. Peanut has represented the Planters Peanuts Company. Today he has his own fan club of collectors who specialize in this area of advertising memorabilia. More than fifteen styles of the glass display jars were made; the earliest was issued in 1926 and is referred to as the 'pennant' jar. The rarest of them all is the 'football' jar from the early thirties. Premiums such as glass and metal paperweights, pens, and pencils were distributed in the late 1930s; after the war, plastic items were offered.

Ash tray, ceramic 60.00
Ball, beach; plastic blow-up, Mr Peanut 22.00
Bank, plastic, Mr Peanut......12.00
Book, Dedication, 1933, EX ..20.00
Bracelet, 6 figural charms 34.00
Can, 5-lb 75.00
Coloring book, Presidents, Mr Peanut 8.00
Coloring book, 1st edition Canada, 1920s, rare, M 85.00
Container, papier-mache, Mr Peanut, 12"...................250.00
Costume, Mr Peanut Parade Man, rare 950.00
Counter bucket, Mr Peanut, large head with blue hat, 10" diameter 25.00
Doll, cloth, yellow & black, 19", NM................................20.00
Game, Saturday Evening Post, Mr Peanut, 1930, uncut.30.00
Halloween costume, Mr Peanut, complete, NM 20.00
Hat, vendor's; early graphics, unused 45.00

Jar, chocolate-covered cashews, label, 1944, 4½ -oz..........**25.00**
Jar, Clipper, original lid........**75.00**
Jar, Fish Bowl, square label.**125.00**
Jar, 4-corner, large blown-out peanut each corner, M .**300.00**
Letter opener, celluloid.........**35.00**
Lighter, peanut figural **85.00**
Marbles in bag, 1940s **25.00**

Plastic Mr. Peanut bank, $12.00.

Night light, Mr Peanut.........**85.00**
Nodder, Mr Peanut figural .**135.00**
Pencil, mechanical; Mr Peanut figural, in original cellophane wrap...............................**22.50**
Profit chart, old Mr Peanut ..**25.00**
Shakers, ceramic, Mr Peanut, pair **85.00**
Shakers, plastic, Mr Peanut, 4½", pair, MIB **15.00**
Tin container, Chopped Peanuts, red, 1952, scarce **90.00**
Tumbler, Mr Peanut Circus, rare, M....................................**150.00**
Wagon, plastic Mr Peanut, 1950s, M....................................**165.00**

Post Cards

The first post cards were printed in Austria in 1869, but it was the Columbian Exposition in 1893 that started the post card craze that swept the country for years to come. Today's collectors tend to specialize in cards of a particular theme or by a favorite illustrator. Among the famous artists whose work you may find are Rose O'Neill, Philip Boileau, Alphonse Mucha, and John Winsch.

Valentine, embossed roses, $3.00; Happy Birthday, ribbon flowers and glitter, signed Horwitz, ca 1912, $2.50.

Alfred E Newman, Me Worry?, linen, EX **6.00**
Attwell, I'll Learn 'Em To Learn Me Music, girl/piano, VG.....**10.00**
Boy's Town, Nebraska, 2 boys in snow, linen, EX..............**10.00**
Clapsaddle, Best Wishes for Your Birthday, girl in green hood, VG **25.00**
Clapsaddle, Easter, girl in red dress with large egg & flowers, VG............................**10.00**
Clapsaddle, New Year, boy offers girl bouquet, EX **12.50**
Comic, Everybody Is Doing It, figure/phonograph, sepia, 1907, unused **8.00**

Drugstore interior view, black & white photo, 1940, NM ... **5.00**

Dwig, SH-ss-sss!!, stork with baby, unused, EX **7.50**

F Earl Christy, lady bowling, light creases, G **3.50**

Fisher, Harrison; Luxury, lady in bed with book, EX **15.00**

Giant Cypress Tree, Largest...in Oklahoma, 1940s, EX **4.00**

Gold Dust Twins, There's a Washout..., VG **27.50**

Griggs, St Patrick's Day, There's...Little Plant, lady & shamrocks, EX **15.00**

Honolulu, Native with hula drum, ca 1910, EX **8.00**

King, Hamilton; Largemont Girl, VG **10.00**

Koehler, Old South Church, hold-to-light, VG **32.00**

Langsdorf, Musical Coons, alligator border, EX **25.00**

Military comic, WWII era, linen, EX **4.00**

Photo, MacDonald Hotel, Honolulu, 1972, used, EX **7.50**

Photo, Women's Club House, La Habra, CA, 1920, M **6.50**

Russel, Buffalo protecting calf, wolves looking on, EX....**25.00**

Shrunken head & 'How To' guide, museum card, NM **1.50**

Sinking of the Pere Marquette, Sept 9, 1910, EX **4.00**

Southern Pacific Motor Car closeup, unused, EX.......**10.00**

Store interior, black & white photo, early, VG.............**20.00**

Theodore Roosevelt, woven-in-silk, Paris, VG **75.00**

Tichnor, Strive for Victory, linen, VG **10.00**

Tuck, Suffragette, Votes For Women,#9498, oilette, VG ...**25.00**

Ullman, Sunbonnet Twins, 1905, used, EX **6.50**

Valentine, comic figures in canoe, 1918, small tear **2.50**

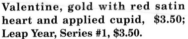

Valentine, gold with red satin heart and applied cupid, $3.50; Leap Year, Series #1, $3.50.

Posters

The most collectible posters are those from the early days of the circus, war posters or those with a patriotic theme, early advertising posters, or those illustrated by noted artists such as Parrish, Fisher, Flagg, and Christy. Condition is important, also consider subject matter. Foxing and fading colors, as with any print, detract from their value.

Advertising, Chesterfield Cigarettes, lady hiker, ca 1935, 28x42" **130.00**

Advertising, Dartmouth Winter Carnival, John Ryland, 34x22", EX.....................**65.00**

Advertising, Eat More Fruit, blonde with fruit basket, 1938, 20x15"...................**80.00**

Advertising, Fatima Cigarettes, heavy stock, early, 34x21", EX **75.00**

Advertising, Nabisco Social Tea Biscuit, I Want You, 1930, 8x12", NM......................**22.50**

Advertising: Victor, Singers and Entertainers, 35" x 25", EX, $500.00.

Advertising, Plow Boy Tobacco, on cloth, 1900s, 40x18".....**125.00**

Advertising, Squibb Aspirin, mother/child, Wilbur, 1940s, 25x45", EX....................**135.00**

Advertising, Union Metallic Cartridge, Indians chase cowboy, 20x14"..........................**355.00**

Advertising, Useful Birds of America, Arm & Hammer, 1917, EX.........................**65.00**

Enlistment, I'm Telling You, Uncle Sam, James M Flagg, 1918, EX......................**100.00**

Exposition, Exposition de Horticulture, Landeau, Paris, 1929, 47x31"................**200.00**

Exposition, Go By All Means..., 1940, 30x20", EX............**65.00**

Magic, Alexander the Man Who Knows, 1920s, 33x44" ...**65.00**

Magic, Irving, An Hour in Chinatown, 1930, 14x42", M ...**25.00**

Minstrel, Mastadon Minstrels, full color, 20x28", EX ...**160.00**

Movie, Laughing at Life, McLaglen/Boyd/Beery, full sheet, 1935, EX........................**12.00**

Movie, Outlaw Tamer, Chandler western scene, full sheet, 1930, EX **35.00**

Theatre, Bachelor's Honeymoon, National Print, Chicago, 42x80", EX.....................**50.00**

Theatre, Cat & Canary, lady scared by black cat, ca 1910, 22x34"..........................**100.00**

Theatre, Chorus Line, Shubert Theatre, 1975, NM.........**25.00**

Theatre, King & I, Yul Brynner closeup, 1970s, M...........**35.00**

Theatre, Sorrows of Satan, devil & surprised man, ca 1900, 20x30" **80.00**

Travel, Australia in the Sun, sheep scene, Trompf, full sheet, EX **35.00**

Advertising: Eclipse Halters, printed by W. Karle, Rochester, NY, 17" x 22", EX, $160.00.

Travel, Cie Gle Transatlantique, French, 39x25", EX......**115.00**

Travel, Egypt, ancient ruins, Roger Breval, 1930s, full sheet, EX **35.00**

Travel, Mountains of France, Nathan, 20th century, 38x25", EX **150.00**

Travel, Visit London, Queen's guard & palace, ca 1947, 25x40" **165.00**

WWI, Fight, HC Christy, laid on board, 30x20", NM.......**165.00**

WWI, Have You a Red Cross Service Flag?, JW Smith, 1918, 29x22", EX.....................**75.00**

WWI, Hold On to Uncle Sam's Insurance, EX **85.00**

WWI, Our Daddy Is Fighting..., children in sailor suits, Dewey, 1917 ....**75.00**

WWI, Seeds of Victory, JM Flagg, color, laid down, repairs, 33x22"............................**85.00**

WWII, Leaders of Royal Air Force, unknown, 1941, 25x38"............................**100.00**

WWII, Ours...To Fight for Freedom from Fear, Rockwell, 20x28" **55.00**

WWII, War Clouds Gather, Army, 1940, full sheet **120.00**

WWII, Your Scrap Brought It Down, burning plane, Broder, 20x28", EX......................**45.00**

Theatre: Charlie Chaplin, The Vagabond, 22" x 14", VG, $500.00.

Primitives

From the early days of our country until the industrial revolution of the latter 1800s, tools, utensils, furniture, and even toys were made almost entirely by hand from readily available materials. Even factory-made items were finished by carvers, smithies, and other artisans who augmented the basic work of the machine with their handiwork. Primitives are evaluated by age, condition, workmanship, uniqueness of form, and desire to own.

Bed warmer, brass, pierced, turned tiger maple handle, 41".................................**265.00**

Box, candle; pine & poplar with worn red paint, square nails, 12" **150.00**

Box, spice; chestnut with stenciled labels, nailed, 8-drawer, 17" **135.00**

Butter paddle, carved maple, 10x5", EX......................**65.00**

Candle mold, 1-tube, pewter, 15", EX................................**100.00**

Candle mold, 1-tube, tin, makes 9" candles, EX **90.00**

Candle mold, 2-tube, tin, makes 10" candles, EX **90.00**

Candle mold, 12-tube, 10½", $135.00.

Candle mold, 4-tube, side handle, tray top, 11"..................**265.00**

Candle mold, 4-tube, tin, crimped top, EX **115.00**

Candle mold, 8-tube (4 each side), cast iron, hinged, Guillon, 11"................................**250.00**

Candle snuffer, metal, 6" **10.00**

Churn, poplar, original red grain-paint with black trim, complete, 35" **300.00**

Churn, staved, brass bands, porcelain handles on lid, complete, 23".....................**155.00**

Churn, syllabub; propeller-type blade, flat ring lid, 9½" ..**65.00**

Clothespin, carved wood, dark tin bands **10.00**

Cranberry scoop, wooden tines, small, EX **100.00**

Dough box, pine, excellent turnings, dovetailed, 2-board top, 28" **500.00**

Foot warmer, cherry with tin liner, pierced, English..**250.00**

Paddle, maple syurp; pine, 3¾" bowl, 25" long.................**65.00**

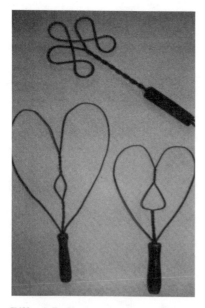

Pillow fluffers, wireware, $25.00 each. Beware of reproductions.

Rack, drying; mahogany, 3-section, 35" **100.00**

Skimmer, tallow; hand-punched tin cone, 11½" iron handle, early................................**85.00**

Smoothing board, feather bed; chip-carved decor, dated 1886, 29"......................**100.00**

Spoon, carved horn, arched handle, 9½" **30.00**

Stocking stretcher, wooden, 7 round drying holes, 31" .**15.00**

Stove leveler, pottery with grown & green running glaze, J Bell, VG...................................**50.00**

Wafer iron, cast waffle with tulip, wrought handles, 30½".**120.00**

Washboard, Common Sense, redware with brown sponging, poplar frame.................**350.00**

Washboard, hand made, all wood, 25"...................................**45.00**

Washboard, National, tin soap rack, blue & white sponged insert, 25".....................**145.00**

Washboard, wooden, blue glass scrub surface **135.00**

Prints

Prints, as with any article of collectible ephemera, are susceptible to certain types of damage. Staining and foxing (brown spots caused by microscopic mold) are usually present to some extent and should be weighed against the desirability of the print. Margin tears may be acceptable if the print is a rare one, but avoid tears that affect the image itself. If margins have been trimmed to less than ¾", the value is considerably lowered. NC: Nathaniel Currier.

Currier & Ives

Agnes, NC, small folio...........**95.00**

American Brook Trout, small folio, NM **325.00**

Currier & Ives, The Old Oaken Bucket, 16" x 24", NM, $1,000.00.

Apples & Plums, First Premium, small folio **150.00**

Autumn on Lake George, small folio **295.00**

Base Hit, small folio **250.00**

Battle of Cerro Gordo, NC, small folio **125.00**

Battle of Spottsylvania, VA, small folio **175.00**

Bolted, small folio **250.00**

Brave Wife, small folio **85.00**

Central Park, The Bridge, small folio **450.00**

Children's Picnic, small folio . **95.00**

Cork River, small folio **65.00**

Darktown Bowling Club, Bowled Out, small folio............. **250.00**

Darktown Opera, Serenade, small folio **250.00**

Deacon's Mare, small folio .. **250.00**

Easter Flowers, small folio ... **55.00**

Eating Crow on a Wager, small folio **250.00**

Evening Star, small folio **75.00**

Feast of Roses, small folio .. **150.00**

Foul Tip, small folio **250.00**

Game Dog, small folio **250.00**

Getting a Hoist, small folio. **250.00**

Ice Cream Racket, Thawing Out, small folio **250.00**

James Monroe, 5th President of US, NC, small folio **150.00**

Jolly Jumper, small folio **250.00**

Kiss Me Quick, small folio **95.00**

Laying Back Stiff for a Brush, small folio **250.00**

Little Daisy, small folio **95.00**

Mambrino, small folio **425.00**

Neck & Neck to the Wire, large folio **900.00**

Peerless Beauty, small folio .. **95.00**

Pioneer Cabin of the Yosemite Valley, small folio **450.00**

Quail on Virginia Partridge, small folio **300.00**

Return from the Woods, medium folio **975.00**

Rose & Lily, small folio **95.00**

Snipe Shooting, small folio . **900.00**

Thistle, large folio **4,000.00**

Through to the Pacific, small folio, NM........................... **1,250.00**

US Steam Frigate Wabash, small folio **450.00**

View on Hudson, Crow's Nest, small folio **295.00**

West Point Foundry, Cold Spring, medium folio **1,500.00**

Wild West in Darktown, small folio **250.00**

Willie & Mary, small folio **95.00**

Currier & Ives, The Last War-Whoop, large folio, trimmed, laid down, $400.00.

Louis Icart

Blue Bandana, pencil signed, ca 1925, 14x18" **1,100.00**

Butterflies, 15x20" **1,300.00**

Courage, My Legions; signed, ca 1917, 22x17" **1,430.00**

Eve, pencil signed, blindstamp, ca 1928, 14x20" **1,650.00**

Girl on Windy Day, pencil signed, 1920, 10x8" **450.00**

Jug of Milk, pencil signed, 1925, 18x12" **1,870.00**

Love Letters, signed, blindstamp, ca 1926, 15x19" **1,050.00**

Mardi Gras, signed, blindstamp, 1936, 20x20" **4,675.00**

Music Lesson II, signed, ca 1934, 15x19" **2,000.00**

On the Beach, pencil signed, ca 1925, 11x16" **1,045.00**

Peaches, signed, 18x13" **725.00**

Red Gate, pencil signed, ca 1925, 12x17" **1,650.00**

Snacktime, signed, blindstamp, ca 1941, 18x12" **2,200.00**

Snow Birds, 17x12" **1,045.00**

Sofa, 1927, 28x17" **1,870.00**

Spilled Milk, pencil signed, ca 1925, 17x11" **1,430.00**

Treasures, pencil signed, ca 1924, 9x11" **550.00**

White Underwear, signed, inscribed, 15x19"...... **2,200.00**

Wounded Dove, signed, blind-stamp, 1929, 21x17" **990.00**

Louis Icart, Seville, 21" x 14", EX, $1,000.00.

Wallace Nutting

A Leaf Strewn Brook, flaming Autumn colors................**75.00**

All Smiles, lady at mirror, interior, 7x9" frame **110.00**

Ambush of a Redcoat, red-jacketed man **385.00**

Blue Lustre Pitcher **275.00**

Gathering a Bouquet, gilt frame, 15"..................................**125.00**

Joy Path, gilt frame, 12x10" .**50.00**

Maple Sugar Cupboard, original frame, 12x15" **125.00**

Mending the Quilt, 4x6", in 12½" frame **110.00**

Wallace Nutting, Mary's Little Lamb, 13" x 16", $200.00.

News in Brief, Ladies at Tea, 13"
frame 145.00
On the Way to Pasture, shepherd
scene 485.00
Overflowing Cup, 1921, 5x7"..40.00
Posing, mother & child outside
front door 125.00
Warm Spring Day, ca 1900, large,
EX 135.00

Maxfield Parrish

Afterglow, 7x9" 55.00
Cleopatra, ca 1960, 12x14" ...18.00
Contentment, ca 1959, 7x11".25.00
Daybreak, ca 1923, framed,
10x18" 145.00
Dinkey Bird, nude on swing,
1905, 13x18".................130.00
Garden of Allah, ca 1918, framed,
11x18" 150.00
Garden of Allah, ca 1954, framed,
9x18"..............................85.00
Hilltop, small.......................160.00
Lute Players, ca 1924, framed,
11x18" 185.00
Lute Players, ca 1924, framed,
18x30", EX 295.00
Peaceful Valley, Brown & Bigelow,
ca 1936, 11x23" 140.00
Quiet Solitude, Brown & Bigelow,
ca 1961, 14x11" 25.00
Quiet Solitude, Brown & Bigelow,
19x16", M.......................75.00
Romance, ca 1925, 14x24" ..475.00

Rubaiyat, ca 1960, 8x29" 18.00
Sea Nymphs, 1908, 12x17".135.00
Sheltering Oaks, Brown &
Bigelow, 1960, 16x19" ...50.00
Stars, ca 1926, framed, rare,
6x10", EX......................125.00
Stars, ca 1959, 7x11" 85.00
Sugar Plum Tree, ca 1902,
framed, 10x15" 75.00
Summer's Eve, 13x16", M.....18.00
The Prince, House of Arts, ca
1925, framed, 10x12".....95.00
Thy Rocks & Rills, 13x16"....18.00
Twilight, Brown & Bigelow, ca
1961, 16x19", M 45.00
Under Summer Skies, Brown &
Bigelow, 16x19", M.........55.00
Wild Geese, 1924, framed, 13x16",
NM...............................185.00
Ye Royal Reception, ca 1950s,
11x14" 18.00

Purinton

Popular among collectors due to its 'country' look, Purington Pottery's dinnerware and kitchen items are easy to learn to recognize due to their bold yet simple fruit and flower motifs created with basic hand-applied colors on a creamy gloss.

Bean pot or marmalade, Apple,
handleless, with cover ...13.00
Bowl, Intaglio, brown, 4" 5.00
Bowl, Maywood, divided veg-
etable; large....................35.00
Canister set, Apple & Pear, 4-
piece..............................75.00
Chop plate, Apple, 12" 15.00
Coffeepot, Apple, 8-cup.........30.00
Coffeepot, Intaglio, brown 35.00
Cookie jar, Apple, oval 25.00
Cookie jar, Heather Plaid 28.00
Creamer & sugar, Apple 15.00
Flowerpot, Apple & Pear, crimped
top, large........................15.00
Jug, Apple, Dutch, 2-pint 12.00

Cruets, oil and vinegar; Apple, $15.00 for the set.

Jug, Apple, Kent, 1-pint **10.00**
Jug, Intaglio, Kent, brown....**15.00**
Mug, beer; PA Dutch **45.00**
Plate, salad; Intaglio, brown . **7.00**
Shakers, Apple & Pear, pair.**12.50**
Shakers, Apple & Pear, range
    type, pair **14.00**
Teapot, Maywood, 6-cup **35.00**
Tray, PA Dutch, Kent............**25.00**
Tray, relish; Apple.................**20.00**
Tray, relish; Intaglio, brown, 3-
    compartment..................**20.00**
Tumbler, Apple, 6-oz **6.00**

Purses

From the late 1800s until well into the 1930s, beaded and metal mesh purses were popular fashion accessories. Flat envelope styles were favored in the twenties, and bags featuring tassels or fringe were in vogue. Enameled mesh bags were popular in the late twenties and into the thirties, decorated in Art Deco designs with stripes, birds, or flowers. Whiting and Davis and the Mandalian Manufacturing Company were two of the most important manufacturers.

Alligator, 12x8x3½" **45.00**
Beaded, jet black, silver frame,
    6½ x7" **60.00**

Beaded bag with church scene, celluloid clasp, $60.00.

Beaded, peacock & flowers on
    black, fringed, 7¼x10" ...**75.00**
Crochet, white, lined, with zipper,
    1930s, 4x7" **10.00**
Leather, black, clutch, 1930s,
    7x17"...............................**12.00**
Linen, birds & floral tapestry,
    gold trim, 7x7¼" **85.00**
Mesh, black & red pattern, red
    frame, Whiting & Davis,
    5x7¼" **75.00**
Mesh, floral, Deco frame, heavy
    handle, 5x9"....................**85.00**
Mesh, floral, Whiting & Davis,
    6x3½" **35.00**
Mesh, floral, Whiting & Davis,
    6x9¾" **95.00**
Mesh, gold bead-lite style, chain
    handle, Whiting & Davis, 3½
    x5" **35.00**
Mesh, ivory, celluloid handle,
    harp frame, 1920s, 19x10",
    EX **35.00**
Mesh, silver, rhinestone closure,
    Whiting & Davis, 4x4"...**50.00**

Mesh, white enamel, chain handle, Whiting & Davis **25.00**
Nylon, yellow & brown drawstring bag, 1930s, 12x10", EX..................................**10.00**

Puzzles

Of most interest to collectors of vintage puzzles are those made of wood or plywood, especially the early hand-cut examples or those that are character related or have a special interest theme.

Donkey Ride, 4 children & donkey at beach, Parker Bros, 1895, EX...................................**75.00**
Horse, McLoughlin, dated 1898, EX in original box........**125.00**
Knight on horseback, Parker Bros, 1901......................**25.00**
Old King Cole & His Fiddlers Three, CM Burd, 1929, 8½ x10½", EX.......................**20.00**
Peg Solitare, 1940, 6x6", M ..**12.50**
Pussy Cat, Ruth Newton, NM in original envelope............**35.00**
Storyland Scroll, Little Bo Peep on cover, McLoughlin Bros, EX.................................**250.00**
Straight Arrow, Indian, Nabisco, 1949, M in mailer...........**20.00**
White Sewing Machines & Bicycles...............................**125.00**
Winter Moonlight, wood, 150-piece, original box **18.00**

Quilts

The appreciation of quilting as an art form and the popularity of 'country' antiques have resulted in an increase in the sale of quilts, and the finer examples are often quite costly. There are several basic types of quilts: (1) appliqued – having the decorative devices applied onto a solid top fabric; (2) pieced – having smaller pieces that have been cut out in a specific pattern, then stitched together to form the quilt top; (3) crazy quilts – made by stitching pieces of various sizes and shapes together following no orderly design; (4) trapunto – devised by stitching the outline of the design through two layers of fabric, one very loosely woven, and inserting padding into the design through openings made by separating the loose fibers of the underneath fabric.

Condition of a quilt is important; intricacy of pattern, good color composition, and craftsmanship contribute to its value. These factors are of prime concern whether evaluating vintage quilts or those by contemporary artists.

Pieced and appliqued: Conventional Rose, ca 1850s, 80" x 84", EX, $425.00.

Amish

Double Wedding Ring, brown shades on beige, extra large, EX.................................**285.00**
Lone Star, blue shades on blue ground, full size **285.00**
Plain, green sateen, fancy quilting, full size, EX..........**365.00**

Red Cross, bright colors, full size,
EX **165.00**
Sunflowers, tan & cream on black,
heavy, full size, EX **325.00**
Sunshine & Shadow, fancy work,
signed & dated, extra large,
EX **485.00**

Appliqued

Flowers & large leaves, 3-stem
design, multicolor, some wear,
large **245.00**
Grapes, pink & lavender with
green & aqua on white, pink
band, large **265.00**

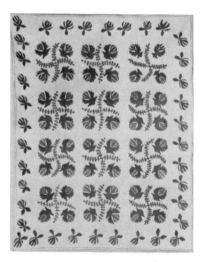

**Appliqued: flower and berry
motif, 75" x 96", EX, $450.00.**

Grapevine Wreath, red & green
on ivory, full size, EX ..**500.00**
Rose of Sharon variation, multicolor, wear, 80x80", EX.**365.00**
Sunflowers, pink & blue, 1920s,
full size, NM **225.00**
Tulips, blue & yellow on white,
82x62", EX................... **225.00**
9 floral motifs, minor fading, crib
size, 45x45".................. **435.00**
9-Patch, old prints with pink bars
& border, crib size, EX.**155.00**

Pieced

Basket, green & red calicos,
1880s, full size **350.00**
Bear Claw, blue & white, minor
wear & stains, 64x70"..**285.00**
Bow Tie, blue & white calico,
76x80", EX................... **265.00**
Cane Bottom, green & white, sawtooth edge, handmade, 1950s,
90x100"......................... **265.00**
Courthouse Steps, jewel tones,
1880s, large, EX........... **275.00**
Crazy, bands of color on black
satin, 56x60", NM **250.00**
Crazy, silks & velvets with much
embroidery, ca 1900, full size,
EX **265.00**
Drunkard's Path, green & pink
with dark pink border,
70x82", EX................... **365.00**
Flying Geese, multicolor on white
with blue lattice, 1920, large,
EX **245.00**
Handy Andy, prints & solids with
pink calico, handmade, 1900,
76x81"........................... **475.00**
Hearts, red on white, with yellow
Wedding Rings, ca 1900,
large, EX....................... **450.00**
Log Cabin Quilt, reds & blues, ca
1890, 73x83", EX.......... **265.00**
Pineapple, browns & reds, 1890s,
70x72", EX **550.00**

**Patchwork silk: Log Cabin, ca
1890s, 90" x 81", $800.00.**

Polka Dots, green & pink calico, 72x80", EX.....................**165.00**

Seven Sisters, multicolor on white, ca 1900, full size, ca 1900, NM.......................**575.00**

Star of Bethlehem, pink on pastels, 83x79", NM...........**650.00**

Star Within Star, bright pastels, extra large, NM **235.00**

Tumbling Blocks, multicolor on white, pink border, old, large, EX.................................**325.00**

Pieced: Blazing Star, 20th Century, 74" x 84", EX, $440.00.

Radios

Collectors of vintage radios are especially interested in those made from the twenties through the fifties by companies such as RCA, Atwater Kent, Philco, and Crosley, though those produced by the smaller manufacturers are collectible as well. Cathedral and breadboard styles are popular, so are Art Deco styles and those with a unique type of speaker, power source, or cabinet.

Arborphone, #27....................**65.00**

Atwater Kent #20, with all tubes, EX original **78.00**

Atwater Kent #32, EX **100.00**

Atwater Kent #49, EX **40.00**

Bendix, end-table style, EX original..................................**65.00**

Charlie MacCarthy, Bakelite, by Majestic, $500.00.

Crosley #10-137, light (faded) green Bakelite, EX **40.00**

DeWald #802 Tombstone, 8-tube, 4-band, restored...........**135.00**

General Electric K-40-A, EX original....................................**45.00**

Kennedy #110, EX..............**500.00**

Kennedy XV, EX..................**160.00**

Magnavox D, pull-out drawer, table model, EX **95.00**

Motorola, light amber marbleized Catalin case **18.00**

Patterson PR-16, EX...........**150.00**

Philco #20, VG.....................**100.00**

Philco #511, metal cabinet, EX original **65.00**

Philco #80, cathedral, EX original....................................**70.00**

RCA #120, cathedral **225.00**

RCA #4T, cathedral, EX......**100.00**

RCA #94BT1, battery **20.00**

RCA X-551, brown Bakelite, table model, M **30.00**

Sentinel, plastic, 1930s.........**75.00**

Stromberg-Carlson #635A Treasure Chest, EX original .**50.00**

Thompson #35, EX original .**95.00**

Traveler, brown Bakelite, EX original **50.00**

Garod, orange and yellow Bakelite, $250.00.

True Tone, plastic, 1930s **35.00**
Watterson, wood cabinet, rectangular, EX.........................**20.00**
Wood Emerson, #544.............**25.00**
Zenith #5-H-40, EX...............**80.00**
Zenith #871, small dial, EX..**85.00**
Zenith T-723, Bakelite, EX ...**25.00**
Zenith Y-723, white plastic, AM/FM, working, EX.....**25.00**

Railroadiana

Memorabilia relating to the more than 175 different railway companies that once transversed this great country of ours represents one of the largest and most popular areas of collecting today. Because the field is so varied, many collectors prefer to specialize. Lanterns, badges, advertising, dinnerware, silver, timetables, locks, and tools are only a sampling of the many types of relics they treasure. Some enjoy toy trains, prints showing old locomotives – in short, virtually anything that in any way represents the rapidly disappearing railway system is of value.

Dinnerware

Bowl, cereal; Challenger, Union Pacific, 6¼" **25.00**
Bowl, soup; Harriman Blue, Union Pacific, 9".............**40.00**
Bowl, Starucca, Erie, 6¼" **50.00**
Celery dish, blue & gold, Union Pacific, 10"......................**35.00**
Celery tray, Flambeau, Chicago & Northwestern, 3¾x7½" ..**20.00**
Cup & saucer, demitasse; Coral, Illinois Central...............**30.00**
Cup & saucer, Maritime, Canadian National **65.00**
Cup & saucer; coffee; Indian Tree, Pullman........................**200.00**
Plate, dinner; State Flowers, Missouri Pacific..................**250.00**
Plate, soup; Centenary, Baltimore & Ohio, Shenango, 9".....**80.00**
Platter, Challenger, Union Pacific, 8", NM............................**35.00**
Platter, DeWitt Clinton, New York Central, 9x6½" **45.00**

Miscellaneous

Badge, cap; Boston & Maine Trainman, nickeled, curved top, 3⅝" long...................**35.00**

Ash tray, aluminum, BLE, 5⅝",
$35.00.

Badge, cap; Pullman Porter, black
 letters on silver metal, 4"
 long **30.00**
Baggage check, Northwestern
 Line logo, 2½x2¼" **45.00**
Book, Curves & Earthworks,
 Allen, 1920, EX **15.00**
Button, uniform; Rock Island
 Lines, star center, gold tone,
 large **4.00**
Button, uniform; Union Pacific,
 silver color, domed, large. **4.50**
Calendar, Burlington Northern,
 1971, 42x25½", EX **10.00**

Brass checks or tags, Erie, 1",
$12.00; B&O, 1⅜", $18.00.

Dish towel, Burlington Rte, safety
 slogans, blue on tan, 18x16",
 NM **8.00**
Fan, Union Pacific Railroad,
 paper folding type, 24 sticks,
 EX **5.00**
Grenade, glass, embossed Chicago
 Northwestern, 18x3" **95.00**

Hand towel, Union Pacific on
 white stripe, 16x16" **8.00**
Hatchet, Wabash...................**32.00**
Headrest cover, Seaboard Coast
 Line, 17x16" **7.00**
Lamp, inspector's; unmarked
 Dietz Acme, tin hood, reflector, kerosene **35.00**
Lantern, conductor's; nickeled
 brass, Pat May 11, 1871 on
 bell bottom **250.00**
Lantern, Frisco, Handlan-Buck,
 clear 5½" globe, twist-off bot-
 tom **200.00**
Letter opener, Northern Pacific,
 red plastic, 8½"............... **5.00**
Lock, Frisco, Pat 2040482 Adlake
 on key drop **10.00**
Lock, Soo Line, brass shackle
 front, Fraim on bk, brass riv-
 ets **10.00**
Luggage sticker, Milwaukee Road,
 purple & orange, 3½" diame-
 ter **8.00**
Luggage sticker, Santa Fe,
 Indian, California Limited,
 3½" diameter.................. **8.00**
Napkin, Burlington Rte, white,
 20x20", M........................ **7.50**
Napkin, Union Pacific, Winged
 Streamliner, 11x16", EX . **7.50**
Neckerchief, Railroad Brother-
 hood, blue cotton, 20x24". **8.00**
Pass, Detroit & Milwaukee, pink
 with vignette, 1873, EX.**15.00**
Pass, Grand Trunk Railway, train
 on bridge scene, 1897.....**18.00**
Playing cards, Burlington Rte,
 riders watch Zephyr, EX in
 box...................................**18.00**
Post card, Erie, Union News pub-
 lisher, ca 1910, used........ **6.00**
Switch key, Chesapeake & Ohio,
 serial number, Adlake ...**12.00**
Tablecloth, California Zephyr
 woven on white, 36x42".**15.00**
Tablecloth, Northern Pacific Yellowstone Park Line, 54x66",
 EX **65.00**

Tablecloth, Rio Grande interwoven, 36x42", EX **12.50**

Tag, Erie RR, brass, 1"..........**12.00**

Timetable, Fitchburg, Hoosac Tunnel Route, 1885........**15.00**

Torch, Baltimore & Ohio, teapot style, hollow handle, 5"..**35.00**

Clothes hangers, $8.00 each.

Razors

Straight razors are prized for their beautifully decorated blades and handles, often portraying nudes, animals, scenes, or slogans popular at the time of their manufacture. Values are determined by assessing the blade style, pattern of the handle, and manufacturer's mark. Corn razors, used to remove corns from the feet, are also collectible. An approximate date of manufacture may be arrived at thorough study of various types of blades. Those made before the 19th century were crude wedge-shaped affairs that evolved through many improvements in shape as well as material to the fully hollow ground blades of the 1880s.

AH Boker, etched blade, winged head & scroll on faux ivory handle **17.50**

Assy Shaheen & Co, Liberty Bell on blade, lady's head on handle **16.00**

Case Bros Cutlery, Little Valley NY, Apollo on blade, extra small **50.00**

Case Brothers, Little Valley NY, yellow swirl handle........**26.00**

Charles Jackson, Sheffield, silver inlay on horn handle......**15.00**

Clark & Hall, black horn handle square-end, 1790s..........**45.00**

Clearcut De Lux etched on blade, pearl tang, black fluted handle **32.00**

Dandelion, Atlantic Barber Supply, owl on branch on handle, EX....................................**24.00**

Diamond, etched blade, jigged bone handle, EX **85.00**

Dixon Cutlery Co Germany, pine cones on faux ivory handle, repinned **16.00**

Ellis Barber Supply, white celluloid handle...................... **5.00**

Ford & Medley, Sheffield, etched blade, black handle........**18.00**

George W Korn Razor Co, Little Valley NY on blade, celluloid handle............................**12.50**

Henry Sears & Son, Queen embossed on handle, mother-of-pearl tang **22.50**

Howell & Sons, hollow ground blade, ivory handle, M...**45.00**

Imperial Warranted, florals on celluloid handle..............**40.00**

Joseph Haywood, Sheffield, mother-of-pearl inlay on celluloid handle **15.00**

Lafayette Cutlery, windmill scene on orange handle, replaced tang **18.00**

Lenox Cutlery, etched blade, black celluloid handle.............. **7.50**

Marsden Warranted, nude & cherub on black handle .**25.00**

Northfield Cutlery, Rattler etched on blade, replaced aluminum handle **10.00**

Parkin Cast Steel, wedged blade, horn handle..................**30.00**

H. Boker, bicycle race etched on blade, black celluloid handle, ca 1900, $50.00.

Rattler, windmill scene on faux ivory handle, rare, EX ...**90.00**

Roberts Warranted, wedge blade, bone handle, 1780s **138.00**

Simmons Hardware, Lilliputian etched blade, jigged bone handle, EX......................**80.00**

Thomas, French, no tang extension, semi-wedge blade, black handle **35.00**

Wade & Butcher, Sheffield, pressed horn handle, wedged blade.............................**135.00**

Wade & Butcher, wedged blade, black horn handle, brass pin covers **17.50**

Westfield Mfg, peacock & branch on faux ivory handle, etched blade **28.00**

Wilbert Cutlery Chicago, Regal etched on blade, faux ivory handle **18.00**

WR Case & Sons, Gold Nugget, clear orange handle **35.00**

Reamers

Though made for the simple task of extracting citrus juices, reamers may be found in fanciful figurals as well as simple utilitarian styles. You may find even wood or metal examples, but the most popular with collectors are those made of glass and ceramics. Fry, Hazel Atlas, Hocking, Jeanette, and McKee are among the largest producers of the glass reamer, some of which (depending on color and rarity) may bring prices well into the hundreds of dollars.

ASCO, clear, unembossed **30.00**

Ceramic, blue, yellow, & white clown, Japan, 5½" **40.00**

Ceramic, green, orange, & white clown, Japan, 6½" **45.00**

Ceramic, orange, black, green, & white clown, Japan, 7½".**45.00**

Ceramic, white, 2-spout, France, 3¼" diameter **10.00**

Federal, amber, tab handle, plain sides.............................**200.00**

Federal, green, pointed cone..**15.00**

Fenton, elephant painted on base, baby size **70.00**

Foreign, crystal, K inside shield mark **15.00**

Fry, opalescent, promotional, common **25.00**

Hazel Atlas, green, measuring & mixing cup......................**22.50**

McKee, jadite, $30.00.

Hazel Atlas, green, tab handle, lemon reamer **7.50**
Hazel Atlas, green, Crisscross, tab handle.............................**12.00**
Hocking, green clambroth, tab handle...........................**100.00**
Jeannette, Delphite, small ...**60.00**
Jeannette, jadite, 2-cup **35.00**
Jeannette, pink, Hex Optic, bucket style **45.00**
Paden City, pink, Party Line, cocktail-shaker style......**80.00**
Paden City, pink, pitcher with reamer top **185.00**
Sunkist, caramel.................**225.00**

Sunkist, clear, unembossed ..**85.00**
Sunkist, custard....................**30.00**
Sunkist, jadite **20.00**
US Glass, green, slick handle, insert near top of cup **32.00**
US Glass, pink, tub shape with reamer top **175.00**
Westmoreland, amber, 2-piece, baby size **135.00**
Westmoreland, pink, decorated, baby size **120.00**

Records, 78 rpms

Records that made it to the 'Top Ten' in their day are not the records that are prized by today's collectors, though they treasure those few which best represent specific types of music: jazz, rhythm and blues, country and western, rock and roll, etc. Instead they search for those cut very early in the career of artists who later became super stars, records cut on rare or interesting labels, or those aimed at ethnic groups.

Common records can often be purchased for $1.00 to $2.00, 45s for even less.

Puddinhead, ceramic, 6", $120.00.

Alberta Hunter, Empty Cellar Blues, Okeh, #8315 ....**25.00**

All-Star Orchestra, Add a Little Wiggle, Victor, #21423 .... **9.00**

Andy & The Live Wires, Maggie, Applause, #1249 .... **8.00**

Apollos, I Love You Darling, Harvard, #803 ....**45.00**

Arcadian Serenaders, Yes Sir, Boss, Okeh, #40562 ....**18.00**

Armstrong, Louis; & His Orchestra, Yours & Mine, Decca, #1369 .... **7.00**

Astaire, Fred; Slap That Boss, Brunswick, #7856 .... **6.50**

Auburn, Frank; & His Orchestra, Goodnight Moon, Clarion, #5450-C **6.00**

Austin, Gene; I Cried for You, Decca, #926 .... **6.00**

Austin, Lovie; & Her Serenaders, Peepin' Blues, Paramount, #12277 ....**35.00**

Barons, Forget About Me, Decca, #29293 ....**15.00**

Batts, Ray; Stealin' Sugar, Excello, #2028 ....**10.00**

Beasley, Irene; Baby's Back Today, Victor, #40092 .... **9.00**

Beiderbecke, Bix; & Orchestra, Sorry, Okeh, #41001 ....**18.00**

Belvin, Jesse; Goodnight My Love, Modern, #1005 .... **9.00**

Birmingham Jug Band, German Blues, Okeh, #8856 ....**85.00**

Birton, Vic; & His Orchestra, Blue, Vocalion, #2974 .....**12.00**

Blake, Charley; California Blues, Supertone, #9534 ....**11.00**

Blythe's Blue Boys, Oriental Man, Champion, #40023 ....**14.00**

Boots & His Buddies, Blues of Avalon, Bluebird, #7187 . **9.00**

Boots & His Buddies, Sleepy Gal, Bluebird, #6968 .... **8.00**

Brigg, Matt; & His Orchestra, Learning, Victor, #22933.. **9.00**

Broadway Rastus, Rock My Soul, Paramount, #12764 ....**45.00**

Brooks, Bob; Wandering Lamb, Columbia, #15676-D **7.00**

Brown, Les; & Orchestra, Lazy River, Decca, #1323 .... **7.00**

Buffalodians, Baby Face, Banner, #1778 .... **7.00**

Buffalodians, Deep Henderson, Columbia, #665-D **10.00**

Cadillacs, Down The Road, Josie, #778 ....**12.00**

Carter Family, Broken Down Tramp, Decca, #5518 ...... **8.00**

Charleston Chasers, Delirium, Columbia, #1076-D **18.00**

Chocolate Dandies, Once Upon a Time, Okeh, #41568 .....**22.00**

Clay, Sonny; & His Orchestra, Jambled Blues, Vocalion, #15078 ....**50.00**

Collins, Sam; Yellow Dog Blues, Gennett, #6146.............**100.00**

Conlon, Peter J; Barn Dance, Okeh, #45030 .... **7.00**

Cookie's Gingersnaps, High Fever, Okeh, #8369 ....**45.00**

Cootie William & His Orchestra, Give It Up, Okeh, #5690. **8.00**

Cornell & His Orchestra, Accordion Joe, Okeh, #41386..**12.00**

Count Basie & Orchestra, Louisiana, Columbia, #35448 .... **6.00**

Crosby, Bing; I Found You, Brunswick, #6248 .... **8.00**

Crosby, Bing; Little Dutch Mill, Brunswick, #6594 .... **6.00**

Davis, Walter; Homesick, Bluebird, #7836 ....**10.00**

Denmon, Morgan; The Two Drummers, Okeh, #45306 ....**10.00**

Desires, Let It Please You, Hull, #730 ....**11.00**

Dixie Jazz Band, My Lovie Lee, Oriole, #269 ....**12.00**

Dixon, Floyd; Come Back Baby, Aladdin, #3151 ....**15.00**

Edwards, Big Boy; Hoodoo Blues, Vocalion, #02932 ....**16.00**

Furry Lewis, Creeper's Blues, Vocalion, #1547 ....**90.00**

Edison Long-Playing, ca 1927, $25.00.

Georgia Tom, Pig Meat Blues, Supertone, #9507 ....**40.00**

Greene, Amos; Memphis Yodel, Supertone, #9671 ....**17.00**

Hackberry Ramblers, Dobie Shack, Bluebird, #2019..**11.00**

Herring, Clara; Beating Blues, Gennett, #6591 ....**35.00**

Jackson, Jim; What a Time, Victor, #38505 ....**18.00**

Johnson, Tillie; Chicago Man Blues, Gennett, #6438 ...**35.00**

Jones, Frankie; My Lincoln, Vocalion, #04206 ....**10.00**

Jungle Band, Dog Bottom, Brunswick, #4450 ....**12.00**

Jelly-Roll Morton & His Red Hot Peppers, Strokin' Away, ca 1930, $75.00.

Kyle, Charlie; Walking Blues, Victor, #38625 ....**60.00**

Lillie Mae, Mama Don't Want It, Okeh, #8920 ....**25.00**

Little Brother, Out West Blues, Bluebird, #6916.............**20.00**

Martin, Sara; Alabamy Bound, Okeh, #8262 ....**18.00**

Miles, Josie; Picnic Time, Ajax, #17083 ....**18.00**

Morris, Gene; Lovin' Honey, Vic, #0287 ....**12.00**

Moss, Teddy; Back Biter Blues, Gennett, #7084 ....**60.00**

Nelson, Red; Empty Bed Blues, Decca, #7185 ....**12.00**

Oak Mountain Four, Medley, Champion, #15874.........**10.00**

Old Southern Jug Band, Hatchet Head Blues, Silvertone, #3061 ....**30.00**

Original Indiana Five, Motem Stamp, Banner, #7084 ... **8.00**

Pacific Coast Players, Jazzing Around, Radiex, #1326 ..**10.00**

Patti Ann, Sorrowful Heart, Aladdin, #3198 ....**22.00**

Patton, Charley; Magnolia Blues, Paramount, #12943 .....**100.00**

Paul, Jerry; Step Out, Holiday, #1001 ....**13.00**

Peters, Teddy; Georgia Man, Vocalion, #1006 ....**60.00**

Piano Red, So Worried, Checker, #911 .... **6.00**

Porter's Blue Devils, Steamboat Sal, Gennett, #5249 ....**13.00**

Pratt, Lynn; Tom Cat Boogie, Hornet, #1000 ....**12.00**

Quarter Notes, Like You Bug Me, Dot, #15685 .... **5.00**

Red Heads, Nobody's Sweetheart, Oriole, #2555 .... **6.00**

Red Mountain Trio, Dixie, Columbia, #15369-D **13.00**

Rythm Wreckers, Desert Blues, Vocalion, #3642 .... **7.00**

Six Black Diamonds, Melancholy Lou, Oriole, #497...........**10.00**

Spand, Charlie; Mississippi Blues, Paramount, #12917 ......**65.00**

Tampa Red, Worthy of You, Bluebird, #5981 ....**12.00**

Taylor, Blind Jeremiah; Mother's Love, Herwin, #93027 ...**45.00**

Walker, James; Lost John Blues, Silvertone, #3553 ....**65.00**

Wheatstraw, Peetie; Santa Claus Blues, Decca, #7129 ....**13.00**

Wikel, Miller; Young Charlotte, Paramount, #3205 ....**20.00**

Williams, Clarence; & His Orchestra, Slow River, Brunswick, #3580 ....**15.00**

Wilson, Lena; Chiropractor Blues, Clarion, #5036-C **11.00**

Wolfberger, Haskell; My Little Girl, Vocalion, #5390......**10.00**

Red Wing

Taking their name from the location in Minnesota where they located in the late 1870s, the Red Wing Company produced a variety of wares, all of which are today considered noteworthy by pottery and dinnerware collectors. Their early stoneware lines, Cherry Band, and Sponge Band (Gray Line), are especially valuable and often fetch prices of several hundred dollars on today's market. Production of dinnerware began in the thirties and continued until the pottery closed in 1967. Some of their more popular lines – all of which were hand painted – were Bob White, Lexington, Tampico, Normandie, Capistrano, and Random Harvest. Commercial artware was also produced. Perhaps the ware most easily associated with Red Wing is their Brushware line, unique in its appearance and decoration. Cattails, rushes, florals, and similar nature subjects are 'carved' in relief on a stoneware type body with a matt green wash its only finish.

Dinnerware

Ardennes, bowl, vegetable..... **7.00**
Ardennes, chop plate, 1947 ..**12.00**
Bob White, cup & saucer **12.00**
Bob White, pitcher, 12" **30.00**
Bob White, plate, dinner........ **9.00**

Bob White, dinner plate, $9.00.

Bob White, sugar bowl **8.00**
Capistrano, bowl, 6"............... **6.00**
Capistrano, cup & saucer **12.00**
Capistrano, platter, 15" **15.00**
Iris, pitcher **25.00**
Lexington Rose, plate, 10½" .. **7.00**
Lute Song, bowl, 6" **6.00**
Lute Song, platter, 13"..........**20.00**
Morning-Glory, creamer & sugar bowl..............................**12.50**
Morning-Glory, cup & saucer. **6.00**
Morning-Glory, plate, 6¼"...... **2.50**
Normandie, cup & saucer **8.00**
Normandie, shakers, pair...... **8.00**
Orleans, shakers, pair **7.50**
Orleans, sugar bowl **6.00**
Pepe, cup & saucer................**10.00**
Pepe, plate, dinner................. **8.00**
Pepe, plate, salad **5.00**
Pepe, shakers, oval, pair **12.00**

Normandy, plate, 10", $8.00; Cup and saucer, $8.00; Creamer and sugar bowl, $16.00.

Pepe, shakers, tall, pair **10.00**
Pompeii, bowl, cereal; 8" **7.00**
Pompeii, plate, 6" **3.00**
Random Harvest, bowl, fruit. **6.00**
Random Harvest, bowl, vegetable; deep **15.00**
Random Harvest, platter......**15.00**

Stoneware

Bean pot, Albany slip, Boston style, marked Red Wing, 1-gal **125.00**
Bowl, Blue Band, 6" **35.00**
Bowl, Greek Key, brown, 10" .**75.00**
Bowl, Saffron, red & blue sponging, large **65.00**
Bowl, Saffron, red & blue sponging, small **55.00**
Butter crock, brown, low, marked North Star, 2-lb **70.00**
Chamber pot, brown, marked Minnesota.....................**125.00**
Churn, leaf on salt glaze, molded, Minnesota, 3-gal **500.00**
Crock, fancy leaf on salt glaze, Red Wing, 15-gal..........**450.00**
Cuspidor, blue & white sponge, unmarked, 6" dia **200.00**

Custard cup, Sponge Band ...**85.00**
Custard cup, white, with advertising, marked Red Wing ..**60.00**

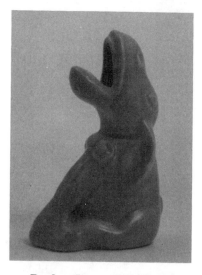

Donkey figure, 5¼", $20.00.

Flowerpot, Albany slip, marked Minnesota, 7" **175.00**
Jar, packing; red wing on white, bail handle, 3-gal **125.00**
Jar, refrigerator; blue bands on white, with bail, 3-lb....**200.00**

Jug, bailed, white, wide mouth, Minnesota, 1-gal **100.00**
Jug, fancy, brown & white, Red Wing, 1-gal **250.00**
Jug, shoulder; brown & white, dome top, marked Minnesota, 1-gal **50.00**

8-Gallon leaf churn, unsigned, $325.00.

Jug, Who Will Win?, miniature, NM **135.00**
Milk pan, brown & white, marked North Star **60.00**
Mug, Happy Days Are Here Again embossed on side............**80.00**
Pitcher, Cherry Band, blue & white............................**125.00**
Pitcher, pipkin; brown & white, Minnesota, 4-pt............**225.00**
Reamer, Sponge Band, marked Red Wing Union...........**500.00**
Refrigerator jar, medium size, pair **95.00**
Snuff jar, white, marked Red Wing, 1-qt......................**75.00**

Redware

Simple utilitarian ware made from easily accessible deposits of red clay was a staple used by the early American settlers. Though available throughout the country, it was utilized to its fullest extent in Pennsylvania, Ohio, and southern Appalachia. Occasionally yellow slip was used to add decorations of straight or wavy lines or simple outlines of birds or tulips. Value is determined by size and form, age, decoration, and condition.

Bank, amber with brown flecks, tooled shoulder lines, ovoid, 5¼" **125.00**
Bank, jug form, red paint, repaired flake at coin slot, 4¾" **65.00**
Bank, purple & brown, knob finial, 5", EX **55.00**
Basket, hanging, 6x5½" diameter, M **500.00**
Basket, yellow & green & brown marbleized, early 1800s, 9x6", NM...............................**350.00**
Bottle, hot water; brown flecks, flat circular form, 8" **80.00**
Bowl, yellow slip with green & brown, 13" diameter **325.00**
Charger, 4-line yellow slip, coggled rim, 11½", NM . **1,050.00**
Churn, green-brown, handles, incised #5, ovoid, 17"......**40.00**
Cup, amber mottle, flared lip, 3¾", EX **85.00**
Dish, 3-line yellow slip waves, rare size, 5½", EX.........**700.00**
Flowerpot, brown runs, attached saucer, marked John Bell, 5", EX **200.00**
Jar, apple butter; clear glaze, tooled, strap handle, 5"..**55.00**
Jar, brown splotches, cylindrical, 9½", VG **95.00**

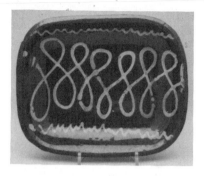

Dish, yellow slip figure-8s, 11½"
long, $700.00.

Jug, puzzle; simple yellow slip,
   minor wear & flakes, 5".**55.00**
Milk pan, glazed interior, 1850s,
   7½" diameter **135.00**
Mold, turk's head, black sponging,
   scalloped, 9¼" **75.00**
Mug, applied star, strap handle,
   tooled lip, 5¼" **125.00**
Pie plate, mustard yellow, cog-
   gled, 11", EX................**275.00**
Pitcher, white with brown mottle,
   pinched spout, repaired, 5",
   EX **65.00**

Plate, yellow slip trailings, minor
chips and wear, 10", $250.00.

Pot, dark brown, open handles,
   wear & chips, 13x16" diame-
   ter **130.00**

Riviera

Made by the Homer Laughlin
China Company, Riviera was a
line of colored dinnerware that
was sold through Murphy's dime
stores from 1938 until sometime
in the late 1940s. A sister line to
Fiesta, Riviera was lighter in
weight, unmarked, and inexpen-
sive.

Baker, oval, 9" **15.00**
Batter set, complete............**185.00**
Batter set, with decals........**135.00**
Bowl, baker; 9" **15.00**
Bowl, cream soup; ivory, with
   liner **40.00**
Bowl, fruit; 5½"...................... **8.00**
Bowl, nappy; 9¼"...................**18.00**
Bowl, oatmeal; 6" **18.00**
Butter dish, cobalt, ¼-lb **190.00**
Butter dish, ½-lb **75.00**
Butter dish, ¼-lb **85.00**

Butter dish, ½-pound, $75.00.

Casserole, with lid **65.00**
Creamer, regular................... **7.50**
Cup & saucer....................... **11.00**
Cup & saucer, demi; ivory **42.00**
Jug, with lid **85.00**
Pitcher, juice; red **175.00**
Pitcher, juice; yellow **55.00**
Plate, deep, 8".......................**13.00**
Plate, 10" **20.00**
Plate, 6" **5.50**
Plate, 7" **7.00**
Plate, 9" **12.00**
Platter, cobalt, 12"................**28.00**
Platter, 11½".........................**12.00**

Salt & pepper shakers, pair .12.00
Sauce boat 15.00
Shakers, pair 11.00
Sugar bowl, with lid 12.00
Syrup, with lid 85.00
Teapot 75.00
Tumbler, juice.......................38.00
Tumbler, with handle............48.00

Rockingham

A type of utilitarian ware favored in America from the early 1800s until after the 1920s, Rockingham is easily identified by its mottled brown sponged-on glaze. While some items are simple and unadorned, many are molded with high relief designs of animals, vines, leaves, cherubs, and human forms. Figural hound handles are often found on pitchers. Some of the finest examples of Rockingham was made at the Vermont potteries of Norton and Fenton, and you may find ill-informed dealers and collectors that mistakenly refer to this ware as 'Bennington.' However, hundreds of potteries produced goods of a very similar appearance; and proper identification of the manufacturer is often difficult, if not impossible.

Bed pan, 16¾" long, M 50.00

Bookends, young girl with books,
7½", EX 260.00
Bottle, embossed morning-glories,
8¼" 85.00
Bottle, Toby form, 9½" 150.00
Bowl, fluted exterior, 2x7"..100.00
Bowl, minor wear, 3x11½"..120.00
Bowl, mixing; with spout, hair-
line, 16"...........................95.00
Bowl, oval, minor wear, 12x8½"
long 100.00
Bowl, straight sides, 3x12".100.00
Bowl, 3½x8"..........................55.00
Candlestick, lip repaired, 8½",
pair 300.00
Frame, embossed/tooled detail,
scalloped interior edge,
13x15", EX...................700.00
Inkwell, sleeping figure, old chips,
4".................................100.00
Jar, embossed vintage, handles,
7½", EX 115.00
Miniature cuspidor, 1½" 110.00
Miniature jug, 1½" 50.00
Miniature pitcher, incised dia-
monds & florals, 2" 60.00
Mold, Turk's head, 3½x8⅛".135.00
Mug, fluted panels, 3⅝".......135.00
Mug, rings at base, 2⅝", EX .30.00
Mug, Toby form, 5¾" 65.00
Pie plate, 11" 135.00
Pitcher, Daniel Boone, 9"....145.00
Pitcher, embossed hunt scene,
8"...................................175.00
Pitcher, embossed portrait bust,
7"...................................75.00

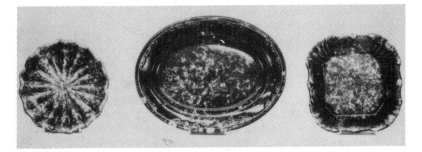

Pie dish, scalloped, 7¾", $140.00; Platter, 13" long, $100.00; Baker's dish, molded edges, 8" square, $170.00.

Pitcher, embossed tulip, 9".225.00
Plate, Gothic arch embossing, canted corners, minor wear, 8¾"..................55.00
Shaker, dome top, chipped lip, 4½"..................85.00
Soap dish, oval, 4¾", NM.....85.00

Rockwell, Norman

His first *Saturday Evening Post* cover was published in 1916; launching him on a lifetime career. He became famous for his ability to portray through his illustrations keen insight and understanding of the American way of life. In addition to his magazine covers, he illustrated advertisements and sheet music. All are highly collectible. Modern applications of his original art – collector plates, figurines, Christmas ornaments, etc. – are also valued.

See also Limited Edition Plates, Ornaments, and Figurines.

Book, Adventures of Tom Sawyer, 1936, EX..................75.00
Book, Norman Rockwell's America, leather bound, limited edition..................85.00
Calendar, cover only, A Great Moment, 1965, large 20.00
Calendar, cover only, Keep Myself Physically Strong, 1964.22.00
Calendar, Pointing the Way, 1962, 8x14½"..................20.00
Greeting card, Santa scene, 1933, 5½x8½"..................13.00
Lithograph, Audubon Paints Passenger Pigeon, 20x25"..275.00
Lithograph, Brooks Robinson, Rawlings, 24x30".........350.00
Lithograph, Donald Art print, 8x19"..................50.00
Lithograph, You Got To Be Kidden, 24x18"..................500.00
Plaque, Freedom from Fear, metal, Curtis Circulation, 11x16"..................280.00
Poster, Fisk Bicycle Club, boys/bike, linen back, 37x25½", EX..................280.00
Poster, Freedom from Fear, 1943, 40x28", EX..................45.00
Poster, Schmidt's Beer, EX ...75.00
Sheet music, Little French Mother, Good-bye..........30.00
Sheet music, Over Yonder Where the Lilies Grow, Rockwell cover..................20.00
Sketch, original, inscribed, signed, 18x48"..........2,000.00
Stein, Looking Out to Sea .225.00

Rosemeade

Novelty items made by the Whapeton Pottery Company of North Dakota from 1941 to 1960 are finding an interested following among collectors of American pottery. Though smaller items (salt and pepper shakers, figurines, trays, etc.) are readily found, the larger examples represent a challenge to collectors who prize them highly. The name of the novelty ware, 'Rosemeade,' is indicated on the paper labels (many of which are still intact) or by the ink stamp.

Ash tray, horse's head embossed on yellow-gold..................32.00
Candle holder, scalloped, thrown, 1½x4", pair..................25.00
Cotton holder, bunny, aqua...58.00
Creamer, stylized horse's head, lime green..................22.00
Figurine, bear, sitting, 3"......32.00
Figurine, buffalo, buff & tan, 2½x3¼"..................40.00

Hors d'oeuvre with pheasant, $45.00.

Figurine, mouse on back legs, gray, 1½".............................**17.50**
Figurine, pheasant, 7", with 12½" wing span........................**225.00**
Figurine, skunk, black & white, 3x3½"...............................**22.00**
Flower holder, stork, 7".........**30.00**
Lamp, TV; pheasant, large .**385.00**
Rose bowl, green shaded, 3" .**17.50**
Salt & pepper, Boston Terrier, bronze & white, pair......**26.00**

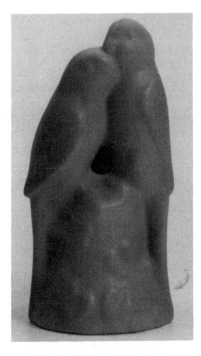

Lovebirds, pink and blue matt, 6", $17.50.

Salt & pepper, Mexican Chihuahua, pair...................**28.00**
Salt & pepper, seal, pair.......**24.00**
Tumbler, wheat, 5¼".............**10.00**
Vase, black with incised wavy lines, ball form, 4"..........**28.00**
Vase, Egyptian, green, 8¼" ..**70.00**
Wall pocket, moon form........**10.00**

Roseville

Founded by George Young in 1892, the Roseville Pottery Company produced quality artware, utility ware, and commercial artware of the finest quality until they closed in the 1950s. Of the major American potteries, Roseville's production pieces are among the finest, and it is a rare flea market that will not yield several excellent examples from the 'middle period.' Some of the early artware lines require perseverance to acquire, while others such as their standard brown-glazed 'Rozane' are easy to locate. During the twenties and thirties they produced several lines of children's serving dishes decorated with Santa Claus, chicks, rabbits in jackets, Sunbonnet Babies, and various other characters, which are today treasured by their own band of devotees. While many pieces of Roseville are marked with some form of the company name, others that originally had paper labels are otherwise unmarked. Careful study of Roseville lines may result in your finding one of the few bargains left at the flea markets today.

Apple Blossom, basket, 309, 8".**80.00**
Artcraft, console bowl, 13" ...**90.00**
Autumn, pitcher, 8½"..........**400.00**
Aztec, vase, blue, 11½"........**300.00**

Bittersweet basket, #810, $80.00.

Azurean, vase, floral, Leffler, #822-7, 15½".............. **1,000.00**
Bank, eagle, 2½"..................**175.00**
Bank, monkey, 6" **150.00**
Bittersweet, basket, 8" **70.00**
Bittersweet, console bowl, #829-12, 12½"..........................**45.00**
Blackberry, jardiniere, small handles, 6" **150.00**
Blackberry, jug, 5"...............**125.00**
Blackberry, vase, 8" **175.00**
Bleeding Heart, plate, #381-10, 10½"................................**50.00**
Blended, umbrella stand, floral, #609, 20".......................**225.00**
Burmese, wall pocket, white, #82-B, 7½" **175.00**
Bushberry, cider pitcher, #1325, 8½"................................**125.00**
Bushberry, mug, #1-3½, 3½".**45.00**
Capri, basket, green, #510, 9" .**75.00**
Carnelian I, fan vase, 6" **28.00**
Carnelian II, vase, 8"............**60.00**
Cherry Blossom, hanging basket, 8"....................................**300.00**
Cherry Blossom, jug vase, with handles, 7"....................**165.00**

Chloron, wall pocket, nude, green, 8½" **400.00**
Clemana, candle holders, 4½", pair **95.00**
Clematis, basket, #387, 7"....**45.00**
Clematis, cookie jar, 10" **125.00**
Columbine, cornucopia, #149-6, 5½" **30.00**
Corinthian, ash tray, 2" **55.00**
Corinthian, jardiniere, 7" **85.00**
Corinthian, umbrella stand .**400.00**
Cosmos, ewer, #951, 15" **175.00**
Cremona, vase, 4" **40.00**
Crocus, vase, 9"...................**400.00**
Dahlrose, vase, 10" **95.00**
Dawn, ewer, #834-16, 16" ...**200.00**
Della Robbia, teapot, bell shape, 6½"............................ **1,275.00**
Dogwood I, bowl, 2½".............**45.00**
Dogwood II, boat planter, 6".**50.00**
Donatella, creamer, landscape, creamware, 3" **55.00**
Donatella, tea set, Gibson Girls, creamware, 3-pc **400.00**
Dutch, pin tray, 4".................**50.00**
Dutch, pitcher, milk; 4½"....**150.00**
Dutch, powder box, 3".........**200.00**

252

Earlam, vase, handles, 6" **60.00**
Early Pitchers, Boy, 7½" **200.00**
Early Pitchers, Bridge, 6".....**55.00**
Early Pitchers, Goldenrod **85.00**
Early Pitchers, Tulip, 7" **50.00**
Falline, vase, handles, 8"....**200.00**
Florane, basket, 8½" **80.00**
Florane, bowl, handles, 5" **50.00**
Florentine, compote, 10".......**45.00**
Foxglove, candle holders, #1150,
    4½", pair **45.00**
Foxglove, conch shell, 6".......**35.00**
Foxglove, tray, 11".................**45.00**

Foxglove, vase, 7", $60.00; Candle holders, #1150, 4½", $45.00 for the pair.

Freesia, cookie jar, #4, 10"..**125.00**
Freesia, cornucopia, 8" **30.00**
Fuchsia, basket, with frog, #350,
    8"...................................**125.00**
Fuchsia, vase, #893-6, 6" **50.00**
Fudji, vase, florals, 10"... **1,350.00**
Futura, window box, blended,
    15½x5"..........................**350.00**
Gardenia, bowl, #600, 4".......**30.00**
Gardenia, tray, #631-14, 15".**60.00**
Holland, tankard, #2, 9" **125.00**
Imperial I, basket, 6"............**55.00**
Imperial II, bowl, 4½" **110.00**
Iris, basket, #355-10, 9½" ..**125.00**
Iris, console bowl, #362-10,
    3½x12½"..........................**50.00**
Ivory II, jardiniere, 6"...........**40.00**
Ivory II, wall shelf, #8, 5½"...**70.00**
Ixia, vase, #862-10, 10½" **50.00**
Jonquil, bowl, handles, 3".....**50.00**

Juvenile, creamer, Santa Claus,
    3½" **95.00**
Juvenile, mug, rabbit, 3" **50.00**
Laurel, vase, 10" **110.00**
Lombardy, jardiniere, 6½" ..**150.00**
Lotus, vase, pillow form, #L4-10,
    10½" **100.00**
Luffa, vase, 8"......................**100.00**
Magnolia, ash tray, #28, 7" ...**45.00**
Magnolia, mug, #3, 3" **45.00**
Matt Color, hanging basket, blue,
    4½" **40.00**
Matt Green, tobacco jar, 6" ...**60.00**
Mayfair, bowl, #1119-9, 10" ..**40.00**
Mock Orange, planter, #931-8,
    9x3½" **35.00**
Monticello, vase, 9" **90.00**
Morning-Glory, vase, 6" **175.00**
Mostique, bowl, 7"................**40.00**
Olympic, pitcher, Pandora
    Brought to Earth, 7". **2,150.00**
Panel, fan vase, nude, 6" ...**185.00**
Peony, basket, #379, 11" **100.00**
Peony, ewer, #8, 10" **100.00**
Persian, jardiniere, large....**175.00**
Pine Cone, console bowl, blue, 11"
    long **75.00**
Pine Cone, pitcher, blue, #415,
    9"...................................**250.00**
Poppy, basket, #347, 10".......**85.00**
Poppy, wall pocket, 8½" **150.00**
Raymor, bean pot, black, with lid,
    #194 ....**25.00**
Raymor, hot plate, #159........**15.00**
Rosecraft Hexagon, bowl, with
    handles, 7½" **75.00**
Rosecraft Yellow, wall pocket,
    10"................................**125.00**
Rozane, jardiniere, floral, footed,
    9½" **200.00**
Russco, vase, handles, 7" **70.00**
Savona, wall pocket, 8".......**250.00**
Silhouette, cigarette box **35.00**
Smoker Sets, ash tray, Fatima,
    3" **175.00**
Snowberry, candle holders, #1CS-
    1, pair **25.00**
Sunflower, bowl, 4"................**75.00**
Sunflower, wall pocket, 7" ..**300.00**

Teasel, basket, #349, 10" ...**100.00**
Thornapple, basket, 10" **95.00**
Tourist, bowl, 4x7" **1,100.00**
Tourmaline, ginger jar........**300.00**
Tourmaline, vase, loving-cup form, 8" **60.00**
Velmoss Scroll, bowl, 9x2½"..**50.00**
Vista, basket, 12" **200.00**

Vista, basket, 6½", $150.00.

Water Lily, basket, #380, 8"..**45.00**
Water Lily, ewer, #10, 6" **35.00**
White Rose, basket, blue, #364, 12"....................................**75.00**
Wincraft, tea set, 3-pc **100.00**
Wisteria, vase, 9" **175.00**
Zephyr Lily, ash tray **35.00**
Zephyr Lily, hanging basket.**60.00**

Rowland and Marsellus

Souvenir and commemorative plates marked Rowland and Marsellus or with an R & M within a diamond were manufactured by various Staffordshire potteries for these American importers who added their own backstamp to the blue-printed wares that were popular in gift shops from the 1890s until 1920. Plates are encountered most often, though cups and saucers, pitchers, etc., were also made.

Cup & saucer, Niagara Falls.**65.00**
Plate, Asbury Park NJ, Casino in center, rolled rim, 10" **50.00**
Plate, Charles Dickens, rolled rim, 10½" **55.00**
Plate, Indianapolis, Soldiers & Sailors Monument, rolled rim, 10" **50.00**
Plate, Mt Vernon, flat **35.00**
Plate, National Monument to the Forefathers, flat **40.00**
Plate, Niagara Falls, rolled rim, 10½" **50.00**
Plate, Philadelphia PA, rolled rim, 10½" **45.00**
Plate, Plymouth Rock, rolled rim, 10½" **45.00**
Plate, Robert Burns, rolled rim, 10½" **55.00**

Plate, Souvenir of Columbus, Ohio, rolled edge, 10", $50.00.

Plate, Standish House, fruit & flower, rolled rim, 10½" .**50.00**
Plate, Syracuse NY, Indian, rolled rim, 10"..........................**55.00**
Plate, Williamsport PA, rolled rim, 10"..........................**50.00**

Royal Bayreuth

Royal Bayreuth was founded in the late 1700s in Tettau,

Bavaria, and since that time has steadily produced fine porcelain dinnerware of very high quailty. In this century, they have become famous for their dinnerware and accessory items made in both figural patterns and series ware themes.

Figurals

Bowl, lobster, blue mark, with lid, 4½"....................................**85.00**
Candle holder, dachshund, blue mark, 4½"......................**250.00**
Chamberstick, elk, blue mark, 7½x4½"..........................**295.00**

Creamer, clown, blue mark, $150.00.

Cup & saucer, demitasse; apple, blue mark **135.00**
Cup & saucer, demitasse; oyster & pearl, blue mark.......**145.00**
Hatpin holder, poppy, red, blue mark **325.00**
Humidor, clown, blue mark, with lid **425.00**
Mustard, grapes, white mother-of-pearl, blue mark, with under-tray **145.00**
Pitcher, bear, blue mark, cream size................................**625.00**
Pitcher, bull, brown, blue mark, cream size....................**130.00**
Pitcher, butterfly, wings open, blue mark, cream size .**295.00**

Pitcher, cockatoo, blue mark, cream size....................**325.00**
Pitcher, crow, black, blue mark, cream size....................**145.00**
Pitcher, duck, marked Deponiert, milk size **165.00**
Pitcher, fish head, blue mark, cream size **145.00**
Pitcher, lamplighter, blue mark, cream size....................**180.00**
Pitcher, leopard, blue mark, rare, cream size **750.00**
Pitcher, orange, blue mark, water size................................**450.00**
Pitcher, St Bernard, blue mark, milk size **245.00**
Pitcher, tomato, unmarked, cream size **45.00**
Plate, lettuce leaf, yellow flowers, blue mark, handle, 7" **40.00**
Shakers, grapes, marked, pr .**95.00**
Teapot, tomato, unmarked ...**75.00**
Tureen, rose, blue mark, oval, with lid, 6"....................**250.00**

Florals, Scenics, and Series Ware

Basket, Rose Tapestry, 3-color, blue mark, 4½x3½"......**265.00**
Box, Snow Babies, blue mark, kidney shape **365.00**
Candlestick, Sunbonnet Babies, blue mark, tall **175.00**

Creamer, tapestry with landscape and goats, 4", $225.00.

Chamberstick, Sunbonnet Babies, washing, shield back, blue mark 425.00
Flowerpot, Rose Tapestry, 3-color, blue mark 195.00
Hair receiver, man with gun, blue mark 125.00
Humidor, pink roses on light blue, blue mark 125.00
Mint dish, Rose Tapestry, blue mark, palette form, 4½x4" 135.00
Pitcher, Devil & Cards, blue mark, cream size 130.00
Pitcher, goat tapestry, blue mark, cream size....................235.00
Pitcher, Sunbonnet Babies, fishing, tall, milk size 255.00
Pitcher, tapestry portrait, blue mark, 3½" 150.00
Salt cellar, Devil & Cards, blue mark, master 200.00
Toothpick holder, Old Man of the Mountain, scuttle form.295.00
Tray, Sunbonnet Babies, diamond shape, blue mark 135.00
Vase, bud; Rose Tapestry, blue mark 200.00
Vase, hunt scene, marked, 5".95.00
Vase, sheep scene, green mark, 6¼x3¾"............................95.00
Wall pocket, Penny in your Pocket Is a Merry Companion, blue mark 165.00
Wall pocket, Sunbonnet Babies, cleaning, blue mark 495.00

Royal Copley

Produced by the Spaulding China Company of Sebring, Ohio, Royal Copley is a line of novelty planters, vases, ash trays, and wall pockets modeled after appealing puppy dogs, lovely birds, innocent-eyed children, etc. The decoration is airbrushed and underglazed; the line is of good quality and is well-received by today's pottery collectors.

Figurine, kneeling Blackamoor, 8½", $15.00.

Ash tray, lily pad with bird, turquoise & pink, 5"........ 5.00
Ash tray, mallard, small 8.00
Creamer, chick, pink & brown, Spaulding, 4¾" 10.00
Figurine, hen, Royal Windsor, 6½" 10.00
Figurine, kingfisher, red & black, 5" 15.00
Figurine, parrot, pink & yellow, 5" 8.00
Pitcher, daffodil, 8" 22.00
Pitcher, Pome Fruit, 8" 24.00
Planter, Balinese girl, 8½"....10.00
Planter, bear cub clinging to stump, 8¼".....................25.00
Planter, bunting, 5"...............16.00
Planter, Chinese boy with big hat, pink, 7½"......................... 9.00
Planter, cocker spaniel with basket, 5½"............................12.00
Planter, gazelle, 9" 17.50
Planter, rooster, walking 10.00
Planter, running horse, 6" 10.00
Planter, water lily, green, 6".. 7.50
Vase, bow & ribbon, pink & gray, footed, 6¼" 7.50

Vase, Carol's Corsage, 7" **12.00**
Vase, Floral Elegance, green shaded, 8" **15.00**
Wall pocket, dancing lady **35.00**

Royal Doulton, Doulton

Though the Doulton Company has been in existence since early in the 19th century, the examples listed here are 20th century products. The company is world reknown for their finely detailed, hand decorated figurines, character jugs, and Tobys, as well as for their many lines of series wares. Among the most familiar of these are their Kingsware, Robin Hood, Dickensware, and Gibson Girl Series.

Values are determined by age, exceptional color and detail, and because of limited availability.

Mine Host, large, $90.00.

Animals and Birds

Cat, Persian, #999, black & white, 5" **90.00**
Dog, Alsatian, #1116, 6" **95.00**
Dog, Bulldog, K-1 ....**45.00**
Dog, Cocker Spaniel, #1187, golden, 5" **95.00**
Dog, English Setter with pheasant, #2529, 8" **300.00**

Dog, Pekingese, K-6 ....**30.00**
Elephant, #2644, 5½" **70.00**
Koala Bear............................**40.00**
Mountain Sheep, #2661 .....**170.00**
Pheasant, #1632.................**225.00**

Character Jugs

Apothecary, D6574, small.....**60.00**
Arriet, D6236, small, A.........**60.00**
Beefeater, D6251, ER handle, miniature........................**25.00**
Blacksmith, D-6571, large ...**95.00**
Cardinal, D6258, tiny **225.00**
Falconer, D6533, bone china, large..............................**95.00**
Fat Boy, D5840, small **85.00**
Gardener, D6638, miniature.**65.00**
Granny, D5521, large............**65.00**
Jarge, D6295, small............**295.00**
Long John Silver, small **50.00**
Mr Pickwick, D6260, tiny ...**225.00**
Neptune, D6548, large **78.00**
Old Charley, D6144, tiny **95.00**
Paddy, D5768, small **60.00**
Robinson Crusoe, small **50.00**
Sairey Gamp, D6146, tiny **95.00**
Samuel Johnson, small.......**275.00**
Sleuth, D6635, small **55.00**
Trapper, D6612, small **45.00**

Uncle Tom Cobbleigh, large, $425.00; White Haired Clown, large, $1,200.00; Punch and Judy Man, large, $600.00.

Walrus & Carpenter, D6608, miniature........................**50.00**
Yachtsman, D6622, large......**95.00**

Figurines

Affection, HN2236 ....**55.00**

Heart to Heart, HN2276, 5½", $400.00.

Amy, HN2958, white dress ...**95.00**
Ballerina, HN2116 ....**250.00**
Bride, HN2873 ....**130.00**
Catherine, HN2395 ....**150.00**
Clockmaker, HN2279..........**250.00**
Debbie, HN2385...................**95.00**
Emma, HN2934...................**110.00**
Fortune Teller, HN2159.....**395.00**
Good Catch, HN2558 ....**150.00**
Hilary, HN2335 ....**135.00**
Jester, HN308 .... **1,350.00**
Lambing Time, HN1890 .....**175.00**
Louise, HN2869 ....**145.00**
Mother's Help, HN2151 .....**175.00**
Penelope, HN1901 ....**295.00**
Rest Awhile, HN2728..........**175.00**
Serena, HN1868...................**675.00**
Thanks Doc, HN2731..........**185.00**
Wood Nymph, HN2192 ....**250.00**

Flambe

Dog of Fo **150.00**
Drake, 6½" **150.00**
Elephant, trunk raised, Sung,
5½"...................................**175.00**
Fox, sitting, 2¾x4" **150.00**

Penguin, 6" **150.00**
Vase, deer, 7" **165.00**
Vase, Sung, multicolor florals on
purple, Noke, 8½".........**545.00**
Vase, woodcut, #1619, 11" ..**285.00**

Series Ware

Bottle, sheep in sunset, hinged
top, marked, 5¼x2¼" **85.00**
Coffeepot, Dickens Ware, Tony
Weller, 7¼x3¾".............**185.00**
Cup, Nursery Rhymes, Old King
Cole, with Mother Goose
saucer **50.00**
Match striker, Dutch People, cou-
ple & crying child, marked,
3x4½" **145.00**
Pitcher, Dutch People, man, lady
on back, 2⅝x1½" **60.00**
Pitcher, Iazzk Walton, Perch or
Pike..., 12½"...................**225.00**
Plate, Coaching Days, William, Ye
Driver, 10" **65.00**
Plate, Old English Inns, King's
Head, Chigwell, 10" **40.00**

Tray, Dickensware, Bill Sykes, Noke, square, 8½" **110.00**
Vase, Dickensware, Barnaby Rudge, marked, 4¾" **70.00**
Vase, Gleaners & Gypsies, woman & children, 2" **70.00**
Vase, Shakespeare, Ophelia in pink, handles, 6⅜x4" ...**135.00**

Stoneware

Beaker, hunt scene................**60.00**
Creamer & sugar bowl, Slater's patent **100.00**
Humidor, figures in relief, brown to tan, marked, 5x4¼"..**120.00**
Jug, cows grazing on tan, Hanna Barlow, marked............**675.00**
Match holder, beehive **70.00**
Mug, King George V..............**55.00**
Ring dish, owl figural, brown & tan, 4x3¼".....................**295.00**
Vase, circus horses, Hanna Barlow, Lambeth, 12" **595.00**
Vase, Nouveau birds, square, FC Pope, 9"............................**80.00**

Toby Jugs

Cap'n Cuttle, D6266, 4½" ...**185.00**
Double XX, D6088, 6½".......**295.00**
Happy John, D6070, 5½" **55.00**
Jolly Toby, D6109, 6½" **65.00**
Mr Furrow, D6701, 4" **45.00**
Reverend Cassock, D6702 ....**45.00**
Sir Francis Drake, D6660.....**95.00**

Miscellaneous

Bottle, liquor; coat-of-arms for Chivas, brown/tan, 8½"..**95.00**
Bust, Sairey Gamp, D6047...**85.00**
Cigarette lighter, Beefeater..**95.00**
Jug, Leatherware with motto, silverplated rim, 8¼x6" ...**135.00**
Loving cup, Captain Cook, basalt, 10" **215.00**
Match holder, Mr Squeers **90.00**

Teapot, Old Charley........ **1,950.00**
Umbrella stand, blue & white florals, 24" **600.00**

Royal Haeger, Haeger

Manufactured in Dundee, Illinois, Haeger pottery has recently become the focus of much collector interest, especially the artware line and animal figures designed by Royal Hickman. These were produced from 1938 through the 1950s and are recognized by their strong lines and distinctive glazes.

Advertising sign....................**25.00**
Bookend, ram, standing, any color, R-132, 9" **18.00**
Bowl, swan, open back, any color, R-955, 11" long **20.00**
Candle holder & vase, Deco style, ball form, pink, 3" **5.00**

Fighting cocks, either style, $25.00.

Figurine, bull, red, 18½".......**50.00**
Figurine, fighting cock, oxblood agate, R-791, 11½".........**25.00**
Figurine, panther, ebony, R-495, 24" long **30.00**
Flower frog, double flying fish, Hickman design, pink & blue, 11½" **20.00**
Flower frog, nude astride fish, any color, R-363, 10" **20.00**

Lamp, table; non-figurine.....**30.00**
Lamp, TV; complete, M **25.00**
Planter, praying Madonna, white,
  original label **8.50**
Planter, shell, upright on waves,
  any color, R-483, 11" **18.00**
Spittoon, green.......................**22.00**
Vase, bird of paradise, any color,
  R-186, 12¾" **25.00**
Vase, deer, running, any color, R-
  706, 15"...........................**20.00**
Vase, deer, standing, any color, R-
  707, 15"...........................**20.00**
Vase, double cornucopia; any
  color, R-246, 16" long **25.00**
Vase, morning-glory, 3 openings,
  any color, R-452, 16" **22.00**
Vase, sailfish, R-271, 9" **22.00**

Roycroft

Elbert Hubbard, whose name
is familiarly associated with the
Arts and Crafts movement, established a community called Roycroft in New York at the turn of
the century. There, in addition to
the original print shop, furniture,
metal items, leather goods, and a
variety of other items were made,
bearing the 'R' in circle mark of
the Roycrofters.

Ash tray, hammered copper, floor
  standing, strap harp & match
  holder, 29x8½"..............**300.00**
Book, Gray's Elegy, Lyric Poem,
  1903, hand illuminated .**95.00**
Book, Pig Pen Pete, leather
  bound, 1914...................**25.00**
Book, Roycroft Story in Verse &
  Prose **20.00**
Bookends, copper, riveted.....**90.00**
Candlestick, copper, stem-like
  standard, 4-petal cup, 14",
  pair **550.00**
Catalog, Few Pieces of Roycroft
  Furniture, 1910, 8x6"...**110.00**

**Bookends, copper and brass,
signed with logo and Roycroft,
4¾", $250.00.**

Crumb set, hammered copper,
  rectangular tray, with
  sweeper........................**140.00**
Frame, desk-top calendar; ham-
  mered copper, small.......**45.00**
Jug, brown, stoneware **25.00**
Lamp, 4 wire sections in hammered
  copper shade, 14" **1,750.00**
Magazine stand #80, 5-shelf, logo
  & maple leaf on each side,
  64" **550.00**

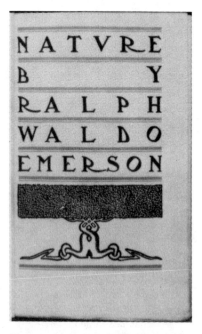

**Nature, by Ralph Waldo Emerson,
printed in East Aurora, 1905,
suede bound, EX, $325.00.**

Purse, hand-tooled floral on leather, mark, 8x6" **375.00**

Tray, hammered copper, worn patina, 11½ x4½ " **130.00**

Tray, hammered copper, 2-handle, #825, polished, 15".......**130.00**

Vase, florals in vertical rows, cylindrical, 9½ "............**450.00**

Vase, hammered copper, dark patina, ruffled, slim, 5".**185.00**

Vase, hammered copper, ovoid, #223, 5"........................**190.00**

Vase, hammered copper, tooled design at top, #236, 5" .**350.00**

Vase, silver design on copper, cylindrical, 6x3"...........**325.00**

Wall sconce, hammered copper, with green Steuben insert, 13x4"...........................**600.00**

Rugs, Hooked

Today recognized and admired as folk art, vintage hooked rugs as well as contemporary examples are prized for their primitive appeal, workmanship, and originality of design.

Cat, gray on green striped ground, small repair, 24½ x47", EX........................**275.00**

Cat on pillow, black on colored ground, minor fading, 20x33", EX.................................**175.00**

Collie, black & tan on gray with red & tan border, minor wear, 23x38" **185.00**

Compass star, faded colors, minor wear, 39" dia.................**400.00**

Dog, white with black details on light blue, dark border, 23x35"...........................**125.00**

Floral medallion, hearts in corners on blue, 23x38", NM.......**250.00**

Florals in light blue oval with dark multicolored border, 20x32"...........................**125.00**

Florals on black wool ground, signed & dated 1889, 30x45", EX **235.00**

Geometric stars, good old colors, minor wear, 26x103" ...**500.00**

Horse with trees & fence, bright colors, 1940s, 30x41"....**135.00**

Medallion of roses, flowered corners, striped borders, 26x38", EX **95.00**

Medallions within a black grid, 31x38", EX....................**175.00**

Moose in olive browns & greens, pink border stripes, 35x50", EX...............................**250.00**

Multicolor stripes with beige & yellow-green border, 26x40", EX...............................**55.00**

Puppies at fence with empty dish between, bright colors, 20x36", NM...................**225.00**

Roses on variegated green-striped ground, wide border, 14x24", EX **65.00**

Rosebuds and other flowers, American, 1800s, 32" x 52", $500.00.

Stylized leaves on blue-gray ground, bright colors, 79x112", EX.............. **2,600.00**

Russel Wright Dinnerware

Dinnerware designed by one of America's top industrial engineers is today attracting the interest of many. Some of his more popular lines are American Modern, manufactured by the Steubenville Pottery Company (1939-'59), and Iroquois, introduced in 1944.

American Modern, divided relish, 10" long, $45.00.

Ash tray, Sterling **65.00**
Bouillon, Sterling, 7-oz **8.00**
Bowl, fruit; sterling..............**65.00**
Bowl, vegetable; American Modern, with lid, 12" **25.00**
Butter dish, Casual, ½-lb......**65.00**
Casserole, spun aluminum, walnut handle, with lid **95.00**
Coffeepot, Casual, with lid ...**65.00**
Cup, American Modern.......... **8.00**
Ice pail, spun aluminum, rattan handle, with tongs, 6½" ..**45.00**
Mug, mug; spun aluminum ..**35.00**
Onion soup, Sterling, 10-oz ..**12.00**

Pitcher, Grass, 9¼", $40.00.

Plate, dessert; Casual, 7½ " ... **5.00**
Plate, dinner; Highlight........**15.00**

Plate, luncheon; Sterling **8.00**
Platter, Highlight, round **25.00**
Platter, Sterling, 13" **20.00**
Relish rosette, spun aluminum, small **50.00**
Teapot, American Modern **45.00**
Teapot, Casual, restyled **85.00**
Tray, spun aluminum, cork apple with stem handle **85.00**
Vase, spun aluminum, spherical, 7".....................................**65.00**

Salesman's Samples

Commonplace during the late 1800s and early 20th century, salesman's samples were small-scale copies of a particular product, often exact working models that enabled the salesman to demonstrate his wares to potential customers.

Album, Raphael Tuck Christmas cards, leather NM........**495.00**
Anchor, cast iron, EX **50.00**
Bat, Louisville Slugger, wood, marked with logo, 8"......**15.00**
Bible, 1886, EX.....................**75.00**
Books, children's, in leatherette case, EX **57.00**
Boot, rubber high top **8.00**
Bowl, cast iron, Griswold **65.00**
Calendar, Winchester, '26 ...**285.00**
Carpet, 2x4"..........................**15.00**
Central Petroleum Co sample kit, 10 bottles in case............**65.00**
Chest, walnut, with cedar lining, EX **125.00**
Dispenser, bulk oil; plated brass, detailed, with carrying case, 8".............................. **2,500.00**
Eyeglasses, small nose-fitting type, folding, with case ..**25.00**
Fry pan, cast iron, Penn Stoves, EX **25.00**
Furnace, Front Rank, fine details, working grates, NM . **2,750.00**
Hat, man's, felt, MIB **25.00**

Kit, Royal Silver, 1895, with catalog of same **95.00**
Padlock, Milwaukee Locks ...**22.50**
Pan, graniteware, Stewart Ware, EX **75.00**
Saddle, tooled leather, unmarked, EX **265.00**
Soap, washing machine form, Bendix, early **35.00**
Spittoon, blue & white graniteware, United States Stamping Co...W VA **750.00**
Step stool, chair, all wood construction, 10½" **400.00**

Table, T. Justinson & Son, 15" x 11", $195.00.

Tin, Libbey's Corned Beef, EX details, 1915, NM..........**35.00**
Vials, 21 containing oil products, ca 1890.........................**185.00**
Waffle iron, Stover Jr, NM..**115.00**
Windmill, Air Charger, partial paper label, 22", VG. **5,700.00**

Salt Shakers

Though salt has always been a valuable commodity, shakers as we know them today were not used until 1863 when a patent was issued for a mechanism capable of breaking up the lumps of salt in a bottle. In 1901 a method was developed that rendered the salt less apt to absorb moisture, and salt shakers began to be produced literally by the thousands in any available material – art glass, ceramics, wood, silver, brass, pot metal, and plastic.

Annie, clear **45.00**
Boot on Shell **20.00**
Bow & Tassel, white.............**22.50**
Bull's Eye & Daisy Variant, green eyes **24.00**
Burmese, ribbed barrel, Mt Washington, pair..................**400.00**
Christmas Barrel, amber, top dated, Dana Alden.......**100.00**
Christmas Panel, sapphire blue, top dated, Dana Alden .**140.00**
Corn Barrel, opaque white & custard, rare **55.00**
Currier & Ives, blue or vaseline, rare **55.00**
Diamond Point & Leaf, blue opaque, rare **60.00**
Egg in Cup, opaque, Mt Washington...................................**90.00**
Flower & Rain, blue or yellow, cased, rare **125.00**
Fluted Scrolls, blue opalescent with decoration, pair **85.00**
Forget-Me-Not, milk glass, tall, pair **45.00**
Heart, blue opaque, Dithridge, 1894-1897, pair **75.00**
Herringbone mother-of-pearl, pink, pewter top **290.00**
Intaglio, emerald green with gold, Northwood, rare, pair ..**250.00**
Leaf Bracket, opaque caramel slag, Indiana Tumbler Co, rare **175.00**
Leaf Mold, cranberry cased, silver flecks, pair...................**145.00**
Lobe Four, white/blue floral on yellow, 6-lobed, Mt Washington, pair......................**185.00**

Melon ribbed with fuchsias, Gillinder, $45.00 for the pair.

Nail, etched, red flashed.......**40.00**
Nestor, blue **22.00**
Optic, rubena with floral, Hobbs, pair in Wilcox frame with swans **190.00**
Panelled Sprig, milk glass with green decor, pair **30.00**
Peachblow, Wheeling, original tops, pair **650.00**
Pillar Ribbed, glossy burmese, Mt Washington, rare, pair.**800.00**
Raindrop mother-of-pearl, blue, rare, pair **410.00**
Rubena, hand-painted butterflies & plants, pair...............**145.00**
Thousand Eye, amber...........**18.00**

Novelty

Burro pulling cart with barrel shakers, Japan, pair **9.00**
Collie head, brown & white, Japan, pair **7.50**
Dog & fireplug, brown & white, Japan, pair **8.00**
Elephant, Dumbo style, black paint on red clay, Japan, 1950s, pair...................... **8.00**
Friar Tuck, Twin Winton, large, pair **35.00**
Kangaroo with baby in pouch, Japan, pair **14.00**

Kitten with real ball of yarn, squeaker in base, Japan, pair.................................. **8.00**
Lamb, sitting upright, white with black hoofs, Japan, 1950s, pair **7.50**
Mouse on wedge of cheese (2nd shaker) Japan, pair **10.00**
Owl doctor, rhinestone eyes, comic, ca 1960, pair **10.00**
Panda bear, black & white, smiling face, Japan, pair **10.00**
Penguin in top hat, 2nd wears scarf, Japan, pair...........**14.00**
Poodle with hat & bow at neck, tall slim form, Japan, 1960s, pair **14.00**
Popeye & Olive Oyl, Vandor Imports, 1980, pair **48.00**

Cottage Ware, salt and pepper shakers, mustard jar on tray, $25.00.

Raccoon, upright, bushy tail, Twin Winton, pair **35.00**
Siamese cat, polka dots & bow tie, Japan, pair **7.50**
Squirrel, long flat form with tail straight out, Japan, 1950s, pair **12.00**
Squirrel & hickory nut, Japan, 1950s, pair...................... **5.00**
Tinkerbell on a flower (2nd shaker), Japan, pair.......**15.00**
Turtle wearing vest & hat, Japan, pair **10.00**

Schoop, Hedi

From the 1940s through the '50s, Hedi Schoop managed a small operation in North Hollywood, California, where she produced novelty wares such as figurines, lamps, and other decorative items.

Bowl, girl, skirt forms bowl, mauve & gold, 12".........**50.00**
Console set, boy trumpeter & dancing girl, footed bowl, 3-piece..............................**130.00**
Cookie jar, Queen of Hearts, 12x12"............................**75.00**

Dutch boy and girl, 10½", $75.00 for the pair.

Figurine, Dutch boy, 11½".....**35.00**
Figurine, flower girl with applied flowers, 9"......................**24.00**

Figurine, girl with basket on shoulder, 11"...................**25.00**
Figurine, Oriental girl with lantern, 11½" **35.00**
Figurine, southern belle, 12" .**40.00**
Flower holder, 2 girls, hands joined, rare, 8"...............**85.00**
Lamp, TV; Comedy & Tragedy, rare, large....................**150.00**
Planter, geisha with umbrella, blue, #223 ....**24.00**

Scouting Collectibles

Founded in England in 1907 by Major General Lord Baden-Powell, scouting remains an important institution in the life of young boys and girls everywhere. Recently scouting-related memorabilia has attracted a following, and values of many items have escalated dramatically in the last few years. Early 1st edition handbooks often bring prices of $100.00 and more; vintage uniforms are scarce and highly valued; and one of the rarer medals, the Life Saving Honor Medal is worth several hundred dollars to collectors.

Blanket, camp; khaki, wool, stamped BSA..................**20.00**
Book, Bear Cub, 1938, EX ...**10.00**
Book, Cub Master's Pack Book, 1939, EX **12.00**
Book, Scout's Test, Saalfield, 1916, EX **5.00**
Book, The History of the BSA, 1937, EX **12.00**
Box, firemaking equipment; early, 26" long, VG **35.00**
Bugle, Rexcraft Official, complete, 1930 ....**30.00**
Calendar, Our Heritage, Rockwell, 1950, 16x30", NM..**15.00**
Calendar, Spirit of America, Rockwell, 1929, 16x30", EX...**50.00**

1966 calendar, Norman Rockwell illustration on each page, 14" x 8", $16.00.

Coin, National Jamboree, silver, 1969, EX **5.00**
Encyclopedia, 1954, VG **6.00**
Field set (telephone & telegraph), early, VG **125.00**
Figurine, GSA, copper & bronze, small **18.00**
Figurine, Rockwell Cub Scout with dog **20.00**
Flag, troop; 1st issue, red & white, 1st class emblem **17.00**
Game, Boy Scout Ten Pins, 1914, VG **22.00**
Game, Scouting for Boy Scouts, Milton Bradley **50.00**
Handbook, GSA, 1947, M **5.00**
Knife, pen; World Jamboree, 1967, VG **10.00**
Magazine, Scouting, Norman Rockwell on cover, G **5.00**
Map, World Jamboree, 1929 . **25.00**
Medal, Scout Contest, 3-color ribbon, 1930s **13.00**

Morse code signaler, MIB **10.00**
Neckerchief, National Jamboree, 1957, VG **8.00**
Patch, National Jamboree, leather, M **15.00**
Patch, World Jamboree, leather, 1967, M **7.00**
Pin, hat; gold-tone, M **4.00**
Plate, Scoutmaster, Knowles, 1977 .... **25.00**
Post card, Boy Scouts First Aid, 1915, G **8.00**
Sheet music, Boy Scouts' March, 1911, VG **8.00**
Sign, BSA, Lawrence Wilber, 1952, NM **10.00**
Signal set, BSA, EX in box ... **20.00**
Tie rack, wood **10.00**
Uniform, complete with pins & patches, GSA, 1929, EX. **50.00**
Uniform, shirt & pants, BSA, 1930s **50.00**

Beadcraft kit, $12.00.

Sebastians

Sold primarily in gift stores in the New England states since the 1930s, Sebastian miniatures were designed by Prescott W. Baston who withdrew the line from production in 1976. At that time, one hundred of the more than four hundred original models were selected to continue in production by the Lance Corporation. The discontinued figures have become highly collectible.

Abraham Lincoln, Marblehead label **60.00**

Aunt Betzy Trotwood, Marble-
head label **55.00**
Becky Thatcher, green label.**35.00**
Betsy Ross, red label **25.00**
Blue Belle Highlander **145.00**
Building Days, pair...............**69.00**
Clown, blue label **95.00**
Colonial Blacksmith..............**35.00**
Colonial Kitchen, no label, Mar-
blehead era......................**55.00**
Commodore Stephen Decatur,
1958 ....**100.00**
David Copperfield & Wife, Mar-
blehead label **60.00**
Gardener Man, 1966...........**210.00**
Gathering Tulips.................**200.00**
Huckleberry Finn, Marblehead
label, MIB.......................**65.00**
James & Elizabeth Monroe.**195.00**
Jell-O Giraffe.......................**275.00**
John Smith & Pocahontas, Mar-
blehead era, pair **215.00**
Lincoln, green label...............**40.00**
Madonna, chair, green label.**40.00**
Neighboring Pews...............**175.00**
Olde James Fort, 1957 ....**190.00**
Our Lady of Laleche, 1954 .**200.00**
Outboard Fishers, blue label.**40.00**

**Phoebe, House of Seven
Gables, 2¾", $95.00.**

Plaque, Marblehead label...**200.00**
Praying Hands, 1956 ....**200.00**

Sam Houston, blue label.......**40.00**
Shaker Man & Woman, Marble-
head era, pair...............**125.00**
Simple Simon, Howard Johnson,
signed PW Baston........**145.00**
Son of the Desert, 1960.......**140.00**
Swan Boat, Boston Public Gar-
den, Marblehead era....**160.00**
The Favored Scholar, 1952 .**150.00**
Weaver & Loom, Marblehead
label................................**55.00**

Sewing Items

Sewing notions from the
1800s and early 20th century
such as whimsical figural tape
measures, beaded satin pincush-
ions, blown glass darning eggs,
and silver and gold thimbles are
pleasant reminders of a bygone
era – ladies' sewing circles, quilting bees, and beautifully hand-
stitched finery.

Basket, wicker, hand-painted flo-
rals, 9" diameter **25.00**
Bodkin, brass, 1870, set of 4 .**65.00**
Crochet hook, ivory, 10".......**20.00**
Darner, blue glass, foot shape,
molded, 5"......................**45.00**
Darner, ebony, sterling repousse
handle, marked, 4½"......**65.00**
Darner, blue iridescent glass with
gray loopings, 5⅜"........**140.00**
Darning egg, wood with fancy
sterling handle...............**50.00**
Emery, bean pod figural, green
satin, 2¼".......................**30.00**
Emery, strawberry form with ster-
ling top, unmarked **25.00**
Kit, marbleized Catalin, advertis-
ing..................................**35.00**
Kit, suede with bullet-type holder,
unmarked **4.00**
Needle case, celluloid, rolling pin
form, blue, 4¼" **40.00**
Needle case, ivory **20.00**
Pincushion, barrel, ivory, cushion
on each end, 1¼" high **65.00**

Needle case, sterling, with thimble inside, 2½", $85.00.

Pincushion, brass, embossed butterfly on leaf-form lid, 1880s, 2¾" **135.00**

Pincushion, leather shoe, plush cushion, 4¼" **28.00**

Punch, eyelet; slide gauge, black wood handle, dated Oct 1909, 5½" **35.00**

Ribbon threader, sterling, fish shape **65.00**

Scissors, embroidery; sterling, stork figural **75.00**

Sewing bird, silverplate, heart key/clamp, Pat 1852, 1940s repro **95.00**

Sewing box, plush with satin interior, unmarked **50.00**

Tape measure, celluloid, bear form **55.00**

Tape measure, celluloid, Lydia Pinkham, large **28.00**

Tape measure, metal, straw hat form, 2" **165.00**

Tape measure, dog in relief, 1" diameter, $55.00.

Tape measure, plastic, house, gray with red roof, 1½" ..**50.00**

Tape measure, red heart shape, Germany **15.00**

Tatting shuttle, ivory **10.00**

Tatting shuttle, mother-of-pearl, EX **55.00**

Thimble, gold overlay, crown mark, USA......................**45.00**

Thimble, gold paneled, Star mark, USA **90.00**

Thimble, sterling, florals, marked Goldsmith/Stern.............**20.00**

Thimble, sterling, birds, Simons shield mark, USA **50.00**

Thimble, sterling, dots & diamonds, Ketcham & McDougall **45.00**

Thimble, sterling, geometric design, Simons shield mark, USA **20.00**

Thimble, sterling, Mother engraved on band, Simons.............**30.00**

Thimble, sterling, raised circles, anchor mark, USA **30.00**

Thimble, sterling with gold & stones, 8-point star mark, Germany.........................**45.00**

Thimble, vegetable ivory, 2", in carved holder.................**95.00**

Thimble, 10k gold, Ketcham & McDougall, USA **100.00**

Thimble, 14k gold, scenic, unmarked **115.00**

Thimble holder, glass shoe, unmarked **15.00**

Thimble holder, goat & cart, unmarked **35.00**

Thimble holder, sterling, reticulated vines & berries, Webster.................................**95.00**

Thimble stand, bronze rooster, Austria..........................**28.00**

Shaving Mugs

Often as elegant as the handlebar mustache sported by its owner, the shaving mug was usually made of china or earthenware, well decorated with floral sprays, gold trim, depictions of the owner's trade, or his name. Today the 'occupationals' are most highly valued, especially those representing an unusual trade or fraternal affiliation.

Before & After, shaving scenes, Lancaster & Sandland Ltd, England **110.00**
Flowers in gold & enameling on porcelain, EX...................**12.50**

Floral, gold trim, unmarked, Germany, 3½", $55.00.

Gold band, hand-painted roses, marked Gold Kante **39.00**
Masonic, gold symbols & rim, eye in center, Royal China International **125.00**
Masonic symbols in blue & yellow with gold, marked T&V Limoges, EX...........................**75.00**
Occupational, artist, palette & brushes, J&C Bavaria .**355.00**
Occupational, blacksmith, horse's head in horseshoe, T&V Limoges **105.00**
Occupational, butcher, tools & steer's head, gold trim .**100.00**
Occupational, cyclist, rider on dirt road, gold trim, EX **525.00**
Occupational, deliveryman, horse-drawn wagon, France ..**265.00**

Occupational, fireman, horse-drawn fire wagon & men, Germany, NM..............**675.00**
Occupational, material shop, clerk & customer, EX **215.00**
Occupational, policeman, man in uniform, Johnson's Barber Supply...........................**155.00**
Occupational, telegraph operater, gold 'key,' Austria, EX .**210.00**
Occupational, waiter, man with tray, gold trim **500.00**
Patriotic, US flag over gold name, Austria, EX.....................**75.00**
Personalized, name & much trim in gold, Royal China International **22.50**
Personalized, name in black, worn gold, T&V Limoges **20.00**
Silverplated with milk glass insert, gold trim, S&L Co, NY, EX............................**35.00**
Sportsman, dog & fox at fence, gold trim, Austria **65.00**
Sportsman, hunter shooting at flying bird, worn gold...**105.00**

Scuttle mug, horse's head, Germany #32, $80.00.

Shawnee

The novelty planters, vases, cookie jars, salt and pepper shakers, and 'Corn' dinnerware made by the Shawnee Pottery of Ohio are attractive, fun to collect, and are still available at reasonable prices. The company operated from 1937 until 1961 marking their wares with 'Shawnee, U.S.A.' and a number series, or 'Kenwood.'

Bank, bulldog **50.00**
Cookie jar, Cookie House, Cottage Line...............................**100.00**
Cookie jar, Dutch Boy, blue/yellow under-glaze paint...........**50.00**
Cookie jar, Dutch Girl.........**120.00**
Cookie jar, Elephant, #60 ....**45.00**
Cookie jar, Jug, #75...............**80.00**
Cookie jar, Lucky Elephant ..**60.00**
Cookie jar, Smiley Pig, blue bandana or shamrocks.........**50.00**
Cookie jar & bank, Winnie .**135.00**
Corn, bowl, mixing; 5"...........**22.00**
Corn, bowl, mixing; 8"...........**35.00**
Corn, bowl, soup or cereal **30.00**
Corn, casserole, 1½-quart.....**50.00**
Corn, dish, 6"......................... **7.00**
Corn, jug, 1-quart.................**50.00**
Corn, platter, 12"...................**40.00**
Corn, relish tray **22.00**
Corn, sugar bowl, #78 ....**20.00**
Corn, utility jar **30.00**

Corn creamer, #70, $15.00.

Creamer, Puss 'N Boots **20.00**
Creamer, Smiley Pig, #86 .....**22.00**
Darner, woman **20.00**
Figurine, gazelle, #614 ....**40.00**

Figurine, Oriental with parasol, #601 .... **8.00**
Figurine, Pekingese **22.00**
Figurine, tumbling bear **22.00**
Pitcher, Little Bo-Peep, #47..**35.00**
Pitcher, Little Boy Blue **45.00**
Planter, bird rests on side.....**12.00**
Planter, boy at fence **6.00**
Planter, boy with chicken **12.00**
Planter, canopy bed, #734 ....**30.00**
Planter, cat playing saxophone, #729 ....**20.00**
Planter, donkey with cart, #538, small **5.00**
Planter, Dutch kids at well ..**12.00**
Planter, gristmill...................**10.00**
Planter, leaf bowl, #3025 .....**12.00**
Planter, Polynesian girl **16.00**
Planter, train set, 4-piece ...**100.00**
Salt & pepper shakers, Chanticleer, small, pair.............**14.00**
Salt & pepper shakers, Dutch boy, pair **16.00**
Salt & pepper shakers, lobster, large, pair......................**15.00**
Salt & pepper shakers, Mugsey, large, pair......................**20.00**
Salt & pepper shakers, Sailor Boy, pair................................... **8.00**
Salt & pepper shakers, Winnie Pig, large, pair...............**25.00**
Teapot, elephant....................**70.00**
Vase, Bow Knot, #819 ....**14.00**

Teapot, Tom Tom, The Piper's Son, $40.00.

Vase, cornucopia, #835.......... 8.00
Vase, doe in shadow box 16.00
Vase, leaf, #823....................20.00
Vase, twin dove, yellow.........15.00
Wall pocket, bow.................... 8.00
Wall pocket, Little Jack Horner,
　#585 ....16.00
Wall pocket, mantel clock.....16.00

Sheet Music

The most valuable examples of sheet music are those related to early transportation, ethnic themes, Disney characters, a particularly popular artist or composer, or with a cover illustration done by a well-known artist. Production of sheet music peaked during the 'Tin Pan Alley Days,' from the 1880s until the 1930s. Covers were made as attractive as possible to lure potential buyers, and today's collectors sometimes frame and hang them as they would a print. Flea markets are a good source for sheet music, and prices are usually very reasonable. Most are available for under $5.00. Some of the more valuable examples are listed here.

American Wedding March, ET
　Paull cover, 1919, EX.....48.00
Barny Google, Rose & Conrad,
　cartoon cover, 1923, VG.12.00
Bibbidi-Bobbidi-Boo, from Cinderella, NM 18.00
Broncho Buster, Madden & Jardon, color cover, 1907, G . 7.50
Buttons & Bows, Bob Hope &
　Jane Russell, 1948.........12.00
Carnival King, black & white
　cover, 1911, small..........20.00
Comin' Through the Rye, Andre,
　color cover, ca 1860, G ...10.00
Crazy Bone Rag, Johnson, Black
　cover, 1913, VG 12.00

Dear Heart, Rolf Armstrong, Church & Co. Publishing, 1919, $15.00.

Dawn of the Century, ET Paull
　cover, EX.......................20.00
Der Fuehrer's Face, Wallace, color
　Disney cover, 1942, VG..12.00
Don't Fence Me In, Cole Porter,
　stars on cover, 1944 ......15.00
For Me & My Gal, Judy Garland
　cover, 1947 ....15.00
I Still Love To Kiss You Goodnight, 1937 .... 8.00
March to Victory, Churchill portrait cover, 1940 ....15.00
Midnight Flyer, ET Paull train
　cover, 1903, EX 35.00
Napolean's Last Charge, color
　cover, 1910 re-issue, VG..12.00
National Emblem March, Bagley,
　1908, VG 5.00
Oklahoma, from Broadway play,
　1943, EX........................12.00
On the Good Ship Lollipop,
　Shirley Temple, 1934 ....14.00
Over the Rainbow, Wizard of Oz,
　picture cover, EX 15.00
Paul Revere's Ride, rider on horse
　color cover, 1905, VG 18.00
Poor Little Rich Girl, Shirley
　Temple cover, EX...........15.00

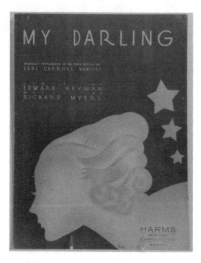

My Darling, Harms Inc., NY, Chappell & Co. Ltd., London, 1932, $15.00.

Riders in the Sky, Burl Ives cover, 1949 ....**14.00**
Rudolph the Red-Nosed Reindeer, 1949 .... **7.50**
Serenade of the Stars, from Mad About Music, 1938 ....**10.00**
Someday My Prince Will Come, Snow White, 1937, NM..**22.00**
Spirit of France, ET Paull color cover, 1919, VG **22.00**
Stars & Stripes Forever, Sousa on cover, 1897, EX **12.00**
That Mysterious Rag, Berlin & Snyder, color cover, 1911, EX...**18.00**
Trolly Car Song, from Meet Me in St Louis, Garland cover, 1944, NM **17.50**
Whistle While You Work, from Snow White, 1937, NM .**22.00**
You're Gonna Lose Your Gal, Kate Smith, 1933, EX.............. **8.00**
Yours for a Song, 1939 World's Fair, EX **15.00**

Slot Machines

Now legal in many states, old 'one-arm bandits' are being restored, used for home entertainment, or simply amassed in collections. Especially valuable are those from the turn of the century, rare or unique models, and those with unusually fancy trim.

Bally Hold & Draw, EX.......**500.00**
Bally Progressive, 1973 .. **1,300.00**
Bally Royal Draw, console model, 1940, VG original.........**700.00**
Bally Spark Plug, countertop, 1934, EX original..... **2,600.00**
Bally 5¢ Reliance, EX..... **3,500.00**
Bally 5¢-25¢ Double Bell, EX original **3,000.00**
Buckley Long-Shot Horse Race, EX original **595.00**
Buckley 5¢ Bonanza, EX **875.00**
Caille Jumbo Success...... **1,600.00**

Caille Roulette, 25¢ table model with oak case, ca 1925, 18", EX, $5,000.00.

Caille Lion, floor model, 1901, M **1,350.00**
Fey Silver Cup, countertop, 1910, EX original **1,250.00**
Genco 1¢ Buster Ball, EX...**250.00**
Horsehead Bonus 25¢, replated, EX **220.00**

Jennings Pace Front, VG....**500.00**
Jennings Sportsman, 1938, EX original **2,100.00**
Jennings 1¢ Little Duke, VG original........................... **1,800.00**
Jennings 25¢ Dutch Boy, EX original........................... **1,500.00**
Jennings 5¢ Duchess, NM . **1,600.00**
Keeney 5¢ Super Bell, VG original **500.00**
Keeney 5¢ Super Bell, console, complete, EX original ..**795.00**
Mills Pilot, EX original... **5,500.00**

Mills, F.O.K. Liberty Bell, 5¢ play, 1936, NM, $2,000.00.

Mills 10¢ Castle Front.... **1,500.00**
Mills 25¢ Futurity, EX.... **2,400.00**
Mills 5¢ Bursting Cherry, 1939, EX original **1,750.00**
Mills 5¢ Lion Front, EX.. **1,700.00**
Pace Races, EX original.. **4,500.00**
Pace 5¢ Comet, EX.......... **1,500.00**

Smurf Collectibles

A creation of Pierro 'Peyo' Culliford, the little blue Smurfs that we have all come to love have found their way to the collectibles market of today. There is a large number of items currently available at reasonable prices though some items such as metal lunch boxes, cereal premiums and boxes, and promotional items and displays are beginning to attract special interest. Because the Smurfs' 'birthplace' was in Belgium, many items are European in nature. The values listed here are for items in mint condition.

Those seeking further information may contact the Smurf Collectors' Club, listed in our Directory under New York.

Bank, Smurf House, porcelain, scarce **18.00**
Book, European, from $8 to .**35.00**
Calendar, European, ca 1983 to 1984, up to **15.00**
Calendar, European, late 1970s, from $15 up to **40.00**
Mug, limited edition, from $7 up to **15.00**
Mug, Travel America Series, minimum value **4.00**
Music box, limited edition, from $25 up to........................**45.00**
Pez dispenser, European........ **3.00**
Plate, limited edition, from $15 up to...............................**40.00**
Post card, European, from $1 up to **5.00**
Smurf figure, European, painted, 1965-1979, 2", up to **150.00**
Smurf figure, pewter, American Pewter, from $10 to........**30.00**
Smurf figurine, European, 1965-1979, 2", minimum value . **3.00**
Smurfagram from France, Belgium, Greece, Portugal, minimum value..................... **4.00**
Smurfette Happy Birthday figurine, porcelain, from $9 up to **15.00**

Snuf-A-Rette Ash Trays

Made in the late thirties and early forties for railroads, hotels, world's fairs, various businesses, and for general home use, Snuf-A-Rette ash trays are gaining in popularity largely because of their fine Deco styling. Available in various shapes and colors, the railroad, world's fair, and advertising trays are most popular and command higher prices.

#25, Stacy China Co..............**11.00**
#26, Stacy China Co..............**11.00**
#801, National Porcelain Co.**17.50**
#802, National Porcelain Co.**10.00**
#810, Ekstrand Mfg Co **20.00**
#818, Ekstrand Mfg Co **14.00**
#820, Ekstrand Mfg Co **17.50**
#821, Ekstrand Mfg Co **17.50**
#834, Ekstrand Mfg Co **14.00**
#835, Ekstrand Mfg Co **17.50**
#841, Ekstrand Mfg Co **20.00**
#842, Ekstrand Mfg Co **20.00**
#852, Ekstrand Mfg Co **14.00**
Advertising, all styles, range from
    $30 to **60.00**
Railroad, all styles, range from
    $25 up to..........................**50.00**
World's Fair, all styles, range
    from $25 up to **30.00**

Soda Fountain Collectibles

The days of the neighborhood ice cream parlor are gone; the soda jerk, the mouth-watering confections he concocted, the high counter and bar stools now a thing of the past. But memories live on through the soda glasses, ice cream scoops, milk shake machines, and soda fountain signs that those reluctant to forget treasure today.

Bottle, Howell's Cherry Julep Syrup, fancy top, M **175.00**
Cone holder, glass, original lid, 13" **300.00**
Cone holder, glass & nickel-plated metal, 15" **300.00**
Container, malted milk; Milkose, glass, aluminum lid **85.00**
Cup, Armour's Bouillon Cubes, china **25.00**
Dipper, Clipper Fountain Supply, VG................................**300.00**
Dipper, Cold Dog cylinder ..**400.00**
Dipper, curved square, VG .**275.00**
Dipper, Gem, size 20 ....**45.00**
Dipper, Indestructo #4 ....**40.00**
Dipper, sandwich; Sanitary, thumb push **250.00**
Dish, banana split; crystal, fluted sides, holding tab **7.00**
Dish, banana split; crystal ...**15.00**

Dispenser, original pump, ca 1915, $1,500.00.

Dispenser, Lash's Orangeade Soda, 1920s, EX **250.00**
Dispenser, Treet, orange lustre glass, incised pump......**700.00**

Display, Eat It All, papier-mache ice cream cone, 21".......**100.00**

Fan, soda fountain related, pre-1950 ....**25.00**

Flavor board, tin, ca 1900...**400.00**

Fountain glass, Canada Dry, crest, with syrup line **15.00**

Fountain glass, Dr Brown's Celery Tonic, side logo.........**25.00**

Fountain glass, Hires, Enjoy Natures Delicious Drink, with logo **40.00**

Fountain glass, Julep, yellow, with syrup line..............**10.00**

Fountain glass, Purox Beverages, with logo **15.00**

Fountain glass, Voegel's ice cream cone, gold diamond **15.00**

Fountain glass, Zipp's Grape-O, grape cluster **25.00**

Fountain glass, 7-Up, green .**15.00**

Jar, malt; clear, embossed circle, Horlick lid, 1-gal **48.00**

Juicer, Arnold Electric..........**45.00**

Malted milk container, Bordens, aluminum.......................**30.00**

Malted milk container, Coors, aluminum **30.00**

Mixer, AC Gilbert **70.00**

Mixer, Hamilton Beach, marble base, early, EX **175.00**

Mixer, malted milk; Horlick's Lum & Abner **35.00**

Mug, Armour's Veribest Root Beer, pottery **50.00**

Mug, Bowey's Old Style Root Bear, buoy trade mark...**50.00**

Mug, Rochester Root Beer, embossed glass, large **20.00**

Mug, Schuester Root Beer **40.00**

Photo, interior view, front counter service, post-1905...........**10.00**

Slicer, Dover Co...................**400.00**

Straw dispenser, Sani Server, round **200.00**

Straw holder, clear, Heisey, open side...............................**500.00**

Straw holder, common, with lid & insert, 12".....................**140.00**

Straw holder, Depression glass, pink...............................**400.00**

Tin container, Runkel's Chocolate, early graphics, NM **350.00**

Trade card, ice-cream related . **5.00**

Wafer holder, Reliance........**250.00**

Window, leaded glass, Ice Cream, ca 1900, 20x29" **425.00**

Spongeware

Utility earthenware from the last quarter of the 1800s decorated with sponged-on colors is popular with today's collectors, especially those interested in primitives, country antiques, and American pottery. Usually the color was applied at random, although occasionally simple patterns were attempted. Blue on white are the most treasured colors; but red, green, rust, black, and tan were also used, sometimes in combination. You may find some items trimmed with gold.

Bowl, blue & white, blue stripes, hairline, 4x10½" **145.00**

Bowl, brown & blue on cream, 4x7" diameter...............**135.00**

Bowl, mixing; blue & white, 6x11", EX.....................**185.00**

Cookie jar, blue & green with red stencil: Cookies, 10".....**300.00**

Ladies' spittle cup, 2", $250.00.

Cooler, blue & white, 2-piece, straight top/ovoid base, 4-gal, EX **995.00**
Creamer, blue & white, ovoid, 4", EX **115.00**
Jar, blue & white, with lid, missing bail, 6", EX **140.00**
Pitcher, blue & white, bulbous bottom, 9", EX..............**185.00**
Pitcher, blue & white, tankard form, 6¾", EX...............**150.00**
Plate, blue & white, scalloped, ironstone, 9", NM **125.00**
Plate, cake; blue & white, side handles, 10½".................**125.00**
Platter, blue & white, Trenton NJ, 12x8"..............................**200.00**

Platter, blue and white sponging, 11" x 8", $165.00.

Platter, blue & white, 12"...**170.00**
Soap dish, blue & white, 6" diameter................................**125.00**
Tray, blue & white, minor stains/pinpoints, 14"....**210.00**
Tray, blue & white, scalloped, 11¼" long **175.00**

Spoons

Since the 1890s, spoons have been issued as souvenirs, to commemorate an event, in honor of a famous person, or on the occasion of a holiday. Today's collectors prefer those with high relief designs on handle as well as bowl, Indian or other full-figure handles, enameled or gold-washed trim,

and examples that are dated or from a limited edition. While the design is more important than the material, silver is much preferred over silverplate.

Alaska, totem pole enameled handle, JM Co **70.00**
Atlantic City NJ on fancy handle; lighthouse engraved in bowl, sterling **17.50**
Bar Harbor, sky view in bowl, fish handle, Shepard......**45.00**
Buffalo in high relief with daggers/rifle/rope on handle, plain bowl.......................**36.00**
California Pacific Expo, made for California Perfume Co...**60.00**
Calla lily figural handle, plain bowl, Watson **27.50**
Catalina Island, Old Abe at handle finial, plain bowl **24.00**
Catalina Island engraved in bowl, large fish finial..............**25.00**
Chicago, bird cutout in handle, plain bowl, Watson........**32.00**
Chicago Fair 1891, Women's Building embossed in bowl, sterling **50.00**
Chicago in bowl, grapevines on handle, monogram **15.00**
Christmas, 1971, Gorham **24.00**
Cincinnati & Soldiers Monument in bowl, scroll handle, Wallace................................**20.00**
Cliff House, San Francisco on handle............................**20.00**
Detroit City seal in bowl, coat of arms on handle, G..........**35.00**
Floral handle, plain bowl, Howard, demitasse **17.50**
Golden Gate embossed in bowl, state seal & miner on handle reverse, 6"........................**18.00**
Grand Canyon etched in bowl, swastika handle finial ...**20.00**
Green Bay WI engraved in gold-washed bowl, bead-edged handle, demi.................**28.00**

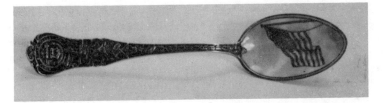

Colorado, sterling with enamel bowl, 1908, 5½" long, $145.00.

Holly around star on handle, Gorham, 1971 ....30.00

Honolulu, beach cutout in frame on handle, 6" 22.00

Illinois State Prison, Joliet in bowl, corn cutout in handle, 6" 110.00

Independence Hall & Liberty Bell on handle, plain bowl.....20.00

Indian handle, scene in bowl, English hallmarks 100.00

Indian head with 1 feather on handle, Ladawga engraved in bowl................................35.00

Jacksonville FL embossed in bowl, alligator handle finial, sterling 55.00

Lake Placid NY in bowl, Indian in canoe at top of handle, Lunt...............................65.00

Los Angeles embossed on handle, plain bowl, demitasse ...25.00

McKinley & eagle embossed on handle, plain bowl, dated handle reverse 50.00

Mexico, Aztec calendar & Mexico on handle, plain bowl 15.00

Montana on handle, cowboy on horse in bowl..................95.00

New Orleans, Jackson monument on handle reverse...........32.00

NY Skyline on handle, Brooklyn Bridge in bowl 80.00

Oregon, scenes both sides of handle, plain bowl................20.00

Peoria IL, Mohammed Temple engraved in bowl, plain handle, 5½" 15.00

Pittsburgh seal, Wm Pitt on handle, plain bowl, Watson..20.00

Portland, letters form handle, plain bowl, marked SM..35.00

Potsville PA engraved in bowl, wavy handle, Shepard ...17.50

Salt Lake City, Temple Square bowl, state seal on handle, 5⅛" 25.00

San Francisco on handle, bear in bowl 40.00

Seattle World's Fair scene on handle, plain bowl, 4⅛".......12.00

Sioux City engraved in bowl, corn cutout handle, Watson...22.00

St Augustine on handle, grapefruit in bowl....................35.00

Stork figural handle, scale embossed in bowl, marked, sterling 50.00

Sumter SC engraved in bowl, holly cutout in handle, Alvin, 5⅝" 27.50

Uncle Sam figural handle, Capitol scene embossed in bowl .80.00

Utah seal & 1896 embossed on handle, demitasse 17.50

Westerly RI, men's head embossed on handle, plain bowl, 4¼" 17.50

Yale Boat House engraved in bowl, oar figural handle, Towle, 5" 17.50

Yellowstone, bear figural handle, plain bowl, Robbins 27.50

Zodiac sign of June, marked Knowlton 45.00

Sports Collectibles

Memorabilia related to sports of any kind is attracting a following of collectors, many of which specialize in the particular sport that best holds their interests.

Baseball punch card, ca 1920s – '30s, unused, $70.00.

Bat, Dave Kingman, Louisville Slugger, 17" **10.00**
Book, Baseball & Tennis Rules, Stahl & Dean, 1924 ......**20.00**
Book, How To Play Tennis, Spalding, 1914, EX..................**37.50**
Cup, cyclist's, collapsible, Pat 1897 ....**30.00**
Menu, Yankee Stadium Club, stadium cover, 1960s, M **15.00**
Nodder, Green Bay Packers, 1967, EX **30.00**
Paperweight, cast iron, baseball form **25.00**
Pennant, Yale, 17", EX.......... **5.00**
Pin-back button, University of Michigan with ribbon & football, NM..........................**60.00**
Plaque, Chicago Cubs, old-style Division Champs, 1984 .**20.00**
Program, Harlem Globe Trotters souvenir, 1954 ....**14.00**
Program, Kentucky Derby, 1945, EX **15.00**
Program, NFL football, Dodgers vs Redskins, 1937 ....**25.00**

Program, University of Illinois vs Michigan, 1927 ....**40.00**
Program, World Series..........**15.00**
Seat cushion, Milwaukee Braves, NM....................................**10.00**
Statue, golfer in knickers swings club, gilded metal, 4" **25.00**
Whistle, athletic; brass, marked Lowe & Campbell, EX..... **5.00**
Yearbook, St Louis Cardinals souvenir, 1967, NM..............**20.00**

Wax packs, 1976, $15.00 to $30.00 per pack.

Staffordshire

The Staffordshire district of England is perhaps the best-known pottery-producing area in the world. Since the early 1700s, hundreds of potteries have operated there, producing wares as varied as their names. While many examples are extremely rare and expensive, it is still possible to find small but interesting Staffordshire items at nearly any good market.

Creamer, farm wagon scene, pink transfer...........................**50.00**
Dog, cocker spaniel, seated, late, 8½" **80.00**
Dog, pekingese on cushion, splashed-on paint, ca 1790, 3½"..............................**250.00**
Dog, poodle, sanded coat, pink purse in mouth, 3", EX .**75.00**
Figurine, boy on back of large dog, ca 1860, 10¼" **200.00**

Figurine, cockerel, gaudy decor, 1835, 6" **300.00**
Figurine, lion, blown glass eyes, 14" long, pair **350.00**
Figurine, man playing French horn, ca 1800, 9" **250.00**
Figurine, man with dog, lady with dog, 7", pair **180.00**
Figurine, Red Riding Hood & wolf, 5" **65.00**
Inkwell, 3 children on lid, 2 inserts, 5", NM **285.00**
Pitcher, child & dog in relief, copper lustre, 2½" **75.00**

Pitcher, lady and dogs in relief, figural dog handle, blue and white, 8¾", $225.00.

Pitcher, Chinese scene, multicolor on white, 7" **85.00**
Pitcher, woman with 4 children, blue transfer, 7" **185.00**
Plate, beggar & figures, brown transfer on white, octagonal, 1840s, 6" **30.00**
Plate, girl & goats, dark blue transfer, 7¾" **70.00**
Spill vase, Red Riding Hood & wolf, 10" **200.00**

Teapot, peacock on pearlware, 1810, 13", EX...............**500.00**
Vase, 2 swans by tree, coleslaw foliage, 4¾", EX..............**65.00**

Stangl

Originally known as the Fulper Pottery, the Stangl Company was founded in 1913 and until its closing in 1972 produced many lines of dinnerware as well as various types of artware. Birds modeled after the prints of Audubon were introduced in the early 1940s. More than one hundred different birds were produced, most of which are marked with 'Stangl' and a four-digit number to identify the species. Though a limited few continue to be produced, since 1976 they have been marked with the date of their production.

Ash tray, Antique Gold **3.50**
Ash tray, bathtub, Town & Country, brown **25.00**
Bird, #3276, Bluebird **80.00**
Bird, #3400, Lovebird **50.00**
Bird, #3401, Wren **50.00**
Bird, #3407, Owl.................**300.00**
Bird, #3421, Duck **260.00**
Bird, #3444, Cardinal **65.00**
Bird, #3446, Hen................**120.00**
Bird, #3449, Parakeet **145.00**
Bird, #3592, Nuthatch **45.00**
Bird, #3592, Titmouse **50.00**
Bird, #3599D, Hummingbirds, pair **225.00**
Bird, #3715, Blue Jay, with peanut............................**550.00**
Bird, #3747, Canary............**165.00**
Bird, #3813, Grosbeak, 5" ..**120.00**
Bird, #3852, Swallow **65.00**
Bowl, Holly, 9¾" **35.00**
Bowl, lug soup; Golden Harvest, with handles................... **8.00**
Bowl, lug soup; Thistle **25.00**

Bowl, Orchard Song, 7½" **25.00**
Butter dish, Starflower.........**35.00**
Butter dish, Thistle...............**20.00**

Gray Cardinal, #3596, $60.00.

Chamber pot, Town & Country,
   honey **65.00**
Coffeepot, Thistle **25.00**
Creamer, Golden Blossom...... **6.50**
Cup, Boy Blue **65.00**
Cup, Provincial...................... **7.50**
Cup, Starflower **10.00**
Cup & saucer, Prelude **10.00**
Mug, Town & Country **20.00**
Pitcher, Star Dust, 1-quart...**15.00**
Plate, Della Ware, 9½" **12.00**
Plate, Lily, pink, 6" **4.00**
Plate, Magnolia, 10"..............**10.00**
Shakers, Magnolia, pair **10.00**
Shakers, Thistle, pair **15.00**
Sugar bowl, Orchard Song, with
   lid..................................... **8.00**
Teapot, Colonial **24.00**
Tidbit tray, Fruit & Flowers, 2-
   tier **20.00**
Tumbler, bathroom; Town &
   Country, yellow **20.00**

Stoneware

   From about 1840 and
throughout the next hundred
years, stoneware clay was used to
pot utility wares such as jugs,
jars, churns, and pitchers.
Though a brown Albany slip was
applied to some, by far the vast
majority was glazed by common
salt that was thrown into the kiln
and vaporized. Decorations of
cobalt were either slip trailed,
brushed on, or stenciled; sgraffito
(incising) was used on rare occa-
sions. The complexity of the decoration has a great deal of bearing
on value, and examples bearing
the mark of a short-lived company
are often at a premium.

Bottle, Albany slip, sgraffito inscription, doughnut form **225.00**
Bottle, Dr JA Brown, blue top, 1-
   qt, EX..............................**60.00**
Bottle, gray salt glaze, doughnut
   form, 9" **145.00**
Bottle, John H Cushing, blue top,
   gray bottom, 10", EX......**65.00**
Bottle, leaf, brushed, cobalt on
   salt glaze, straight sides, 9",
   EX **225.00**

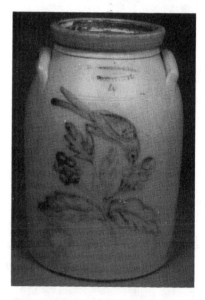

**Churn, bird on flowering branch,
W. A. Macquoid & Co., New York,
1870s, 15", VG/EX, $550.00.**

280

Churn, floral, brushed, cobalt/salt glaze, ovoid, unmarked, 1850s 450.00
Churn, FT Wright, bird on branch, cobalt on salt glaze, 3-gal, M........................750.00
Churn, IM Mead, tulip, brushed, cobalt on salt glaze, 17", EX 600.00
Churn, Ottman Bros, bird on stump, cobalt on salt glaze, 4-gal, EX.........................900.00
Churn, Whites Utica, bird, quilled, cobalt on salt glaze, repaired........................625.00
Cooler, Albany NY, sunflower, cobalt on salt glaze, ca 1880, 2-gal......................... 1,200.00
Cooler, floral, brushed, cobalt on salt glaze, midwest, 1860s, 4-gal................................220.00
Cooler, Hart Bros, bands & handle highlights, cobalt on salt glaze, lg........................150.00
Cooler, Whites Utica #5, floral, quilled, cobalt on salt glaze, EX.................................475.00
Crock, #6 & flourish, quilled, cobalt on salt glaze, 13".70.00
Crock, bird on branch, quilled, cobalt on salt glaze, 11", EX 250.00
Crock, butter; leaves, cobalt on salt glaze, handles, no lid, 6x10", VG 260.00
Crock, C Hart & Son, bird/flourish, quilled, cobalt on salt glaze, 12" 300.00
Crock, chicken pecking corn (dotted), cobalt on salt glaze, 10", NM...............................450.00
Crock, floral, #5, brushed, cobalt on salt glaze, handles, 14", NM...............................500.00
Crock, floral, cobalt on salt glaze, late 1870s, 5-gal...........240.00
Crock, floral, handle accents, cobalt on salt glaze, with lid, 12"................................125.00

Crock, floral, quilled, cobalt on salt glaze, 11", VG 95.00
Crock, FT Wright & Son, bird on branch, cobalt on salt glaze, MA, 1-gal......................375.00
Crock, horse tied to post, 1860, cobalt on salt glaze, 14", EX............................... 1,800.00
Crock, leaves around top, brushed, cobalt on salt glaze, 1-gal..............................125.00
Crock, NA White & Son, floral, quilled, cobalt on salt glaze, 12", EX 475.00
Crock, NA White & Son Utica, bird/flowers, cobalt on salt glaze, 4-gal 450.00
Crock, NY Stoneware Ft Edward NY, dragonfly, cobalt on salt glaze, 1-gal 250.00
Crock, partridge in pear tree, cobalt on salt glaze, 1870s, 6-gal 550.00
Crock, Whites Utica, fan-tail bird, cobalt on salt glaze, 4-gal, EX..........................600.00
Figurine, dog, seated, blue face & ears, 8"...................... 1,800.00
Flask, salt glaze, 5½" 85.00
Footwarmer, Dorchester Pottery, EX....................................45.00
Jar, Albany slip with brushed ochre florals, ca 1880, 3-gal, NM...............................345.00
Jar, Burger & Lang, tulip & leaf, cobalt on salt glaze, 1870s, 3-gal 300.00
Jar, canning; floral, brushed, cobalt on salt glaze, 8".575.00
Jar, canning; horizontal lines, cobalt on salt glaze, 7".100.00
Jar, canning; lines & foliage scroll bands, cobalt on salt glaze, 10" 550.00
Jar, canning; lines/stars, stenciled/brushed, cobalt on salt glaze, 7" 400.00
Jar, canning; squiggles & drips, cobalt on salt glaze, 8" .175.00

Jar, Demuth's Snuff, Lancaster PA, stenciled, unmarked, 1890s 60.00

Jar, ES&B New Brighton PA, stenciled, 1890s, 2-gal....65.00

Jar, floral, cobalt on salt glaze, 13", EX..........................135.00

Jar, floral, cobalt on salt glaze, 8½" 165.00

Jar, floral/#2, brushed, cobalt on salt glaze, 11", NM.......175.00

Jar, Hamilton & Jones, floral, brushed, cobalt on salt glaze, 4-gal..............................225.00

Jar, slip-cup flower, Lyons, 14½", $325.00.

Jar, Hamilton & Jones PA, stenciled, brushed swirls, 5-gal, NM..............................350.00

Jar, James Hamilton Greensboro PA, stenciled, cobalt on salt glaze, 2-gal....................115.00

Jar, swirls/1860, cobalt on salt glaze, semi-ovoid, unmarked, 3-gal..............................325.00

Jar, tulips on vines/rickrack, cobalt on salt glaze, hdls, 14", EX..................................725.00

Jug, batter; floral under spout, cobalt on salt glaze, bail handle, 1-gal......................325.00

Jug, Burger Bros, floral, #3, cobalt on salt glaze, ovoid, 17", NM 350.00

Jug, Edmonds & Co MA, grapes & leaves, cobalt on salt glaze, 2-gal..................................475.00

Jug, Haxstun-Ottman & Co, bird on branch, cobalt on salt glaze, 12" 350.00

Jug, J Bennage 1837, splash, cobalt on salt glaze, ovoid, 2-gal..................................240.00

Jug, N Clark Jr Athens NY, floral, cobalt on salt glaze, ovoid, 2-gal 150.00

Jug, S Hart, inscribed in quillwork, cobalt on salt glaze, ovoid, 11" 150.00

Jug, Thompson & Tyler, bird on branch, cobalt on salt glaze, 1-gal..............................675.00

Jug, Whites Utica, bird, cobalt on salt glaze, 14", EX........625.00

Jug, Whites Utica, floral, cobalt on salt glaze, 14", NM .275.00

Meat tenderizer, edge trim, cobalt on salt glaze, edge chips, 4", EX 450.00

Mug, band top & bottom, cobalt on salt glaze, hand thrown, EX 120.00

Mug, CNY Pottery, bands, cobalt on salt glaze, M............120.00

Pitcher, floral, brushed, cobalt on salt glaze, 10", VG........475.00

Pitcher, Pat Sexton, floral & bird embossed, cobalt & buff, 9", NM..............................175.00

Salt dish, brushwork, cobalt on salt glaze, 3" dia, EX....500.00

Shaving mug, floral, brushed, cobalt on salt glaze, hairline, 5"................................ 2,400.00

Spittoon, leaf, brushed, cobalt on salt glaze, unmarked, ca 1850s, 7" dia.................325.00

Urn, Thos Haig, floral spray, cobalt on salt glaze, 2-piece, large..............................800.00

Store Collectibles

Items that once were part of the country store scene are being collected and enjoyed by many, especially those whose interest's focus on primitives or advertising memorabilia. Today small glass and oak showcases often display collections of miniatures; or, filled with green plants and a few special pieces of glass or pottery, they may be used as coffee tables.

Display case, copper and glass, 9" x 12", $200.00.

Bag rack, tin & wire, Snow King Baking Powder, 17"......**235.00**

Bag rack, wire, 6 wire shelves, unmarked, 27" **45.00**

Bag rack & string holder, pyramidal, 2-piece, VG............**185.00**

Bag rack & string holder, wire ware, hangs from hoops, 12x14" **150.00**

Buggy whip holder, tin & wire bottom, wire top, chain hanger..........................**75.00**

Cabinet, ribbon; with racks, maker's tag, 48x26" **900.00**

Cabinet, 30-compartment, red paint, 1890s, 16x28......**200.00**

Candy jar, glass, pedestal base, swirled collar & stopper, 30", NM..............................**850.00**

Case, collar; IL Showcase Co, ca 1910, 48x6x7"..............**225.00**

Cheese slicer, wrought iron bow with wire, turned wood handle, 22"..........................**125.00**

Hand stamp, mechanical, brass, Arvin, patent 1891 ....**10.00**

Lamp, brass font, iron hanger, tin shade, 1890s, 33" **330.00**

Printing set, wood in wood box, ca 1920, complete **33.00**

Scoop, brass, funnel shape, 18x7½", EX **58.00**

Scoop, candy; brass, ca 1880, 9½" long **26.00**

Showcase, wood & glass, floor standing, 48" long..........**75.00**

String Holders

Until the middle of this century, spools of string contained in devices designed for that purpose were a common sight in country stores as well as many other businesses. Early examples of cast iron or wire and those with advertising are the most desirable and valuable, but later figurals of chalkware or ceramics are also quite collectible.

Apple & berries, chalkware..**18.00**

Army campaign figural, Smokey Bear-style hat, 4"...........**44.00**

Black porter, Fredericksburg Art Pottery........................**145.00**

Cat, ceramic **15.00**

Chef's face, ceramic, gold trim, large...............................**55.00**

Court jester, plaster **40.00**

Dog with fly, Art Deco style, ceramic, NM **50.00**

Indian's head, plaster **68.00**

Lady knitting, cat playing with string ball, tin **15.00**

Mammy, ceramic, large **50.00**

Mammy, full figure, plaid dress, ceramic, Japan...............**65.00**

Mexican's head, plaster **30.00**

**Mexican's head, chalkware, 8",
$30.00.**

Pumpkin face, ceramic **48.00**
Puppy face, ceramic **50.00**
Smiling Buddha, white china .**10.00**
Spanish lady, chalkware, large,
    EX **65.00**
Top hat with face, chalk........**35.00**
White chef with bottle, ceramic,
    EX **60.00**

Sugar Shakers

Once a commonplace table
accessory, the sugar shaker was
used to sprinkle cinnamon and
sugar onto toast or muffins.

Acorn, pink opalescent with gold
    florals............................**115.00**
Acorn, sapphire blue...........**165.00**
Apollo, etched, original top...**75.00**
Argus Swirl, peach bloom...**175.00**
Beatty Rib, blue opalescent..**92.00**
Bubble Lattice, cranberry satin,
    scarce............................**600.00**
Bulging Loops, blue cased .**215.00**
Chrysanthemum Base Swirl,
    cranberry opalescent ...**295.00**
Coin Spot, blue opalescent, 9-
    panel **110.00**
Cone, green opaque.............**105.00**
Egg shape, pansies on peach to
    white, Mt Washington .**225.00**

**Bubble Lattice, blue opalescent,
$175.00.**

Erie Twist, satin..................**265.00**
Flower & Pleat, clear & frosted,
    original lid....................**120.00**
Forget-Me-Not, chartreuse .**100.00**
Jumbo & Barnum **145.00**
Leaf Mold, yellow or lime green
    satin **175.00**
Leaf Umbrella, blue cased .**250.00**
Leaf Umbrella, spatter, North-
    wood **165.00**
Medallion Sprig, clear to cobalt,
    original lid....................**195.00**
Medallion Sprig, rubena.....**275.00**
Melligo, blue opaque **95.00**
Quilted Phlox, blue opaque..**125.00**
Reverse Swirl, canary yellow
    opalescent......................**125.00**
Ribbed Lattice, clear opalescent,
    tall..................................**75.00**
Ribbed Pillar, cranberry spatter,
    frosted **195.00**
Sawtooth Band (Atlas), US Glass,
    1890 ....**45.00**
Tomato figural, ornate top, Mt
    Washington **235.00**
White satin with green shamrocks
    & blue dots, Dithridge .**115.00**

Swanky Swigs

During the 1930s through the 1950s, Kraft cheese products were sometimes packed in glassware tumblers decorated with various animals, flowers, stripes, etc., ranging in size from about 3½" to 4½". Some of the more valuable are the Texas Centennial tumblers, valued at $20 to $25.

Black dots, 4¾" **8.00**
Black tulips in pot, 3½".......... **3.50**
Blue cornflowers with green leaves, 3½"........................ **2.50**
Blue sailboat, 3½" **10.00**
Blue stars, 4¾" **5.00**
Blue tulips in pot, 4½" **6.00**
Bustling Betsy, 3¾" **2.50**
Cat & rabbit, 3¾" **2.50**
Churn & cradle, 3¾" **3.00**
Circles in dots, blue, 4¾" **7.50**
Daisies, 3¾" **5.00**
Dog & rooster, 3¾" **3.00**
Duck & horse, 3¾".................. **2.50**
Forget-me-nots, any color with green leaves, 3½"............. **2.50**
Lamp & kettle, 3¾" **2.50**
One red band, 3⅜"................... **2.50**
Red checkerboard, 3½"..........**17.50**
Red tulips with green leaves, bands at top, 3¾"............. **2.50**
Squirrel & deer, 3¾"............... **2.50**
Two red & black bands, 4¼" . **4.00**
Violet, Jonquil & Cornflower bands, 4½".......................**12.00**

Syrups

Syrup dispensers have been made in all types of art glass, china, stoneware, and in many patterns. Together they make a lovely collection.

Apple Blossom, milk glass .**175.00**
Banded Portland **75.00**

Button & Band, 6¾" **75.00**
Button Arches, original pewter lid, 7"..............................**75.00**
Coin Spot, blue opalescent, ring neck **175.00**
Coin Spot, green, bulbous ..**125.00**
Cord & Tassel **125.00**
Coreopsis, EX decoration....**145.00**
Eyewinker **120.00**
Feather, green **345.00**
Galloway...............................**65.00**

Grape and Leaf, blue opaque, 5¼", $165.00.

Guttate, cranberry, squatty, scarce...........................**325.00**
Hobnail, blue, original pewter lid, dated.............................**235.00**
Ivy in Snow...........................**70.00**
Leaf & Flower, amber **100.00**
Lincoln Drape, flint, eagle embossed on tin lid **195.00**
Locket on Chain **235.00**
Michigan...............................**75.00**
Moon & Star, original lid **125.00**
Optic, rubena, Hobbs **125.00**
Priscilla **110.00**
Prize, ruby flashed..............**235.00**
Rope & Thumbprint, canary yellow **125.00**
States....................................**65.00**

Torpedo, pewter lid **80.00**
Tree of Life, milk glass..........**70.00**
Valencia Waffle, blue **125.00**
Venetia, cranberry **295.00**
Wildflower, amber, scarce ..**195.00**
Wisconsin **85.00**

Tea Leaf Ironstone

Ironstone decorated with a copper lustre design of bands and leaves became popular in the 1880s. It was produced by potters in both England and America until the early 1900s.

Bowl, fruit; scalloped, H Burgess, 10".....................................**75.00**
Bowl, sauce; square, Wedgwood, 4" **20.00**
Butter pat, unmarked, 3" **15.00**
Coffeepot, Fish Hook, Meakin, large...............................**175.00**
Cup & saucer, Chinese shape, Shaw...............................**95.00**

Cup and saucer, Meakin, $65.00.

Cup & saucer, ribbed, Adams, ca 1870 ....**35.00**
Egg cup, unmarked, 3½" **395.00**
Gravy boat, Fish Hook **50.00**
Mug, child's size **195.00**
Nappy, Chinese, Shaw **22.00**

Nappy, Wilkinson, 4½" **20.00**
Pitcher, milk; Blanket Stitch, Alcock, 8¾" **120.00**
Pitcher, wash; Chrysanthemum, Burgess, NM **225.00**
Plate, dessert; Meakin..........**12.00**
Plate, dessert; Wilkinson **12.00**
Plate, dinner; Pepper Leaf....**25.00**
Plate, dinner; Wedgwwod **25.00**
Plate, luncheon; Meakin.......**13.00**
Plate, soup; Shaw, 8¾" **35.00**
Platter, Meakin, 16x12".......**45.00**
Platter, Shaw, 12½x9"...........**45.00**
Relish dish, oval, reticulated handles, Wilkinson **45.00**
Relish dish, Plain Square, Wedgwood, 9x5", EX **25.00**
Saucer, deep, Meakin, 6"........ **8.00**
Shaving mug, Chinese, Shaw, 3¼" **165.00**
Sugar bowl, Cable, with lid ..**65.00**
Sugar bowl, Furnival, no lid.**40.00**
Sugar bowl, Lily, Shaw **125.00**
Sugar bowl, Wedgwood **55.00**
Teapot, Morning-Glory **265.00**
Tureen, sauce; Fish Hook, with lid, Meakin **95.00**
Waste bowl, Pepper Leaf Variant, Elsmore & Forster **75.00**

Teapots

Among the most popular types of teapots on today's market are the figurals – animals of all sorts are especially common. Examples that are easily identified as to manufacture are usually more valuable. Though teapots date back to 16th-century China, most encountered today are from the late 19th century through the present.

Austria Victoria Carlsbad, fine china with florals...........**30.00**
Barge, South Derbyshire, England, brown, embossed name, large **75.00**

Charles & Diana, marked Wales
CM, brown pottery, 2½".**75.00**
Double spout, earthenware, slip
decoration, ca 1890 ....**80.00**

**Children's teapot, cupids in relief,
European, $60.00.**

Ellgreave, Wood & Sons, England,
ironstone with florals.....**35.00**
Grimwades, Royal Winton, England, cozy set, flower-forum
handles **55.00**
Ming Tea Co, made in Japan, with
label, 1½-cup **15.00**
Old English Sampler, H & K England, 6-cup, EX................**45.00**
Snow White & Seven Dwarfs,
Walt Disney Productions,
musical **50.00**
Spode's Tower, England, blue &
white transfer, London shape,
VG..................................**45.00**
SYP, Wedgwood, bone china, blue
& white with gold trim, ca
1905 ....**110.00**
Wade, Scotty, marked, 1953-1955,
9"....................................**45.00**

Teddy Bears and
Related Collectibles

Only teddies made before the
1940s can be considered bona fide
antiques, though character bears
from more recent years are also
quite collectible. The 'classic' bear
is one made of mohair, straw
stuffed, fully jointed, with long
curving arms tapering at the paw
and extending to the knees. He
has very long skinny feet, felt
pads on all paws, embroidered
claws, a triangular, proportion-
ately small head, a long pointed
snout, embroidered nose and
mouth, and a hump on the back
torso at the neck. But above all,
he is adorable, endearing, cuddly,
and he loves you.

**American, fully-jointed mohair,
14½", $280.00.**

Bear, fully jointed, gold mohair,
glass eyes, skinny, 8" ...**150.00**
Bear, fully jointed, gold mohair,
Petz, 1940, 24", EX **350.00**
Bear, fully jointed, gray frosted
fur, Hermann, 11" **95.00**
Bear, fully jointed, long gold
mohair, Chad Valley, 1940,
23", EX **750.00**
Bear, fully jointed, mohair, England, 1934, 33" **285.00**
Bear, fully jointed, mohair, metal
eyes, Schuco, 3"............**250.00**

Bear, fully jointed, mohair, straw filled, glass eyes, 16"....**290.00**
Bear, fully jointed, mohair, straw filled, with buttons, Steiff, 10".................................**500.00**
Bear, fully jointed, mohair, straw filled, with hump, 7"....**150.00**
Bear, fully jointed, mohair, vest & bow tie, Chad Valley, 1930s, 15"...............................**295.00**
Bear, fully jointed, red mohair, with hump, glass eyes, 4", EX..............................**175.00**

Steiff, with ear button, well worn, new ribbon, 10", $300.00.

Bear, fully jointed, silvery mohair, with hump, Hermann, 1955, 12"...............................**135.00**
Bear, fully jointed, cotton plush, Ideal, 1923, 15", VG.....**365.00**
Bear, fully jointed, tan mohair, felt mouth, Clemens, 1950, 10"............................**155.00**
Bear, gold cotton & wool, red felt paws, Merrythought, 1960, 12"...............................**175.00**
Bear, growler, fully jointed, straw stuffed, with tag, Hueneg, 17" **200.00**
Bear, growler, honey fur, hump, long nose, 12", EX........**150.00**
Bear, musical, fully jointed, mohair, felt mouth, Reuge, 12" .**250.00**

Bear, not jointed, wool plush, glass eyes, straw filled, German, 15" **60.00**
Bear, pin-jointed, gray wool, Holland, 1940s, 14" **115.00**
Bear, squeaker, gold mohair, hump, English, 12", EX...........**135.00**
Bear, squeaker, mohair, with tag, Hermann, 9" **85.00**
Bear, squeaker, not jointed, long mohair, with tag, Hermann, 11"................................**150.00**
Book, Mother Goose's Bears, Cavally, 1907, EX **325.00**
Book, Teddy Bears, Towne, ca 1907, 8 volumes **625.00**
Bottle warmer, white, straw head, glass eyes, 12" **150.00**
Dish, teddy bears transfer, ABCs, china............................**125.00**
Puppet, black ears, embroidered nose, Chad Valley, 10"....**95.00**
Puppet, mohair, straw-filled head, embroidered nose, glass eyes, 9"...................................**150.00**
Tea set, teddy bears play soccer, Japan, 1920s, 16-pc **550.00**
Tip tray, Roosevelt bears, dress shop ad, 1906, EX........**350.00**

Telephones

Early phones are quite different in appearance than those we have become accustomed to, and the various stages of advancement over the years since the telephone was invented have resulted in hundreds of modifications. Oak wall phones, simple or with ornate carvings, are only one type that is highly sought. Collectors also seek related memorabilia such as Bell Company paperweights, public telephone signs, and advertising ephemera.

Century Telephone Mfg, oak fiddleback style................**375.00**

Chicago Supply, Elkhart IN, magneto box **45.00**

Federal cradle style, brass and Bakelite, ca 1905, $250.00.

Kellogg, candlestick, brass, 1907, VG **85.00**
North Electric, desk, 1937....**50.00**
Railroad, portable, in leather case, with 4-part connecting pole, EX **70.00**
Railroad dispatcher, candlestick style **75.00**
Stromberg-Carlson Mfg, candlestick style **85.00**
Stromberg-Carlson Special, #1534, WWII era.............**25.00**
Sumter Mfg, oak wall-crank style, small...........................**235.00**
Western Electric, brass & black metal candlestick, pat 1904, EX................................**135.00**
Western Electric, candlestick style, Pat 1915 ....**95.00**
Western Electric Spacesaver, with dial................................**75.00**

Tiffin Glass

Founded in 1887 in Tiffin, Ohio, the Tiffin Glass Company was one of several companies comprising the U.S. Glass Company. They made tablewares and decorative items. They are most famous for their black satin glass, which they made during the 1920s. U.S. Glass was sold in 1959; in 1962 the plant closed for a short time but soon reopened as the Tiffin Art Glass Company. Their main products were tableware, stemware, and various types of decorative items.

Advertising sign, light blue ..**20.00**
Ash tray, Empress, green & crystal, #6590 ....**65.00**
Bowl, Cherokee Rose, crimped, 12" **25.00**
Bowl, Empress, red & crystal, #6561............................**165.00**
Candlestick, blue, pair..........**30.00**
Candlestick, Modern, crystal, #6326, pair **75.00**

Candlestick, enameled bird on black satin glass, 8½", $60.00.

Candy box, Modern, cut, blue, #6455 ....**130.00**
Cellini bowl, Modern, citron & crystal, #6067 ....**115.00**
Champagne, Classic..............**22.00**
Claret, Flanders, pink...........**55.00**
Cocktail, Cherokee Rose.......**24.00**
Cocktail, June Night.............**20.00**

Cordial, Flanders **55.00**
Cornucopia, wisteria............**135.00**
Cup & saucer, Flanders, footed
    style **35.00**
Goblet, Paulina, topaz, 5½" ... **7.00**
Lamp, hurricane; crystal, #6408,
    2-piece..............................**60.00**
Pitcher, Empress, Twilight &
    Kilarney **250.00**
Pitcher, water; Classic **175.00**
Plate, Flanders, pink, 6" **13.00**
Sherbet, Cherokee Rose........**12.00**
Sundae, Cerice etching, #071, 6-
    oz.....................................**15.00**
Tumbler, ice tea; Byzantine, crys-
    tal with black base.........**22.00**
Tumbler, juice; June Night,
    footed, 5"..........................**16.00**
Vase, bud; Cherokee Rose.....**15.00**
Vase, Empress, blue & crystal,
    #6551.............................**165.00**
Vase, Modern, crystal, cornucopia,
    #6301.............................**150.00**
Vase, poppies in relief, blue vel-
    vet, 8½"............................**48.00**
Whiskey, La Fleur, Mandarin Yel-
    low, 2¾".............................**20.00**
Wine, June Night, #17403 ....**20.00**

Tinware

From 1800 until the early
20th century, American tinsmiths
imported sheets of tin plate from
Europe from which they hand
fashioned kitchenware items, foot
warmers, lamps, etc. Some pieces,
such as lamps and lanterns, were
sometimes decorated with simple
pierced designs. Often they were
painted, either freehand or stenciled; this type of decoration is
referred to as tole. Cookie cutters,
very popular with today's collectors, were made in every shape
imaginable. The very early, more
unusual detailed forms sometimes
sell for well in excess of $100.00.
See also Toleware.

Basket, berry; old red paint, ca
    1880, 1-quart................**110.00**
Bill clip, horseshoe form, wall
    hanging............................**12.00**
Birdcage feeder, ca 1870.......**80.00**
Box, spice; multicolor stencils, ca
    1900, 9½x7x5" **70.00**
Cabinet, spice; 8-drawer, original
    black paint & stencils, hang-
    ing..................................**195.00**
Cake mold, butterfly form, ca
    1900, 14x10x3"...............**65.00**
Cake pan, Christmas tree form,
    10x11" **25.00**
Candle box, black finish, round,
    tab hangers, 13"...........**235.00**
Candle holder, cup shape,
    stoneware drip cup, ring han-
    dle, pair **125.00**
Candle lantern, pierced, Paul
    Revere type **145.00**
Candle snuffer, cone shape,
    twisted wire handle, 1860s,
    4½"...................................**45.00**
Candle stand, weighted cone base,
    2-socket, 28", VG............**80.00**
Chandelier, double cone with 6
    curved arms, 1800s, 30"
    diameter **400.00**

**Chandelier, early 1800s, 20",
$500.00.**

Coffeepot, child's, 5"..............**28.00**
Colander, strap handles, on ring
    base **22.50**
Cookie cutter, rabbit, full bodied,
    6x4"..................................**25.00**
Cookie cutter, horse, prancing,
    bobtailed, 6½x7"...........**250.00**

Cookie cutter, violin, 5½".......**55.00**
Cookie cutter, heart, 3x2½" ..**14.00**
Cracker pricker, scalloped edge, 8 sharp points, handle......**85.00**
Cream whipper, 4-loop, crank handle, 1880s, 9½".........**65.00**
Dust pan, 2" hood, flat ring handle, 1860s, 7½x5", EX **28.00**
Egg coddler, ornate base, burner, complete, 4-piece.........**225.00**
Funnel, side strap handle, 6½x6¼".............................**25.00**
Grater, half-round, on 1-piece board with handle, ca 1820, 13"....................................**85.00**
Ice cream dipper, cone shape with key **25.00**
Ink cup, with spring clip to fit ledger, ca 1800, 1½".......**39.00**
Kraut cutter, with sliding tin box, large **50.00**
Match holder, original blue paint, 2-pocket, wall hanging ..**20.00**
Measure, slant sides, strap handle, ½-pint size **18.00**
Oil lamp filler, brass cap, dated April 2, 1861...................**65.00**
Pie crimper, repaired, 7¾" **22.50**
Sconce, punchwork, mirrored backplates, 10", pair ...**225.00**
Sconce, rectangular with crimped crest, 12", pair **250.00**
Scoop, round with fancy wood handle, large **30.00**
Sieve, cheese; heart shape, ring foot, 5" **175.00**
Skimmer, dark, round strap handle, 8" **45.00**
Soap saver, screen wire top & bottom, patented, 1875 ....**25.00**
Spatula, fish slice; rounded blade, with punchwork, wood handle **65.00**
Syrup pitcher, brown japanning, hinged cover, 3½"..........**40.00**
Teakettle, straight sides, cast pewter finial, 5¾" **135.00**
Toddy warmer, funnel shape, pouring lip, side handle.**95.00**

Tobacciana

Now gone the way of the barber shop and the ice cream parlor, the cigar store with its carved wooden Indian at the door and the aroma of fine tobacco in the air is no more. But the clever figural cigar cutters, the hand-carved Meerschaum pipes, the cigar molds, and humidors are still enjoyed as reminders of our country's younger days and for the workmanship of long-ago craftsmen.

Ash tray, bronze, LaFendrich 100th Anniversary, 1850-1950 ....**20.00**
Ash tray, cast iron, man smoking pipe relief.....................**15.00**

Bakelite pipe with brass trim, in case marked Redmanol, $85.00.

Cigar box, Sear's Golden Jubilee, 1866-1936, EX...............**15.00**
Cigar box, Temptation, Black advertising, VG..............**15.00**
Cigar box, Two Birds, cartoon roosters, 1909 stamp......**30.00**
Cigar case, brass, scrolling dragon applied on lid, 5¼x2½"...**60.00**
Cigar cutter, brass, monkey on potty, EX........................**70.00**
Cigar cutter, brass, repousse florals, steel blades **80.00**
Cigar cutter, sterling, Nouveau lady each side................**85.00**

Cigar cutter, Tom Benton Cigars, early, EX.....................**295.00**
Cigar mold, wooden, makes 10, EX...................**25.00**
Cigarette card, Anderson's Henry character, set of 50, M .**100.00**
Cigarette dispenser, cast iron mechanical elephant, 1900, rare...............................**125.00**
Cigarette holder, sterling, engraved thistle, amber stem, England, 2"....................**48.00**
Cigarette urn, monkey with top hat, wrought iron, tail is cutter..................................**85.00**
Coupon, Corn Cake Tobacco . **3.00**
Cutter, plug; Spearhead......**150.00**
Cutter, plug; steel blade, Bradford Clonmell, 1800s..............**75.00**
Cutter, plug;Black Beauty, horse's head figural..................**300.00**
Humidor, figure of a lady taking snuff, German, 10" **150.00**
Humidor, happy hippo, majolica, 8"....................................**135.00**
Humidor, head of Blackamoor in turban, pottery, 9"........**175.00**

Humidor, monkey with pipe, pottery, 1910, 6" **100.00**
Humidor, Nouveau lady's head, Austria **95.00**
Indian chief, plaster, ca 1900, countertop size.............**575.00**
Lighter, Lektrolite Flameless, Deco style, 5x15"..........**195.00**
Pipe, Charatan, Perfection Winston, #323 DC.................**50.00**
Pipe, meerschaum, lady's hand at bowl, silver ferrule, 5¾" .**85.00**
Pipe, meerschaum, sultan's head, amber mouthpiece, EX .**65.00**
Pipe, Perfection, straight pot, extra large......................**67.50**
Pipe, Stanwell, Deluxe, #44, oval shank..............................**25.00**
Pipe holder, meerschaum, detailed carving, EX **30.00**
Pipe rack, walnut, wall hanging, drawer, ca 1800, 18" **700.00**
Pipe rest, German shepherd, cast iron figural, 3" **25.00**
Plug press, Brown's Mule, embossed metal, 1920s, 12" square.............................**10.00**

Prancing horse tobacco cutter, 1890s, 16" long, $600.00.

292

Sack, Big John Tobacco, unopened, 1940, NM **7.00**
Snuff spoon, wood with jeweled end, ca 1840, EX **100.00**
Spittoon, blue & white stoneware, embossed scroll **95.00**
Spittoon, cast iron, blue-gray paint, traditional shape.**55.00**
Spittoon, Indian Head Redskin Brand, brass **35.00**
Table lighter, Parker Silent Flame, nude **16.00**
Tobacco tin tag, Cut Short **30.00**

Toleware

Hand-painted or stencil-decorated tinware is refered to as 'tole.' The most valuable was made by the Pennsylvania Dutch in the 17th century. Color, design, age, and condition are the most important worth-accessing factors.

Basin, flowers on black, American, mid-1800s, 11¾" diameter **110.00**
Bowl, flowers, on multicolor, 3x4", VG **45.00**
Box, deed; floral spray, 3-color, square panels, 9" long ..**300.00**
Cache pot, vases & florals on black, gilt twig handles, 8"......**425.00**
Candle lamp, double, gold on green, lyre base, French, 17", pair **1,000.00**
Candlestick, flowers on black, American, 1850s, 7⅜" ..**110.00**
Coal bin, floral, 25" **500.00**
Coffeepot, floral, 3-color on black, side spout, 8", NM.... **1,050.00**
Creamer, brushstrokes, 3-color on dark brown, 4", VG **90.00**
Creamer & sugar bowl, multicolor fruit/florals, straight sides, 1800s **900.00**
Lamp, floral, oil can on straight stem, dished base, 7" ...**700.00**

Coffee canisters from a general store, sliding glass fronts, 28", $350.00 for the pair.

Taper holder, stripes & vines, yellow & gold on black, 4" .**40.00**
Tea caddy, leaves, gold on black, pewter foot, brass bail .**165.00**
Tea caddy, multicolor hand-painted florals, oval, with lid, 3x4x6" **135.00**
Teapot, flowers on black, American, 1850s, worn, 10"...**120.00**
Tray, bread; Oriental scenes, 6-color paint on black, 1875, 14" **250.00**
Tray, floral band in red & green, 8-sided, 12" long...........**250.00**
Tray, landscape with boats, 23x29", on 21" stand **990.00**
Tray, peaches & berries, yellow borders, PA, ca 1840, 13" long NM **1,900.00**
Tray, tavern view, English, 1800s, 30" long..................... **1,100.00**
Tumbler, gold stenciled flowers & birds, 1850s, 3x3"...........**50.00**

Tools

Considering the construction of early tools, one must admire the hand-shaped wood, the smithy-wrought iron, and the hand-tooled leather. Even factory-made tools from the late 1800s required a good deal of hand finishing. Most desirable to tool collectors are those with the touch mark of the craftsman or early examples marked by the manu-facturer. Value is determined by scarcity, condition, usefullness, and workmanship.

Brace, Sheffield, beech, unplated, coca bola head, EX **95.00**
Calipers, Roker, fine-adjust screw, bowed style, 8" **12.50**
Chisel, pocket; Stanley Everlast-ing, 8", EX **18.00**
Gauge, mortise & marking; Stan-ley #77, NM **35.00**
Gauge, mortise; rosewood, brass-faced fence, 8½" **45.00**
Gauge, veneer-slitting; beech, wedge type **18.00**
Jointer, Stanley #7, patented 1910, rosewood knob & han-dle, EX **50.00**
Level, machinist's pocket; Stanley #38½, 4", EX...................**17.50**
Level, Stanley #5, patented 1894, 30"...................................**22.00**
Level, Stratton Bros, brass-bound rosewood, patented 1870, 12", EX **245.00**
Plane, block; Stanley #101 ...**20.00**
Plane, double rabbet; Sargent #81, EX **65.00**
Plane, jack; Stanley #5, ca 1910-1920, VG **25.00**
Plane, jack; Stanley S-5, decal on handle, EX **90.00**
Plane, rabbet; Stanley #190 .**30.00**
Plane, Stanley #129 ....**35.00**
Rule, Stanley #62 ....**20.00**

Wood-worker's shave, composed of alternating light and dark woods, ca 1900, 12" long, $200.00.

Saw, hand; Harvey Pace, dated 1869 ....**20.00**
Scraper, Stanley #80 ....**20.00**
Spoke shave, rabbet; Stanley #68, steel, NM japanning **35.00**
Tape, Lufkin, cloth in leather case, 50-ft **25.00**
Tin snips, Bartlet, knuckle-jointed, lever action **22.00**

Toothpick Holders

Toothpick holders have been made in hundreds of patterns, in art glass, pattern glass, opales-cent, and translucent glass of many colors, in novelty designs and figural forms. Today they are all popular collectibles, relatively easy to find and usually afford-able.

Acorn, pink, decorated..........**80.00**
Amberina, tricorn top **225.00**
Baby Thumbprint, amberina, 2½" **175.00**
Beaded Swirl & Disk, amber.**50.00**
Begger's Hand, vaseline **25.00**
Bull's Eye & Fan **12.00**
Button Band, ruby **22.00**
Champion **28.00**
China, roses, hand-painted, gold rim, Nippon **35.00**
Colorado, clear......................**21.00**
Colorado, green **32.00**
Cord & Pleat, cobalt.............**95.00**
Daisy & Button, with V Orna-ment, vaseline **45.00**
Delaware, green with gold ...**95.00**
Diamond Spearhead, sapphire opalescent......................**85.00**
Double Arches, red satin.....**110.00**
Empress, green **175.00**
Feather, Cambridge **35.00**
Fruit Panels **30.00**
Galloway...............................**20.00**
Hobnail, vaseline, Hobbs **20.00**
Iris with Meander, blue opales-cent **75.00**

Iris with Meander, sapphire blue
    with gold..........................**55.00**
Jefferson Optic, custard........**35.00**
Little Lobe, white..................**80.00**
Maine, pink stain, rare.........**95.00**

**New Hampshire, amethyst top
with gold trim, $85.00.**

One-O-One, milk glass **45.00**
Panelled 44, gold flashed **37.50**
Peek-A-Boo, amber **42.50**
Pineapple & Fan, green with EX
    gold, Heisey...................**195.00**
Quartered Block....................**25.00**
Rib & Bead, ruby stain.........**25.00**
Royal Ivy, rubina **125.00**
Scrolled Shell, milk glass with
    goofus.............................**12.00**
Silverplate, barrel & fireman's
    helmet, Pairpoint **165.00**
Spiral Rib, vaseline...............**60.00**
Square Urn, purple slag.......**45.00**
Stars & Bars, blue, rare......**220.00**
Tarentum's Tiny Thumbprint,
    custard............................**55.00**
Tree in Meadow....................**80.00**
Wild Bouquet, white opalescent
    with pastel decoration .**135.00**
Wreath & Shell, vaseline opales-
    cent with hand-painted deco-
    ration **195.00**

**R.S. Prussia, roses and gold trim,
marked, $120.00.**

Toys

Toy collecting is a very popular hobby; and, if purchases are
wisely made, there is good potential for investment. Toys from the
1800s are rarely if ever found in
mint condition but should at least
be working and have all their
original parts. Toys manufactured
in the 20th century are evaluated
more critically. Compared to one
in excellent condition, original box
intact, even a slightly damaged
toy may be worth only about half
price. Character-related toys,
space toys, toy soldiers, and toy
trains are among the more desirable. See also Character Collectibles.

Diecast

Corgi, Bentley Continental, #224,
    NM in box.....................**95.00**
Corgi, Citroen Safari, no luggage,
    #436-A1, G **40.00**
Corgi, Dick Dastardly's Racing
    Car, #809, M in box........**55.00**
Corgi, Oldsmobile Sheriff's Car,
    #237, M in box...............**85.00**
Corgi, Studebaker Golden Hawk,
    #211S, G **20.00**

Dinky, Armored Command Car, #602, M in box **75.00**
Dinky, Cinderella's Coach, #111, M in box **35.00**
Dinky, Maserati Race Car, #231, M in box..........**50.00**
Dinky, Rambler Station Wagon, #193, M in box..............**45.00**
Hot Wheels, Peterbilt Tanker, Shell logo, M in box........**20.00**
Hot Wheels, Racing Series set, 4 vehicles, M in box..........**20.00**
Matchbox, Cement Truck, #19, M in box **8.00**
Matchbox, Chieftan Tank, Battle Kings #103, M in box.....**15.00**
Matchbox, Fire Pumper, Code Red series, M in box **7.50**
Matchbox, Goofy's Sports Car, Disney, #9, M in box **10.00**
Matchbox, Greyhound Coach, #66, M in box..........................**25.00**
Matchbox, Hot Rocker, #67, M in box.................................. **6.00**
Matchbox, Sherman Tank, Battle Kings #101, M in box.....**15.00**
Matchbox, Volkswagen Camper, #34, NM in box..............**30.00**

Matchbox, Jiminy Cricket, copyright 1979, $15.00.

Fisher-Price

#118 running bunny cart, pull toy, 1957 ....**10.00**

#131 Happy Hoppers, push toy, plastic with wooden handle, 1969-1976 .... **6.00**
#131 milk wagon, 1965-1972, complete, 9x8x6" **9.00**
#132 pony chime, pull toy, 1965-1967, 9¼x12x7¾" **22.00**
#139 Tuggy Turtle, xylophone, 1959-1961, 9x7x5¼" **9.00**
#145 Husky dump truck, 1961-1963, 12" long.................. **6.00**
#145 musical elephant, 1948-1950, 10¼x4¼x8" **34.00**
#151 Little Miss Muffet doll & pillow, squeaker, 1977-1980. **4.00**
#156 music box TV radio, Baa Baa Black Sheep, 1966 ... **5.00**
#162 Roly Poly Boat Chimes, 1967-1969, 6" diameter... **4.00**
#181 Snoopy Sniffer, pull toy, 1961-1980, 14" long......... **8.00**
#189 bluebird music box, The Children's Prayer............ **6.00**
#305 walking duck cart, 1957-1964, 9x4½" long............**11.00**
#410 fun flower, infant squeaker, 1973-1979 .... **1.50**
#440 Pluto pop-up kritter, 1936-1949 ....**30.00**
#445 hot dog wagon, pull toy, 1940-1941, 10¾" long **30.00**
#451 Shake 'N Roll rattle, 1973-1979 .... **2.00**
#462 Barky, pull toy, 1958-1960, 5x4½" **9.00**
#476 Mickey Mouse drummer, pull toy...........................**35.00**
#540 Granny Duck, pull toy, 1939-1942 ....**28.00**
#549 lunch kit, 1972-1979, 5x2x4½" **3.00**
#635 Tiny Teddy, xylophone pull toy, 1962-1966, 6x7¼" **10.00**
#641 Toot Toot Engine, pull toy, 1962-1964, 6" long.......... **4.00**
#653 Allie Gator, pull toy, 1960-1962, 10⅛x4¼"................. **7.00**
#656 Bossy Bell, cow, pull toy, 1959-1963, 6x6".............. **8.00**

Fisher Price, Gabby Duck, ca 1952-53, $12.00.

#662 Merry Mousewife, pull toy, 1963 .... **7.00**

#7 Looky Fire Truck, 1950-1954, 12x4½x5" **25.00**

#8 Bouncy Racer, pull toy, 1960-1970, 9¾x6⅝x4" **9.00**

Guns

Daisy, Buck Jones #107, BB gun, NM **185.00**

Daisy Model #35, BB gun **40.00**

Daisy Red Ryder, BB gun **90.00**

Johnny Ringo, Fastest Gun in the West set, Marx, NM **175.00**

Little Burp Gun, Mattel, #5545, M **200.00**

Red Fox Missile, Hubley, M in worn box **155.00**

Ricochet carbine, Marx, bullet ejecting, EX **55.00**

Shell Shooting Detective pistol, Marx, minor wear **175.00**

Shotgun, pump action, shell ejecting, Marx, EX **60.00**

Submachine gun, realistic sound, Marx **37.50**

Texan Jr, Hubley, 9", jeweled leather holster, M in box............**155.00**

Male Action Figures

Action Marine, sold by Sears, complete in box **200.00**

Adventure Team GI Joe, Kung Fu Grip, M in box **100.00**

Captain Action Super Hero, Aquaman disguise, M..**175.00**

Captain Action Super Hero, Phantom disquise, M...**175.00**

GI Joe Adventure Team, Black Adventurer, NM..........**120.00**

Green Beret, original clothes & accessories, 1969 ....**300.00**

Japanese Imperial Soldier, original clothes, 1966 ....**400.00**

Marine, #770, camouflaged fatigues, jump boots.....**125.00**

Palitoy of England, Action Man Soldier, M **75.00**

Palitoy of England, Space Ranger Space Pirate, M..............**95.00**

Schildkrot of Germany, Action Team Fire Fighter, M.....**60.00**

Takara of Japan, #2, M.........**95.00**

Talking Man of Action, $125.00.

Marx

Coca-Cola Truck, tin, 1940s, 18" long, EX **75.00**

Daredevil Motor Drome, tin windup, 1930s, 9", EX .**120.00**

Dump Truck, tin, friction motor, 1950s, 12" long, EX........**70.00**

George the Drummer Boy, tin windup, 1930s, 9", EX..**145.00**

Hot Rod #23, tin, friction motor, Japan, 1967, 8", M **28.00**
Junior Typewriter, metal base, plastic knobs, 1957, EX .**10.00**
Lazy Day Farms Truck, metal litho, 18" long, EX.........**20.00**
Monkey Cyclist, tin windup, 1930s, VG **80.00**
Pinnochio, tin litho windup walker, eyes move, EX .**120.00**
Racer #3, tin litho, 5", EX...**150.00**
Woody Sedan, tin, friction motor, 7½", NM..........................**35.00**

Models

American Firefighters, Revell, 1953, M, sealed **25.00**
Church, with accessories, Marx, 1950s, M in box **50.00**
Design-A-Plane, Pyro, 1950s, VG in original box **75.00**
Dr Jekyll As Mr Hyde, Aurora, 1964, unopened............**200.00**
Duesenberg Town Car, metal kit, Hubley, G **65.00**
Flintstones Rock Cruncher, Hanna Barbera, 1974 ....**50.00**
German Tiger Tank, Lindberg, 1966, M in box................**15.00**
John F Kennedy, all plastic, Aurora, M in box **150.00**
King Kong, the Last Stand, Mego, 1975, sealed **30.00**
Mercury/Gemini, Revell, 1964, NM.................................**40.00**
Nasa Space Shuttle, Monogram, 1986, NM........................**22.50**
Neanderthal Man, Aurora, 1971, M, sealed **35.00**
Space Shuttle Challenger, Revell, M in sealed box **45.00**

Space Toys and Robots

Atomic Disentegrator, cap gun, Hubley, 1930s, 6"...........**50.00**
Buck Rogers Punch-O-Bag, official **40.00**

Buck Rogers rocket ship, he & Wilma in window, Marx .**150.00**
Buck Rogers water pistol, red & yellow, 1930s **90.00**
Buck Rogers 25th-Century Space Pistol, XZ-31, 1934, original box **100.00**
Cape Canaveral missile set, Marx, boxed...................**85.00**
Flash Gordon Ray Gun, air pump type, Flash Gordon decal, metal............................**120.00**
Flash Gordon Rocket Fighter, tin windup, Marx, 1930s ...**100.00**
Lost in Space robot, plastic, Remco, boxed, 16" **145.00**
Mighty Robot with Apollo, plastic windup, robot pulls Apollo rocket............................**65.00**
Mister Mercury, battery-operated remote control, Marx, Japan, 13" **275.00**
Robot Sam, The Answer Man, Jaymar **30.00**
Robot-7, tin windup, bullet shape, Japan, 4"........................**15.00**

Robert the Robot by Ideal, 1950s, 14", $200.00.

Satellite, battery operated, Cragstan, 9" diameter ...50.00
Space Man, gray with red feet, tin windup, Japan 100.00
Space Pilot telescope, tin, 1950s, M 20.00
Space Racer #3, tin litho windup, bullet shape....................85.00
Spaceman, windup, Linemar, Japan, 6".........................90.00
Star Wars C3PO robot doll, plastic, Kenner, 1970s 40.00
Star Wars X-Wing Fighter Ship, Kenner, 1978 version, 13½", M................................25.00
Tom Corbett Space Cadet Atomic Rifle, Marx, 24"............45.00

Star Trek

Action figure, Dr McCoy, plastic, Mego, 1979, 3¾"............ 7.00
Action figure, Scotty, molded plastic, Mego, 1974, 4" 8.00
Bank, Kirk with communicator, Play Pal Inc, 1975, 11½".12.00
Binoculars, plastic with decals, Larami, 1968 ....10.00
Doll, Captain Kirk, vinyl, Mego, 1974, 8" 18.00
Doll, Klingon, with skull ridges, Mego, 1980, 12" 35.00
Doll, Romulan, vinyl, Mego, 1974, 8"...................................45.00
Doll, Spock, Cabbage Patch, hand-sewn, 1986............50.00
Film viewer, red & black, plastic, 1967 ....12.00
Flashlight-Ray Gun, plastic with decals, Larami................12.00
Frisbee, Flying USS Enterprise, Remco, 1967, 8½" 9.00
Helmet, white plastic, motorcycle style, Enco, 1976............35.00
Phaser gun, electronic dueling set, Milton Bradley........75.00
Play case, Starship Enterprise Flight Deck, vinyl, Mego, 1974 ....65.00

Play set, Mission to Gamma VI, Mego, 1976, 21x19x16"..50.00
Play set, USS Enterprise Bridge, Mego, 1980, 24x12"........20.00
Spaceship, Enterprise USS, die cast, Dinky Toys, 1977...45.00
Walkie-talkies, blue plastic with silver insignia, Mego 50.00
Water gun, black & chrome colored, Azrak-Hamway, 6". 8.00

Toy Soldiers

Auburn Rubber, bomb thrower, #234, NM 18.00
Auburn Rubber, doctor, #224, EX 20.00
Auburn Rubber, signalman, #236, VG.............................. 8.00
Auburn Rubber, soldier charging with gun, #238, EX........10.00
Barclay, cook, #769, VG 7.50
Barclay, cowboy on horse, #90, EX 12.00
Barclay, fireman with axe, #187, VG..................................10.00
Barclay, grenade thrower, #76, EX 12.50
Barclay, Indian chief, #754 .... 6.00
Barclay, sharpshooter, stands to fire, NM 12.00
Barclay, soldier at attention, EX 12.50
Barclay, soldier with gas mask, #778, EX.........................10.00
Barclay, train conductor, #161, NM...............................10.00
Grey Iron, dog, American Family series, #12, EX................. 2.50
Grey Iron, doughboy officer, #6A, EX 10.00
Grey Iron, Indian on horse, #11M, VG..................................15.00
Grey Iron, newsboy, American Family series, #10, M 12.00
Grey Iron, pirate with dagger, #16/3, VG......................12.50
Grey Iron, Royal Canadian policeman, VG 10.00

Grey Iron, US Marine, NM...**16.00**
Manoil, cannon loader, #42...**16.00**
Manoil, machine gunner, stretched out, #12, EX ...**10.00**
Manoil, policeman, #49.........**12.00**
Manoil, sniper, #48, EX **12.50**
Manoil, boxer, #100, EX........**45.00**
Manoil, soldier in poncho, #523, EX **20.00**

Lionel trolleycar with passengers, original box, 7" long, $300.00.

Trains

American Flyer, electric locomotive, 0 gauge, working headlight, EX **85.00**
American Flyer, sand car, 0 gauge, red, EX................**38.00**
American Flyer L2002, Erie steam engine, Standard gauge, EX **165.00**
American Flyer 4000, locomotive, Standard gauge, VG.....**115.00**
American Flyer 480, tank car, 0 gauge, NM **12.50**
American Flyer 622, box car, Standard gauge, EX.......**20.00**
American Flyer 9900, locomotive, 0 gauge, windup, EX....**155.00**
Ives 17, locomotive with original tender, VG **150.00**
Ives 1779, derrick, Standard gauge, VG.....................**200.00**
Ives 189, truck car, Standard gauge, white, VG..........**385.00**
Ives 24, refrigerator car, black & white, VG........................**70.00**
Ives 30, electric locomotive, tin with cast frame, VG **235.00**
Ives 3258, locomotive, 0 gauge, brass plates, EX...........**125.00**
Ives 40, tender, Standard gauge, tin, G............................**120.00**
Ives 550, baggage car, 0 gauge, green & black, EX **35.00**
Ives 62, parlor car, green & orange, EX.....................**35.00**
Lionel 1110, Scout steam engine, 027 gauge, VG................**15.00**
Lionel 119, tunnel, Standard gauge, EX **45.00**

Lionel 2029, steam engine with tender, 0 gauge, EX........**32.00**
Lionel 204, steam engine, 0 gauge, black, VG............**37.50**
Lionel 233, steam engine with tender, 027 gauge, NM ..**28.00**
Lionel 338, observation car, Standard gauge, VG..............**37.50**
Lionel 60, trolly, 027 gauge, blue lettering, VG **50.00**
Lionel 6017, caboose, 027 gauge, brown, EX........................ **4.50**
Lionel 602, baggage car, 0 gauge, dark green, 7", EX..........**35.00**
Lionel 959, barn set, plastic, 23 pieces, complete, EX **7.50**
Marx 352, Venice gondola car, blue & black, EX............**35.00**
Marx 4583, Deluxe flat car, plastic, black & white, 8 wheels, EX **3.00**
Marx 556, cable car, tin, 4 wheels, 6", M **12.50**
Marx 586, Rock Island caboose, plastic, 8 wheels, NM...... **2.50**
Marx 597, locomotive, stamped steel, clockwork, NM......**42.50**
Marx 901, diesel locomotive, plastic, 8 wheels, NM **12.00**

Miscellaneous

Alps, strutting penguin, tin windup, M in box **45.00**
German, soccer players kick ball back & forth, windup, 1910, EX **650.00**
Gilbert, microscope set, 1956, NM in box **38.00**

LineMar, Ham 'N Sam, 1950s, scarce, EX 850.00
LineMar, Pluto, windup walker, 1950s, NM in box 450.00
Martin, violin player, tin windup, 1890s, EX 650.00

Charlie Chimp, Hula Expert, made in Japan, MIB, $75.00.

Girard, Air Mail biplane, tin windup, 1920s, EX 750.00
Hartland, Cheyenne, with horse, saddle, & hat 90.00
Hartland, Davy Crockett, with horse, saddle, & hat 200.00
Hartland, General Lee, with hat & sword 65.00
Hartland, Maverick, with horse, saddle, & hat 235.00
Hartland, Paladdin, with horse, saddle, & hat 125.00
Hartland, Roy Rogers, with horse, saddle, & hat...............125.00
Hartland, Thunderbird, with horse 95.00
Japan, Mercedes-Benz, tin friction, #8, 9", EX 35.00
Japan, station wagon, friction, 1940s, 5", NM 30.00
Japan, turn-over monkey with cymbals, tin, battery operated, M in box 38.00
Japan, woodpecker, tin windup, rare, 9"...........................160.00
Keystone, Deluxe Service Station, NM................................175.00
Klingsbury, fire truck, tin windup, 1915, EX 450.00

Marching Drummer Bear, made in Japan, MIB, $75.00.

Metalcraft, Heinz Pickles Truck, 1930s 350.00
Occupied Japan, cat with ball, celluloid windup, EX 25.00
Occupied Japan, Cherry Cook, celluloid windup 25.00
Occupied Japan, Chevrolet, tin windup, M in box 75.00
Occupied Japan, Studebaker, tin windup, M in box 75.00
Rempel, Friskey stick horse, 2 wheels at base, 36", EX .17.50
Schuco, Old Timer Mercer car, tin, M....................................70.00
Smith-Miller, Sand Digger Steam Shovel, 28", VG 165.00
Strauss, Parcel Post Truck, 1920s, EX 850.00
Strauss, taxi with driver, tin windup, 1920s 750.00
Sun Rubber, Town Car, 5¾"..22.00
Wolverine, Shoot-A-Loop, tin litho spiral marble game, EX . 7.50

Wolverine, Sonny-Andy tank, tin,
EX **180.00**

Traps

Recently attracting the interest of collectors, old traps are evaluated primarily by their condition. Traps listed here are in fine condition, that is with the trademark legible in its entirety, with strong lettering.

Arrow Jump #1, single under
spring...............................**30.00**
Black Hole, throw-away mousetrap, plastic **8.00**
Clayton Killer.....................**300.00**
Cooper #1, clutch jaws, single
long spring......................**40.00**
Diamond #34, offset jaws, double
long spring......................**40.00**
Duke #1½, coil spring............. **4.00**
Eclipse #1, under springs **40.00**
Evans, mousetrap, brass **150.00**
Fenn #1 Killer, English.........**15.00**
Funsten Submarine, float-type
trap **225.00**
Helfrich #750, coil spring......**20.00**
Jack Frost, Never Lose, coil
spring.............................**19.00**
Kliflock #1 Killer..................**20.00**
Montgomery Digger #2, coil
spring **35.00**
Nash, mole trap, Kalamazoo MI,
cast iron **15.00**
Pendelum Trigger #3 Killer.**160.00**
PS&W #1 Good Luck, single long
spring **65.00**
Runway, mousetrap, metal...**10.00**
Sargent #14, round pan, double
long spring......................**70.00**
Star #3, double under spring.**45.00**
Sure Shut, Chicago Ill, fruit jar
trap **30.00**
Trailzend #3, double long spring,
Nelson Boode Co **150.00**
Triumph #0, single long spring,
with T cut in pan **100.00**

Up to Date, mousetrap, metal,
catches from both ends .**20.00**
Victor #10, rabbit trap, single long
spring...........................**150.00**
WR Feemaster, mousetrap, aluminum, Brooklyn MI **15.00**

Universal

Located in Cambridge, Ohio, Universal Potteries Incorporated produced various lines of dinnerware from 1934 to the late 1950s, several of which are especially popular with collectors today.

Ballerina, bowl, vegetable; wine,
handles, 9"....................... **8.50**
Ballerina, cup & saucer, dark
green................................ **3.50**
Ballerina, plate, wine, 9" **4.00**
Ballerina, shakers, pair......... **6.00**

Calico Fruit: Covered jug, $35.00; Lug soup bowl, $13.50; Lug fruit bowl, $6.50; Milk pitcher, $16.00.

Cattail, bowl, berry; 5¼" **4.00**
Cattail, cake tin **20.00**
Cattail, canteen jug..............**19.00**
Cattail, casserole, 7" **16.50**
Cattail, cup & saucer **9.50**
Cattail, custard **4.50**
Cattail, scales, metal **25.00**
Cattail, tumbler, iced tea.....**10.00**
Cattail, tumbler, 4¾"............**17.50**

Valentines

Valentines that date from the early decades of the 1900s can often be found at today's flea markets. Watch for dealers whose merchandise includes other types of ephemera such as post cards, calling cards, and trade cards. Collectors often specialize from among several possible areas, for instance: comic cards, mechanicals, or those signed by a well-known artist.

Accordion-type foldout, Cupid at wheel of car, 4", $7.00.

Blue Fairy, mechanical, Walt Disney Productions, 1939, 5¼", EX **20.00**
Cherub holds heart, 1918, 3"..**2.00**
Cherub plays mandolin, cupid with message cutout, fold-out, 7".....................................**15.00**
Children in swing, fold-out...**15.00**
Cupid & child, fancy, fold-out, 1920s, 10".......................**12.00**
Cupid & urn, fancy, fold-out, 1920s, 8".........................**10.00**
Edwardian cherubs & children, Germany, ca 1918, 14x10" sheet **5.00**

Girl at soda fountain, mechanical, Germany, early, large...... **8.00**
Girl with phone lifts receiver boy appears, 1930, 6x6", EX.................................**10.00**
Hand cut, lacy, circular form with verses, ca 1900, EX........**75.00**
Heart, mechanical, celluloid, old, large...............................**35.00**
I'd Like To Capture You, mechanical, boy with gun, 1940s . **8.00**
I'd March a Million Miles..., soldier, 1940s, 5", EX........... **6.00**
I'm No Jitterbug..., boy dancing, 1930s, 6", NM................. **5.00**
Many flowers & verse, Prang, 1881, 6x8".......................**24.00**
Roller coaster with boy & girl, stand-up, 1930, EX......... **8.00**

Van Briggle

Van Briggle pottery has been made in Colorado Springs since 1901. Fine art pottery was made until about 1920 when commercial wares and novelties became more profitable products. The early artware was usually marked with the date of production and a number indicating the shape. After 1920 'Colorado Springs' in script letters was used; after 1922 'U.S.A.' was added. Van Briggle is most famous for his Art Nouveau styling and flat matt glazes.

Ash tray, Hopi Indian, turquoise, pre-1922, 6"...................**65.00**
Bookends, bear on stump, blue & black, 8", pair..............**250.00**
Bookends, peacock, turquoise, no marks, 5", pair **75.00**
Bowl, spade leaves, maroon & blue, USA, 10"..............**125.00**
Bowl vase, dragonflies, blue over red, exposed clay, 3x5" .**500.00**
Candle holder, double; plum, dated 1931, 6x5", pair....**95.00**

Ewer, medium green with red at top, #435, 1905, 7" **200.00**
Flower frog, duck figural, green & brown **35.00**
Lamp, Damsel of Damascus, rose, original shade...............**200.00**
Lamp, Grecian urn, turquoise, original shade, 11½" **55.00**
Lamp, Maiden at the Well, ca 1930 ....**150.00**
Lamp, 2 racing deer, Ming Blue, 11" **125.00**
Mug, green, dated 1905, 5".**175.00**
Shakers, rose, floral, pair **42.00**
Teapot, turquoise with purple, bamboo-reeded handle, with cover **135.00**

Vase, bears at rim, mulberry, 15½", $1,000.00.

Vase, Arts & Crafts-style flowers, green, #382, 1906, 5" ...**425.00**
Vase, bell flowers, medium blue, #197, dated 1903, 6" **900.00**
Vase, bud; maroon, dated 1914, 8", pair **150.00**
Vase, Despondency, maroon with green, ca 1925, 12".......**575.00**

Vase, green, cream-brown body, #734, '08-11, 7½" **350.00**
Vase, iris, turquoise, 6" **40.00**
Vase, leaves, dark on light blue, #848, 7½" **60.00**
Vase, Lorelai, blue, EX mold, ca 1920s, USA, 10" **850.00**
Vase, Ned Curtis marks, maroon, #793, 1914, 5½" **225.00**
Vase, rose, floral, 4½"............**48.00**
Vase, slim leaves, mustard yellow, 1907, 5"........................**500.00**
Vase, 3 Indian heads, turquoise, pre-1922, 11" **200.00**
Vase/planter, conch shell, blue, 6x16" **45.00**

Vernon Kilns

From 1931 until 1958, Vernon Kilns produced hundreds of lines of fine dinnerware, which today's collectors enjoy reassembling. They also made novelty items designed by famous artists such as Rockwell Kent and Walt Disney, examples of which are at a premium.

Ash tray, Kentucky, red **12.00**
Brown-Eyed Susan, bowl, 9" . **9.00**
Brown-Eyed Susan, chop plate, 12½" **12.00**
Brown-Eyed Susan, creamer & sugar bowl **13.00**
Brown-Eyed Susan, plate, 6". **3.00**
Brown-Eyed Susan, salt & pepper shakers, pair **8.00**
Fantasia, bowl, Satyr..........**115.00**
Fantasia, bowl, Sprite, pink, #125, 1940 ....**125.00**
Fantasia, figurine, Baby Pegasus, 1940 ....**175.00**
Fantasia, figurine, Centaurette, recumbent, #17 ....**300.00**
Fantasia, figurine, Donkey Unicorn, #16.......................**250.00**
Fantasia, figurine, Ostrich Ballerina, #28 or #29 ....**600.00**

Fantasia, sugar bowl, with cover, individual **25.00**
Fantasia, vase, Goddess, white with light green, #126 .**200.00**
Gingham, bowl, chowder; tab handles................................ **7.00**
Gingham, casserole **30.00**
Gingham, coffee decanter **18.00**
Gingham, creamer & sugar .**12.00**
Gingham, platter, 14" **12.00**

Gingham: Platter, 14", $12.00; Cup and saucer, $7.00.

Gingham, tumbler.................**15.00**
Homespun, pitcher, 2-qt **20.00**
Homespun, plate, 9¾"............ **5.00**
Monterey, creamer & sugar ..**12.00**
Organdie, bowl, chowder; tab handles................................... **5.00**
Organdie, bowl, vegetable; round, 8" **8.00**
Organdie, chop plate, 14" **11.00**
Organdie, coffee carafe **18.00**
Organdie, pitcher, iced beverage; large................................**18.00**
Organdie, teapot, 6-cup **18.00**
Plate, Bit of Old England **28.00**
Plate, Eastern Star **12.00**
Plate, Eisenhower **13.00**
Plate, General MacArthur....**10.00**
Plate, Music Master, 8½" **12.00**
Plate, Will Rogers **13.00**
Salamina, plate, in pewter frame, 9½" **125.00**
Salamina, plate, 14"............**150.00**
Salamina, sugar bowl, with cover, regular size....................**35.00**

Tam O'Shanter, casserole, with cover................................**25.00**
Tam O'Shanter, pitcher, water ; large...............................**25.00**
Tam O'Shanter, soup, flat **8.00**
Ultra California, sugar bowl, yellow................................... **6.00**
Ultra California, tumbler, green, 5¼" **13.00**

Watch Fobs

Watch fobs were popular during the last quarter of the 19th century and remained in vogue well into the 20th. Retail companies issued advertising fobs, and these are especially popular with collectors. Political, commemorative, and souvenir fobs may also be found. They were made from brass, cast iron, bronze, copper or celluloid.

Abraham Furs, triangular..**250.00**
American Boy Scout.............**48.00**
American School of Correspondence, blue enamel on porcelain, NM **25.00**
Atkins Saws, silver metal **20.00**
Boston Store Silver Jubilee, silver metal, 1925....................**18.00**
BPOE, 1923, EX **45.00**
Buick, blue enamel on porcelain, NM................................**48.00**
Butte MT, copper, M.............**65.00**
Cambria Spring Co **40.00**
Commercial Travelers AA of America, multicolor enameling..................................**28.00**
Cyrus McCormick Centennial of the Reaper, brass, 1931 .**48.00**
Disciples of Christ Centennial, brass, Whitehead & Hoag, 1909, EX **15.00**
Flat Rock Coal Co, mother-of-pearl, EX.......................**40.00**
George Washington Bicentennial, 1732-1932, lead-like.......**15.00**

International Harvester, bronze with 2-color enamel **15.00**
Jap Rose Soap, multicolor celluloid, brass rim, EX **55.00**
Kellogg's Corn Flakes, box form, brass **50.00**
Michigan Shovels & Cranes, embossed scene **35.00**
Mining & Metallurgical School, Organized 1871 ....**15.00**
Mohawk Trail, Chief's protrait, with green enamel band on bonnet.............................**25.00**
National Cash Register, register shape, old........................**20.00**
Pacific Coast Association of Fire Chiefs....................................**45.00**
Pharmacy, Cincinnati College, sterling, 1901 ....**45.00**
Polarine Frost & Carbon Proof Oil, plated brass, EX......**60.00**
Railsplitters Society, Cincinnati OH, enameling...............**20.00**
Red Diamond Overalls..........**18.00**
Rome Fire Dept, Rome GA ..**75.00**
Sanico Stoves, brass..............**65.00**
Sun Insurance **30.00**
Taft 1908 ....**45.00**
Wallis Tractor.......................**60.00**
Wear-Ever Aluminum, aluminum, EX **16.00**

Warco, from the Riddle Co. of Bucyrus, Ohio, $95.00; LaPlant – Choate, yellow and blue porcelain inlay, $85.00.

Watt

Since making an appearance a few years ago in a leading magazine on country decorating, Watt Pottery has become highly collectible. Easily recognized by it's primary red and green brushstroke patterns on glossy buff-colored backgrounds, these items often carry a stenciled advertising message in addition to designs of apples, tulips, starflowers, and roosters. It was made in Crooksville, Ohio, from about 1935 until the plant was destroyed by fire in 1965.

Bean pot, Apple, #76............**75.00**
Bean pot, Starflower, #76 ....**45.00**
Bowl, Apple, #39, spaghetti serving..................................**65.00**
Bowl, Apple, #8 ....**40.00**
Bowl, Pansy, #8 ....**30.00**
Bowl, Pennsylvania Dutch, mixing, #65 ....**50.00**
Bowl, Poinsettia, tab handles, #18, with cover..............**45.00**
Bowl, Rooster, #68................**45.00**
Bowl, Rooster, #73, with advertising....................................**38.00**
Bowl, Starflower, spaghetti serving....................................**55.00**
Canister, Pennsylvania Dutch, #80, with cover **125.00**
Casserole, American Red Bud, with cover, 8"..................**50.00**
Casserole, Apple, #600.........**65.00**
Casserole, French; Rooster...**85.00**
Chip & dip set, Apple **85.00**
Creamer & sugar bowl, Autumn Foliage **85.00**
Cup & saucer, Pansy.............**45.00**
Ice bucket, Apple, with matching cover **65.00**
Pie plate, Apple.....................**95.00**
Pie plate, with advertising ...**55.00**
Pitcher, Apple, #15................**40.00**
Pitcher, Apple, #15, with advertising **45.00**
Pitcher, Cherry, #15 ....**35.00**
Shakers, Poinsettia, pair **65.00**
Sugar bowl, Apple, #98, with cover................................**85.00**

Weller

Sam Weller's company made pottery in the Zanesville, Ohio, area from before the turn of the century until 1948. They made lovely hand-decorated artware, commercial lines, garden pottery, dinnerware, and kitchenware. Most examples are marked with the company name, either in block letters or script.

Arcola, lamp base, grape cluster, no mark, 10" 95.00
Athens, vase, no mark, 15".350.00
Baldin, bowl, apples, 4" 45.00
Blue Drapery, planter, marked Weller, 4" 30.00
Blue Drapery, wall pocket, no mark, 9" 65.00
Breton, bowl, marked, 4" 35.00
Brighton, Bluebird, marked Weller, 7½" 325.00
Brighton, Woodpecker, no mark, 5" 200.00
Bronze Ware, plaque, dogs, 7½x7½" 200.00
Burntwood, vase, 7" 40.00
Cactus, cat, marked, 5½" 80.00
Cameo Jewell, jardiniere & pedestal, no mark, 34" .700.00
Candis, console, 11x2½" 20.00
Candis, hanging basket, no mark, 5½" 40.00
Chase, fan vase, 8½" 200.00
Chengtu, ginger jar, 12" 120.00
Chengtu, jar, with cover, 8" ..80.00
Claywood, candle holder, no mark, 5" 35.00
Claywood, mug, 4½" 50.00
Copra, basket, floral, 11" 125.00
Copra, jardiniere, tulips, 8" .70.00
Creamware, planter, 2" 35.00
Dickens III, creamer, Charles Dickens, #0034, 4" 350.00
Dupont, planter, square, 4" ..30.00
Dynasty, vase, no mark, 6" ...30.00
Elberta, nut dish, 3" 25.00

Eocean, vase, owl on branch, signed EB, 10½" 900.00
Etched Matt, vase, marked Weller, 10" 80.00
Etched Matt, vase, marked Weller, 14" 140.00
Evergreen, candle holder, triple, 7½" 65.00
Fairfield, bowl, 4½" 30.00
Fairfield, vase, no mark, 8" ..50.00
Flemish, comport, with cover, marked Weller, 8½" 225.00
Flemish, inkwell, 7x4½" 600.00
Florala, wall pocket, marked Weller, 10" 55.00
Floretta, ewer, 10½" 135.00
Floretta, vase, 5½" 75.00
Forest, window box, 14½" ..250.00

Forest, window box, 12" long, $250.00.

Fruitone, wall pocket, 5½" ...45.00
Glendale, vase, birds, 12" ..325.00
Glendale, vase, birds, 10" ...195.00
Hobart, candle holder, no mark, 6", pair 80.00
Hobart, girl with flowers, no mark, 8½" 65.00
Hunter, vase, deer, handles, #343, 6½" 400.00
Ivoris, ginger jar, 8½" 40.00
Ivoris, powder box, with cover, marked Weller, 4" 30.00
Ivory, jardiniere, 5" 15.00
Ivory, window planter, 15" 60.00
Jap Birdimal, mug, geisha with cat, marked Weller Rhead Faience, 5" 550.00
Klyro, candle holder, 9½" 40.00
Knifewood, tobacco box, marked Weller, 3½" 125.00

L'Art Nouveau, bud vase, ...**100.00**
La Sa, lamp, signed, 14½" ..**375.00**
Lorbeek, candle holder, 2½"..**22.50**
Louwelsa, mug, signed EA .**125.00**
Mammy, teapot, marked Weller,
8"...................................**250.00**
Marbleized, vase, 9"............**100.00**
Matt Floretta, tankard, apples,
signed CD, 13½"..........**450.00**
Melrose, basket, 10"............**180.00**
Minerva, vase, flamingos, marked
Weller, 8½"....................**395.00**
Mirror Black, bowl, marked
Weller, 11".......................**30.00**
Mirror Black, strawberry jar, no
mark, 6½" **65.00**
Monochrome, comport, 8" **55.00**
Montego, vase, 9½" **60.00**
Muskota, girl, no mark, 4"..**100.00**
Muskota, nude on rock, 8" .**200.00**
Noval, candle holder, marked
Weller, 9½", pair **80.00**
Noval, vase, no mark, 6".......**45.00**
Paragon, vase, marked Weller,
7½" **50.00**
Parian, vase, no mark, 8½" ..**65.00**
Parian, wall pocket, 10" **80.00**
Pastel, planter, #P-3, 4x7" **35.00**
Pearl, basket, 6½" **130.00**
Pearl, bud vase, marked Weller,
7"....................................**40.00**
Pumila, wall pocket, 7" **60.00**
Raydance, vase, 8" **35.00**
Roma, candlestick, 11½" **45.00**
Roma, comport, no mark, 5".**40.00**
Rosemont, jardiniere, apples,
marked Weller, 5"...........**85.00**
Sicard, bowl, no mark, 5" ...**525.00**
Sicard, vase, signed Weller
Sicard, 5".....................**500.00**
Silvertone, basket, 13"........**225.00**
Stellar, vase, marked, 5½" ..**110.00**
Tivoli, vase, no mark, 9½" .**100.00**
Velva, bowl, 3½x12½"............**20.00**
Velva, vase, marked, 6"........**20.00**
Voile, jardiniere, 6" **60.00**
Warwick, basket, 7" **80.00**
Woodcraft, bowl, marked Weller,
3½" **80.00**

Zona, baby plate, squirrels, rolled
edge, 7½"........................**40.00**
Zona, jardiniere, 7" **100.00**

Western Collectibles

Items such as chaps, spurs,
saddles, and lariats represent
possibly the most colorful genre in
the history of our country, and collectors, especially from the western states, find them fascinating.
The romance of the Old West lives
on through relics related to those
bygone days of cowboys, Wild
West shows, frontier sheriffs, and
boom-town saloons.

Branding iron, Lazy JW **15.00**
Bridle, heavy brass, English work
type **45.00**
Bull ring, brass, with set screw,
3½" **10.00**
Bust, plaster, General Custer,
Civil War uniform **220.00**
Chaps, buffalo fur, Miles City
Saddlery, EX.................**300.00**
Dietz Lantern, rustic, globe miss-
ing, not usable................**20.00**
Gauntlets, studded leather, old,
EX **50.00**
Miner's pan, rustic, pre-1900 vin-
tage, usable **30.00**
Moneybelt, old calfskin.........**15.00**
Pick head, rustic, handle missing,
shows wear **10.00**
Railroad lock, brass, railroad ini-
tials, rustic **25.00**
Skull, buffalo, with horns...**100.00**
Spurs, lady's legs, straps,
Renalde, pair **135.00**
Stirrups, steel, pair **30.00**
Stockman's whip, 12-ft.........**45.00**

Westmoreland

Originally an Ohio company,
Westmoreland relocated in

Grapeville, Pennsylvania, where by the 1920s they had became known as one of the country's largest manufactures of carnival glass. They are best known today for the high quality milk glass which accounted for 90% of their production.

Ivy bowl, milk glass, $27.50.

Ash tray, Panelled Grape, milk glass, 6½".......................... 8.00
Basket, English Hobnail, milk glass, tall 20.00
Basket, Panelled Grape, purple slag, oval, 6½" 35.00
Bowl, Beaded Grape, milk glass, square, footed, lid, 7" 28.00
Bowl, Old Quilt, milk glass, bell shape, footed, 9" 50.00
Butter dish, Old Quilt, milk glass, ¼-lb 30.00
Cake salver, milk glass, pedestal base, #1875 ....38.00
Candy dish, English Hobnail, milk glass, 3-footed 28.00
Candy dish, purple slag, dolphin foot 50.00
Cigar holder, clear, etched design, #352 ....15.00

Cookie jar, Cherry & Cable, hand-painted on milk glass.....85.00
Creamer & sugar bowl, Della Robbia.....................................22.50
Creamer & sugar bowl, swan, cobalt carnival, with lid (reproduced)...................40.00
Gravy boat, Panelled Grape, milk glass, with tray 50.00
Pitcher, Panelled Grape, milk glass, 1-qt 40.00
Pitcher, syrup; Old Quilt, milk glass 22.50
Plate, child's, embossed castle, milk glass 32.00
Plate, dogs, lacy edge, hand-painted milk glass.........22.50
Plate, Zodiac signs, white on blue mist, 5½".........................20.00
Shakers, Della Robbia, pair..35.00
Sherbet, Panelled Grape, milk glass, low 17.50
Slipper, blue mist, hand-painted decoration.......................18.00
Vase, Old Quilt, aqua ice carnival, ruffled, footed, 7"............35.00
Wedding bowl, plain, milk glass, with lid 35.00

Wicker

Wicker became a popular medium for furniture construction as early as the mid-1800s. Early styles were closely woven and very ornate; frames were of heavy wood. By the turn of the century the weaving was looser and styles were simple. Today's collectors prefer tables with wicker tops as opposed to wooden tops, matching ensembles, and pieces that have not been painted.

Basket, arched handle, early 1900s, 7½x9x5¾".............45.00
Footstool, square base, round top with upholstered insert, 9½x12"........................100.00

Highchair, simple Victorian style, woven braid trim..........**150.00**
Lamp, table; simple style, with shade, 24".......................**75.00**
Plant stand, circular top, cabriole legs, fancy apron **350.00**
Rug beater/fluffer.................**30.00**
Stroller, doll; Victorian, high wheel, original paint & upholstery..............................**495.00**
Tea cart, tight weave, bottom shelf, front wheels, top tray, EX...............................**265.00**

Willow Ware

Inspired by the lovely blue and white Chinese exports, the Willow pattern has been made by many English, American, and Japanese firms from 1750 until the present. Many variations of the pattern have been noted; mauve, black, green, and multicolor Willow ware can be found in limited amounts. The design has been applied to tinware, linens, glassware, and paper goods, all of which are treasured by today's collectors.

Ash tray, square, Royal Doulton, 6"....................................**28.00**
Baking dish, Hall, 3x8".........**16.00**
Baking dish, oven proof, Japan, 2½x5" **16.00**
Batter jug, frosted glass, Hazel Atlas, 8½" **50.00**
Bone dish, dagger border, Minton, 8¼"..................................**48.00**
Bowl, salad; square, ca 1927, Ridgway's, 4x9" **60.00**
Bowl, soup; 1930s, Homer Laughlin, 8" **12.50**
Bread tray, scenic, scalloped edge, ca 1912, Booth's, 12"......**90.00**
Butter dish, Buffalo, 8".........**80.00**
Butter pat, Grindley **22.00**
Cake plate, flat, Cook, 12"....**36.00**
Cake plate, red, Japan..........**30.00**

Cake stand, unmarked English, 2½x8½" **175.00**
Candle holder, Doulton, Flow Blue, 7½", pair **335.00**
Candle lamp, Japan, 11½"....**20.00**
Chamber pot, Doulton, Flow Blue, 5½x9¼" **240.00**

Cheese keeper, numbered, 7¾" long, $85.00.

Clock, round, tin, Smith's.....**85.00**
Coffee jar, unmarked Japan .**30.00**
Coffeepot, Wedgwood, 8".......**80.00**
Creamer & sugar bowl, gold trim, Booth's **120.00**
Cruet, unmarked Japan **25.00**
Gravy boat, with attached underplate, Booth's, 4x8½"......**70.00**
Lamp, kerosene; with reflector, Japan, 8" **65.00**
Pitcher, milk; McCoy, 9"........**25.00**
Plate, brown, Doulton, 8½" ..**50.00**
Plate, hand-painted, Wood & Sons, 9"....................**28.00**
Plate, pink, Buffalo, 9½".......**35.00**
Plate, scroll & floral border, Mason's, 10"....................**25.00**
Platter, birds, Japan, 12"......**30.00**
Platter, Meakin, 14".............**70.00**
Punch bowl, 6x9¼"..............**165.00**
Salt box, wooden cover, Japan, 5x5"..................................**65.00**
Shakers, unmarked, 5½" **14.00**
Spice set, Japan, 6-piece **60.00**
Spoon, soup; Japan, 5½" **7.00**
Spoon & fork, salad; Willow handles, pr **12.50**
Spoon rest, double, Japan, 9" .**25.00**
Sugar bowl, gold trim, ca 1912, Booth's, 3"......................**50.00**

Teapot, Booth's, 7"..............**125.00**
Teapot, 1875-1908, Maling ...**90.00**
Teapot, 1880, Ashworth, 6" ..**95.00**
Toaster, Pan Electrical Mfg, American, 7x7"...........**400.00**
Toby jug, Staffordshire **400.00**
Toothpick holder, Buffalo **35.00**
Wall plaque, brass plate in oak frame, England, 7"........**90.00**
Wash bowl & pitcher, ca 1891-1902, Doulton.............**750.00**

Winchester

Originally manufacturing only guns and ammunition, after 1920 the Winchester Company produced a vast array (over 7,500 items) of sporting goods and hardware which they marked 'Winchester Trademark, USA.' The name of the firm changed in 1931, and the use of the trademark was discontinued. Examples with this mark have become collectors' items.

Air rifle, walnut stock, EX..**195.00**
Air rifle shot, red, yellow & blue tube, blue cap, M............. **5.00**
Bullet mold, 32-caliber **48.00**
Bulletin, Trapshooters, June 1921, EX **25.00**
Can opener, VG **45.00**
Catalog, 1907, EX **110.00**
Chisel, ripping; 1" **20.00**
Chisel, ¼", VG **20.00**
Comic book, EX **35.00**
Flare kit, M in box **37.50**
Fly rod #5705, steel, 3-piece .**60.00**
Folder, tips on roller skating, 1926, EX **16.00**
Golf ball, M...........................**150.00**
Hammer, claw; VG **95.00**
Hammer, machinist's, 32-oz .**45.00**
Hatchet, shingling; NM **48.00**
Ice skates, clamp-on style.....**35.00**
Letter opener, dated 1922 ....**90.00**
Level, iron, 24", EX.............**100.00**

Level, wooden, 30", EX.........**75.00**
Lock, 6-lever, with key, VG.**135.00**
Meat grinder #12, clean........**29.00**
Paperweight, 1910, VG **41.00**
Pencil box **75.00**
Plane, bull nose; 4", EX........**65.00**
Pliers, slip joint, M **38.00**
Poster, Jr Rifle Corps, EX...**850.00**
Receipt **10.00**
Rule, folding, with caliper, 12", EX.....................**65.00**
Saw, keyhole; EX..................**25.00**
Screwdriver bit......................**15.00**
Sharpening stone, round, M.**39.00**
Spatula #7637, nickel silver rivets & fitting, 12" blade, EX.**65.00**
Tennis racquet, EX..............**175.00**
Thermometer, very clean....**135.00**
Wrench, monkey; 12", EX.....**40.00**
Wrench, open end; EX..........**20.00**
Wrench, telephone linemen's; 12½" long, EX **65.00**

Woodenware

Most of the primitive handcrafted wooden bowls and utensils on today's market can be attributed to a period from late in the 1700s until about 1870. They were designed on a strictly utilitarian basis, and only rarely was any attempt made toward decoration. The most desirable are those items made from burl wood – the knuckle or knot of the tree having a grain that appears mottled when it is carved – or utensils with an effigy-head handle. Very old examples are light in weight due to the deterioration of the wood; expect age cracks that develop as the wood dries.

Board, cabbage slicing; walnut, early, EX **15.00**
Bowl, burl, ash with EX figure & color, 2¼x5½"................**135.00**

Bowl, hewn, dipper-like handle, small **5.00**

Bowl, worn original blue exterior paint, 14" diameter **140.00**

Bread board, BREAD on rim, 11" diameter **35.00**

Bread peel, hewn handle, tapered rectangle, 1820s, 21x6"..**85.00**

Butter paddle, bird's-eye maple, 9¼x4" **35.00**

Charger, birch, ca 1800, 19½x20", EX................................**495.00**

Cheese drainer, oblong box shape, EX **95.00**

Cookie board, early auto with driver, 14x9"...................**85.00**

Cookie board, hex signs, hearts & initials, octagonal, 7x9" .**65.00**

Cutting board, maple, 1¼x11x13", EX **65.00**

Dipper, grain forms concentric circles in bowl, 6½".............**80.00**

Draining board, 1-piece, all wood, 19x24", EX **165.00**

Funnel, maple syrup, 1-piece, ca 1800, 8½x4½"..................**95.00**

Jar, turned, urn form, with lid, 6"......................................**45.00**

Lemon squeezer, pierced cherry inserts, 1750s, 11½".......**65.00**

Reamer, mushroom knob handle, ca 1870 ....**75.00**

Rolling pin, tiger maple, elongated handles, 17".........**95.00**

Scoop, carved, slant sides, hook handle, small..................**55.00**

Spoon, maple, ca 1850, 3½" bowl, 11" **50.00**

World's Fairs and Expositions

Souvenir items have been distributed from every fair and exposition since the mid-1850s. Examples from before the turn of the century are challenging to collect, but those made as late as the 1939 New York and San Francisco fairs are also desirable.

1893 Columbian, Chicago

Award medal, bronze, marked American Bronze Co, 3" diameter, EX **100.00**

Catalog, Osborne Harvesting Machinery **30.00**

Coin purse, leather, metal frame & snap, embossed scene, France, EX....................**40.00**

Columbian Exposition, paperweight, signed Libbey, 4" long, $75.00

Fan, folding, panoramic view of grounds..........................**50.00**

Paperweight, glass, Kansas State Building, Libbey **42.00**

Pin dish, frosted glass, leaf form, signed Libbey, EX **25.00**

Plate, Horticultural Building, blue, Wedgwood, 8" **35.00**

Plate, white satin glass, Machinery Hall, Mt Washington, 11½" **350.00**

Print, Pleasures of Anticipation, full color, 9x12"...............**15.00**

Ticket, Chicago Day **7.50**

Tray, heavy metal, diamond shape, pierced edges, 4".**22.00**

Tray, silverplate, Columbus bust, buildings, 7½" dia **65.00**

1898 Omaha

Bowl, US Government Building in, angel on handle, 4¼" .**25.00**

Medallion, brass, heart shape, Nebraska Building, 1¼".**25.00**

Pin-back button, celluloid, Pennsylvania Day, Oct 5 ......**40.00**

Plate, Trans-Mississippi, Manufacturer's Building **48.00**

Trade card, boy in Storm King Rubber Boots, multicolor, 3½x5½"............................ **8.00**

1901 Pan American

Bookmark, celluloid, Libby foods, NM...................................**15.00**

Cup, aluminum, collapsible, buffalo head at top **28.00**

Knife, made from huge nail..**25.00**

Letter opener, buffalo figural, brass, EX **45.00**

Paperweight, Electric Tower, paper label on base, 4"...**35.00**

Photo, lady's portrait, mounted, marked & dated 1901, 3½x2½"............................ **5.00**

Silk, Electric Tower, 10", M ..**40.00**

Spoon, Indian head, Niagara on handle, 4½" **18.00**

Watch fob **15.00**

1904 St. Louis

Letter opener, bronze, with eagle handle............................**50.00**

Plate, glass, Festival Hall & Cascades, lacy edge **20.00**

Plate, porcelain, 3 scenes, openwork rim, Carlsbad, 9" ..**80.00**

Scarf, silk, Expo St Louis 1904, Festival Hall, 20x20" **50.00**

Stamp case **35.00**

Thimble holder, brass, inscribed, Festival Hall shape, 3" .**78.00**

Watch fob, Government Building, state seal, 3-part **75.00**

1915 Panama Pacific

Book, Architecture & Landscape Gardening of Exposition, 202-page **40.00**

Book, Official Souvenir Views, 40-page, 9½x12½" **25.00**

Folder, Painted Desert Exhibit, illustrated, 3x6", EX **7.50**

Pin-back button, celluloid, Indian on horse, Dec 4, 1915.....**40.00**

Pin-back button, celluloid, lady & 2 bears, EX....................**22.50**

Tablecloth, blue felt, bird's eye view of Exposition, 16x25", EX................................**40.00**

Tray, metal, 5 Exposition buildings, 5" dia....................**17.50**

1933 Chicago

Blotter, Travel Building, Johnson Gasoline & Oils, 4x9".....**15.00**

Book, Official Guide, 1933 edition, 194-page, EX **17.50**

Bracelet, silver-colored metal, 6 scenes, EX **25.00**

Buckle, mother-of-pearl with comet, 1¼x1½", EX **25.00**

Cane, wood, beer-barrel handle, EX................................**45.00**

Cent, Skyway & Observation Tower, elongated, EX **10.00**

Plate, white china, fair scene, marked Pickard, 8½" **32.00**

Puzzle, fair overview, over 350 pieces, in box **38.00**

Thermometer, Electric Group by Night, 7½"......................**18.00**

Tray, metal, buildings & scenes, oblong, worn, 6½x3½" **8.00**

Wagon, Toy Radio Flyer, with fair sticker, 2x4"..................**85.00**

1939 New York

Ash tray, ceramic, figure of Trylon & Perisphere match holder, NM **50.00**

Bottle, milk glass, embossed globe, Deco Trylon neck, no cap...............................**17.50**

Cup, enameled tin, NM **55.00**

Knife, clear glass, 3-star handle, 9¼", in original fair box .**12.50**

Pencil, Westinghouse NY, 3½",
NM **3.00**
Spoon, silverplate, Textile Build-
ing, NM **12.00**

1939 San Francisco

Bookmark, enameled brass, blue
tassel on card, 4½" **15.00**
Cloth, silk or rayon, fair scenes on
rose, 20" square **20.00**
Compact, Court of Hemispheres
on lid, mirror inside, 3" diam-
eter..................................**25.00**
Ice pick, wooden handle, marked
World's Fair, 1939 San Fran-
cisco **30.00**
Medallion, blue enamel on brass,
embossed decoration, 1"
diameter **12.50**
Pencil, mechanical; building &
bridge, blue on gold........**25.00**
Towel, terry cloth, Golden Gate
Bridge, white & green,
27x15", EX **32.00**

1964 New York

Ash tray, multicolor Unisphere in
relief, 7½x5" rectangle ...**12.50**
Bank, metal Unisphere **25.00**
Bread tray, bright silver plastic,
wheat rim, Unisphere center,
11x7" **10.00**
Coloring book, Deluxe, M **15.00**
Spoon, demitasse; silverplate,
Vatican Pavillion............. **7.50**
Thermometer, metal, Unisphere
form, 6½", EX **7.50**
Tray, smokey glass, White Horse
Scotch & Unisphere, oval,
8¼x6¼".............................. **6.50**
Tumbler, Federal Pavillion ... **5.00**

Wrought Iron

Before cast iron became commonplace in the mid-1800s, hand-
forged (or wrought) iron was the
metal used most extensively. You
can often judge the age of an iron
piece by studying its surface.
While rusty wrought iron appears
grainy, cast iron pits to an orange-
peel texture.

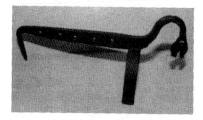

**Skewer rest, primitive animal
form, ca 1700s, rare, $300.00.**

Andirons, gooseneck curves, conical finials, 1880s, 16", VG,
pair **65.00**
Calipers, double, 18¾", VG ..**50.00**
Candle holder, primitive, round
base, 15" **165.00**
Eye hook, with spike, 4¼".....**65.00**
Fork, bold details, 3 tines, 22"
long **65.00**
Kettle stand, cabriole legs,
pierced sheet iron at top,
11x10x11" **250.00**
Kraut cutter, serpentine shape,
maple handle, old patina, 9"
long **400.00**
Leg irons, Civil War style, 19",
with key, EX **75.00**
Pie crimper, turned handle, brass
ferrule, 6⅝" **25.00**
Pie crimper, twisted handle, brass
bushing in wheel, 7" **125.00**
Rack, utensil; 4 hooks, scrolled
crest, 14" long..............**150.00**
Rack, utensil; 8 hooks on 10½"
ring, scrolled & twisted
details, EX....................**145.00**
Roaster, 6 hooks, short feet, long
swivel handle, 24" **185.00**
Roasting stand, tripod base,
penny feet, adjustable rack,
26" **650.00**

Skewer holder, with 2 non-matching skewers, primitive ..**70.00**
Sugar nippers, stamped mark: R Timmins & Sons, 9" **275.00**
Thumb latch, with primitively scrolled door plates **40.00**
Toaster, swivel rack, twisted details, fleur-de-lis ornaments, 15x13" **50.00**
Tool, with sliding needle, used for thick material, 22" long .**65.00**
Trammel, round twisted links, 37" long **95.00**
Utensil rack, scrolled & twisted details, 18" long............**100.00**
Wagon jack, iron & wood, old red & black paint, dated 1793, 17" **115.00**
Wheelwright's tool, pitted, 14" long **25.00**

Yellow Ware

Utility ware made from buff-burning clays took on a yellow hue when covered with a clear glaze, hence the name 'yellow ware.' It is a type of 'country' pottery that is becoming quite popular due to today's emphasis on the 'country' look in home decorating. It was made to a large extent by the Ohio potters, though some was made in the eastern states as well. Very seldom do you find a marked piece. Bowls, pitchers, and pie plates are common; mugs, rolling pins and lidded jars are more unusual and demand higher prices – so do items with in-mold decoration or mocha-like decoration.

Bank, pig; daubs of green & amber, hairlines & chips, 5" long **45.00**
Bowl, mixing; brown band, RRP Co, Roseville, OH, 7".......**28.00**

Casserole, ribbed, 6x10" **70.00**
Chamber pot, white band, ca 1850s **65.00**
Custard cup, blue band.........**23.00**
Custard cup, brown sponging, early 1900s, 3x4"............**14.00**
House, bungalow style, open windows & door, IA, 7" **200.00**
Humidor, ca 1900 ....**150.00**
Jar, seaweed, white band & dark brown stripes, with cover, 6x7", NM.....................**700.00**
Milk pan, marked Jeffords, 3x10½" diameter **100.00**
Mold, grapes, 3½x6x7" **85.00**
Mold, rabbit form **95.00**
Mug, blue bands, unmarked, ca 1850s............................**50.00**
Pie plate, 8" **32.00**
Pitcher, blue bands, 8", EX...**85.00**
Pitcher, white bands, unmarked, 8½" **75.00**
Rolling pin, ca 1900 ....**325.00**
Salt box, 3 white bands, 'Salt' in black lettering, 7".........**175.00**
Soap dish, rectangular, unmarked, ca 1890s.........**125.00**
Teapot, hexagonal, 6"..........**195.00**
Toothpick holder.................**265.00**

Pitcher, green mocha seaweed with brown stripes, 4", $385.00.

Index

Directory

The editors and staff take this opportunity to express our sincere gratitude and appreciation to each person who has in any way contributed to the preparation of this guide. We believe the credibility of our book is greatly enhanced through their efforts. Check these listings for information concerning their specific areas of expertise.

You will notice that at the conclusion of some of the narratives, the advisor's name is given. This is optional and up to the discretion of each individual. We hope to add more advisors with each new edition to provide further resources to you, our readers. If you care to correspond with anyone listed here in our Directory, please send a SASE with your letter.

Arizona
Lund, O.B.
13009 S. 42nd St.,
Phoenix, 85044
602-893-3567
Specializing in milk bottles

California
Santi, Steve
19626 Ricardo Ave.,
Haward, 94541
415-481-2586
Specializing in Little Golden Books and look-a-likes
Author of *Collecting Little Golden Books,* published by Books

Americana. This book contains 266 pages of information and approximately 600 black and white photos. You can purchase the guide from Steve by sending $10.95 plus $2.00 postage and handling to Steve at the above address. If requesting information, please include SASE.

New York
Smurf Collectors' Club
24 Cabot Road West,
Dept. P
Massapequa, 11758
Specializing in Smurf memorabilia, 1957-1990

Ohio
National Button Society
Miss Lois Pool, Secretary
2733 Juno Place, Acron,
44333-4317
216-864-3296
Specializing in buttons: fabric, metal, glass, enamels, military, pearl, etc. Be sure to include SASE when requesting information.

Oregon
Flager, Gloria
2564 Fox Haven Dr. SE,
Salem, 97306; 581-9019
Specializing in Little Golden Books

Schroeder's Antiques
Price Guide

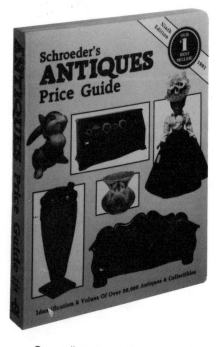

Schroeder's Antiques Price Guide has become THE household name in the antiques and collectibles field. Our team of editors work year around with more than 200 contributors to bring you our #1 best-selling book on antiques and collectibles.

With more than 50,000 items identified and priced, *Schroeder's* is a must for the collector and dealer alike. If it merits the interest of today's collector, you'll find it in *Schroeder's*. Each subject is represented with histories and background information. In addition, hundreds of sharp original photos are used each year to illustrate not only the rare and unusual, but the everyday "fun-type" collectibles as well – not postage stamp pictures, but large close-up shots that show important details clearly.

Our editors compile a new book each year. Never do we merely change prices. Each category is thoroughly checked to spot inconsistencies, listings that may not be entirely reflective of actual market dealings, and lines too vague to be of merit. Only the best of the lot remains for publication. You'll find *Schroeder's Antiques Price Guide* the one to buy for factual information and quality.

8½x11", 608 Pages   **$12.95**

COLLECTOR BOOKS
A Division of Schroeder Publishing Co., Inc.